# THE ROAD
# LESS
# TRAVELED

PHILIP ZELIKOW

# THE ROAD
# LESS
# TRAVELED

## THE SECRET BATTLE TO END THE
## GREAT WAR, 1916–1917

PUBLICAFFAIRS

*New York*

PublicAffairs
Hachette Book Group
1290 Avenue of the Americas, New York, NY 10104
www.publicaffairsbooks.com
@Public_Affairs

Printed in the United States of America

First Edition: March 2021

Published by PublicAffairs, an imprint of Perseus Books, LLC, a subsidiary of Hachette Book Group, Inc. The PublicAffairs name and logo is a trademark of the Hachette Book Group.

The Hachette Speakers Bureau provides a wide range of authors for speaking events. To find out more, go to www.hachettespeakersbureau.com or call (866) 376-6591.

The publisher is not responsible for websites (or their content) that are not owned by the publisher.

Library of Congress Cataloging-in-Publication Data
Names: Zelikow, Philip, 1954– author.
Title: The road less traveled: the secret battle to end the Great War, 1916–1917 / Philip Zelikow.
Other titles: Secret battle to end the Great War, 1916–1917
Description: First edition. | New York: PublicAffairs, 2021. | Includes bibliographical references and index. |
Identifiers: LCCN 2020044440 | ISBN 9781541750951 (hardcover) | ISBN 9781541750944 (ebook)
Subjects: LCSH: World War, 1939-1945—Peace. | World War, 1914-1918—Diplomatic history. | Peace-building—History—20th century. | Peace movements—Europe—History—20th century. | Germany—Foreign relations—1888-1918. | France—Foreign relations—1914-1940. | Great Britain—Foreign relations—1901-1936. | United States—Foreign relations—1913-1921.
Classification: LCC D613 .Z45 2021 | DDC 940.3/12—dc23
LC record available at https://lccn.loc.gov/2020044440

ISBNs: 978-1-5417-5095-1 (hardcover); 978-1-5417-5094-4 (e-book)

LSC-C

Printing 1, 2021

FOR PAIGE

# CONTENTS

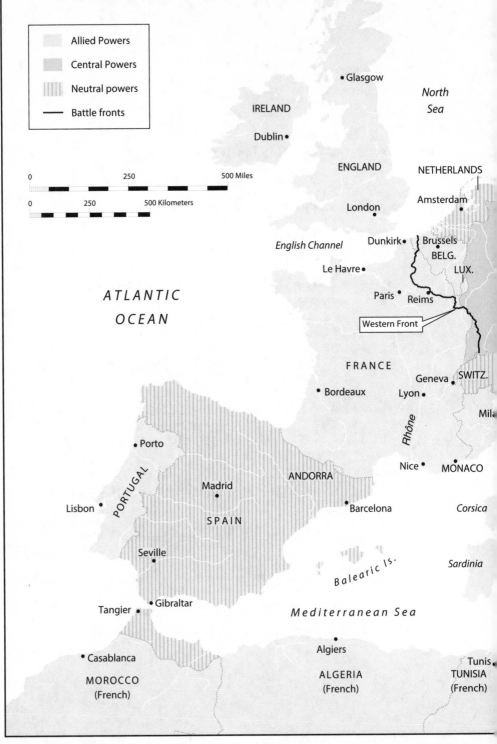

# BATTLE LINES IN EUROPE, AUTUMN 1916

Allied Powers

Central Powers

Neutral powers

—— Battle fronts

0       250       500 Miles

0    250    500 Kilometers

Glasgow

*North Sea*

IRELAND

ENGLAND

NETHERLANDS

Dublin

Amsterdam

London

*English Channel*

Dunkirk • Brussels

BELG.

LUX.

Le Havre

Paris • Reims

*ATLANTIC OCEAN*

Western Front

FRANCE

Geneva • SWITZ.

Bordeaux

Lyon

Mil

*Rhône*

Porto

ANDORRA

Nice • MONACO

PORTUGAL

Madrid

Lisbon

SPAIN

Barcelona

*Corsica*

Seville

*Balearic Is.*

*Sardinia*

Tangier • Gibraltar

*Mediterranean Sea*

Casablanca

Algiers

Tunis

MOROCCO
(French)

ALGERIA
(French)

TUNISIA
(French)

# THE ROAD
# LESS
# TRAVELED

# Two Roads Diverged

EDWARD THOMAS COULD NOT decide what to do. An emerging poet, Thomas, thirty-seven years old in the summer of 1915, was balancing his time between literary London and the home he loved in the beautiful Hampshire countryside of southern England. Married, with children, he had not yet been conscripted into the war that was already taking so many of his country's young men.

Thomas was torn. Should he enlist, join the war, and serve his country at the front? Or should he leave it all far behind and go to America?

Thomas had a real offer of refuge in America. His friend and soulmate, a fellow poet named Robert Frost, had gone back to his beloved farmlands of New Hampshire. Come join me, Frost had offered.

Frost and Thomas had become friends when Frost had moved to England in 1912, hoping that there he might make an impression with his work. Over many visits together, the two men had encouraged each other's writing, each other's dreams. They often took long walks through the woods, relishing the outdoors. "Thomas and I had become so inseparable," Frost recalled, "that we came to be looked on as some sort of literary Siamese twins."

Earlier in 1915, Frost and his wife, Elinor, had returned to America. With them, Edward Thomas sent his eldest child, his fifteen-year-old son. Thomas had an open invitation to come along too.

So, now, Thomas faced his choice: Should he join up and go to war or seek peace with his American friend? Thomas had often talked to Frost about his dilemma. "These last few days," Thomas wrote in June 1915, "I have been looking at 2 alternatives, trying to enlist or coming out to America."[1]

Frost replied by sending his friend a draft poem. He called it "The Road Not Taken."

> *Two roads diverged in a yellow wood,*
> *And sorry I could not travel both*
> *And be one traveler, long I stood*
> *And looked down one as far as I could*
> *To where it bent in the undergrowth;*
>
> *Then took the other, as just as fair,*
> *And having perhaps the better claim,*
> *Because it was grassy and wanted wear;*
> *Though as for that the passing there*
> *Had worn them really about the same,*
>
> *And both that morning equally lay*
> *In leaves no step had trodden black.*
> *Oh, I kept the first for another day!*
> *Yet knowing how way leads on to way,*
> *I doubted if I should ever come back.*
>
> *I shall be telling this with a sigh*
> *Somewhere ages and ages hence:*
> *Two roads diverged in a wood, and I—*
> *I took the one less traveled by,*
> *And that has made all the difference.*

Thomas took the message of the poem very personally. He was hurt by it. He felt Frost was accusing him of dithering and that the accusation was unfair. "It's all very well for you poets in a yellow wood to say you choose, but you don't."

Frost wrote back, assuring his friend that he was only teasing: "Methinks you strikest too hard in so small a matter. . . . the sigh was a mock sigh, hypocritical for the fun of the thing."

Thomas was unconvinced. "You have got me again over the Path not taken & no mistake."

A week later, he wrote to Frost to say that now his mind was made up. "Last week I had screwed myself up to the point of believing I should come out to America & lecture if anyone wanted me to. But I have altered my mind. I am going to enlist on Wednesday if the doctor will pass me."

The doctor did pass him. After training, Thomas reported for duty to become an officer in the Royal Artillery. The date was August 25, 1916.[2]

When Thomas took on his commission, the Great War had been under way for two years. The summer of 1916 had been the most monstrous yet. Already that season's gigantic concussions had passed into the common vocabulary; one needed only to say "Verdun" or "the Somme." No one in Europe had ever lived through such a war. It had passed well beyond any known experience.

Earlier, in 1916, Thomas wrote a poem that closed with the words

> *Now all roads lead to France*
> *And heavy is the tread*
> *Of the living; but the dead*
> *Returning lightly dance.*[3]

If they danced lightly in memory, the collective tread of the lost millions was heavy enough in the consciousness of the living. By August 1916, with no end to it in sight, all the leaders of the warring powers, at least in private, confronted the scale and cost of the slaughter, the unremitting hardship weighing on their societies.

Like Edward Thomas, the leaders also faced a fateful choice. They too looked out at two divergent roads. Down one path was ever more war. The other, perhaps, led to peace.

As they looked down the war path, no good military options were left. Money, food, munitions, and people were running short.

Yet the road to peace seemed daunting too. How to get there? How to take the first steps?

Exhausted nations, drummed onward by patriotic duty, sought meaning from their appalling sacrifices. Bureaucrats wrote papers speculating about annexing this or that strip of land. But to some of the leaders, on both sides, such aims seemed banal, almost trivial, in relation to the scale of what was being sacrificed. Was anything, beyond defense of home and country, worth all this? Yet, if they had doubts, how could they acknowledge them? What could they say? How could they be the first to go before their suffering people and offer to end the war without a heroic conclusion?

For Edward Thomas, the other path—away from war—led toward America. Those wartime leaders who confronted their own secret doubts also looked to America. The US president, Woodrow Wilson, held the key that could release them from their awful dilemma.

A week before Edward Thomas reported for duty, on August 18, 1916, the chancellor of Imperial Germany made the first big move. He sent a momentous and secret cable to his able ambassador in Washington. Britain had cut direct telegraph connections from Germany to America. So the chancellor's message had flashed over the wires first to neutral Stockholm. From there it was relayed to neutral Buenos Aires. From there his coded message was dispatched again, on to the German embassy in Washington. There the chancellor's words were laboriously decoded.

"We are happy to accept a mediation by the President to start peace negotiations among the belligerents who want to bring this about," the German chancellor instructed. "Please strongly encourage the President's activities in this regard."

To avoid giving any impression that his country was weak or desperate, the chancellor's plea was utterly secret. The German mediation request was unconditional. The chancellor sought President Woodrow Wilson's help to arrange both a peace conference among the belligerents to end the war and another, more general peace conference, with participation by the United States and other neutrals, to set postwar plans to secure the peace. The other path now beckoned.[4]

---

THE IMPERIAL CHANCELLOR who made that plea, the sixty-one-year-old Theobald von Bethmann Hollweg, had been in his job for seven years. He was a tall, firmly built, angular man, graying with a short mustache and beard.

He was not an elected politician. He was an imperial official, appointed by and serving at the pleasure of the kaiser. Bethmann was the supreme civilian leader and foreign minister both for the German Empire as a whole and for its largest member state, Prussia.

He had never attempted to become the kaiser's friend. His style was to be the quintessential dispassionate public servant. Deliberate, plain-spoken, and truthful, he offered appraisals and advice in a professional, careful, didactic style. Others in the court occasionally resented and mocked him; yet they respected him.[5]

Before the war started, Bethmann had been melancholy, his mood darkened by his wife's death in May 1914. As the conflict wore on and his son died at the front later in 1914, he became still more somber. By early 1915, Bethmann wondered aloud, to friends, about what share of the blame he should carry for the hurried and negligent diplomacy that had led to war in July 1914. "If one talks about guilt for this war—we also have our share of the responsibility, that we have to confess honestly," he confided. "And if I say this thought depresses me that would be too little—the thought does not leave me. I live in it."

Bethmann put some of the blame on xenophobic popular movements, including in his own country. "There we have our part of the guilt, the pan-Germans (*Alldeutsche*) have their guilt. In our domestic and foreign policy, we have lived in lies."[6]

By 1916, Bethmann was in plain opposition to the right-wing factions. They were doing all they could to bring him down. To some he seemed worn down, "tense, tired, and nervous," a colleague observed in the spring of 1916. "His hair has become white; his face is lined with deep furrows."[7]

But in August 1916 Bethmann had won the kaiser's approval to step out, for the first time, on the road to a general peace. The path, the German peace strategy, looked to Woodrow Wilson, the only leader of a great power not yet embroiled in the war, to bring the warring sides to the table.

And Wilson was eager to do it. And in Paris, and in London, other leaders too were eyeing the peace road. Bethmann's timing was better than he knew.

———

ON AUGUST 17, 1916, the day before Bethmann sent his request to Wilson, King George V granted an audience at Buckingham Palace to

Francis Bertie. Bertie, the second son of an earl, had spent fifty-three of his seventy-two years in diplomatic service until he was awarded a title of his own, Baron Bertie of Thame. The king had something he needed to tell Bertie. Since 1905, seemingly forever, Bertie had been Britain's envoy in Paris. The king had some startling information to pass on about France.

The king had just returned from a then secret visit to the British troops in the field. A key stop was at Val Vion, a handsome four-story brick mansion, about a mile east of the village of Beauquesne in northern France, that was the forward headquarters of the British commanding general in France, Douglas Haig. Val Vion was about twelve miles west of the networks of interlocking trench lines.

The gigantic Battle of the Somme had been raging for the past seven weeks. It would continue for months to come. The battle had already snuffed out more lives than any other that had ever been fought in the long history of the British Isles. From Val Vion, the king could hear the rumble of the guns.

France's president, Raymond Poincaré, came up to Val Vion for a private talk with the king. The king came out to greet him, wearing a beribboned khaki military uniform appropriate to the occasion.

The two men, the king and the president of France, were already well acquainted. Poincaré had been president since 1913. President Poincaré stepped forward in a more somber kind of uniform, a livery of mourning. Poincaré wore black from head to toe, without a bit of adornment or decoration. Poincaré knew the toll the war was taking. Seeing the king, on August 12, he had been "preoccupied by the numerous letters in his postbag calling for a peace settlement."[8]

To the French public, Poincaré was a symbol of the united war effort. He was a conservative nationalist. He was competent and worked hard. He had very much been part of and supported France's moves toward war in 1914. He personified France's "sacred union" to wage that war. A few months before he saw the king, in May, he had given a firm speech reiterating France's determination to fight on to impose a proper peace.

That was the public man. But in private, with the distant thunder of the guns in the background, Poincaré had a sober message. He confided to the king that he was in favor of "bringing the war to a conclusion as soon as possible."

How could this be done? Poincaré had his eye on the American path to peace. He expected the American president, Woodrow Wilson, to offer mediation by October. "When an offer of American mediation comes," the French president explained, "the Allies should be ready to state their terms for peace."

Poincaré believed that, understandably, the French public was "too optimistic." The people did not know the full situation. He also felt "great anxiety in regard to the state of affairs in Russia." That ally had just suffered yet another season of horrific losses. The political turmoil there was more and more obvious to all observers.[9]

Receiving this report from the king about what Poincaré had said, Bertie was greatly disturbed. The aged diplomat viewed any talk of peace with haughty disdain. Just six days before this royal audience, Bertie had in fact tried to persuade the foreign secretary, Edward Grey, to dismiss any peace move from Wilson.

Grey had not agreed. He had long been eyeing the peace path from America, much more than Bertie knew. To his blustery ambassador, Grey did not explain all this. Grey did predict, correctly, that Germany would ask Wilson to mediate. Britain, he told his ambassador, could not "make a blank refusal" of such a move by Wilson. Britain would have to consult with allies and dig into the terms. Britain's leaders did not dare to "put America against us."

Arguing with Grey, Bertie had played the French card. He "had not seen any signs of the French being ready to listen to peace proposals," he assured Grey, "they not being afraid of America as we are." How discomfiting it was now to Bertie. Having just made that argument to Grey, confidently describing French opinion, he might now have to report that, from no less a source than the king himself, it turned out that the famously patriotic president of France was very much "ready to listen to peace proposals."[10]

Grey would indeed soon learn about what Poincaré had said. To that he could add his own awareness of just how much the entire British and Allied war effort and food supplies depended on America. Grey also knew, as Bertie did not, the greatest secret of them all: that Britain's ability to pay for these supplies, to sustain its whole war effort, was running out.

On August 30, the British prime minister, Herbert Henry Asquith, began getting ready in earnest. He secretly asked the members of his cabinet's War Committee to submit their views on the terms for a negotiated peace.

The War Committee well knew that Woodrow Wilson was anxious to mediate an end to the war. Wilson had hoped that the British would ask him to do it. In the first half of 1916, the British government had in fact been sorely tempted. Yet, after round upon round of secret debates, the British had put off the American peace option. They and their allies decided they would first try out their long-planned gigantic summer offensives.

Those bloodily foundered. So, as hopes of a military breakthrough faded once again, as the shocking casualty lists touched families in every part of the land, the British debates began again. So, in August, for the first time, all the stars finally came into alignment for a real chance to end the war. On both sides, those who knew the most were pessimistic about the future and willing to consider ways to bring the war to an end. The one great power still on the sidelines was ready and willing to help them do it.

––––––

FOR MORE than five months, from August 1916 until the end of January 1917, leaders secretly struggled to end the Great War. They did so far out of public sight, one reason their battle is still little understood today.

Other supposedly pivotal moments in the war have long been the subject of intense scrutiny. For generations, the spotlights have been trained on how the war started. Scholars have minutely studied every move and countermove in the "July crisis" of 1914.

The great battles, however inconclusive, have been scoured for their significance. There is even a book dedicated to the war's last week, when its conclusion was inevitable.

In many ways, these choices not to end the war are more interesting than the choices that started it. In July 1914, the choices were rushed; options were murky and consequences hard to imagine. Between August 1916 and January 1917, the leaders worked for months on the peace road. By that time the stakes were tragically visible. But there are no books on why the war did not end in late 1916 and early 1917.

Few know that the German government secretly sought peace and pleaded for Wilson to mediate a peace conference. This was no informal feeler. It was a direct move made at the top, coordinated with allies and key political figures in Germany.

Few know that Wilson entirely recognized the significance of this move and sought to act on it as quickly and emphatically as he could. He placed it at the top of his agenda as soon as he was reelected. Wilson also knew he had practically absolute leverage—mainly financial—over the Allied ability to continue the war. Given the political climate in the warring countries, it was the Americans who could give the peacemakers in all the warring capitals the face-saving way out.

Few know that the divided British coalition government was intensely, secretly debating its own growing pessimism about the war and its imminent bankruptcy in the dollars to sustain it. These debates were quickened by a still deeper layer of secret knowledge. British intelligence had learned of the secret German peace move.

Few know any of these things because, to outsiders then and to most historians now, it seemed that nothing happened.

———

DURING THOSE five months of speculation, arguments, and choices behind closed doors, the future of the war, and the world, hung in the balance as never before.

The 1916–1917 phase of peacemaking was a unique opportunity. After 1916–1917, there would be other discussions about peace. But the alignment of possibilities slipped away. In March 1917, the Russian Revolution began. The Russian war effort slowly collapsed. That collapse eased some major problems for Germany and its allies. It gave them hope to carry on.

After 1916–1917, the British and French also had fresh reason to hope. They had America on their side. That sustained them, quite literally. In their darkest days, later in 1917 and in 1918, the rising American support always spurred them on. So, what in August 1916 were two years of agonizing war had by November 1918 turned into more than four. Those further years of widening war changed the whole course of world history.

The winter of 1916–1917 was pivotal for the history of the United States. Six months before America entered the war, few Americans (or British leaders) predicted it would. Even in January 1917, urged to look to the readiness of the armed forces, Woodrow Wilson, who had just been reelected with the slogan "He kept us out of war," turned sharply on his adviser. "There will be no war," the president said. "This country does not intend to become involved in this war."[11]

Until April 1917 the United States in its 141-year history had never sent a single soldier or sailor to fight on the continent of Europe. During the next year and a half, the United States, then a country of about one hundred million people, would send two million of them across the Atlantic Ocean to war. Neither Europe nor the United States would ever be the same.

There is a public story of why and how America's historic neutrality came to an end. It is a story catalyzed by a debate over German submarine warfare. That story is well understood.

But behind that public story is the secret story. The Germans resumed their full U-boat war, the public road to wider war, because some German leaders concluded that the alternative road, the secret road, the peace road, had, after months of trying, reached a dead end.

The Americans faced the end of neutrality because they too had run out of options: President Wilson's alternative, his peace diplomacy, had also failed, although—then and later—he never really understood quite what had gone wrong. This book is the secret understory of why and how America's historic neutrality came to an end and America embarked on a new course in world history.

———

THE STORY is, however, about much more than what happened to the United States. The consequences of these failures and Britain's own fateful choices in these months rippled far outward. The French historian Georges-Henri Soutou calls this period of late 1916 and early 1917, and the flurry of efforts to bring the war to an end, the *tournant*, the great turning. He is right.

"The transition from 1916 to 1917 marked a decisive turning point in the war," writes a German historian, Jörn Leonhard. "For the historian,"

Bentley Gilbert observes, "the autumn and winter of 1916 provide clearly a division in the course of the First World War. More to the point, many contemporary thinkers as well as the great suffering mass of Europe, saw events in the same way."[12]

A number of leaders realized that, by the latter half of 1916, their societies were on the edge of a precipice. All the major warring powers had pushed their countries to the outer limits of what a modern nation-state could do to turn governments into absolute machines of war. As the war continued and widened, from 1917 on, the once-mighty Liberal Party in Britain disintegrated as a political force. Germany, the United States, and France all explored how to further transform and militarize their entire societies. In that story too, "1916 was a pivotal year." These experiences became the models for the total-war states still to come.[13]

Had the war stopped in 1916, it would have given way to a scarred, bitter peace. There would have been more turmoil, just as years of turmoil followed the end of the Napoleonic Wars. But the outlook would have been better. As in a patient ravaged by illness, the immune system more and more compromised, every further year of terrible warfare lowered the world's odds for a healthy recovery.

To pick just one example: without a continuation of the war, it is hard to work out any plausible scenario in which the Bolsheviks would have seized power in Russia. As the war continued, profoundly damaged most of all, beyond the countless individual human tragedies, were the future prospects for core regions of the world—Europe and the Middle East.

As horrific as the war had been until the end of 1916, the conflicts of 1917–1918 pushed Europe and the Middle East over the edge. The historian Robert Gerwarth has recently chronicled that descent. "Notably in its final stages, from 1917 onwards, the Great War changed in nature.... It was in this period that a particularly deadly but ultimately conventional conflict between states—the First World War—gave way to an interconnected series of conflicts whose logic and purpose was much more dangerous."[14]

By the end of 1918, when the armistice stopped the shooting in western Europe, other wars were already well under way, including the revolution and civil war in Russia that began in 1917–1918, the violent decomposition of the Austro-Hungarian domains, and the wars that tore apart the former domains of the Ottoman Empire. The regions slid irreversibly into years of violent torment that continued on into 1923.

These further wars in central and eastern Europe, Asia, and the Middle East inflicted some of the worst traumas of the whole era. The scars and burdens—psychic, financial, physical, and political—crushed ideals, dimmed hopes, and infected European society with every conceivable social and political virus.

———

IN 1919–1920 the Reichstag of the new German republic conducted a remarkable investigation of two aspects of Germany's diplomacy related to the war. Part of the work was on the outbreak of war in 1914. But there was also a second report, one that inquired into why the German peace moves of 1916–1917 had failed.[15]

Lacking any evidence about the British, French, or American behavior, the early German investigators tended to point fingers of blame among themselves. Soon, those arguments about those peace moves were put aside, swamped by the overwhelming attention given instead to the great and public debates about 1914 war guilt and the unending waves of documentary releases and arguments about the "July crisis" of 1914.

After the war, knowledgeable British and American sources had no great interest in revisiting the question of whether they could have ended the war in 1916–1917. Wilson's emissary, Edward House, for example, wrote a memoir with the Yale historian Charles Seymour, edited with the help of the former British intelligence agent William Wiseman, that was immensely influential but carefully omitted and edited key material.

Wilson's great biographer Arthur Link began pulling together some of the key German and American material and kept revising his interpretation of it. At first, he thought the Germans were never serious. Then he thought they had not given Wilson enough time. In his last work, Link began also blaming members of Wilson's own team for the American failure. But Link never had any clearer idea than Wilson did of just what had gone wrong. Nor did Link have the evidence now available about the crucial British debates and the way they interacted with the other stories. Another Wilson biographer, John Milton Cooper Jr., came closer, noticing several key clues over the years, but never squarely turned his full attention to the peace story.

The historical work has continued to be limited by national interpretations. To this day, British historians of the period mistakenly assume that any peace was impossible because the Germans would not compromise. Mirroring that, the German historians tend to mistakenly assume that peace was impossible because the British would not compromise. Both sides thus inadvertently echo arguments made back in 1916 by the hard-liners in London and Berlin.[16] And neither group tends to look hard enough at what the Americans could have done, given the situation and the strong cards the Americans held in their hand.

Also, since there was no British peace diplomacy during this particular period, some historians on both sides of the Atlantic assumed, as many people did at the time, that British leaders were generally optimistic about the war. That assumption is mistaken. Or they assumed that British leaders were not interested in a negotiated peace. That assumption is, at best, misleading. An intense crisis about whether or how to continue the war was what really precipitated the fall of the Asquith government in December 1916, and that did not quiet the issue.

As I wrote in the study of the 9/11 attacks by the 9/11 Commission, "The path of what happened is so brightly lit that it places everything else more deeply into shadow."[17] Much of what happened in this history, the secret debates and hidden crises, was already in shadow to begin with. This history should see the light, because, beyond the tragedy, it is also a story of inspiring possibilities.

––––––––

THIS BOOK originated in the late 2000s, while I was working on another project with Ernest May, who had written one of the foundational accounts of the end of American neutrality. We concluded that the peace debates of 1916–1917 deserved another very hard look. May passed away in 2009. I kept chipping away and started publicly presenting early versions of the argument.

I was fascinated by the momentous puzzle of why the secret German peace move of 1916 had failed. Reconstructing the story required historical detective work in German, British, and American sources. I analyzed the proposals and arguments with a professional's eye, as a former policymaker and diplomat.

After I presented on this topic at Harvard in 2017, a British scholar there connected me with Daniel Larsen at Cambridge. Sharing our work, we realized we had independently noticed some of the same questions, and Larsen, focusing on the British story, had arrived at some analogous conclusions.[18] I also invited Holger Afflerbach to review an early paper and found that he had just published a book, focused on the German story, in which he too had independently noticed "a historic opportunity to bring the First World War to an end... and spare Europe and the world the enormous costs of the last two years of war."[19] Showing how all the stories intertwine finally brings that "historic opportunity," that road not taken, into view.

———

TWO ROADS diverged. Both were uncertain. One led toward peace, the other toward a wider war. The secret battles to end the war were not a blur of explosions and gunfire, the battles that kill thousands. They were the quieter, more secret kind that determine the fates of millions. This is the story of how a small number of leaders, mainly in London, Washington, and Berlin, faced their two roads.

Analytically, one can distill some of the miscues into cold isolates: the unfortunate timing of the American presidential election season, the division and paralysis of Britain's governing coalition, the ambitions of David Lloyd George, the dissembling of Edward House, the resurgent faction of German militarists. But, as in the greatest tragedies, what stands out are human beings, flawed as they are, striving courageously to avert catastrophe. They wrestled with a challenge that, in its way, was as great as any of the mud-spattered heroics in Flanders or Galicia, at Verdun or Belleau Wood.

The story of the lost peace would be easy if it were merely a story of governments with irreconcilable goals. But, as this book shows, the chancellor of Germany and the president of the United States had a vision that could mesh with the vision that held sway in much, if not most, of the British cabinet, at times including both of the relevant prime ministers. The possibilities for peace were tantalizingly within reach.

Some leaders rose to the occasion. Others did not. Some demonstrated the greatest civic courage; others, its absence. It was one of those times that reveal a person's deepest strengths and weaknesses, in ability and in character.

"Peace is on the floor waiting to be picked up!" the German ambassador to the United States pleaded in November 1916. He was right. But with the war in full bloody bloom, peace depended on enough people choosing the less obvious outcome: they had to step onto the road less traveled by.

# CHAPTER 1

# Wilson Makes a New Peace Move

## Woodrow Wilson, Pragmatist

For two years, from the moment the war began, the American president had been hoping and waiting for one of the warring powers to ask him to mediate an end to it. Each year, Woodrow Wilson had dispatched his personal eyes and ears, Edward House, the private adviser who had become practically a member of his family, to talk to the leading people in London, Paris, and Berlin, take soundings, and see what was possible.

In 1914, House had gone out while Europe was still at peace. He could see that Europe was divided into two large alliances. On one side were the French and Russians, hoping for British backing. On the other side were the Germans and Austro-Hungarians, warily fearing they would be encircled and crushed, especially as Russian power—financed mainly by France—was growing and modernizing. House sensed the disturbing way German military arrogance mixed with German anxiety, surrounded by possible enemies.

House was an upper-class Texan who assumed white Anglo-Saxon superiority. He never thought or cared much about Russia, or Asia. Therefore, back then, in the spring of 1914, he sought to reconcile Germany and Britain, perhaps by easing their naval competition. House's other big idea (which Wilson did not know about) was that Britain, Germany, the United States, and France might get together and jointly figure out how to manage the "waste places of the earth."[1]

Everyone seemed to like House and regard him as well-meaning. But no one in London and no one actually running the German government took these ideas very seriously.[2] Most recent crises had come out of the Balkans, worrying Austria-Hungary and engaging Russian interests. House knew little about the Balkans.

When another Balkan crisis erupted during the summer of 1914, House did, though, know enough to advise Wilson that "Germany is exceedingly nervous and at high tension and she knows that her best chance of success is to strike quickly and hard, therefore her very alarm may cause her to precipitate action as a means of safety."[3]

In early 1915, with Europe at war, Wilson sent House back to Europe to float the idea of an American mediation to negotiate peace. The mediation would be based on German agreement to withdraw from Belgium, pay an indemnity for damage done, and join this with some large effort at general disarmament.

At that point, none of the warring powers were interested. With all of their initial military plans having been tested, both sides were determined to try out a revised set of military plans in 1915, for another full year of fighting. The Entente Allies, whom Americans often just referred to as the "Allies," added Japan and Italy to the core alliance of Britain, France, and Russia (and Serbia, where the war had started). The Central Powers, Germany and Austria-Hungary, added the Ottoman Empire to their alliance and, late in 1915, added Bulgaria as well.

Using their superior navy, the British tightened their blockade of the enemy powers. In response, the Germans declared a war zone in waters near Britain and Europe. Their small but growing submarine force would try to create a blockade of its own, sinking vessels without warning.

In May 1915, shocking the whole world, a U-boat torpedoed the great luxury liner *Lusitania* just off the coast of Ireland. The 1,198 who went down with the ship included 128 Americans. The year between May 1915 and May 1916 was probably the peak of anti-German feeling in the United States. Yet then, and later, Wilson, like most Americans, still did not want to join the war.

———

WHEN THE WAR began during the summer of 1914, Americans understood its origins no better than the average student does today. Another Balkan war, the third in three years, had set off a European war. To Americans then, like almost all people now, the reasons why this turned into a general European war and the ultimate responsibility for that seemed obscure.[4]

Americans did understand, though, that Germany had attacked and overrun neutral Belgium in order to get at France. The Germans looked and often acted like ruthless invaders. It was the Germans whose troops were occupying Belgium and part of France. The simultaneous Russian invasion of Germany and Austria-Hungary was practically invisible in the American press. And, in any case, by 1915 the Russian invaders had been thrown back.

Among the warring powers the details of the "July crisis" of 1914 were also obscure, but the war began to take on a much larger meaning after the fact, after their peoples were fully engaged. Somehow, they were at war. Now that they were, the highest principles were said to be at stake.

For the Allies, it soon was a war for "civilization." For the Germans and Austro-Hungarians, it was a war to preserve culture, their moral community and way of life, against Slav conquest or the domination of amoral Anglo-Saxon materialism.[5] Translating such exalted goals into any sort of meaningful war aims was a less lofty exercise, to which bureaucrats or military officers might dedicate their imaginations.

Many Americans reading the news, reading how each side was justifying its cause, were just glad to be well clear of the war. To the extent Americans rooted for one side or the other, opinion leaders tended to favor the Allied side. For historical and cultural reasons, Americans in that era sympathized more with France than with Britain. Tens of thousands of young Americans volunteered to help the Allies, as soldiers or pilots, in hospitals or driving ambulances.[6]

———

BY 1915, American public opinion about the war clustered into three broad groups.

First, there were the Americans who disdained any foreign entanglements. This included a significant number of pacifists, who were concentrated in the Democratic and Socialist Parties. America had a small but significant Socialist Party back then, a little smaller than the Labour Party in Britain and much smaller than the large Social Democratic Party in Germany.

Pacifist or not, the citizens in this camp agreed that America could safely stay out of the war. They insisted on a pure adherence to neutrality. Those who wanted to sell goods to either side or to travel across the Atlantic might just have to do so at their own risk.

William Jennings Bryan, who had contested the White House for the Democrats in three presidential elections, represented this view. He resigned his position as secretary of state in May 1915 because Wilson did not sufficiently share his ideals.

A second faction wanted American intervention on the side of the Allies. This group thought America, as a great nation and great power, had a duty to stand up and fight for justice and civilization. They thought Germany dominated by brutal, antidemocratic "Prussian militarism." Russia's membership on the Allied side was downplayed as an unfortunate necessity.

The most vigorous spokesman of this faction was former Republican president Theodore Roosevelt. He regarded neutrality as craven, a cowardly refuge for those who did not care who was right or who was wrong.

Wilson lined up with the third faction, the "moderates." The "moderates" wanted America to stay engaged in the world, support international law, protect American "neutral rights" to trade and travel, and stand up for American "honor." But they preferred to stay out of the war. They thought America was not immediately endangered by it.[7] This faction was predominant in both major parties, Democratic and Republican.

To a principled activist like Roosevelt or a principled pacifist like Bryan, Wilson seemed to have no strong principles. To them, his high-minded rhetoric was the gloss used by a temporizing opportunist.

This was not how Wilson saw himself. His formative years in the post–Civil War South had, for him, dispelled heroic or romantic ideals of war. Also he, like most of his fellow progressives, "believed that America's unique mission was to purify herself in order to provide an example of democracy triumphant over social and economic injustice and a model of peaceful behavior." As Wilson put it, "If we have had aggressive purposes and covetous ambitions, they were the fruit of our thoughtless youth as a nation and we have put them aside. We shall, I confidently believe, never again take another foot of territory by conquest."[8]

Wilson derided hyphenated Americans who might feel divided loyalties. He was for "Americans for Big America," who "look forward to the days in which America shall strive to stir the world without irritating it or drawing it on to new antagonisms, when the nations with which we deal shall at last come to see upon what deep foundations of humanity and justice our passion for peace rests."⁹

Therefore, in thinking about the Great War, Wilson regarded himself as a dispassionate realist. After the sinking of the *Lusitania* in May 1915, Wilson said there was such a thing as being "too proud to fight." The other sides both derided him for this phrase, either because it did not project pure neutrality or because it sounded weak and Quakerish to some American ears. Both sides misunderstood the essential attitude behind Wilson's choice of words. "Too proud to fight" was not an expression of pacifism. It was an expression of condescension.

Wilson was not interested in exploring what happened in 1914 in order to judge who was guilty or innocent. He sized up the European war as a colossal tragedy for which all the major European powers shared some measure of responsibility. In his analysis, their whole system of imperialist rivalry, opposing military alliances, and arms races had shown itself to be catastrophically dangerous.

To Wilson, the great and obvious lesson of the war was the need to develop some new basis for managing world politics. He had no well-formed idea of what this world order should look like. He did know that it should be different from the system that had caused the war. It would presumably rest on some shared hopes for peaceful cooperation, a check to destabilizing arms races, the development of international law, and no more wars of conquest. He also knew that the United States was becoming immensely powerful economically and might somehow play a vital role in shaping whatever new system might emerge after the war.

Wilson thought it was important to take a cold-blooded view of American national interests. The war was, he thought, a great danger to those interests, since, as it continued, it would damage the future prospects and prosperity of the whole world. But Wilson saw no great case for American intervention to help the Allies win the war. America, he said, should save its strength "for the anxious and difficult days of restoration and healing which must follow." What Wilson saw was a great case for American intervention in the cause of peace, to help end the war as soon as possible.

Wilson's stance on German submarine warfare revealed the way he calculated American interests. He did not demand that Germany stop all submarine attacks. Instead, he carefully and quite personally crafted a compromise position—that Germany had to cease *unrestricted* submarine warfare or face ruptured relations and war with the United States.

Wilson's proposed restrictions evolved into a final ultimatum delivered to Germany in April 1916. Germany could attack warships without warning. But German submarines should not attack passenger or cargo vessels without warning, since these were presumed to be unarmed. In such attacks, the submarines should obey the traditional rules of "cruiser warfare," approaching on the surface to at least give warning.[10]

With this position, Wilson did not protect American cargo, carried in British vessels, from being sunk. He did not protect American passengers from having to take to the lifeboats. He was just trying to persuade Germany to use its new naval weapon in conformity with traditional rules and customs of international law. Such rules might avoid future humanitarian catastrophes like the *Lusitania* tragedy. They might reveal whether Germany was willing to be a rule-abiding nation at all—which would then show whether any durable peace could be made with that government. Politically, by taking this position, he could satisfy those who wanted America to draw at least some sort of line to regulate German sinking of unarmed ships.

To present-day readers, the attention of Wilson and many others around the world to international law and possible arbitration of disputes may seem a bit quaint. Yet, on this topic in 1916, Wilson was no outlier. All three of the American factions treated international law as having cardinal importance. The pacifists were even more ardent in their hope of using arbitration to end all war. The interventionists, like former president Theodore Roosevelt, were even more zealous in their desire to enforce international law and justice on "outlaw" states. One of Roosevelt's chief allies, former secretary of war Elihu Root, was also the first president of the American Society of International Law.[11]

This was an age when, for all its violence, the warring parties all took questions of international law quite seriously. Regard for international law, at least ostensibly, marked a nation as civilized. For a hundred years, all the great powers had participated in elaborate conferences to settle their differences. They had accepted various forms of third-party arbitration even on some serious disputes.

Thus, in the America of 1915–1916, Wilson's position was more practical and less rigid in its approach to international law than the positions of either of the other factions. Even as it infuriated the men of principle on both wings of opposition, Wilson's moderate stance won broad acceptance among politicians and opinion leaders in both parties.

In late 1915 and early 1916, there was another national debate, this time about military preparedness. It too split into about the same three camps.

Again, Wilson took the centrist position. When his secretary of war, Lindley Garrison, wanted a larger buildup of the army, Wilson forced him to resign. The middle ground was that some meaningful modernization and extra preparedness were needed, especially to build up the navy. But the measures the Wilson administration enacted during 1916 were not intended to get America ready for any imminent entry into the war. The land forces were conceived more for home defense and modest long-term professionalization. The planned naval buildup was more impressive. But it too was presented as defensive, intended to equal the size of the British navy and protect American neutrality. Even that naval plan would not reach fruition until the early 1920s. And these measures represented the outer limit of what a bitterly divided Congress was prepared to support.[12]

———

WOODROW WILSON is caricatured as a stiff-necked idealist with fanciful notions of making the world safe for democracy. People who style themselves as "realists" regard themselves as attentive to power and practicalities. They contrast themselves, in this imaginary paradigm, with wooly-headed, would-be secular messiahs like Wilson.

There was nothing unusual about Wilson's appeal to ideals in this age of reform. "All the major figures in public life during the first two decades of the twentieth century proclaimed themselves idealists. Roosevelt and Bryan did so proudly."

What distinguished Wilson in 1916 was his seeming openness to compromise and aversion to confrontation. That was why a biographer of both Roosevelt and Wilson, John Milton Cooper Jr., observed that "nothing infuriated Roosevelt more than to hear Wilson called an idealist."

In Wilson's world of progressive reformers, he "came off as one of the most careful, hard-headed, and sophisticated idealists of his time."[13] Wilson's attitude toward the Great War showed his instinct for balance and compromise.

To develop concrete ideas and plans of action on the great legislative issues of the day, Wilson usually was offered a rich mix of ideas already being prepared by others, with their advocates in Congress and the press. One key issue on Wilson's desk in 1916 was a landmark bill to establish an eight-hour workday. Arguments and evidence flowed into his in-box. Wilson applied fine judgment as he sorted through the evidence and arguments. His strength was his ability to react, analyze the information, size up the politics, correspond with the players, and judge well how best to secure the bill's passage. If the flow of information was strong, Wilson could steer with the current.

In the foreign policy realm, however, there was no gush of information or predictable course. If Wilson wanted to make a major policy proposal, he or someone else had to develop an analysis of it, perhaps from scratch. Wilson was unconscious of what he lacked. He did not know enough about the necessary staff work to know that he did not have it.

Wilson knew he had a different and more personal responsibility in foreign affairs. He knew that went with the job of being president. He had become skilled in handling, often drafting, the relatively narrow exchanges of notes and threats in nearly a year of submarine and blockade diplomacy with Germany and Britain. He had learned a lot from early mistakes in handling problems with Mexico, and by 1916 he was able to steer a careful course to limit America's involvement in that country's civil war.

But in the world war, Wilson's skills and process as a potential mediator and peacemaker were untested. There was a great precedent: in 1905, Theodore Roosevelt had mediated the peace negotiations that ended the last war among great powers, between Russia and Japan, and he had been awarded one of the new Nobel Peace Prizes for this achievement. Wilson knew little about the details of exactly how Roosevelt and his team had done this. Wilson and House had no comparable experience with serious diplomatic choreography.[14]

Wilson did recognize the scale of the test he faced. On October 3, 1916, he gave a long interview to a journalist he admired, Ida Tarbell. In his mind was his plan to take up the secret German initiative requesting his mediation to end the war, but to Tarbell, who knew nothing of this, Wilson only spoke generally about the challenge he would face in trying to end the war.

All along he had tried, he said, to keep emotion from swaying his judgment. He told her, "I have tried to look at this war ten years ahead, to be a historian at the same time I was an actor."

"There were people," Wilson explained, who felt they could settle the war "on what they knew, but usually they came to me with general statements. It bores me to have men waste my time in general terms."

"What I want to know," Wilson explained, "is how it is to be done. I am never interested until that point is reached.... I am not interested until a practical method is proposed—that is, I suppose that in government I am a pragmatist: my first thought is, will it work?"[15]

## Woodrow Wilson and Edward House

In person, the president was a charming, highly intelligent, perceptive, and well-read man. He liked to have time alone to think and reflect. He liked

*Wilson*

an orderly routine. He spent most of his time with an extremely small inner circle.

Until her death in August 1914 from Bright's disease, Wilson's first wife, Ellen, had been his vital partner in everything. Wilson had been terribly lonely and depressed when she died, but during the second half of 1915, he fell in love with and ardently courted Edith Galt, who became his second wife and another close confidante (though Edith does not seem to have matched Ellen's qualities of judgment). He often shared papers with Edith, who—as with Ellen—became his constant sounding board.

Wilson had no speechwriter or policy team: he usually drafted his own speeches or notes on what to say. He relied on an Irish Catholic secretary, Joe Tumulty, to schedule and handle routine business, including some press management. He looked to a young man who was the White House doctor, Cary Grayson, as a kind of family member and daily golf companion.

Wilson's only really close male friend was Edward House. Accompanied sometimes by his wife and always by his secretary, House visited Washington and the White House from time to time. Or, if he was in New York, Wilson might stay at House's pleasant but not lavish apartment there.

In his academic career, before becoming president of Princeton, Wilson had been a professional scholar of government. He had written with great sweep about the general qualities of political institutions, for instance, contrasting the American and British systems.

In his brief and successful tenure as governor of New Jersey, then again in his first term as president, Wilson was at his best leading and managing the passage of reform legislation. He did not craft policy programs in the way people might think of this today. Instead, his talent lay in the careful choice of people and positions. He would express these positions, above all in speeches, which the many newspapers and magazines then so widely read would cover and often publish in full.

Wilson was an articulate public speaker but not fiery. He was eloquent, in the manner of an earnest, candid, and very knowledgeable teacher, which is exactly what he had been. In 1914 the radical journalist John Reed interviewed Wilson. "The window curtains swayed in a warm breeze; things were unhurried, yet the feeling in that room was of powerful organization." Reed had "never met a man who gave such an impression of quietness inside.... Wilson's power emanates from it."[16]

---

To HANDLE his diplomacy during his first term in office, Wilson's foreign policy process was simple. In 1916 there was a quite competent new secretary of war, former Cleveland mayor Newton Baker. The secretary of the navy, a former newspaper editor, Josephus Daniels, had a vigorous assistant secretary, a New Yorker from a good family, Franklin Roosevelt. But these cabinet officers were hardly involved in or informed about the diplomacy surrounding war and peace. The military departments had developed no serious plans for what to do if America entered the Great War, and nor had the Treasury, being run by the president's son-in-law, William McAdoo. Wilson had no call for such war plans and didn't want to see them elaborated.

There were important voices in the Congress, of course. The chairman of the Senate Foreign Relations Committee was a Democrat, Bill Stone of Missouri, a pacifist close to Bryan. The voices in Congress offered next to no input on strategy. Like most outsiders, they were content to offer broad and breezy opinions about America's general "position."

So, when it came to the war, Wilson rarely solicited advice about what to do from anyone. His policy process consisted of his writing desk and his in-box, filled day to day by the State Department, which would relay messages or letters from his ambassadors or notes from a foreign government.

William Jennings Bryan's replacement as secretary of state, Robert Lansing, had been Bryan's deputy. Lansing was an experienced international lawyer, a veteran of property arbitrations and boundary disputes, and had no meaningful experience of what we might now call geopolitics.

Wilson attended faithfully to meetings and correspondence with Lansing, whom he regarded as a handsome, intelligent clerk. Lansing would forward important foreign reports and might offer a draft reply. Lansing's workday during the war was very much nine to five. He occasionally made tactical suggestions, rarely offering any broad policy advice. Those ideas he vented only in memos left in his diary.

Wilson studied the reports that came in to him from foreign governments or his ambassadors, sometimes reading them aloud to his wife or to Edward House, if his friend was in town. When House was away, as was usually the case, Wilson and House relied on frequent letters back and forth.

House got along with Lansing, who understood the way things worked. House had also arranged the appointment of Lansing's deputy, his counselor, Frank Polk. Polk was more broad-gauged than Lansing, better at sizing up people and situations. He had been corporation counsel of New York City, as well as a private lawyer. Polk had gotten to know House through exchanges about which New York politicos to put in which jobs. But Polk had no particular international experience.

————

CONSEQUENTLY, WOODROW WILSON'S foreign policy advice came almost exclusively from one man. Although Edward House was a presidential adviser on many subjects, domestic and foreign, his role was strange and unique in American history.[17] He was not, and never had been, a government official on a public payroll. He did not regularly go to work in or near the White House. He was a private citizen with an exceptional network of personal contacts and correspondents.

Born in 1858, House was the youngest child of one of the wealthiest men in Texas, where his father was an extremely successful merchant, banker, and plantation owner. Educated at Cornell and setting up his home in Austin, Edward House formed a network of other affluent up-and-comers who, with him, created a political network to advise and help direct money to their preferred Democrats.

These were "New South" men. They preferred local businesses and banks, run by up-and-comers like them. They campaigned against the power of the railroads and trusts based in distant northern states like New York and New Jersey. House and his friends had a run of supporting successful candidates for governor and other offices. One of the first of those, "Big Jim" Hogg, made House an honorary Texas "colonel." Although the tag "Colonel House" stuck, he never saw any actual military service.

By 1902 House had secured his portion of the family inheritance, which was more than enough to support a genteel lifestyle. He retreated from Texas to a life in the Northeast, splitting his time between New York City, New England in the summer (usually by the seashore), and annual grand tours in Europe. He continued to dabble knowledgeably in Democratic

Party politics and remained a friend of the perennial candidate, William Jennings Bryan.

House met Wilson just as the latter was organizing his first presidential run in 1911. Wilson's best friend from Princeton days had turned against him in a battle over the future of the university. House happened to step into the void. In House, Wilson found a man who hobnobbed with the East Coast elite and was of his own cultivated social class.

House's political ideals were also those of a reform Democrat, what in England were the ideals of the "radical" faction within the Liberal Party. These ideals mixed a desire to tame the power of big business, interest in social insurance, devotion to small, local government, and a preference for peaceful cooperation in world affairs. Wilson and House were instinctively very sympathetic to the Liberal leaders in England like Prime Minister H. H. (Herbert Henry) Asquith and his charismatic Treasury secretary, David Lloyd George.

In addition to his gentility and reform ideals, House was a savvy political operator. That did not mean he was expert in policy and administration. House had never actually run an agency or program, or in fact anything beyond his family business interests. He had stayed out of the hurly-burly of daily administration of any large public operation. But he was an expert in the people side. This was an era when wielding patronage, picking and deploying the right man to represent your faction or fill a job, was a principal part of party politics.

House had no public style. He was the quintessential inside man, slender in build, "a small man with strange cat-like eyes, a broad forehead and a thin face." He spoke in a low, modulated voice, "almost as one might speak to another in a cathedral."[18] His style was that of the sympathetic listener, low-key and discreet.

For someone like Wilson, House had the added charm of not seeking any particular job for himself. He just wanted to be the president's good counselor. So, although he became a clearinghouse helping pick who got what jobs in the Wilson administration, for himself he wanted nothing. He kept a regular distance, never living in Washington, DC, and continuing his habit of summering in New England and touring Europe.

In Europe, before the war, he spent his time, as he wrote a friend, with "races, polo, pigeon shooting, fencing, concerts, grand opera, etc." Yet,

*House*

beneath the veneer of the diffident, polite, and knowledgeable man of the
world bubbled odd, utopian ambitions. He would entertain friends and
family with elaborate fantasies about how, if he were the kaiser, he might
fight a European war.[19]

As he was getting to know Wilson, in 1911 and 1912, House articulated
his fantasies in a novel. Privately published the month before Wilson's election in November 1912, the book listed no author. It was advertised only as
being written by "a distinguished public man." House's anonymous novel
imagined the rise in America of an all-powerful reformer, in *Philip Dru:
Administrator, a Story of Tomorrow, 1920–1935.*

Dru is an army officer, a "young knight" who becomes America's dictator. With this mighty power, Dru takes on the bosses. America descends
into civil war. Dru leads the righteous forces to victory in a gigantic battle.
He cleanses the country with sweeping reforms. Then, having restored free
elections to his now much happier land, Dru sails off into the Pacific with
a beautiful, admiring wife.

The slightly futuristic novel that dramatizes political ideas was a popular genre of the prewar generation. H. G. Wells was an exponent, in a more futuristic setting, as was William Le Queux, whose novels were popular with Asquith. But House's book is not in their league. The writing is wooden, didactic, and awkward, and the whole thing is somewhat embarrassing to read.

House distributed copies to his friends, including Wilson, who reacted politely, unlike the reviewer in the *New York Times*, a young Walter Lippmann, who did not know the author. Lippmann, then twenty-three, was already making a mark as a leading thinker of the Progressive movement, embarking on the career that would make him America's leading political journalist.

"Now, if the author is really a man of affairs," Lippmann wrote, "this is an extraordinarily interesting book. It shows how utterly juvenile a great man can be. If he is really an 'insider,' then we who are on the outside have very little to learn. If he is really an example of the far-seeing public man," Lippmann went on, "then, in all sincerity, I say, God help this sunny land. The imagination is that of a romantic boy of 14 who dreams of what he would do if he had supreme power and nobody objected. But if Philip Dru is a projection of an anonymous great man, the only adequate comment is that of the girl whom Dru marries: 'How you do enthuse one, Philip.'"[20]

———

IT's NOT immediately obvious what the studious and solitary Wilson saw in House's odd mix of savvy and dilettantish dabbling. One key is that House was, in some ways, the opposite of Wilson—a good listener and an observer, attuned to what he was hearing in society, and happy to put the hours in socially to get to the interesting people, none of which appealed to Wilson. House was a reasonable judge of people and their abilities, colored of course by whether they agreed with him.

When he stayed in Washington, he would sit with Wilson and his family in the parlor in the evening as they read poetry or essays to each other.

Lippmann later came to know both Wilson and House about as well as any journalist in America. (He apparently never made the connection between House and the anonymous author of the Philip Dru book he had blistered years earlier.) After House's death, Lippmann explained,

The things which Colonel House did best, meeting men face to face and listening to them patiently and persuading them gradually, Woodrow Wilson could hardly bear to do at all. The President was an intellectual, accustomed to acquiring knowledge by reading and to imparting it by lecturing and by writing books. Wilson was annoyed, quickly bored, and soon exhausted by the incoherence, the verbosity, and the fumbling of most talk, especially the talk of practical men of affairs.... Colonel House, on the contrary, was as nearly proof against boredom as anyone imaginable. Lacking all intellectual pride, having no such intellectual cultivation as Woodrow Wilson, he educated himself in the problems of the day by inducing men of affairs to confide in him.[21]

Wilson did not rely on House to develop specific positions on policy. Wilson launched landmark domestic programs in his first term, and House's influence on them was marginal. A perennial foreign policy issue throughout Wilson's time in office was how to deal with the enormous civil war in Mexico that had begun in 1910 and continued through all his time in office. Again, even though he was a Texan, House had marginal influence on the substance of that subject.

But when it came to Europe, House could draw on his supposed familiarity from all those summer travels and from his social set there. He became Wilson's unique bridge to European politics—and European war.

He was especially empowered because Wilson and Lansing did not wish to entrust confidential work to the obvious usual channel: US and foreign ambassadors. Wilson and Lansing disliked the British ambassador to Washington, Cecil Spring-Rice, a man of intemperate disposition who also had the misfortune of being a close friend of America's leading Wilson-hater, Theodore Roosevelt.

Nor did Wilson and House wish to rely on their own ambassador to London, Walter Hines Page. Page was a serious thinker and writer, first as a journalist and later as a major publisher and editor. His had been one of the most important American voices among Democratic Party reformers. However, Page was an ardent advocate of American entry into the war on Britain's side. By 1915, Wilson no longer trusted his objectivity.

To Berlin, Wilson had sent James Gerard, a New York lawyer and politician long supported by New York's powerful Tammany Hall political machine. Gerard spoke and wrote impulsively and tactlessly, rarely bridling his quick temper or thinking much about what he was saying. Reading one of Gerard's reports from Germany, Wilson once commented, "Who can fathom this? I wish [the Germans] would hand this idiot his passports [sending him home to America]."[22]

The one diplomat in Washington who impressed both Wilson and House as a statesman, however, was the German ambassador, Count Johann von Bernstorff. They were prepared to listen to him.

## Wilson and House Plan a New Peace Mission

In the autumn of 1915, Wilson and House redoubled their efforts to mediate an end to the war. The context was that war with Germany seemed quite possible, even likely. Americans were then at a high pitch of anger about German submarine warfare and German espionage activities in the United States.

Rather than try to persuade Congress and the country to go to war over some particular submarine incident, House came up with the idea of using a peace mediation offer as a strong, clear basis to bring America into the war—which at that time he thought was inevitable. His scheme was this: The United States would offer, in good faith, to open peace negotiations. House expected the Germans to reject the offer. Then, once Germany had cast aside the proffered olive branch, Wilson could go to Congress and ask for a declaration of war.

House's essential partner in this scheme would be his friend, the British foreign secretary, Edward Grey. In all of House's visits to London, no one in the top of the British government had been more tolerant and sympathetic.

By this time, Grey had been leading the Foreign Office for more than ten years. He was an institution, if a lonely one.

In his youth, Grey had been one of those young men who seemed to excel at anything he tried, whether with books or on a playing field, but never cared to try too hard. He was not a partier; he was just naturally relaxed and aloof, preferring above all to spend his time outdoors, fly-fishing in a nearby stream. Leaving Oxford, a hereditary baronet with an assured income, he found he enjoyed politics and became a Liberal MP for the border constituency of Berwick upon Tweed.

*Grey*

Political life and marriage sharpened Grey's commitment to his work. In 1892, he received a subcabinet appointment in the Foreign Office. When out of office, he became a leading member of the opposition, and when the Liberals came back in at the end of 1905, Grey was appointed as the foreign secretary.

Only a few months later, Grey's beloved wife died in a carriage accident. Grey turned inward, devoting himself monastically to his work, with the beckoning streams and countryside as his great outlet (he was a keen student of birds and fishing). His style was careful and honest. He knew the contours of diplomacy well, and by 1916 he had become the longest continuously serving foreign secretary in British history.

———

WILSON ASKED HOUSE to go to Europe in December 1915, just before the president's wedding to Edith Galt. As usual, House would receive no salary, though the government would pay his travel expenses. Formally, if anyone asked, he was going out to confer on Wilson's behalf with America's ambassadors in London, Paris, and Berlin.

In fact, House had a secret mission. His job was to see if the British and French governments would agree to an American call for a peace conference. House wrote ahead to Grey, explaining his idea and that the peace conference would agree on ways to end "militarism and navalism."[23]

House still saw the American peace mediation plan as a clever entry ramp to set up the argument for American involvement in the war. But Wilson did not see it that way at all. He wanted to play the game straight and seek support for a genuine, neutral mediation. To House, Wilson had "visibly weakened." The president "seemed to think we would be able to keep out of the war."

Wilson had his way. There was no need to set up a pretext for American entry. Also, Wilson wanted both sides to regard him as fair. He "did not wish to let the Allies know we are definitely on their side."

Grey liked House. But Grey was not sure the time was right to call for peace talks. As for terms, practically from the start of the war, by December 1914, Grey had in mind only two "absolute" objectives for peace. One was the German evacuation of Belgium, compensation to the Belgians, and reestablishment of Belgium's independence. He now repeated to House that "the minimum to avoid disaster" was the restoration of Belgium and "preservation" of France.

The other objective was some "durable peace that will secure us and our Allies from future aggression."[24] Germany did not need to be crushed. A "secure peace is not to be obtained in that way." The durable peace could be accomplished by some league of Great Powers. That could preserve peace if the United States was a party to it.[25]

This talk of "militarism and navalism" made no sense, Grey wrote House. Instead, the real issue, Grey insisted, in letter after letter, was to form a postwar "league of nations" that could keep the peace. This idea was being promoted by some English Liberals and by the more muscular American believers in international law, led by former presidents Theodore Roosevelt and William Howard Taft. In June 1915, this group had founded an organization to support a future League to Enforce Peace, led by Taft. Were the Americans willing to commit to that idea?

"The British are in many ways dull," House grumbled. But, nonetheless, he wrote back with Wilson's approval, affirming that the United States would go along with Grey's concept. The Americans were willing to commit to a postwar league of nations. Wilson was privately sympathetic to such an idea, though it would be years before he developed his own version of how it might actually work.[26]

---

WILSON GAVE HOUSE clear written instructions. The United States would press for peace talks. The United States would take no position; it would "have nothing to do," he wrote, with the territorial terms of peace.

The United States would, however, address Grey's other objective. Wilson promised that America would participate in a postwar settlement to help guarantee "the future peace of the world." The "only possible guarantees" of such a peace would be "(a) military and naval disarmament and (b) a league of nations to secure each nation against aggression and maintain the absolute freedom of the seas."

If only one side accepted this plan, Wilson instructed House, his demand for peace would be enforced on the recalcitrant side by "our utmost moral force." Again, this was not at all the plan House originally had in mind. House's original scheme was a secret promise to support the Allied cause at the peace conference, to tempt them to say yes to the peace conference, with America planning to enter the war when the Germans said no. Now he was instructed to make a neutral plea to come to a peace conference, promising only American help with postwar guarantees of the peace and with no promise to enter the war.[27]

As House was en route to England, the submarine issue was still unsettled. News arrived that the Germans might have torpedoed another British liner, near Crete, with the loss of a few American lives. Wilson cut short his honeymoon and returned to Washington. Tumulty, his secretary, told him that the United States had to take some "vigorous action" against Germany, that American public opinion was concerned about a lack of leadership.

Wilson "stiffened up in his chair," his secretary noted later that day. "Tumulty," he said, "you may as well understand my position right now. If my re-election as President depends upon my getting into war, I don't want to be President." During his honeymoon, he had had "lots of time to think about this war and the effect of our country getting into it." He wanted Tumulty to understand, "I have made up my mind that I am more interested in the opinion that the country will have of me ten years from now than the opinion it may be willing to express today." Wilson said he understood the public mood. "But I will not be rushed into war, no matter if every damned congressman and senator stands up on his hind legs and proclaims me a coward." He believed "that the sober-minded people of this country will applaud any efforts I may make without the loss of our honor to keep this country out of war."[28]

## The War Situation

Crossing the Atlantic with his wife and secretary on a neutral ship of the Holland-America Line, Edward House reached England on January 5, 1916. As the president's eyes and ears in Europe, House wanted to obtain a good sense of the military situation, and fortunately, when he arrived, the battlefronts between the two sides—the Entente Allies and the Central Powers—were relatively quiet.

The battle lines in 1916 can be seen on the map supplied at the front of this book. On the western front, the Germans still occupied almost all of Belgium, some of northern France, and bits of territory in eastern France. During 1915, the French and British had mounted major offensives, with the French carrying most of the burden. The offensives had utterly failed. Italy had joined the Allied side and attacked Austria on their shared mountainous border. The attacks failed.

In the East, the Germans, Austrians, and their new Bulgarian allies made major gains. They had repelled the 1914 Russian advances into East Prussia and Galicia and, by the end of 1915, occupied portions of the pre-war Russian Empire, including Russian Poland (there had not been an independent Polish state since 1795) and multiethnic populations in parts of what today are Lithuania, Latvia, Belarus, and western Ukraine. The front line ran roughly from Riga on the Baltic Sea south to the Carpathian Mountains and the Romanian border. Romania was neutral but wavering.

In the Balkans, where the war had begun, Serbia had been overrun by the Central Powers. The remnants of the Serbian army were refugees in Greece. The Allies had landed forces near the city of Salonika (present-day

Thessaloniki) but had received little support from a weak Greek government reluctant to join either side. The Allies had hoped to use this Balkan front to threaten Austria. They failed, being shut in mainly by the Bulgarians.

Joining the war in November 1914 on the side of the Central Powers, Ottoman Turkey had cut off the main Allied supply routes to Russia through the Dardanelles and the Black Sea. The British Empire, with French support, made a major naval and land effort against Turkey, landing a large force on the Gallipoli peninsula, on the European side of the Dardanelles, to try to open the strait and threaten the Ottoman capital, Constantinople. The whole operation became a disaster, and by the end of 1915, London had decided to evacuate its forces and abandon the effort.

The battles of 1915 had exacted truly staggering costs in lives and treasure. France, Austria-Hungary, and Russia all ended the year badly weakened.

The Allies planned another series of giant offensives for 1916 on all fronts, in the West, the East, and the Middle East. Their hope was to bleed the Germans and their allies to death on the battlefield and starve them into submission with a tightening naval blockade.

The German leadership had no great illusions that they could win a decisive land victory in 1916. They planned to launch a limited offensive against the French, at Verdun, to force the French to make endless, ruinous counterattacks. The German leaders' response to Britain's "hunger war" at sea was a submarine blockade of their own. But unrestricted submarine warfare risked war with America.

––––––––––

THAT WAS the state of the war that House found on his arrival in Europe as the year 1916 began. Sent to explore possibilities for peace, he tried to learn more about what each side hoped to gain from more fighting. House could well imagine that all the warring powers had secret wish lists of war aims, including various annexations to take account of promises they had made to their allies. But he knew little about the specifics.

In January 1916, only the Germans and Austro-Hungarians actually already had possession of territories they wanted. On the Allied side, each country had drawn up wish lists of their own of territories they wanted.

Other than some German colonies that had been snapped up, their desired annexations in Europe—pieces of prewar Germany, prewar Austria-Hungary, and prewar Ottoman domains—could only be attained if the Central Powers were defeated. There was no prospect of that happening anytime soon. Millions more people would probably have to die in order to accomplish it.

However, these secret wish lists did not make much difference to the people doing the fighting. And their views mattered, because the war had become a war of entire populations.

The week before House arrived in London, the new Asquith coalition of Liberals and Conservatives, reshuffled in 1915, had pushed through a bill to expand conscription. The conscripted, and their families and communities, had different war aims. They were not fighting for annexations. They worked so hard and sent their sons off to fight because they deeply believed they were fighting *in self-defense*, not for conquest.

To the Allies, the war was Germany and Austria-Hungary's fault. Those countries had started it, beginning with Austria-Hungary's aggression against Serbia. Russia and France had just come to Serbia's aid. Then Germany's invasion of France through neutral Belgium had brought Britain in.

To the Central Powers, the war had been plotted by their encircling enemies, abetted by Britain. Serbia had tried to subvert Austria-Hungary and sponsored the terrorism that killed the Austrian heir. It was an ambush. When Austria and its German ally had responded in a local way, the Entente powers seized their moment to gang up on Germany. Russia had immediately invaded both Germany and Austria-Hungary, ravaging lands and driving people from their homes. Germany had struck out in the only way it could to fight off the encircling enemies. Now the British naval blockade, its "hunger war," was targeting noncombatants, systematically and deliberately starving millions of innocent civilians.

So, as House could see, each side had its own narrative of self-defense. Yet he could also see that in every country he visited, the public was exhausted and feeling great strain. In London, the conscription bill would nearly double the size of the army. Beneath the veneer of general patriotic support for the war effort, political leaders on all sides were visibly divided about how much further they should or could go.

## House Goes to London and Berlin

In Britain, the two largest parties—the Liberals and the Conservatives (then also called Unionists because of opposition to Irish home rule)—were about evenly balanced. As in all the major powers, the leading politicians disagreed about the best way to conduct or conclude the war.

In Britain, the Liberals tended to be more open to possibilities for a compromise peace. Opposing them, a large faction within the Conservative Party, but by no means all the Conservatives, supported all-out measures and the most unlimited war aims. They wanted to smash "Prussian militarism," break up and redistribute the Austro-Hungarian and Ottoman Empires, and expand British imperial possessions.

Herbert Henry Asquith had been prime minister for eight and a half years—already one of the longest tenures of any prime minister in more than a century. He was the undisputed leader, since William Gladstone, of Liberal England. He had led the country through historic changes and struggles in its domestic life before the war began.

*Asquith*

His white hair a bit unkempt, Asquith bore a look of "dignified, benevolent slovenliness." His mind was quick. He had the former barrister's and skilled parliamentarian's ability to digest facts, cut to the core of an issue, and rapidly compose an argument. He was not an aristocrat, but he was classically educated, gracious in manner, and honest; he bore few grudges and readily gave others credit and took blame when anything went wrong. He was, in other words, much loved in his Liberal Party.

"He had managed his party superbly through the vicissitudes that the six years of his peacetime premiership had thrown at him between 1908 and 1914," judges historian Simon Heffer. "His handicap" was the education that had "provided his own social mobility from the middle to the upper middle class: an education designed for a world of certainty, peace, and a Whiggish idea of progress...an attitude ill-equipped for total war."[29]

Time in office and the war had been wearing Asquith down. Even by the summer of 1915, he seemed "spent" and more and more "carried on the current."[30]

If Asquith's fire was cooling, his cabinet colleague and occasional rival for public stature among the Liberals, the charismatic politician and Welsh former solicitor David Lloyd George, was burning bright. When House returned to London in January 1916, Lloyd George was turning fifty-one. He had "boundless energy, resilience and determination, courage and imagination, creativity and vision, a sharp and open mind, a strong nerve, a silver tongue, an unfettered intellect, extremely good health, a capacity for hard work, a thick skin, and an intuitive grasp of political realities."

Lloyd George's ambition was colored by "his egocentricity, his vanity, and his search for comfort and praise." Conscious of his gifts, he felt a sense of "innate superiority" and personal destiny.[31] He relished fights with those who chose to oppose him.

Lloyd George used the establishment yet was always willing to challenge it. His base of support was in the public and the press, which he endlessly cultivated. Influential editors liked him in return, as they always like high officials who are talkative, witty, gossipy, and a tiny bit wicked. Effectively separated from his wife, Lloyd George found devoted companionship with his mistress, Frances Stevenson, who was also a private secretary in his office.

*Lloyd George*

By January 1916, as House returned to London, Lloyd George had become a figurehead for the all-out war effort. When war came, he had taken charge of munitions production, winning much praise. Lloyd George had impressed the US ambassador in London as "the most agile and most thoroughly convinced popular agitator of our time. A year ago he was the most hated man in England—among the upper classes."[32] Now, well into the war, Lloyd George seemed like the one man who inspired confidence that he could get things done.

Lloyd George had built a personal coalition of supporters drawn from old Liberal allies and new allies of convenience among some Conservatives because of his apparent devotion to winning the war and their hatred of Asquith. He had, though, alienated many of the radical Liberals whom he once caucused alongside.

Asquith's relationship with Lloyd George was complex. They had been political partners. Asquith had used his own immense prestige to save Lloyd George in 1913, when the Welshman was implicated in an ugly corruption scandal. But late one night in 1915, Asquith jotted a note about his longtime colleague. Lloyd George "is a wonderful person in some ways," but he "is totally devoid of either perspective or judgment: and on the whole during these 7 years he has given me more worry than any other colleague."[33]

By the beginning of 1916, plenty of editors and politicians were complaining about Asquith. The Conservative Party leader, however, told one leading editor that the balance in Parliament made it inevitable that any other prime minister would still have to be a Liberal. Since the only other Liberal alternative was Lloyd George, who Conservatives thought "had shown a certain instability and lack of judgment of late," they were on the whole "more disposed to put up with Asquith."[34]

———

DURING THE two wintry weeks he spent in London that January, House dined and met with most of the top officials in the new coalition government. Everyone was friendly and happy to share his opinion on what was going on in the war and in British politics.

House followed the guidance Wilson had given him, neutrally offering American mediation to call a peace conference to end the war and negotiate a lasting peace. No one he met seemed eager to pick up on Wilson's proposal.

In his meetings with House, Foreign Secretary Grey was usually accompanied by an old friend and political rival, now coalition colleague, Arthur Balfour. Balfour, sixty-seven, was a Conservative Party elder statesman, a former prime minister (1902–1906), who in this coalition was the civilian head of the navy, the first lord of the Admiralty. Incisive and analytical, Balfour took policy proposals seriously, often dissecting them in writing. It was Balfour who cross-examined House on the substance of the postwar ideas. How, he quizzed House, would these ideas about a postwar league actually work? Grey was more soothing.

During this visit, House's most interesting meeting was with Lloyd George. Accompanied only by his close friend Lord Reading, the minister of munitions had asked to see House.

The little group dined at the Savoy in a private room. They chatted about America. Lloyd George had just seen the movie *The Birth of a Nation* and "was much interested in [House's] account of the Reconstruction period in the South." House found Lloyd George "as ignorant as ever" about the political world in the United States.

Coming to his main point, Lloyd George told House that the war would go on indefinitely unless Wilson intervened to stop it. The two men agreed, House reported to the president, that "the war could only be ended by your intervention."

Lloyd George thought that Wilson's big peace move would have to wait until September 1, when "the big battles of the summer would have been fought and...a forecast could then be made of what the final end might be." They had therefore "settled tentatively upon that date."

Lloyd George had "a fantastic idea of the power the President may exert at the peace conference," House noted in his diary. With America's economic might, Wilson could practically dictate the peace terms. If Wilson proposed mediation, Lloyd George "thought each belligerent government would object, but would soon be brought to accept by public opinion."

The two men then surveyed the map of Europe and its possible postwar disposition. House recorded of Lloyd George, "His mind acts quickly, largely upon impulse, and he lacks the slow reasoning of the ordinary British statesman."[35]

But Lloyd George's plan for American mediation was no momentary impulse. He had been developing the idea for some time. A month earlier, in mid-December, Lloyd George confided to his favorite Liberal editor (of the *Manchester Guardian*) that "it was nonsense to talk about 'crushing' Germany; it was neither possible nor desirable. The best thing that could happen would be when the two sides were seen to be evenly matched America should step in and impose terms on both." " 'There,' he told the editor, 'I think I've talked enough treason.' "

At the time, the editor could not "say exactly how far [Lloyd George] was talking seriously or only 'in the air.' " Lloyd George was serious. He had followed up with House in their meeting the next month, in mid-January 1916.

At the end of January, two weeks after he saw House, Lloyd George saw the editor again. He again went over his plan for American mediation, explained that it should occur when both sides were getting exhausted, and implied that House had encouraged it.[36]

Right after his remarkable conversation with Lloyd George, House went back to Grey and Balfour and told them what Lloyd George had said.

They replied that Lloyd George had not discussed any of this with them. They guessed (rightly), "He has probably thought the thing out and seized upon your being in London to discuss it with you." Their colleague, they impressed on House, was "brilliant and unstable." They guessed (rightly) that he would probably share some of his thinking with "his newspaper friends."

Yet, unfortunately, Grey and Balfour argued, it was not yet prudent to raise the plan for American mediation with the rest of their cabinet or with their allies, like the French. "The difficulties are many." More importantly, the people could not be told about a peace move unless they could also be told how such a negotiation would help Great Britain.

House felt deflated. Talking a few days later with a Liberal scholar both he and Wilson admired, Lord Bryce, House said he wished Lloyd George could be the prime minister and Grey his foreign secretary. Those leaders, he thought, would have the "boldness" that was needed.[37]

---

HOUSE THEN traveled on to Berlin. He crossed the channel and journeyed by train through France, Switzerland, and then Germany. As in London, all doors were open to him.

In any peace negotiation, the Germans and Austro-Hungarians had an obvious and substantial advantage on the ground: they occupied enemy territory in both the West and the East. But they did not have everything their way. Their offsetting big, visible disadvantage was that they were running short of food and other important resources. The blockade and the war were causing great hardship.

House had a long meeting with the American army's attaché in Berlin, Colonel Joseph Kuhn. Kuhn was an invaluable source of information. House took away, early in 1916, a sense of continuing German military strength. Kuhn "sees no lack of either men or munitions," House noted.

House picked up a hint about the imminent German assault against the French fortress of Verdun. He later passed that speculation along to the British, about a week before the German offensive began.

House and Kuhn doubted that either side could gain a major breakthrough anytime soon. But Kuhn's information rekindled House's determination to find some way of getting Wilson to mediate an end to the war, before it took a decisive turn, possibly against the Allies.[38]

House's most important meeting in Berlin was with Theobald von Bethmann Hollweg, the chancellor. After a large dinner at the American embassy, they went into a side room to talk. Chatting for an hour and a half, they needed no interpreter since Bethmann spoke English fluently.

House told Bethmann that the British government was so deeply divided politically that it was difficult for the leadership to take action to seek peace. He said Lloyd George and Grey were most receptive to eventual negotiations. He assured Bethmann that Wilson was genuinely neutral.

House did not press the Germans for any action. Bethmann therefore had no need to engage in any substantive discussion about possible peace terms. The Allies, he said, were not interested in peace. Why should Germany beg for peace if it had not been conquered? His country would not be starved into defeat.

During his visit, House heard plenty about Bethmann's internal battle against the navy and the leader of the army, Erich von Falkenhayn, over the issue of whether to give in to the American demands to restrict submarine warfare. House thought Bethmann might lose that fight and would not be able to stay in power much longer.

The two of them sat and talked in the parlor at the embassy, called the Blue Room, well into that cold winter evening in Berlin. Bethmann downed beer after beer brought in by a waiter, with no obvious effect. House prided himself on sticking to mineral water.

As the conversation went on, Bethmann talked about how much he deplored the war "and its ghastly consequences." The chancellor said he had "reached a condition," drained of passion, "in which he neither loved nor hated. He repeated this several times," House observed, "just why I do not know." After the war, Bethmann would talk about the challenge for leaders to free themselves from the "machine of war passion." He may have been trying to communicate this to House.

Dictating his diary later that night, House was also struck by another of Bethmann's comments. The chancellor had said that "he was the only one in authority among the belligerents who had spoken for peace." He "could not understand why there was no receptive echo anywhere."

When Bethmann said that, House had pushed back, saying that Bethmann's "peace talk was interpreted merely as Germany's desire to 'cash in' her victories." The Allies thought they could improve the situation, that

Germany could not "hold her own from [then] on, and that another story would be told before the end." The British, House said, "were a stubborn race and felt no concern as to the ultimate result."

Finishing his dictation, before he went to bed after a very long day, House mused for a moment about these exchanges he had just had and about the rest of what he had heard so far in London and Berlin. "The thought occurs to me time and again," he said, "that this war is not so much a breakdown of civilization as it is the failure of our statesmanship."[39]

# CHAPTER 2

# The British Are Tempted

IN THE FIRST DAYS of February 1916, House retraced his journey across western Europe, returning from Berlin, back through Switzerland, to Paris, and then on to London. In London, he again urged the Allies to move at once to accept Wilson's mediation offer.

If the Allies waited too long, House now stressed, their situation might get much worse. House came away from Berlin impressed with Germany's continued strength, capabilities, and determination. House thus had the special authority for his French, then British, listeners of having just come from their enemy's camp. The Germans, House argued, might knock Russia out of the war. If the Allies waited too long, their situation might be so dismal that the United States would give up on trying to mediate a fair peace.

Meanwhile, writing to Wilson, House revived his idea of setting up a German rejection of peace mediation as the best way to get America into the war. In February 1916, House assumed that the Germans would not talk peace and that the next submarine sinking or some such incident would provoke Wilson to seek a declaration of war.

House knew Chancellor Bethmann Hollweg wanted a compromise to avoid war with America. But House, underestimating Bethmann as "an amiable, well meaning man with limited ability," thought the chancellor would be swept aside by the German military leaders. Thus, if Wilson insisted on his demands, war would follow. As before, House thought that going to the Congress for a declaration of war over one more submarine incident was not ideal. It would be better, he thought, to go to the Congress with a nice clear story of how the Germans had rejected the path of peace.

House's plan was unchanged from before: once the Allies gave the go-ahead, Wilson would offer to mediate. There were two possible outcomes. The Germans would accept, and there would be a conference and an end to the war. Or the Germans would refuse, thereby rejecting peace, and Wilson would then have his story for the Congress. House doubted that the Germans would accept Wilson's offer.

House's plan was biased in favor of the Allies because he thought the militarists were about to overthrow Bethmann. If those Germans won the war, on their terms, "the war lords [would] reign supreme and democratic governments [would] be imperiled throughout the world." House's fear was that the Allies might wait too long to set up American entry in the war, until it was too late. There was also the possibility, which he rarely talked about, that Wilson might be voted out of office that November.

"I cannot begin to tell you by letter," House wrote to Wilson from Paris, "how critical the situation is everywhere.... In my opinion, hell will break loose in Europe this spring and summer as never before and I see no way to stop it for the moment." Probably remembering Lloyd George's timeline, targeting September 1 for the time when the American peace move would surely be ripe, House assured Wilson, "I am as sure as I ever am of anything that by the end of the summer you can intervene."[1]

## What House Didn't Know

In Paris, House did not tell French ministers about his and Wilson's peace mediation plan. He planned to work on that with his British friends. He explained only that something might happen later in the year that would bring American intervention. The French heard this as an expectation of intervention into the war on the Allied side. This naturally sounded a bit mysterious to the French, who did not know what to make of it all.[2]

House was concentrating on London, where he would make his argument that they should ask for peace mediation, the sooner the better. He crossed the channel by troopship, then made his way on to the great capital by train. There he immediately found that, somehow, the atmosphere had changed.

During House's January visit to London, everyone had been polite. There had been many questions about his ideas. But no one, except Lloyd George, had taken his proposal seriously enough to get down to work on any actual plan of action. Even Lloyd George had only mused about a move that would not happen until later in the year, around September 1, after the summer offensives had been tried.

Yet when House returned to London in February, suddenly people like Edward Grey and Arthur Balfour seemed eager to take his proposal very seriously indeed. Why the change of heart?

If House had paused awhile to reflect on why there was now so much interest in the American peace option, which he did not, he still would have had trouble figuring out what was really going on. He did not know that, for weeks, the British leaders had been locked in grim, drawn-out debates about whether there should be a summer offensive at all. They were debating their whole outlook on the future of the war. House and Wilson's proposal became an option in *those* debates, about which House knew practically nothing.

————

HERBERT HENRY ASQUITH, although he had been prime minister for eight and a half years, had a leadership style that was not one of outspoken command; it was wary, reactive, and tactical. Opponents mocked him as "Squiff" to evoke an image of a passive Asquith, too genteel. In 1916 the powerful newspapers and magazines controlled by the press baron Lord Northcliffe were attacking Asquith almost daily, trying to bring him down.

Asquith did sometimes seem indolent, seeking relief in small diversions, relaxing by writing witty notes to friends. Like Wilson, to relax he usually preferred the friendship and conversation of women.

To amuse himself, Asquith once wrote a little play in which he was called to final judgment before "the infernal tribunal." In the play, he used the judge's summary to size himself up. The judge found that poor Asquith was neither genius nor saint. The judge did allow that the man was endowed with "luck" and "qualities of temperament." These qualities included "energy under the guise of lethargy" and "a faculty for working quickly," along with the ability to see the other side's point of view, "a growing sense of proportion," and "a rather specialized faculty of insight and manipulation" in dealing with his varied colleagues.[3]

Asquith led a remarkably talented and experienced cabinet. British government was "cabinet government," a concept that Americans, with their presidential system, do not easily grasp. It was a collective government of ministers, a carefully arranged composition of political interests and talents. These ministers were drawn almost entirely from members of Parliament. Ministers had great autonomy over how they ran their departments, with accountability to the cabinet. The cabinet, in turn, was designed to sustain a governing majority in Parliament. The prime minister could guide and set an overall tone and direction to the whole.

By 1916, Asquith's original Liberal cabinet had been reshuffled to become a wartime coalition that included some Conservatives. This reflected both the hope of more unity in wartime and the thin plurality Liberals had held in Parliament since the last general election, in 1910. The cabinet's core in early 1916 was the War Committee, shown below. This War Committee was much smaller than the full cabinet, which had about two dozen members. The War Committee met more than a hundred times between late 1915 and the end of 1916.[4]

Horatio Kitchener, the war secretary since August 1914, was a large public figure, a military man, not a member of Parliament, whose reputation was won in colonial wars in Africa. The Great War had exposed the limits of his abilities. Asquith reorganized the government to reduce his authority,

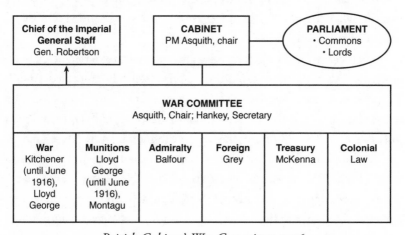

*British Cabinet's War Committee, 1916*

and in 1915 the huge job of managing war production was put in the new Ministry of Munitions, led by Lloyd George. In 1916, the cabinet gave the job of recommending military strategy to a greatly empowered and newly appointed chief of the Imperial General Staff, General William Robertson.

Robertson was a rare officer in a British army then still dominated in its upper ranks by men of high birth. He had worked as a servant in his teens, had enlisted in the British army as a common soldier, and had risen to the highest ranks through a remarkable combination of competence and rugged physical ability. A veteran of intelligence and staff jobs, Robertson impressed others with his clear, forceful views about strategy.

By the beginning of 1916, his plain strategy was to concentrate all possible British ground forces against the main enemy, Germany, on the main battlefield, the western front. That meant an end to the ceaseless "eastern" diversions that had turned out so disastrously, all through 1915, in Ottoman Turkey, in the Balkans, in Egypt, and in Mesopotamia (modern-day Iraq).

In Robertson's view, one of the two sides would wear the other down to defeat, or else the war would end with mutual exhaustion. To wear down Germany and the German reserves, his campaign plan for 1916 was to support offensives to put pressure against Germany on all fronts, centered on a massive offensive in France led by the largest British army ever fielded in the country's history. This would become the campaign later known as the Battle of the Somme.

Robertson's style was clear and blunt. He would "give his best professional advice and then refuse to debate." The civilian politicians would then do what they would do, a fact that Robertson regarded with barely concealed irritation.

Robertson worked to protect himself from civilian interference. He had powerful allies in the pro-war Northcliffe press, which he cultivated. And the king was on his side. The king had once been a career naval officer, was conscious of his special sovereign relationship to the forces, and regarded Robertson as an admirable epitome of the rugged common man risen to high rank.[5]

The War Committee's secretary was the one civil servant who might be said to have a cabinet minister's clout. Maurice Hankey was an officer in the Royal Marines who in early 1916 was about to turn thirty-nine. His biographer titled his life story *Man of Secrets*. Insiders knew his importance; to outsiders he was practically invisible.

*Hankey*

Hankey had long been detached to Whitehall, in naval intelligence and then to support interdepartmental work on imperial defense. His dispassionate skill, remarkable tact and discretion, and seemingly inexhaustible capacity to work made him invaluable. He was a forerunner of what Americans now think of as a national security adviser.

Hankey was not a powerful principal in his own right. But behind the scenes he was quite influential, advising Asquith, managing the process, and maintaining a high-quality flow of written records and written analysis. He knew most of what was going on. He lunched, dined, and sometimes weekended with the ministers he was seeing so often, most of whom confided in him and used him as an informal conduit they could trust. In August 1916, Asquith called him "the most useful man in Europe—he has never been wrong." Hankey had developed a trusting relationship with the king as well. Retaining his outward tact, he kept quite candid diaries of his war work, opened to researchers many years later, after his death.[6]

When House returned to London in February 1916, Hankey had just played a hidden, central part in defusing a continuing crisis. There had been a great public debate over extending conscription to fill the armies for the coming summer offensive. Some Liberals were opposed on principle to more conscription. Others challenged whether the government could balance military claims on resources with the need to keep the economy going. Hankey had come up with the solution. It was another cabinet committee, this one on the coordination of military and financial effort, sometimes just called the Military-Finance Committee. Its job was to balance ends and means.

It was a select committee, at first with only three members. Asquith chaired it, joined by his Treasury secretary, Reginald McKenna, and a Conservative (then running the India Office), Austen Chamberlain. In the spring a fourth member was added, another Conservative, who had run both the Foreign Office and the War Office in past governments: Lord Lansdowne.

This secretive process to balance ends and means tackled the most important, yet least understood, part of the equation that would determine Britain's whole approach to the war. After committing to hugely enlarging its army with compulsory war service, Asquith's coalition faced two other fundamental questions, both of them well out of public view: Should Britain use this larger army to undertake a massive land offensive in France? Could Britain sustainably pay for such an army and such an offensive?

———

*SHOULD BRITAIN launch a massive offensive in France?* We now remember the Somme offensive of 1916 as practically shorthand for "meaningless bloodbath." Some in the British government foresaw that disastrous possibility. For months in early 1916, ministers secretly argued about whether the country should go ahead with this offensive. But House knew little or nothing of this discussion.

In that secret debate in the War Committee, Balfour led the opposition to the planned general offensive. It was supposed to exhaust the Germans. Instead, Balfour warned, this giant assault might fail bloodily, like the campaigns in 1915. Instead it was the British and their allies who might face exhaustion and ruin.

Lloyd George preferred to at least delay the offensive from spring until summer, until more munitions could be assembled. A decision was put off.

As for Grey, like Balfour, he doubted the offensive would work. But no one was presenting any other option. Facing what he called "the paralysis of all strategy," Grey had an alternative to put on the table.

*Balfour*

If "Germany will be exhausted before another year is over, and... the same is true of others; and, if things remain as they are, I think that there will be a sort of general collapse and inconclusive peace before next Winter." By "inconclusive," Grey meant a peace in which neither side decisively beat the other. Both sides would have to settle for, in effect, a kind of draw that, at best, might bring things back to about where they were before the war.

Grey therefore offered an alternative. The British could either "hammer the Germans hard" in the summer or, as an alternative to that bloodbath, they could now go straight to where matters might likely end up anyway and "make up [their] minds to an inconclusive peace" sooner rather than later.

Balfour had a different alternative, a third option: Go on the strategic defensive, unless the offensive was "absolutely necessary to assist the Russians." Let the Germans attack and ruin themselves if they wished.

The War Committee agreed that the giant offensive at least needed to be readied. But they deferred a final decision on whether to go forward with it.[7] When House returned to London in February, that decision was still hanging in the air.

*COULD BRITAIN sustainably pay for such an army and such an offensive?* One could recommend in principle, as General Robertson did, mounting a giant offensive in France to help wear down the Germans. Balfour pointed out that this might "prove a military luxury...too expensive for our means."

If the government took many more men into the army, it took them out of industry, farming, and trade. Consequently, Britain would earn less money to pay for its imports. And it would rely more on those imports because its own production would go down. A general offensive would spend munitions much faster.

Underneath all this was a basic fact, large and fundamental, yet never widely understood. Britain and its allies were waging a war well beyond their means and beyond their own productive capacity. Even after drawing what they could from imperial dominions and colonies, a large, vital part of the Allied war effort used American workers and farmers to replace and supplement their own.

These vast American resources had to be paid for in dollars, on cold, commercial terms. America was neutral. Farmers and firms liked the Allied purchases, liked the higher prices they could charge, but their own economy was growing, and they were not so dependent on Allied purchases that they were going to give anything away. All credit was backed by hard collateral, deposited in America, like gold or American stocks and bonds that had a clear market value and could readily be sold.

No one had a greater responsibility for tracking this problem than the man who had taken over from Lloyd George as chancellor of the Exchequer and had also supplanted him as Asquith's "political chaplain and confessor," Reginald McKenna.[8] He and his wife, Pamela, were personally quite close to Asquith, who called them the "McKennae."

Grimly competent, McKenna was now taking on his fourth cabinet post. His professional ability had earned him unusually high regard among Whitehall's career civil servants. The promising young economist John Maynard Keynes was an important member of McKenna's team at Treasury.

But McKenna was respected more than liked. Asquith remarked of McKenna, "Tho' generally right, [he] is singularly rasping and unpersuasive in manner." Lloyd George and McKenna already disliked each other, an antipathy that was deepening into mutual hatred.[9]

Studying the numbers, McKenna looked at Britain's options and resources. In the late summer of 1915, he began warning his colleagues that "Britain could serve as the paymaster for the Entente or risk bankruptcy by trying to do too much." He concluded, "We have already reached the prudent limits of safety." Allied imports from the United States were already equal to or larger than the amount France was spending on its whole war effort.[10]

Financially, the offensive plans for 1916 had become a huge, secret gamble. They were betting, the war leaders grudgingly agreed, that Germany could be defeated by August 1916. If that bet failed, the Allies would be "done for." Why? "Unless the allies could gain some military victory before the economic pressure on them became as great as it was on Germany, the allies might make peace." They would be financially paralyzed by the spring of 1917.[11]

Britain's finances were now supporting much of the whole war effort for itself and all the major allies, including France and Russia. Grey had noted to his War Committee colleagues, "If we were to withhold the support that we give to the Allies, they could not continue the war. We could probably bring about this result even by withholding financial support alone."

Grey's point, though, was that Britain could not use its financial leverage to demand that the Allies do more. Those same Allies had the option of making a separate peace with Germany "on comparatively favorable terms, if they would separate themselves from us." Britain was stuck with its burden.[12]

Britain's dollar deficit was the government's most important secret in the war. If outsiders even started to question the government's creditworthiness, a trickle of doubts could turn into a ruinous cascade. Not only would purchases be harder, but the sterling exchange rate, which controlled the price of private imports—such as food—would sink. At the beginning of 1916, that secret financial outlook—known only to a few—had slid from merely gloomy to dire.

During the fall of 1915 the great British idea to address the nation's dollar deficit was to start selling Anglo-French bonds to the American public.

Since the end of 1914, J. P. Morgan & Co. had been managing Britain's and France's financial work in America in the largest set of financial operations ever handled in history: "The history of commercial banking offers little or no basis for comparison."[13]

By the beginning of 1916, it was clear that the bond issue had failed. The American public was not interested. The underwriters were stuck with most of the bonds. In the short run, the British and French had gotten their money from the underwriters, money those governments had spent as soon as they got it. But there would be no more of that.

The secret failure of the Anglo-French loan "marked a turning-point in the Allies' plan to finance their mounting need for American supplies." It meant that the British had to use increasingly desperate measures to find dollars or dollar collateral. To obtain more collateral, the Treasury bought or borrowed every decent American stock or bond held in private hands in Britain. But that would only stretch so far. Morgan could front some dollars to handle temporary shortfalls or bolster the exchange rate, but that too was risky because the failure of Morgan itself would devastate Britain's ability to continue the war.[14]

So, in parallel with the secret debate over whether to launch the general offensive in France, an even more secret debate raged over dollar finances. McKenna did not quarrel with General Robertson about military strategy. But he, like other ministers responsible for the economy, notably the capable commerce minister (president of the Board of Trade), Walter Runciman, just did not see how Britain could afford its war effort much longer.[15]

During the War Committee debate on the question of a general offensive, on January 13, after Lloyd George proposed delaying its start until the summer, Kitchener warned that the offensive would need to pound away for some months. His theory of victory was to push back the Germans in the spring, the Germans would start talking peace, and a second offensive would push the Germans back to the Rhine in the autumn; only then would the war end.[16] Kitchener admitted, "If [there is] no final decision" by the winter of 1916–1917, Britain would face "the exhaustion of [her] resources."

McKenna drily pointed out that, unless the effort was successful, the British, not the Germans, would indeed be exhausted, but with this difference: "The failure of the British in such a case would be different from that of any others [like the Central Powers]," who had internal resources, whereas the British had none.

Lord Kitchener was taken aback. He asked, if British resources were exhausted, have "we nothing"?

If we become exhausted, we are done, McKenna answered.[17]

McKenna, joined by Asquith and Conservative minister Austen Chamberlain, went over these issues in the cabinet's new select Military-Finance Committee created by Hankey (and for which he took the notes). Its members all agreed on the bleak situation. The financial expedients now being used to raise dollars "could only be done once," Chamberlain acknowledged.

Chamberlain wanted the government to "concentrate on making a great military effort in 1916." That little committee's consensus, on February 3, given the military advice from Kitchener and Robertson, was to go ahead and prepare the general offensive. But that might be a last great throw of the dice. If they went forward with it, they were, historian Daniel Larsen observes, "gambling everything."[18]

Asquith and the others had their three options. Go ahead, as Robertson wished, with the big offensive, which might degenerate into a bloodbath and worsen the grim financial outlook. Take up Grey's idea and seek "an inconclusive peace" (this was the Wilson peace offer). Or follow Balfour's advice and go on the defensive and stand pat, hoping that the Germans might ruin themselves in fruitless assaults.

Each option had its problems, generating mounting anxiety among the ministers. That was the setting as Edward House returned to London on the evening of February 9.

## The House-Grey Memorandum

Grey received House at his office the next day, February 10. House now found, for reasons he did not understand, that his push to consider Wilson's peace mediation was now pushing on an open door.

House went through his argument about "the plight of the Allies and the possibilities of defeat." He said the Germans were "in no great economic distress" and that the Allies should not wait too long before calling on Wilson to mediate. There was, too, the chance that the Germans would say no, which might bring America into the war on the Allied side.

Grey went to work. For the reasons House did not understand, Grey quickly needed to create the "inconclusive peace" option, possibly very soon.

Grey now dispensed with the conditions that he had originally attached to the Wilson proposal. Those had concerned plans for postwar security, like a league of nations with American participation. While House was gone, Balfour had actually sat down and analyzed, in writing, the disarmament and league ideas—something neither Grey nor House had done. His memo broke down a series of practical problems (foreshadowing arguments that would become better known a few years later). Facing the crises in the winter of 1916, Grey dropped the league idea and any demand for American assurances about future security.[19]

Grey wanted to create a simple policy option, to allow the British to ask secretly for American mediation. If they exercised this option, the British would secretly invite Woodrow Wilson to call a conference to end the war. Period.

That day, the two men agreed "it was best for the President not to set any conditions whatsoever, but merely to demand that war cease, and a conference be held." Knowing nothing of the potential disaster scenarios that were torturing the British cabinet, House was surprised, he reported to Wilson, that Grey had taken matters "further than I had any idea that it was possible to do." Wilson approved.[20]

Suddenly, there was a notional path for peace. House continued to believe that the Germans would reject American mediation and the process would end with America joining the war. "If my plan was adopted, I believed it would inevitably lead to an alliance between the United States and Great Britain, France, and Italy, the democracies of the world."[21]

Grey did not bother to dispute House's supposition. But neither Grey nor any of his War Committee colleagues shared House's confidence that the American peace option would end up bringing America into the war on their side. It was nice to think it might, but they never thought it a good bet. Grey's job was to supply an American peace parachute, if going forward either with the offensive or the "stand pat" options just seemed too dreadful.

House and Grey reviewed the peace option with Asquith, Lloyd George, Balfour, and Lord Lansdowne. McKenna and Hankey also knew what was going on. McKenna had decided to support Grey. He preferred peace negotiations as the alternative to the summer offensive. Hankey distrusted Wilson, believing the president was more interested "in returning to office next November" than in making peace or joining the war.[22]

Grey and House agreed that the peace conference should be held in the neutral Netherlands, at The Hague. House was sure Wilson would be willing to travel to Europe to chair the peace conference in person.

They did not get into a key detail: that there would actually have to be two sets of negotiations at the peace conference. One would be among the warring powers, to end the war. The other set, on postwar plans, would involve at least some neutrals like the United States. The British focus, the "essential feature," was only that Wilson should call for a halt to the war and demand a conference. "I did not expect to go beyond that," House noted, "and I was quite content."[23]

Lloyd George and Asquith wanted more. They wanted some American commitment from Wilson to help them, as best he could, obtain desirable peace terms in the set of negotiations among the warring powers. If Wilson convened the talks, he might play at least an informal role in pressuring the belligerents to develop reasonable, compromise terms to end the war. House went along with this. He agreed that Wilson would help get a reasonably fair agreement on the peace terms.

Grey wrote up their understanding in a document known to historians as the "House-Grey memorandum." If the Allies accepted Wilson's proposal for a peace conference and Germany rejected peace talks, "the United States would probably enter the war against Germany." Note that word "probably." House could not yet commit Wilson, nor could Wilson commit Congress, to a declaration of war.

To satisfy the request from Lloyd George and Asquith, the House-Grey memorandum added House's "opinion" that the conferees would secure peace "on terms not unfavourable to the Allies." If they did not, the United States would join the Allied side in the war. Once he saw the document a couple of weeks later, Wilson added a "probably" qualifier to that too. It was his only edit.

What did "not unfavourable to the Allies" mean? It meant the restoration of Belgium, the transfer back to France of Alsace and Lorraine (ceded to Germany in 1871), and "the acquisition by Russia of an outlet to the sea." Those were the only specifics mentioned. Belgium was key for Britain; the point about Alsace and Lorraine would placate France; and the third point, "outlet to the [Mediterranean] sea," was something for Russia. Grey foresaw that the Allies could not agree to attend a peace conference that did not at least promise to push very hard for these things. Grey ignored what Italy or Japan might want. Germany, the memorandum said, might have to be "compensated by concessions to her in places outside Europe."

––––––

THIS HOUSE-GREY memorandum was very closely held. Few in the British government were aware of its existence. Grey had pared the list of aims down. A peace roughly along these lines would be something close to a draw. Grey sought to ensure that German conquests in the West would be renounced, especially Belgium. If the war was being waged for self-defense, the British and French could argue that they had succeeded.

Composing this list, Grey, like most British and French citizens, was indifferent about the borderlines in the East. The British leaders also knew that any peace conference would have a dynamic of its own, given the German-Austrian-Ottoman-Bulgarian positions on the ground.

These aims were fundamentally moderate. There was no pretense of trying to overthrow the existing governments of Germany, Austria-Hungary, or the Ottoman Empire.[24] Therefore, a continuation of the war would mean that millions would die for an argument over marginal strips of territory about which relatively few people cared.

## The British Debate the American Peace Option

Grey shared Balfour's deep worries about the high risks of the forthcoming offensive and all the other bloodletting to come that year. Grey was in favor of invoking the American offer immediately. He preferred immediate action, he told House, "so that the lives of millions of men might be saved, and the havoc which would follow another spring and summer campaign might be avoided." He became emotional, a rare break in his usual diplomatic reserve. This might be, he said, the "most important moment since July 1914."

Grey, like Lloyd George, thought an unadorned call for peace would be unpopular. He imagined that angry mobs might even attack his home. But it was the right thing to do. "History," Grey told House, "will lay a great charge against those of us who refuse to accept your professional services at this time."[25]

Lloyd George and Asquith demurred. All along, Lloyd George's position had been to wait until after the summer offensive. He still thought September 1 was the moment to turn to the Wilson option.

As for Asquith, he had not yet made up his mind. He agreed with Grey, in front of House, that the planned offensive might not do much more than make a dent in the German lines. He did not tell House that the government had not yet decided whether to go forward with it.

———

The War Committee first considered the American peace option in February, just before House left for home.[26] In that first clash, Grey pushed for immediate action. Lloyd George wanted to wait.

McKenna drew the discussion back to the likely scenario. The Germans might accept the peace offer and try to get a "status quo" peace. This would be some kind of draw. He was "certain" the Americans expected "that the end of the war would be a draw." In that pure status quo situation—the mid-war, not the prewar, status quo—Britain might not even get its minimum aim, which was the restoration of Belgium.

"To the Allies," Asquith said, given the current situation on the ground, "a draw [would be] much the same as a defeat."

True, Grey admitted. The Germans could "call it a victory."

Could the Americans, they wondered, use "coercive power" to force Britain to end the war? Not in 1916, Lloyd George thought. The British still had some time.

But Grey thought that, at some point, "the economic factor would bring about a decision."

For Wilson, Asquith commented, the prospect of the upcoming election "controlled everything else."

Grey agreed that "it would be the greatest coup for President Wilson if he were able to say afterwards that he had intervened in this great War and been able to restrain Germany."

The consensus, for the moment, was to delay. Lloyd George summarized that there was "nothing to be done at present." Balfour was silent.[27]

Grey, Lloyd George, and McKenna continued the argument the next day over lunch. Afterward, Lloyd George told his mistress and secretary, Frances Stevenson, "Grey is frankly pessimistic and is for making peace at once." As for terms, Grey said "status quo." McKenna agreed with Grey.

Lloyd George thought "public opinion would not stand it."

"Well, perhaps not just *now*," McKenna replied, "not on the 23rd of February; but let us say in June or July perhaps."

Lloyd George asked McKenna what Asquith thought.

"He says there will be peace within the year." But Asquith put faith in Kitchener's hopes that the coming offensive might push the Germans back to Germany. Asquith might want to wait until the offensive had been tried.

Lloyd George also still preferred to wait. But, he admitted to Stevenson, "Unless the U.S.A. come in to help us, we cannot hope for victory."

Lloyd George had been badly shaken by a trip to France where he visited a friend's son in the hospital. The young man had been grotesquely wounded in the head, smashing part of his brain. As Lloyd George stood by his bed, the young man twisted in his dying agonies. "I ought not to have seen him," Lloyd George told her. "I feel that I cannot go on with my work, now that the grim horror of the reality has been brought home to me so terribly."[28]

———

HOUSE WENT home. Pleased with his adviser's work, Wilson confirmed the House-Grey memorandum of understanding, making just the one edit to clarify that America could not guarantee the peace terms at the conference. With House nearby, Wilson himself sat down and typed out a message to Grey to confirm the American offer. Wilson's renewal of the offer went to London on March 7.

Grey brought the matter back to the War Committee. He believed the whole question now turned on the military estimate. Grey put the choice simply. If "the war went wrong," he explained, Britain "would have missed a great opportunity either to get a decent peace or to bring in the U.S.A." If, on the other hand, "we were likely to be completely victorious it would be better to ignore it." There was a middle ground, to just hope for the best, "but this would probably be to miss our opportunity [to make peace with American help]."

Hankey found Grey's argument convincing. A few days earlier, he had noted in his diary that Robertson "ought to be asked whether in his opinion we could defeat the Germans this summer or not, and to be warned that after the summer economic pressure [the dollar deficit] would probably compel a reduction in our maximum effort." If Robertson could defeat the Germans that summer, then the government would be justified in going ahead. "Otherwise in my view they ought to test Col. House's suggestion in order either (1) to discuss peace before we passed our zenith, or (2) to get the U.S.A. behind us, in which case we could go on forever."[29]

In the March discussion of the American peace option, there was a new dimension. Now it seemed that the British offensive might have to go forward, regardless, if just to support the French. The enormous German assault on the French at Verdun had begun. The French were pleading for the British to do their part to relieve the pressure. Also, the Russian offensive plans were well advanced and about to start. How could Britain not support its allies? The War Committee formally approved the Somme offensive later in March.

As it now seemed clear that the offensive would have to go forward regardless, this time the War Committee debated Wilson's peace option without any real urgency. Asquith "affects," Hankey diarized, "to regard the whole thing as humbug and a mere manoeuvre of American politics." One of Asquith's friends in the cabinet, Edwin Montagu, wrote to Asquith at length to convince him to reject the Wilson peace option or, at the very least, postpone action on it. Still, Asquith went ahead and put the issue up for discussion on March 21.

Grey presented it. "This decision," he said, "depends upon the opinion of military and naval authorities on the prospects of the War."[30]

Forewarned by Hankey to be ready to answer this question about "prospects," General Robertson refused to be pinned down. He said only that "all his own instincts were opposed" to the American peace option.

Bonar Law, the Conservative leader, was opposed too. He thought any peace conference would only end up with the prewar status quo, which he believed public opinion would see as a defeat for the Allies.

Balfour had given up the fight to find some alternative to the summer offensive. "At present," he said, there was no question about how to proceed. The only reasons not to go forward with the war, the only "urgent problems" at this point, were "money and ships." McKenna thought the money would at least last through July 1916.

Asquith summarized the conclusion of this very secret discussion: the American peace proposal was "put aside for the present."[31]

————

IN PUBLIC, during April, the British government went through another huge debate over "compulsion," this time debating whether to extend the draft to millions of married men, though this would actually yield relatively few troops anytime soon. Bonar Law threatened to resign if the bill was not passed; so did Lloyd George.

McKenna sharply criticized Lloyd George's behavior to his face. Such resignations would bring down the government. He would be forcing many of his fellow Liberals, the "anti-compulsionists," to perhaps form a new coalition with the fledgling Labour Party. At a full cabinet meeting on April 19, an Asquith friend, Lewis Harcourt, argued that the breakup of the British government might well lead the French to leave the war. Germany would likely offer to withdraw from all occupied territories in France and even cede part of Alsace. France "would accept such a peace."

Grey called the situation "the most serious since August 2d [1914]," the day Britain had decided to enter the war.

Asquith, chairing the meeting, observed that it was now 2:45 in the afternoon. And he needed to give a statement "in the House of Commons at 3:45." What was he to say? he asked his colleagues.

Balfour was blunt: "That the British Constitution is bankrupt." "That we have broken down and are unfit to conduct the war, and tell the allies to make the best peace they can and soon as they can."

"Am I really to say that?" Asquith probed.

"It is the bare truth," Balfour replied.[32]

Asquith and the other resistant Liberals in the coalition gave in. They passed the compulsion bill that Lloyd George and the Conservatives had demanded.

On April 24, as the latest "compulsion" crisis started to subside, a new crisis flared with a violent revolt of Irish rebels in Dublin, what is now called the "Easter rising." Asquith, riding in a car with Hankey to an evening event, commented that "within the next 3 or 4 months there would be an overwhelming demand for peace from all the countries engaged in the war." Hankey agreed.[33]

———

THOSE WERE the crises the public could see. In secret, the cabinet's small Military-Finance Committee, now augmented by Lord Lansdowne, kept working on how to match ends and means. All its members (the two Liberals, Asquith and McKenna, and the two Conservatives, Austen Chamberlain and now Lansdowne) were dismayed by the numbers. Chamberlain told Kitchener, with brutal candor, that "the nation [could] only stand the financial strain" of these forces "for a very short period, and this period would be followed by a very rapid decline afterwards."[34]

Hankey was the scribe for all the meetings. His unease could find full outlet only in his diary. On April 27, he had lunch with Jack Seely, whom Hankey had known for years.

General Seely truly straddled the civil-military divide. He had maintained simultaneous careers for most of his adult life as both an army officer (decorated for valor) and a Liberal member of Parliament. Before the war, he had been a cabinet minister, heading the War Office. When the war began, Seely returned to active army service. He was now commanding a Canadian brigade.

Visiting London and lunching with his friend Hankey, Seely vented about how bad the British generals were. "Not one in a thousand," he said, "had the brain power of the worst Cabinet minister." Noting this in his diary, Hankey, the retired Royal Marine officer, added, "I rather agree."

To be specific, Seely warned, "the proposed offensive had no earthly chance of success." Hankey agreed with this too. Seely "laughed to scorn the corps to which he is attached, which is termed the 'army of pursuit.'"

In his diary, Hankey raged, "The Army want a regular orgy of slaughter this summer." It was "a plan which no member of the Cabinet and none of the regimental soldiers who will have to carry it out believe in, a plan conceived in the heads of the red-hatted, brass-bound brigade behind, who know little of the conditions at the actual front and are out of touch with real regimental opinion."

Supposedly the summer fighting was to save the Russians, Hankey observed. But he recalled that the French had tried that the previous year, "with the result that they are now bled white and have no reserves left." Yet Britain would now "repeat the process, notwithstanding that it may jeopardize the financial stability of the country on which the whole future of the Allies rests!"[35]

Meanwhile, his victory in the public battle to extend "compulsion" had become another defining political moment for Lloyd George. He had confidently promised the House of Commons, sitting in secret session, that Britain could "outstay, and outstay for years, anything Germany could do."[36]

On May 19, McKenna secretly gave the cabinet quite a different prediction. On present trends, he wrote, giving the numbers, "the facts describe a danger of our being unable to meet our liabilities in America.... We are likely, therefore, to face the last quarter of the calendar year [1916] without any resources in sight."[37]

As a result, the War Committee decided it had to take yet another look at the American peace option. That pressure coincided with another push—from Wilson.

## Wilson Decides to "Get Down to Hard Pan"

Back in March, Wilson and House thought they were on the verge of a great move to end the war. It was exciting. House—who only four years earlier had written his anonymous utopian fantasy about an imaginary reformer—now entered into his diary, "The life I am leading transcends in interest and excitement any romance."

House had talked to the German ambassador, Bernstorff. He now believed Germany might go along with a peace conference "if we can get the Allies to give the word."

Wilson and House began working on who would attend the conference in The Hague. Their tentative plan was to invite only heads of government and foreign ministers from the warring powers and one representative each from the neutral countries. They envisioned two concurrent sets of negotiations at the conference. In one, the belligerents would have "voice and vote" on the peace settlement to end the war. In the other, the whole group would work on the postwar arrangements to secure peace, such as "the future conduct of war, restriction of armaments, freedom of the seas during war, etc. etc."

Wilson worried about how to manage the logistics; House assured him that he would handle it. He planned to compose an organization of advisers to provide information "just as available as if I were in a library with every book at my command."[38]

During March and April, as House had anticipated, America had come to the brink of war with Germany over submarines. The culminating crisis was over the sinking of the *Sussex*, a passenger ship that a U-boat had mistaken for a warship, a minelayer, and torpedoed without warning. Wilson worked hard to find a way out. Continually reworking draft notes that Secretary of State Robert Lansing or House prepared, Wilson carefully crafted an ultimatum that gave the Germans a chance to step back.

It was a close call. Leaving Berlin in January, House had thought the German military would have its way, that Chancellor Bethmann Hollweg would lose his job. House had misjudged the situation. Bethmann was strong and determined enough to defeat his opponents in the army and navy, at least this time around.

With Bethmann steering the policy, Germany decided to accept Wilson's restrictions. In what became known as the "*Sussex* pledge," Germany agreed that the U-boats would obey the rules of "cruiser" warfare: they would warn civilian ships and give them a chance to surrender and get passengers and crew into the lifeboats.[39]

Having come to the edge of war with Germany over its submarine blockade, Wilson and American opinion refocused on complaints about the British surface naval blockade of Germany. The circumstances surrounding Wilson's peace offer had changed.

———

HAVING COME to the brink of war and avoided it, Wilson was impatient with the British delay in accepting his offer of mediation. To help persuade

London, Wilson and House recalled Grey's earlier wish that America participate in a postwar league to guarantee security. On May 9, Wilson and House decided that the president would publicly endorse this idea. As the occasion for this endorsement, they picked an address to the League to Enforce Peace, chaired by the former president, and Wilson's Republican opponent in 1912, William Howard Taft.

On Wilson's orders, House wrote to Grey. He told him, "There is an increasingly insistent demand here that the President take some action towards bringing the war to a close." It seemed as if "the Allies [were] more determined upon the punishment of Germany than upon exacting terms that neutral opinion would consider just."

Grey, knowing that in March the War Committee had decided to put the peace option off until after the summer offensive, replied that the peace move was still "premature." House wanted to let the matter rest there. Wilson would not.

Wilson directed House (by letter, since House was, as usual, operating out of his apartment in New York) to "get down to hard pan." The United States "must either make a decided move for peace (upon some basis that promises to be permanent) or start confronting Britain" over its blockade of neutral commerce. "Which does Great Britain prefer?"

As to terms, the warring powers should address whatever immediate interests they "may be able to agree upon." At the conference, they would have their set of negotiations to end their war.

"Our interest is only in peace and its guarantees," Wilson wrote to House. But on that, he confirmed that the United States was willing to help guarantee the peace by defending "freedom of the seas" and to prevent wars of aggression.[40]

Joe Tumulty, Wilson's secretary, urged Wilson on. "The time is now at hand," he stressed, "for you to act in the matter of *Peace*. The mere process of peace negotiations may extend over a period of months." If Wilson waited too long, "the militaristic element" in the warring countries would be preparing their 1917 campaigns. "*The time to act is now when these drives [in 1916] are spending their force.*" He added, "Everybody admits that the resources of the nations involved cannot last through another year without suffering of an untold character."[41]

By this time, in mid-May 1916, all of the assumptions House had believed at the time of the February House-Grey memorandum no longer held. House had originally conceived of the mediation move as, at least in part, a way to persuade Congress to support American entry into a war that, House thought, America was about to join anyway. But Germany and the United States had settled the submarine issue, at least for the time being.

House had used American support for Allied territorial aims at the peace conference as a way to induce British support. Now Wilson was making plain that America would stay clear of that set of negotiations at the peace conference.

Instead, Wilson had revived the postwar league idea that Grey, in February, had put aside. Remaining was whether the British were ready to ask for peace talks immediately, even with the current conditions on the ground.

"The President and I are getting into deep waters," House noted uneasily. "If he will play our hand with all the strength within our power, I believe we can make them do as we wish. But if he does not, we will lose some prestige and perhaps the good will of the Allies."[42]

House did as Wilson asked. He wrote to Grey and pushed hard. "The time is critical and delay is dangerous."

While arrangements were made for a peace conference, there would still be time, House also assured Grey, for the British to try their planned summer offensive. They would still have a chance "to demonstrate whether or not Germany [was] indeed in a sinking condition and the deadlock [could] be broken."[43]

———

For Asquith and the War Committee, it was a jolting coincidence that this message from House to Grey arrived on May 19, the very same day that McKenna had circulated his alarm about Britain running out of dollars to maintain the Allied war effort. The British government was committed to the great offensive. But now the leadership was not sure the money could last even through the end of the year.

For that reason, the American peace option was put back on the agenda for discussion on May 24. This time the intrigues were intense. The British leaders had also just received a message from the choleric British ambassador in Washington, Cecil Spring-Rice. He weighed in to attack Wilson, portraying the American president's peace interest as just a political ploy designed to secure his reelection.

General Robertson and other army leaders escalated their opposition. They began threatening to resign if the War Committee pursued peace. Robertson schemed to go to the king about it. He was determined to go ahead with the planned offensives.[44]

Unsurprisingly, when the War Committee convened on May 24, there was a "frightful row." The military men, including Hankey, were told to wait outside. No one remained in the cabinet room at Number Ten Downing Street except the civilian cabinet members who sat on the War Committee. The military leaders waited, cooling their heels, for nearly an hour.

With Hankey also sitting outside, no notes were made of what was said. But McKenna debriefed Hankey later on what happened. This, with other records, allows a reconstruction.

Asquith, Grey, McKenna, and Balfour wanted to accept "President Wilson's good offices, owing to the black financial outlook." Asquith's interest was a significant shift.

Grey had drafted a forthcoming message back to House and Wilson. The ministers debated it. Balfour, the former Conservative prime minister, was supportive, but he wanted to offer an alternative draft that might rally broader support.

We have not reached a decision, McKenna said. Bonar Law and Lloyd George are still against the Wilson offer, as they would "not admit to the seriousness of the financial situation." Nonetheless, McKenna predicted that the American option would end up being accepted.[45]

Balfour prepared and sent around his fresh draft of what the British government could say to Wilson. His draft makes clear what the advocates of the American peace option thought they needed from the American president. Balfour's draft reply to Wilson was a very significant document. If this cable was sent, it could set in motion the process to end the war.

Balfour and his allies knew the Germans would go into peace talks with a relative advantage on the ground. They needed Wilson to promise to at least try to ensure the peace was fair. Otherwise, the German militarists and their allies would think they had won the war. No such peace would be durable.

The peace group, for whom Balfour was writing, wanted Wilson to commit to at least help, as best he could, on Belgium and Alsace-Lorraine, as well as to see conquered Russian Poland "relieved from German domination [and] the status of Turkey profoundly modified." This short list was not much different from the list of goals in the February House-Grey memorandum, which Wilson had endorsed in March.

Balfour had added the line about Poland. He carefully avoided the issue of whether German-occupied Poland would be returned to Russian rule or granted some form of independence. The Russians would oppose Polish independence, but some British officials supported that.[46]

The British were not sure that the promise of a postwar league was helpful. Balfour and Hankey, for instance, had their doubts about whether international arbitration to determine who was the aggressor would really work. They also wondered whether America, which required congressional approval to declare war, could follow through on a league's commitments.

One red flag, to the British, was American language about postwar guarantees of "freedom of the seas." That would seem to prohibit future blockades. For generations, blockades and sea control were the main instrument of British power. How could they give that up? They would need this power if Germany ended the war relatively undefeated.[47]

In his draft to nail down Wilson's offer, Balfour was mindful of domestic politics. There was no chance that, at that stage in the war, Britain's leaders could simply announce, in effect, "We quit!" and raise a flag of truce.

If they sought peace, they had to have a way to explain this to their war-battered public, which had sacrificed much over the previous two years. They knew the end result might be very close to the prewar status quo. They knew this would be a compromise peace. If the Americans could at least reassure London of support on a few points like these, the peace advocates could make their case.

They could say that German aggression had been stopped and thrown back, that the Americans were committed to help ensure that the German conquest of Belgium was renounced, and perhaps more. If those aims seemed possible, the British and French leaders who knew much more of the story, and eventually their publics too, could then reexamine the costs and dangers of going on.

If the Americans would not offer to help with such minimum goals, then perhaps it was best to wait and see how the summer offensives turned out. This was tempting, especially for Asquith, who had to juggle both the substance and the politics of holding together his government. That government was under renewed strain in dealing with a serious cabinet crisis over how to handle the aftermath of the Easter Rising in Dublin. The British had bloodily put down the revolt, but now the government was embroiled in a renewed and divisive debate about whether to grant Irish home rule.

As a reminder to Asquith of the political enemies he would face, Lord Curzon, the most forceful and pompous Conservative in the cabinet, wrote to the prime minister later that same day, May 24. Curzon complained bitterly about the idea of the American peace move. It was just a Wilson reelection ploy, he huffed. "Even the discussion of a premature and inconclusive peace," he threatened, "would in my opinion wreck the Government, and be a breach of faith with the nation."

A couple of days later, Asquith wrote Curzon a one-line note saying he agreed with him.[48] Whether or not he really did (since McKenna had a different impression of Asquith's views), the War Committee prepared to decide on Balfour's draft message responding positively to Wilson's peace move. That meeting would be on May 29.

## Thoughtful Speech, Thoughtless Diplomacy

Wilson had decided to give a public speech announcing American support for a postwar league of nations to keep the peace. Such an announcement would be historic, a break from traditional American reluctance to join in any "entangling" foreign commitments.

House did a draft that Wilson rewrote. His speech was scheduled for delivery on May 27 to former president Taft and the assembled members of the League to Enforce Peace. "It may be," Wilson thought, "the most important I shall ever be called upon to make."

Wilson stood before his audience in Washington and proclaimed that American responsibility had to grow along with the nation's size and

strength. It was time to step beyond the supposed age-old American doctrine of "no entangling alliances," of staying out of European or world
affairs. The United States should be willing, he said, to join future efforts
to keep the peace.

America should represent to the world a few core principles. A few days
earlier, to clarify his own thinking, Wilson had distilled these principles as

1. the right of every people to choose the sovereignty under which they
   shall live;
2. the right of small states to the same respect for their integrity and
   sovereignty that big states expect to enjoy;
3. the right of the world to be free from every disturbance of the peace
   that proceeds from aggression; and
4. the willingness of the United States to go into a partnership for
   these objects, wanting nothing for herself and seeking to limit herself along with the others.

"We have ourselves upon occasion in the past been offenders against
the law of diplomacy which we thus forecast," Wilson acknowledged. "But
our conviction is not the less clear, but rather the more clear, on that account." Surely this terrible war had advanced the thinking of the statesmen
of the world.[49]

In the hall and beyond, Wilson's address was extremely well received.
Most American commentators thought Wilson had spoken for the great
majority of Americans. They thought he had found the right balance. Facing reelection, Wilson had again positioned himself in the center of the
ongoing political debate, between those clamoring for a more interven-
tionist stance and those determined to stay entirely apart.

Wilson had hoped his speech would help the British peace advocates
carry the day so that London would accept his mediation offer. After all,
that was the major reason the speech was being given at all. Guiding House
in his initial drafting of the speech, Wilson wrote, "Would you do me the
favour to formulate what you would say, in my place, if you were seeking
to make the proposal as nearly what you deem Grey and his colleagues to
have agreed upon in principle as it is possible to make it when concretely
formulated as a proposal?"[50]

But the House-Wilson draft did not do this. His speech ignored all the territorial desires listed in the House-Grey memorandum, goals that Wilson had endorsed in the secret message sent to London back in March. If the Americans did not wish to get into specifics in a public speech, Wilson could, at least, have endorsed the general goal of persuading the belligerents to renounce their conquests. Or—aiming at the British—the speech could have called out the significance, widely supported in the United States, of the restoration of Belgium.

Yet, instead of offering any solace about the actual peace terms that would end the war, House and Wilson wrote words expressing indifference to those terms. Wilson said only that it was up to the warring powers to end the war on any terms they could agree upon, given their "immediate interests." Adding distance to indifference, Wilson went on to say that Americans "were quite aware" that they were "in no sense or degree parties to the present quarrel."

This was not a call to return to something like the prewar status quo. Wilson was implying that he could accept the *mid-war* status quo. That, given the territory Germany and its allies occupied, was tantamount to asking the British to concede that the Allies had on balance lost the war. Most of the British government, including key centrists like Balfour, were not yet desperate enough to try to sell that to their publics.

Moreover, to further show his neutrality, Wilson gratuitously said of the war, "With its causes and its objects we are not concerned." Wilson was right, in his speech, to avoid taking sides on the causes of the war. But he could instead have displayed his empathy for the narratives honestly believed on both sides. He did not need to articulate disdain.

Discussing postwar futures, Wilson spotlighted a possible league of nations. That was the central theme of his speech. But he chose, again, also to emphasize freedom of the seas.

———————

GREY HAD warned House, in advance, that on Monday, May 29, the cabinet might have a decisive discussion of Wilson's peace offer. Grey hoped to telegraph House the answer then.[51]

Grey sent that warning on May 27. But that same day Wilson gave this speech, which, instantly transmitted to Britain, entirely knocked the struts out from under Balfour and the peace group. They were proposing a message, asking for American support on a few core, moderate peace goals, most of them goals they knew Wilson had already endorsed. Wilson's speech seemed to publicly step away from all of that.

At the last minute, House seems to have realized that he needed to offer Grey and his colleagues the reassurances that Wilson's speech so conspicuously omitted. So, on the day of the speech, he sent Grey a reassuring letter. His letter explained, crucially for the British, that the United States was firmly opposed to a peace "on the basis of the map as it stands today. This cannot mean anything but a victorious peace for Germany." House continued, "If England and France, under our invitation, should go into a peace conference now, it would probably lead either to Germany's abandonment of this position or war with us. I thought I would call your attention to this, although I take it you have considered it."[52]

This message could have been very constructive. It was the natural complement to the response Balfour was urging his colleagues to accept. If the British had received that letter before Wilson's speech, it might have helped enormously.

Instead, House sent it on the day of the speech. And—perhaps to be sure it could not be intercepted—he sent it *as a letter*. It had to be carried to London by ship across the ocean and then by train. It could not possibly arrive in time to influence the decisive meeting on May 29 that Grey had warned House about.

House's letter arrived by courier in early June. By then, reacting only to the reports of Wilson's speech, the British had already angrily cast Wilson's offer aside.

———

WILSON HAD hoped his speech would put matters "in a way that it would be very hard for the Allies to reject, as well as for Germany,"[53] but the Allies did not find it hard at all to reject Wilson's words. When the War Committee met on May 29, Wilson's speech had alienated even the potential advocates of an early peace, like Balfour and Hankey.

Later that day, Grey wrote to House to give him the bad news. He had, of course, still not received House's letter. Grey therefore explained, diplomatically, that any peace terms "must be sufficiently favourable to the Allies to make the German people feel that aggressive militarism is a failure." A "premature" call for peace by President Wilson "would be interpreted as meaning that he desired peace on a basis favourable to Germany."

The French ambassador to Washington saw House and reported back to Paris that the Americans did not seem to grasp how they had ruined their own plan. "Neither the President, in fact, nor his most heeded adviser, seems to have foreseen or believed ... that the advances in favor of peace in the address of May 27 could not have produced anything but misunderstandings and would ruin the very plans of the speaker had those plans been feasible in the first place, which is not the case."[54]

─────────

YET WHAT about the "black financial outlook"? That had been a key reason for reconsidering Wilson's offer. McKenna himself had helped put off that disaster for a few more months.

In late May, while preparing for the climactic debate about Balfour's proposed reply to Wilson, McKenna organized an emergency response to the imminent dollar crisis. Before, the government had tried to coax private holders of American securities to sell or loan them to the Treasury. Now, using new, coercive taxes, the government would force those private citizens to turn over their American stocks or bonds so the government could use them as collateral for dollar loans.

Also, during the last week of May, the Treasury asked J. P. Morgan to come up with a plan for a gigantic new loan to Britain. "Every source of dollars was tapped, and potential new ones explored."

Fortunately for Britain, Morgan "succeeded in keeping the gravity of Britain's financial position largely unknown. Most Wall Street leaders were unaware of it. There were the usual rumors that Britain was seeking a loan, but only the senior officers of the banks extending the credits knew the actual facts of the situation." Morgan limited the number of those banks.

The Morgan partners worked with the British on the new loan plan. They would use, as collateral, British-owned American securities and the best British securities, such as UK or Imperial railway stocks, or any other marketable foreign stocks and bonds that the British government could get by persuasion or coercion.[55]

In sum, Wilson's speech had damaged the case of the British peace group, while McKenna's emergency measures had put off the fatal dollar crisis. The peace window closed for a time. The military would get its chance, in the summer offensive, to change the situation on the ground.

Wilson's May move to press his peace option for immediate action had failed. Wilson failed to persuade because, instead of helping the British peace advocates, as he wished to do, he unwittingly undercut them. Wilson failed to coerce because he did not yet understand that his power of coercion over the British, through finance, was practically absolute. He would come to that realization later in the year.

One of the best histories of Wilson's diplomacy in this period was written by a famous British judge, Patrick Devlin. Judge Devlin chose, late in his career, to become a historian. As British judges do, Judge Devlin summarized the evidence about the role House had played in these spring debates: "It is possible to assess House as a shrewd and intelligent man and at the same time to accept that in common with most Americans of his time he thought that there was nothing to learn about diplomacy." To Judge Devlin, "there is something of the too clever amateur about House's devices, something of the raw smartness of the litigant in person when he feels that his natural ingenuity has alighted upon a good technical point."[56]

What a peace process in May needed was demonstrative empathy for the Allies from Wilson and a discreetly wielded financial stick; what it got was chilly neutrality and a president who did not yet realize he had a stick at all.

---

WILSON WAITED and waited for the British to pick up his offer to call the peace conference. He simmered with frustration. As the slaughter continued every day, he and House complained to each other about the foolish stubbornness on all sides, especially the British and French.

As 1916 went on, public sentiment in America and the White House also swung more against Britain, partly because of British actions in the enforcement of their sea blockade and partly due to the way the British military had suppressed the Easter Rising in Dublin, executing a number of the captured Irish rebels. To many in America, Britain looked like a vicious imperial power that had turned its face against any idea of peace.

As Wilson saw it, writing to House on June 22, the behavior of the warring powers indicated "a constantly narrowing, instead of a broad and comprehending, view of the situation. They are in danger of forgetting the rest of the world, and of waking up some surprising morning to discover it has a positive right to be heard about the peace of the world." To his diary, House commented, "The British and French are prolonging this war unnecessarily."[57]

As the summer went on, as he prepared to concentrate fully on the reelection campaign, Wilson decided that he would not wait much longer. He would decide when the moment was right. Then he would just make his peace move.

"I conclude that it will be up to us to judge for ourselves when the time has arrived for us to make an imperative suggestion." Imperative? "I mean a suggestion which they will have no choice but to heed, because the opinion of the non-official world and the desire of all peoples will be behind it."[58]

CHAPTER 3

# The Germans Secretly Seek a Compromise Peace

## The View from the Castle

Berlin and its allies believed the war had placed them under a gigantic siege. London led the encircling besiegers.

With their history, Europeans intuitively understood the principles of a siege. The besiegers would try to wear down and starve out the defenders, men, women, and children alike. Those under siege would resist as long as they could, hoping—as often had happened in medieval sieges—that the besiegers would run low on supplies or willpower.

In 1916, the besieging Allies launched assaults on all fronts. They all failed—in France (the Somme offensive), in eastern Europe, and in Italy. In faraway Mesopotamia (modern-day Iraq), they did worse than fail: a British-Indian army had marched up to Ottoman Baghdad, retreated back down the Tigris Valley, and then, humiliatingly, had to surrender what was left of its forces.

The Germans launched an assault of their own at Verdun, a site they correctly believed the French would exhaust themselves to defend. There the Germans and the French wore each other down, at a cost of hundreds of thousands of lives.

No one can say for certain how many died just in 1916. The number was in the millions. Beyond the loss of life and limb, new weapons that the Germans introduced in 1916, like flamethrowers and a new type of poison gas, added to the ambient terror. As one German army group commander in the Somme commented, "The effect of overwhelming enemy artillery fire, existing in the shell holes, not enough rations, the stench of corpses, and all the other difficulties of a lengthy battle quickly consume the nerves of leaders and men."[1] Most of those who died that year were soldiers or sailors, but civilians were dying in larger numbers too, victims of military operations or, more commonly, malnutrition and related disease.[2]

As a third year of campaigns wore on, the losses of life and limb on every front, sustained by every major combatant, were now so vast as to be far beyond anything any living person had experienced. They were beyond anything in national histories. Battles and losses on this scale had never happened before. War weariness and exhaustion were universal.

Even though the besiegers, the Entente Allies, had lost more, the besieged Central Powers were also very badly worn down. The year was especially hard on Austria-Hungary, which became much more dependent on Germany. German officers and units were blended directly into the Habsburg army.

The siege was now playing out on a continental scale. Remaining resources, like farmers and their draft animals, went first to the military, exacerbating the quite serious shortage of food. People in the besieged Central Powers stood in long queues for groceries, lost weight, and fell prey to illness. German cities experienced hunger riots.

By August 1916, the warring countries were reaching their limits: limits to mass tolerance of the agony; limits in the numbers of men available to man front lines, factories, and farms; limits of money; and limits of food and other resources.

———

FROM THE towers of their besieged castle, German leaders surveyed their options in the summer of 1916. None saw any need, just yet, to raise the white flag. Yet their prospects for breaking the siege were not encouraging. The military options were completely unpromising on land and risky and uncertain at sea. They had three strategic possibilities.

First, they could just hold out and wait for one or another of the besiegers to quit and make terms. They tried to tempt Russia or France into giving up.

Second, the defenders in the castle could plan a giant counterstroke to turn the tables. In medieval warfare those under siege might attempt to disrupt the besiegers, using a tunnel or some other ruse to sally out and cut them off from their supplies. In 1915 and 1916, the navy proposed going underwater, using submarines to cut the supply lines of the besiegers.

This counterstroke was the only choice that might win a full military victory, the kind of victory the right-wing parties preferred, the kind that would yield far-reaching annexations that these parties thought would placate the strained, uneasy public. The risk of the strategy was that, if it brought the United States into the war on the Allied side, America could give the besiegers unlimited supplies and, perhaps eventually, even American forces to join the assaults. So, the counterstroke might blow back catastrophically.

The third basic choice for those in the castle was to seek peace, a negotiated peace that was neither a full victory nor a complete surrender. Such a compromise peace was called "inconclusive," a "status quo/status quo ante peace," or a "peace of understanding."

————

FOR THOSE in the castle who preferred this third option, the compromise peace option, the question was, How to get there? There was no trust between the two warring sides. A request for talks on either side would be seen either as a trick or as a sign of weakness.

In the Middle Ages, sometimes a dignitary of the church would step in to help mediate the negotiated conclusion of a siege. In 1916, though sometimes people looked to the pope, the president of the United States increasingly seemed like the most natural potential agent for mediating peace. Every diplomat remembered that only about ten years earlier, in 1905, an American president had mediated an end to the last war among great powers, the war between Russia and Japan.

An astute German observer put it this way: "The war had become on both sides a war of the people, and he who was desirous of bringing about peace had to handle the belligerents as you handle two fighting bulldogs when you separate them; he had to be in a position to sprinkle pepper on their noses. He was bound to have the means of exerting pressure. Therefore it was quite obvious from the start that secondary neutral Powers could accomplish nothing. The only Power which could do it was America."[3]

FIRST, GERMANY had to decide whether it was willing to seek a compromise peace. The German Empire was a federation of twenty-five separate states, represented in a federal council, or *Bundesrat*. Most government functions were handled by the constituent states. One of those states, Prussia, had a preponderant role, although other states mattered too. For example, Bavaria was an important part of the federation that made up Germany. It had a king of its own, with an ambassador representing Bavaria in Berlin.

But Prussia had about two-thirds of the territory and 60 percent of the population. The Prussian king was also the empire's kaiser. The Prussian prime minister was also the imperial chancellor. The chancellor/prime minister was a civil servant, not an elected politician, and was appointed by the kaiser/king.

Foreign and military policy were even more centered in these imperial institutions. The king/emperor gave the civilian leadership, leadership of the "political branch," to his chancellor. The chancellor was also the imperial foreign minister. The diagram indicates the structure and officeholders as of August 1916.

The army and navy leaders, heading the "military branch," also reported directly to the kaiser, not to the chancellor. The kaiser was the personal commander in chief of the armed forces. The political branch,

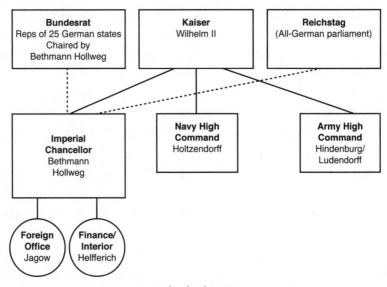

*German war leadership, Autumn 1916*

the army, and the navy had liaison officers at the kaiser's court who also helped the kaiser make personnel appointments.

A major part of the chancellor's fiendishly difficult job was to manage the kaiser, Wilhelm II. Wilhelm was fifty-seven in 1916. He had been on the throne for twenty-eight years. By this time his neuroses and instability were long familiar to everyone at court. In recent years, and even more after the war began, the kaiser had become detached from most political life, rarely seen or heard by the public. In his usually symbolic role as commander in chief of the armed forces, the kaiser spent most of his time well away from Berlin, living near the general headquarters, which at this stage of the war was most often at Pless, in eastern Germany (now in present-day Poland, near that country's southern border).

The divide between the worlds of Berlin and Pless was like the divided, schizophrenic worlds of the German government itself. Berlin, the capital of Prussia, a center of art, music, and scholarship, was one of the great cities of the world, proud and growing. The Chancellery and Foreign Office were adjacent on Wilhelmstrasse, in the very heart of the city, an easy walk from the Brandenburg Gate.

But while the civilian government might rule in Berlin, the army and the kaiser ruled in Pless, three hundred miles away. For Chancellor Theobald von Bethmann Hollweg or his aides to get to Pless was an overnight or all-day train trip, each way. Bethmann thus often dealt with that half of the government through cables sent to or received from his liaison there.

Pless was rural, aristocratic Germany. It was the seat of a duchy in Silesia, and the kaiser and the army high command had taken over much of the magnificent castle of the prince of Pless. The prince had married an Englishwoman, a great beauty, "Daisy" Cornwallis-West. When the newlywed princess arrived at the castle in 1891, she noted her first impression: "hectares of terraces and gardens as well as many indistinguishable sculptures. A wonderful order of a stately residence of a heavy luxury but with no comfort or convenience."[4]

The kaiser provided little operational direction to the conduct of the war. He sat every day for his briefing on recent developments. Mostly, he drifted in an aimless routine. "Wilhelm's vacillations also gave the people around him the impression that he was helpless. As in peacetime, he liked to flee from brutal reality into other worlds, and would have newspaper reports read to him for hours about, for example, Hittite translations. Or he would go hunting in moments of crisis, appearing at dinner in the uniform of a *Hofjagdmeister* [court master of the hunt]."

But at key moments, the kaiser's role could be pivotal. On several occasions, only he could settle the ultimate arguments, like the one about submarine warfare and war with the United States.[5]

———

THE CHANCELLOR advocated for the government's policies in the parliament, the Reichstag. When the war began, the kaiser had called for a *Burgfrieden*, a peace among the parties, but by 1916 that political peace was fraying.

There were the regional divisions (like the differences between the Prussians and practically everyone else), religious divides, especially between the majority Protestants and a large minority of Catholics, and deep social and class divisions in a country that had grown, industrialized, and urbanized quickly.

The most recent general election to the Reichstag, in 1912, helped define the three major camps that the chancellor, Bethmann, sought to balance.

To his right there were aristocrats, industrialists, and others—like the Prussian military elite—who tended to support the most conservative parties. They had about one-third of the delegates. These groups feared the democratic trends in German political life. To those more familiar with American history, there is an analogy between the way many Germans (and others) saw the rural Prussian landowning elite, with their large estates east of the Elbe River, and the way many Americans in the North, before the Civil War, regarded the disproportionate power of the plantation elite of slaveowners and their dependents in the South—the "slave power." Some Germans would refer to *Ostelbia* the way a northerner might have referred to the "Deep South."

During the war, these conservative factions supported all-out German victory, an all-out U-boat war to get it, and large territorial gains that they hoped would secure the dominance of a pan-German empire (uniting all ethnic Germans) and placate the masses. They imagined taking much if not all of Belgium to open Germany up more easily to the Atlantic and get Belgian iron ore. They imagined keeping the rich Briey-Longwy coalfields and iron ore deposits in eastern France that German forces had occupied during the war. They imagined other large gains in the East, extending up the Baltic coast, to be colonized by German farmers. Their future state would be even more authoritarian than before.

To Bethmann's left there were the Social Democrats, then a Marxist-oriented party of democratic socialists. They represented Germany's large, powerful trade unions and had 35 percent of the seats in the Reichstag. They detested the conservatives, manned their battle lines against the industrialists, and distrusted the militarists. The Social Democrats had generally supported the war—but only as a war of self-defense to defend the fatherland, mainly against Russia. They were suspicious of right-wing annexationist dreams, which they regarded as symptoms of capitalist and militarist greed.

In the middle were the Center and Progressive Parties, which held one-third of the seats in the Reichstag. They too largely thought of the war as one of self-defense, and they were open to a compromise peace, while they also hoped Germany might make at least some modest territorial gains.

By political necessity, expediency, and personal conviction, Bethmann identified with these centrists. Bethmann relied not only on the kaiser's continued backing but also on his own continuing influence, which the kaiser recognized, among the centrists, the Social Democrats, and the governments of the various German states. He tried to maintain a difficult balance. He had developed "a conception of peace" that would embed Germany "in a European order" that was "especially opposed to pan-German plans, privileged restraint and tolerance over force and chauvinism."[6]

Bethmann's strategic priority was to keep the Americans out of the war. Then, once tensions settled down and German opinion was not so hostile to President Wilson, there might be an American role to play in negotiating a compromise peace. "If America is finally settled, peace is also probable this year without a U-boat war," one of Bethmann's closest aides noted in his diary.[7] In May, Bethmann had accepted the U-boat restrictions Wilson had demanded.

The next month, on June 13, Bethmann had an evening alone with that long-trusted aide, Kurt Riezler. To his diary, Riezler wrote that the chancellor "was wonderful—full of passion and, in his strange way of grasping everything concretely, clairvoyant in the capture of dangers and depths, the tragic...seeing the true reality behind all the human opinions—but glowing in his faith in the people."

Bethmann thought the only path to peace was compromise. He expected that there might be some kind of "revolution" after the war, a "nightmare" prospect that weighed on him. The returning men in "field-gray" would have "huge claims, disappointment about the peace."

The war would therefore lead to a fundamental political transition in Germany. Bethmann viewed this prospect philosophically. Now, he explained, there were parties "that could maintain themselves only through incitement of passions against the Left, but [were] so hollowed out on the inside that they [had] nothing more to say." After the war, the parties would have to reinvent themselves into something "quite new," completely reshaping the public spirit. Otherwise, "Germany would go into the ground [*geht zu grunde*]." It seemed impossible to change the "East-elbian" elite; it was they who would have "to be broken—go under."[8]

Bethmann believed his job was to chart a practical path to end the war and manage such a transition. He had no fixed plan. He had to improvise, he explained to the Bavarian ambassador, devising "ad hoc ideas which could be influenced through changes in the fortune of arms."[9]

*Bethmann Hollweg*

Some historians deride Bethmann as a hypocritical expansionist who never wanted a compromise peace.[10] In fact, while Bethmann temporized and kept adjusting his views, he was never an enthusiast about annexation. By 1916, Bethmann had consistently and with great determination opposed the pan-German conservatives for a year. By the middle of 1916, although censorship muffled public debate, the right-wing factions hated Bethmann personally. They had fixed on him as their public enemy.[11]

"I was no annexationist," Bethmann testified a year after the war to a knowing group of mainly centrist and leftist German parliamentarians, who had come to power after just the kind of revolution Bethmann had foreseen. "All Germany knew this, in fact." Bethmann reminded them that he had wanted "a peace of understanding" with "moderate peace aims." It was exactly for these reasons "that a bitter fight was being waged against [him] by political parties and the press."

The pan-German conservatives wanted the U-boat war because they believed it could provide a complete victory. Bethmann understood, as his aide put it later in June, that if he was able to negotiate a compromise peace, "the screamers" would argue that such a peace, which was bound to be "much worse than people thought," could have been avoided by using the U-boat weapon. "We had victory and world domination in our hand," these "idiots" would say.[12]

Many Germans were tempted by the U-boat panacea just because they were so desperate for anything that would bring the war to an early end. The popular right-wing line to attack Bethmann, a line that found its way to many soldiers, was "Our youth is shedding its blood in the trenches because the Chancellor has not the guts to start an aggressive U-boat campaign."

This line got passed back to the kaiser's naval liaison, Admiral Georg von Müller, from his brother-in-law serving at the front. Müller wrote back to him angrily, "Can an officer really be so stupid as to imagine that the Chancellor would not rather demand unrestricted U-boat warfare today than tomorrow if it could force England to make peace? But an England allied to America means, among other dangers, the certain prolongation of the war."[13]

Opposed to doing anything that would bring America into the war against Germany, Bethmann steadily argued against the all-out U-boat

war. To that end, working with the kaiser, he forced the great German naval advocate, Admiral Alfred von Tirpitz, out of the government. Tirpitz's
ouster mobilized even more conservative agitation against the chancellor.

Bethmann then faced off against another internal foe. The powerful
chief of the general staff, the head of the army high command, Erich von
Falkenhayn, had joined the submarine advocates. Falkenhayn was not an
annexationist and was willing to accept a compromise peace. His usual
line had been that the war would be a "drawn game" and that "if we don't
lose the war, we have won it." He discouraged wild talk about large annexations, "foggy war aims," as Falkenhayn called them. The louder and
more indiscriminate such claims were, the more difficult it would be to
persuade any of Germany's enemies to give up. But Falkenhayn supported
the expanded U-boat war as a way to force the British to sit down and talk
peace.[14]

Bethmann took the opposite view, believing that American entry into
the war would prolong it and make Britain more likely to keep fighting.
The kaiser was fond of Falkenhayn, but in the summer of 1916, Bethmann
began intriguing to persuade the kaiser to dismiss him. Bethmann's plan
was to bring in a team of German military heroes from the East, the pair
who had turned back the Russian invasion: Paul von Hindenburg and Erich von Ludendorff. Hindenburg was a stolid, affable, elderly, and majestic
general; Ludendorff, his ruthlessly competent partner and chief of staff.
Hindenburg had become Germany's great symbolic military hero.

––––––––––

PART OF BETHMANN'S plan to bring in Hindenburg was that, with this
move, he would be able to negotiate a compromise peace. Bethmann wrote
to Moriz von Lyncker, the kaiser's army liaison, that people might accept a
setback if Hindenburg was in charge "as they would [accept] a peace over
his name."

In July, as the Allied offensives pounded away at the German and Austrian lines, Bethmann made his move. He arranged an important set of
meetings at the end of July with the kaiser and the kaiser's staff. Bethmann
told the kaiser bluntly that his Hohenzollern dynasty was at stake.

"With Hindenburg," Bethmann explained, I can "make a face-saving
peace." Without him, I can do nothing. The time has come, Bethmann
concluded, to seek Wilson's help.

The chancellor assumed that the American president would demand that Germany demonstrate its willingness to compromise. "It might be necessary," he warned the kaiser's naval liaison, "to approach Wilson to mediate for peace on the understanding that we would be prepared to evacuate Belgium."

The kaiser was persuaded. He accepted the premise of some sort of compromise peace. Several times that year he had said he thought the war would end in a draw.[15]

By August, as the Russian summer offensive helped bring Romania into the war on the Allied side, the kaiser took the final step of dismissing Falkenhayn. He summoned Hindenburg and Ludendorff to take over the army.

———

IF, IN the late summer of 1916, the Germans could take comfort as they read news about war weariness in Russia, as well as in Paris and London, they also felt the fatigue. One observant German officer, home from the front, strolled through central Berlin on August 1. "This evening I encountered on Luisenplatz and at the Oranienburg Gate troops of boys and girls who had come there to protest against the war," he noted in his diary. "Many policemen but everything took place peacefully. The movement is not threatening. But a great war weariness prevails in all circles."

It was hard to see any good military way out. "Actually only a miracle can rescue us," one of the kaiser's top military aides confided to his wife. These were "quite secret thoughts," thoughts that no one could say out loud. As summer turned to autumn, such views were common among the leaders of Germany and its dependent ally, Austria-Hungary.[16]

The German leaders decided to launch the process of negotiating a general peace. They turned to America. But they weren't sure what to make of President Wilson.

## Bethmann's Man in Washington

To explain Wilson, the German government relied above all on its representative in Washington, Count Johann von Bernstorff. He was well suited to this responsibility. Bernstorff had been born to diplomacy. It was truly the family's trade.

For 150 years, Bernstorffs had been diplomats and high ministers for Denmark, Hanover, Prussia, and Germany. Johann was born in London in 1862, while his father was Prussia's ambassador to Great Britain, and he spent his first eleven years in England.

Johann's path to a diplomatic career had been disrupted, however. His older brother—already a diplomat in Washington—"showed more interest in the Y.M.C.A. than in politics," Johann cryptically recalled. The brother was sent home. There his brother made matters worse, supporting political foes of Germany's then chancellor, Otto von Bismarck. It looked like Johann's political prospects were finished.

Having married a German American woman born in New York, Johann settled instead for the life of a Guards officer in Berlin society. There, having restored his family's good name with the Bismarcks, he received a diplomatic post after all. He then served across Europe and the Middle East, including a return to London as the deputy head of the German mission there.[17]

By the end of 1908, Count Bernstorff was regarded as one of the brightest stars in the diplomatic service. He was selected to be ambassador to the United States. His success there during the presidencies of Theodore

*Bernstorff*

Roosevelt and William Howard Taft added to his stature. When high officials speculated about candidates who might succeed Bethmann as chancellor, Bernstorff made the shortlist.[18]

Bernstorff was content in America and with Americans. His style was lively and charming. Empathetic, he listened, observed, and analyzed.

The outbreak of war in 1914 caught Bernstorff on summer leave in Europe. He was just able to get back to Washington before British warships made such voyages impossible, but he had to leave his wife behind.

At the American embassy in Berlin, the ambassador was a patronage appointee, James Gerard, an eminent lawyer and judge from New York who had been Tammany Hall's failed candidate for the US Senate in 1914. The Germans regarded him as high-strung and tactless and hoped for his recall. To assess Wilson and his government, the German government relied almost entirely on Bernstorff.

The German government was, to a remarkable degree, cut off from the United States. Since Britain controlled the seas and the telegraph lines, communications between Berlin and Washington were challenging. Dispatches could go by clandestine courier, sometimes (rarely) through a visiting submarine, or through coded telegrams sent by circuitous routes. Short, telegraphed cables used elaborate cyphers that coded a set of numbers for each letter. These messages, coded and decoded by hand, could be transmitted through neutral "roundabouts," for instance, by inserting them (with permission) into Swedish diplomatic traffic sent from Washington to Buenos Aires, from there to Stockholm, and then from Stockholm to Berlin.

If the message was especially urgent, the Germans would ask the United States to transmit their cable, in code, through the American embassy in Berlin. In that case, Bernstorff would deliver a coded German message to the State Department, to be inserted into one of its cables to the American embassy in Berlin. The embassy would then deliver the coded message to the German addressee. The Americans provided this service only if they were assured the message was related to peacemaking, not war making.[19]

———

Bernstorff got along reasonably well with both Wilson and House. He had a nuanced appraisal of both. "Audiences with the President," Bernstorff recalled, "when they were obtainable at all, proceeded on the lines that the visitor put forward his suggestions, upon which Wilson delivered a more or less detailed exposition of his own views. Then the audience was at an end, unless the visitor was very persistent, in which case he did not fail to forfeit the President's favour, who would in the end hand him over to House."

Wilson was, Bernstorff believed, "the most brilliant and most eloquent exponent of the American point of view." Writing after the war, when many German readers were very bitter about Wilson, Bernstorff explained, "There can be no question that, as a result both of his origin and his training, the President is very much under the sway of English thought and ideals. Nevertheless, his ambition to be a Peacemaker and an *arbiter mundi* certainly suggested the chance of our winning him over to our side, in the event of our being unable to achieve a decisive victory with the forces at our disposal." "In this case," Bernstorff explained, "Wilson, as the democratic leader of the strongest neutral Power, was the most suitable person to propose and to bring about a Peace by arrangement." Bernstorff never wavered from this view.

Bernstorff understood that the reliance on Wilson had drawbacks. These were more practical. He observed that Wilson did not "devote the same energy and consistency to the execution of his various programmes as . . . to their formation."

Once he had settled into a position, Wilson's "obstinate dogmatism and his inclination for solitary work made him little suited to foreign politics." The problem was that "internal questions can be solved by a theorist from his own writing table, if he has gone into them with proper care," Bernstorff allowed. "But foreign affairs can only be mastered in actual practice. Eloquent orations can sway a nation and convince a parliament, but they are of little use when the interests and armed might of foreign Powers are vigorously engaged."

Still, Bernstorff believed Wilson was sincere in his desire to make peace. The American president was not a hypocrite, "as anyone can testify who knew Wilson well." Nor did Bernstorff question Wilson's integrity. "At that time," he testified shortly after the war, "I considered him an absolutely honorable mediator."[20]

And Bernstorff was sure that American mediation was essential. It was "the only possible way out of the war." He was sure that "if the American

Government established a peace conference, this would be sure to lead to peace itself. It could not be imagined that, in view of the nations' need of peace, such a conference could break up without having reached any result."[21]

────────

IN THE early summer of 1916, Bernstorff had been going back and forth about the Wilson mediation option with Bethmann's deputy in Berlin, the state secretary managing the Foreign Office, Gottlieb von Jagow. Jagow had been uneasy about Wilson, but by July he was more sympathetic,[22] at which point Bernstorff laid out a detailed argument in favor of Wilson's mediation. Because of the message's sensitivity and length, he sent it via clandestine courier. It took a month for his analysis to get to Berlin.

In that analysis, Bernstorff reassured Berlin that Wilson had expressly disclaimed any desire to dictate territorial terms. Wilson, he argued, just wanted to be the peacemaker.[23]

Bethmann read Bernstorff's long message. He and the kaiser were already inclined to try this peace path, using Wilson. The chancellor himself wrote the telegram that went out in reply to Bernstorff right away, on August 18. It gave Bernstorff just the green light the ambassador had sought: "We are happy to accept a mediation by the President to start peace negotiations among the belligerents who want to bring this about." The agenda was wide open: the Germans set no preconditions.[24]

This message was a watershed moment. It was the first time in the war that any leader of a warring power had sought a peace mediation from an outside power. And Germany was asking, very secretly, for a peace mediation from the leader of the most powerful neutral country in the world, a leader who was eager and waiting to take up this challenge.

At the end of August 1916, as Romania joined the war on the Allied side, posing a new threat to Austria-Hungary, Bethmann went through yet another prolonged debate with the military high command. Once more, the navy pushed hard for the all-out U-boat war. Bethmann held them off, but he took stock of the situation with his key advisers.

About this time, a photographer snapped Bethmann talking to two of them on the steps of the Chancellery in Berlin. Bethmann stood on the left, Jagow on the right, and Jagow's chief aide, Arthur Zimmermann, in the middle.

*Bethmann, Zimmermann, and Jagow*

Everything should be done to end the war, Bethmann concluded. But the only way to secure peace was through President Wilson.

As to terms for compromise, Bethmann was open to important territorial adjustments with France. He was interested in a bargain that might cede some of the territory in Alsace and Lorraine, annexed by Germany in 1871, perhaps in exchange for concessions in the valuable Briey-Longwy area of eastern France, which the Germans had occupied during the war.

Depressed by the news about Romania, the kaiser said he too was convinced that Germany must have peace, almost whatever the terms. He was indifferent to everything else, he said.[25]

To further encourage Wilson, Bethmann and Jagow agreed to assure the American president, as a sign of good faith, that Germany was prepared to restore Belgium. They expected to work out suitable conditions for this in negotiations already begun with the Belgian king.

On September 2, the chancellor sent another telegram to his ambassador, concisely giving the German leadership's view of the war situation. "Hope to conclude peace before winter...would peace mediation by Wilson be possible and successful if we were to guarantee Belgium's conditional restoration?"[26]

———————

WHEN BERNSTORFF received his first instruction, the August 18 message, he, like almost everyone else who could, had fled the Washington summer for cooler climes. He was staying on the north shore of Long Island Sound, in Rye, with ready access to communications in New York City.

Only days earlier he had reunited in New York with his wife, whom he had not seen in the two years since the war started. He had arranged permission for her to travel through the blockade on a neutral vessel sailing from Copenhagen. The chancellor himself had met with her before she departed Germany, in mid-August, and said, "Tell your husband that if he cannot bring about a peace in the meantime, we shall be forced to declare unrestricted U-Boat war on February 1st." Bethmann's alarms eased a bit while she was en route. Via cable, he assured his ambassador that there was no current intention to declare such a U-boat war. But Bernstorff certainly understood what the chancellor wanted.[27]

Armed with his August instruction, Bernstorff immediately sought out House, not waiting for him to return from his summer vacation at a cottage on Lake Sunapee, in New Hampshire. Bernstorff and his wife arranged to visit him there. The ambassador used the cover story that he and his wife were going to stay with friends over the Labor Day weekend. He called House the day before to ensure he was welcome. Then the couple made the daylong drive (in an early automobile) and arrived for a late lunch on a summer day, by the lake, so that Bernstorff could spend a couple of hours with House.

In their wide-ranging conversation House was very clear: Wilson would go forward with the peace move—but not until he had been reelected in November. Once reelected, House said, Wilson could speak "with the voice of America back of him." In arranging the peace conference, House assured Bernstorff, Wilson still did not plan to try to dictate the terms among the warring powers (in keeping with the stance he had taken in his May speech).

It was a pleasant visit. "Bernstorff is the only one of the Ambassadors among the belligerents who has retained his equilibrium," House noted in his diary. He "has been able to smile upon the present and philosophize as to the future."

Returning from his lakeside meeting, Bernstorff promptly reported back to Berlin. As that report was going out, Bethmann's September 2 message, including the German offer to restore Belgium, came in. Bernstorff immediately answered that too.

His message to Berlin was that yes, Wilson was eager to move but could not do so right away. He needed to wait until after the November election. Once reelected, which Bernstorff thought likely, "the President will immediately take steps towards mediation. He believes that then he will be strong enough to force a peace conference." He forecasted that the Wilson peace move for mediation was "very likely to occur before the end of the year."

Accurately summarizing what he heard from House, Bernstorff reported, "Wilson considers it in America's interest that neither belligerent should win a decisive victory." As for territorial terms, Bernstorff wrote that if Wilson "mixed into that," which he had said he would not, then yes, Belgium was "the primary American interest." This was "almost exclusively" what concerned American public opinion. Politically, Belgium was *the* issue.

Bernstorff also warned again that an escalation of U-boat warfare would "unquestionably" mean war with America. Such a campaign would not end the war. Instead, the conflict "would simply be prolonged."[28]


## Bethmann Presses for Action

From August 1916 through the rest of the year, "the wish to bring about general peace negotiations via Washington . . . now occupied a central position in German foreign policy," observed Swedish scholar Karl Birnbaum. "Now an American diplomatic initiative seemed the only way open to peace. Moreover, it also appeared the only means of avoiding a rupture with the United States."[29]

Bethmann could keep the gateway to peace open for a while, at least for some months. But he probably could not hold that gate open indefinitely. The U-boat advocates were also offering to end the war—their way.

The chancellor now also had to live with the consequences of his effort to depose Falkenhayn and replace him with Hindenburg and Ludendorff. Hindenburg was indeed popular, but this gave him a political base of his own, matched with Ludendorff's energetic agenda, which was to prepare Germany for total war, making every instrument of government answerable to General Headquarters. "In his boundless pride and ambition," one top General Headquarters staffer warned, Ludendorff "will wage war until the German people are completely exhausted, which will saddle the monarchy with the blame."[30]

At first, Hindenburg and Ludendorff concentrated on the Romanian crisis and an all-out mobilization of manpower. The Germans began bringing that situation under control, invading the country with Austro-Hungarian and Bulgarian help. The Russians and other allies were unable to help the Romanians.[31]

Bethmann carried a tremendous load. An American diplomat visiting Bethmann's office noticed how "the Chancellor was continually going out of the room and returning for a few moments, only to be called away again." The once handsome Chancellery on Wilhelmstrasse was itself run-down, looking to one of Bethmann's friends "more like a seedy boardinghouse."[32]

Impatient public agitation for use of the U-boat weapon increased. The general war weariness made the idea of a quick breakthrough especially attractive. The Reichstag reconvened on September 26. The conservative parties in the Reichstag, with about a third of the delegates, used a resolution on the U-boat issue as a way to bring Bethmann down. At secret hearings, the navy minister asserted that the military significance of the United States' participation in the war, if it were to join as a belligerent, would be "zero."

Aided by his younger vice-chancellor, Karl Helfferich, who had a strong background in finance, Bethmann was very practical. There was still no need, the chancellor said, to resort to a "policy of desperation."

Still, during October, Bethmann's pillar of support in the Reichstag, the centrists, voted for a resolution saying that while they would back him on the U-boat issue, he needed to have the support of the high command. Once the military leaders felt ready for another full confrontation, Bethmann's position would again be very difficult, unless by then the peace option showed some promise.[33]

So, in late September and October, Bethmann pushed harder to persuade Wilson to take action as soon as possible. He still had the kaiser on his side. In early October, Wilhelm bluntly told the navy's leaders that "there should be no possibility of launching the U-boat war in the near future"; it was out of the question while negotiations were under way with the United States.[34]

Bethmann reached out again to Wilson. He used both the German ambassador in Washington and the American embassy in Berlin. To Bernstorff, Bethmann sent out a cluster of telegrams detailing his instructions. The U-boat advocates were pressing. Germany would welcome the peace move. But no one should see that the Germans had asked for it. The Germans did not want to look weak or desperate. Wilson's move had to "appear spontaneous to those viewing it from without."

Bethmann stressed that the president should move as quickly as possible. "If Wilson desired to wait until shortly before or after his election, he would scarcely be left any further opportunity for taking such a step." Everyone would then get caught up in preparing their military moves for 1917.[35] The chancellor was saying, in unusually direct language, that if Wilson waited until he was reelected, he would then need to move very quickly indeed.

"Germany anxious to make peace," Gerard meanwhile reported from the US embassy in Berlin. Through that channel, Bethmann reiterated that "if the President will make offer of good offices in general terms," using the model President Roosevelt had used in 1905 for the Russo-Japanese War, "Germany will accept in general terms immediately and state readiness to send delegates to proposed peace conference."[36]

———

WILSON DOES not seem to have understood anything of the German sense of urgency at first. House did not tell Wilson about his lakeside talk with Bernstorff over the Labor Day weekend. In fact, he did not talk at all to Wilson about foreign issues until late in September, by which time everyone was consumed with the reelection campaign. Gerard's message from the American embassy conveying Bethmann's plea for the peace move did, however, go directly to Wilson on September 30.[37]

Bernstorff saw House in person again on October 3. Armed with the latest instruction, he again pressed. Was there any chance that Wilson might move before the election? Out of the question, House reiterated. Writing to Wilson a couple of days later, House did not mention this second visit. He seemed impervious to the German urgency.

Bernstorff at last had the chance to speak directly with Wilson. He was at the White House to discuss humanitarian relief in Poland. The two men were friendly. Wilson stressed that his "sole wish was to remain neutral and help end the war, since he considered a decision by arms out of the question." It was "better to make peace today than tomorrow."

Having just explained to House (under instruction) that the initiative had to look like it came from the Americans, so that Germany's enemies would not think the Germans were anxious or desperate for peace, Bernstorff carefully explained to Wilson that the warring powers could not formally be seen to be asking Wilson to mediate. But Bernstorff liked what he heard from Wilson. He confirmed to Berlin that, if reelected, Wilson might then be emboldened to make the peace move.

Bernstorff went back up to New York to see House at his Midtown Manhattan apartment, where the ambassador could come and go without notice by the press. Yet again, Bernstorff pressed for action. Yet again, House said nothing could be done before the election. Bernstorff was "disturbed," House noted.

The ambassador again wanted assurance the Americans understood both that it had to look like the Americans were making the peace initiative on their own and that Germany was ready and eager to welcome this move. House told Bernstorff not to worry. When Wilson wanted to move, he would. He would not need a formal request.[38]

Heartened, Bernstorff cabled Berlin. If Wilson is reelected, "he will try peace mediation very soon and will be successful."[39]

To urge Wilson to move more quickly, the kaiser himself decided to write directly to the president. In his ham-handed way, Wilhelm wanted to emphasize the pressure he was feeling. He wrote that he knew that Wilson might offer "his good services to the belligerents for the promotion of peace." He warned that, if there was no peace, the German government would eventually have to regain its "freedom of action" in the use of submarines, which might jeopardize the president's peace move if Wilson was delayed until "towards the end of this year." Conveying the kaiser's indelicate message, Berlin reassured Bernstorff that "a more ruthless submarine war [would] not be waged for the time being," and passing the message to House for Wilson, Bernstorff emphasized that the kaiser's message was not meant as a threat.[40]

Wilson did not need this added spur. He had already made up his mind. He would make his peace move as soon as possible—after the election was over.

On November 4, three days before the election, he wrote, "The minute the campaign is over, I shall be obliged to prepare some of the most important papers I have yet had to prepare." A few days after the election, just before returning to the White House, he wrote to another friend, "Now the burden upon me is heavier than ever."

"If we can escape entering the war and bring about a rational peace, it is something worth living and dying for," Wilson wrote. "I believe the country feels that way or it would not have re-elected me."[41]

## Preparing for a Compromise Peace

As Americans went to the polls, Bethmann had been hard at work, for months, to pave the way for negotiations that would produce a compromise peace. During October, given their federal system, this meant secret discussions with key civilian leaders in the German federal and state governments.

Bethmann, with Vice-chancellor Helfferich, briefed these leaders and conditioned them for compromise. "We do not want to prolong the war one day more than necessary because of wild annexations," they said.

Bethmann outlined the kind of terms that he expected a peace process might require. The end result, he said, would look a lot like the prewar status quo. Such a peace might seem "meager." The chancellor was candid. "The glowing hopes we entertained in the years 1914–1915 are now probably beyond fulfillment. Unfortunately the war has not gone the way we had expected."

Bethmann and others appealed to a very well-known analogy in German history. The Seven Years War (1756–1763) had established Prussia as a great power. Then the kingdom was led by Frederick the Great. Yet, toward the end of that war, Prussia's situation was dire. Defeat loomed.

In 1763, Prussia salvaged the situation by negotiating a compromise peace with Austria. Both sides effectively relinquished their conquests. The previous year, Prussia had struck a compromise with Russia. Instead of complete defeat, the Peace of Hubertusburg had allowed Prussia to survive the war, ensuring that it would remain a great power.

It was time again, Bethmann said, for such a "Hubertusburg" peace. The majority of German political leaders could accept this. Most Germans sincerely believed they were fighting a defensive war. Parliamentarians in the moderate Center Party and some leaders of the powerful Social Democrats quietly let Bethmann know they would support a negotiated peace.

Talking with some of Prussia's more conservative leaders, Helfferich was blunt. If the Allies would accept a status quo ante peace, Germany would have to agree. Like it or not, he warned them, in such a situation, politically, Germany would be unable to continue fighting. The Social Democrats' position would be clear. They would support such a peace. The centrists would not wish to continue either. The right wing could not force Germany to fight on. None of the Prussian leaders disagreed with Helfferich's analysis.

Germany's real goal was to show it could not be vanquished, Bethmann explained in his meetings. "If we stand up to the overwhelming enemy superiority and come out of it able to negotiate, we shall have won." Pursuing the Hubertusburg analogy, he argued that if Germany could just defend its potential for growth and the achievements of 1870, which had unified and created a great country, "we should thank God."

Bethmann's great fear, expressed time and again, was that at some point "the governments will no longer be able to stop the war." In that case, the war would "finally be concluded by the people" in a revolution. So, rather than let matters "merely drift with events," Germany had to take the initiative.[42]

Germany's ally, Austria-Hungary, also sought peace as soon as possible. The Habsburg emperor, Franz Josef, was old and near death. His heir, Karl, was twenty-nine years old and full of energy. From the start, Karl's view, as one historian put it, was that "instead of war aims, peace aims were to be drawn up. Karl wanted to content himself with maintaining the integrity of the Monarchy. Nothing else was needed."[43]

Bethmann had probably read a memo composed back in July 1916 by a Bohemian nobleman, one of the Habsburg Empire's ablest diplomats, Count Ottokar von Czernin. Czernin was then serving in Romania (he would become Austria's foreign minister in December, once Karl became the new emperor). In July, Czernin wrote a memo titled "Thoughts About the Ending of the War" and gave it to his German colleague in Bucharest, who sent it on to Berlin.

Czernin was pessimistic about the war, foreseeing eventual defeat with "mathematical certainty." The key point, he thought, was to judge the right moment for the Central Powers to bring the war to an end. He believed that moment had come.

Czernin thought the peace should have a few basic elements. The Central Powers would renounce any territorial expansion. Every warring state would take care of its own costs and damages. Belgium would be restored, and all the warring powers would help rebuild it.

The peace conference should also address disarmament and take other measures to prevent a future world war. The last point might seem utopian, he wrote, but after this horrific war, he thought a world coalition committed to arbitration of disputes was not necessarily a utopian dream.[44]

In the last week of October, Bethmann read reports of a speech Edward Grey had given in London. Grey had chosen to emphasize issues of postwar security, including a possible league of nations, and the role that neutral leaders like Wilson could play in that.

Bethmann decided that he would make a public address of his own in reply. Addressing the Reichstag on November 8, he declared that Germany was willing "to enter into a League of Nations at any time; yes, lead an organization which curbs those disturbing peace." Bethmann added that Germany had "never called for the annexation of Belgium."[45]

———

IN SECRET, with the German Bundesrat and with Prussia's state ministers, Bethmann outlined specific goals for the peace talks. His wish list included restoration of Belgium with some undefined guarantees for German security, an independent Poland created out of former Russian

Poland, annexation of German-occupied Baltic lands in provinces of the Russian Empire located in present-day Lithuania and western Latvia, a restoration of Serbia, and some sort of exchange with France involving the Briey-Longwy region and parts of Alsace and Lorraine. There would also be some sort of vague compromise about colonial lands (much of which Germany had already lost).[46]

"We are not leading a war of conquest," Bethmann reminded his ambassador in Vienna at the end of October. At an open-ended peace conference, Germany and its allies might get some modest gains for security. But they would not annihilate other nations. "The existence and freedom of development of [our] peoples did not conflict with respect for the rights of other nations." It was time for peace. "Hundreds of thousands of the best human lives" had already been sacrificed, just waiting for peace talks to begin.[47]

Bethmann also worked with the Austro-Hungarian foreign minister, Baron István Burian, on preparations for a peace conference. Returning to Vienna after his talks with the chancellor, Burian secretly confided to the head of the Austro-Hungarian army, on November 5, "The key to the [peace] situation lies in the West. If Germany gives away France and Belgium and a bit more, then peace will come. The Chancellor has promised me, in strict confidence, to make the sacrifice."[48]

––––––

THE SECRET internal discussions about goals for peace talks were a tricky bureaucratic and political exercise for the chancellor. It was hard to state maximum objectives, as there would be no indication of readiness to compromise. It was hard to state minimum objectives, because those would be more controversial at home and could then just be the starting points for bargaining with the enemy.

But the various wish lists, that "thick book," as Bethmann called them, had to be put aside or managed. He especially had to manage the unbalanced expectations of the German high command. To do that, Bethmann's political strategy was to sand down the proposed terms, to say as little as possible about them.

Most important for him was just getting to the talks, without setting any preconditions for holding them. At the peace conference there would be a new situation, politically and bureaucratically. At the peace conference, Bethmann, not the generals, would be in charge. They ran the war; he ran foreign policy. At the peace conference, he would have greater freedom of action and more possibilities to work compromises among the various participating countries. After long haggling, step by step, all the sides would slowly see that they would have to abandon most or all of their military gains. Bethmann was convinced that he needed "only to get Asquith and Grey to sit with him at the table in order to get peace."[49]

The Wilson route was the best way to get to the peace table with the fewest constraints. If, instead, the Germans had to make a common peace proposal jointly with their allies (the route Vienna preferred), the Austro-Hungarians could—and did—demand that, in advance, they and the Germans must come to a binding, written understanding about terms. Bethmann did not want to be confined by that. On the other hand, if the Americans convened the conference, then the Germans could just say yes to the American proposal.

The same was true on the Allied side. They had their own book of wish lists and prior understandings with each other. If they had to act together to make a peace move, they would also have to negotiate the terms for doing that. For them too, Wilson's calling the conference would create a new political situation in which any country could just say, "Yes, we will come."

It is a waste of time, Bethmann told one of his aides, to take seriously some "imaginative catalog of war aims drafted by some nameless General Staff officer." As Bethmann put it to Hindenburg at one point, at the negotiating table, peace planning would be "the art of the attainable." Bethmann later explained: he knew "perfectly well that the moment I present a tangible chance for peace to the Kaiser, I shall have my way with him." Yes, there would be trouble with the high command and there would be political attacks. "But peace will be made all the same."

"Unless it was our desire to keep fighting at all costs," Bethmann observed, "all these statements of war aims would be of little or no practical value." Once there was a real chance to move, "all earlier statements of war aims would be dissipated into thin air."[50]

# CHAPTER 4

# The British Debate Reaches Breaking Point

## After the Summer Offensives

By the end of May 1916, British leaders had submerged their doubts and gone ahead with the great gamble on their summer offensive on the Somme, assisted by the French, to support the Russian offensive. The peace option had been tabled, at least until the end of the summer (Lloyd George's original suggestion), to see how they did. By early August, a picture was starting to emerge, but it was anything but clear.

What was clear was that none of the Allied offensives had secured large, lasting gains. What was clear was that the toll had been staggering. The chief of the Imperial General Staff, General William Robertson, who had vigorously pressed for the offensive, still believed that any decisive gain could only be made on the western front. But even he actually knew frustratingly little about the real situation in the field.

"The telegrams sent to me," he wrote privately to his commander in France, Douglas Haig, "as a matter of fact do not contain daily more than is in the Press Communiqué." This information was not sufficient for him to explain matters to the cabinet's War Committee.

The great offensive of the British Empire and French forces in the watershed of the Somme, in northern France, had relieved some of the pressure on the French at Verdun. It was unclear if the Somme offensive had accomplished much else.

On July 29, Robertson wrote again to Haig. "The Powers that be are be-ginning to get a little uneasy in regard to the situation.... In general, what is bothering them is the probability that we may soon have to face a bill of 2 to 300,000 casualties [about one-third of them dead] with no very great gains additional to the present." Haig resented Robertson's implied reproach, but his headquarters did give Robertson more to work with, feeding the argument that the Somme campaign was successfully "wearing out" the Germans.[1]

At the beginning of August, Winston Churchill decided to voice a furi-ous dissent. Churchill had been Arthur Balfour's predecessor at the Admi-ralty. Out of government and out of favor, Churchill had returned to the army and commanded a battalion of the Royal Scots Fusiliers during the first half of 1916. This added a bit of credibility to his passionate critique. He arranged to circulate, among the cabinet, a memo sharply criticizing the whole conduct of the Somme campaign.

Facing such criticism, Robertson closed ranks with Haig. He loyally presented Haig's "wearing out" argument to the War Committee. Haig added greatly exaggerated estimates of German losses, reflecting the mer-curial optimism of his intelligence chief. Robertson was served by a more somber and clear-eyed intelligence adviser and did not necessarily believe all the happy talk. He did, however, share a grim determination that the only possible strategy was just to continue to pound away on the western front. So, as he confided to Haig, all this just showed "the necessity of giving me the necessary data with which to reply to the swines"—their civilian critics, such as Churchill.

Robertson and Haig argued that the attacks would need to continue for months to come. Robertson observed that, since the British had started to field giant armies in France relatively recently, its losses in the war were only about one-fifth the scale of those France had suffered to date. The current loss rates should not, Robertson said, "be considered in any way excessive" if "judged by the standards of this war."[2]

The trouble with that argument was that the war's standards were horrific and unprecedented, as Robertson well knew. So the question of whether this was "excessive" could only be answered by also pondering, Losses for what?

Among the civilian leaders, the reaction to all this was confused. They wanted to believe the military claims that the Germans were reaching their limits. Asquith, having acquiesced to all this carnage, did not want to accept Churchill's criticisms. It was hard to know what to believe.

---

PRIME MINISTER Asquith's eldest son, Raymond, had a better idea about the state of the fighting. He was serving at the front. Raymond was then thirty-eight years old, an officer in the Grenadier Guards. Handsome, greatly admired by his contemporaries, and a gifted athlete and poet, Raymond had been a flourishing barrister when the war began, about to begin a glittering political career of his own. When the war began, he immediately volunteered for active service, and by the summer of 1916 he was a seasoned officer, rotating in and out of the line. Raymond had spent time at headquarters, and he frequently dined with senior officers when out of the line, well aware that a staff billet was always there for him if he wanted one. But he felt his place was with his regiment.

One of Raymond Asquith's duties as an officer was to censor the letters his men wrote home. From them, even by December 1915, Raymond saw that the soldiers were expecting the civilians to end the war. "Nothing will persuade the men that the war is not practically over now and that they are merely marking time out here while the details of peace are being settled," he wrote a close friend. "I wish I could think so."

*Raymond Asquith*

Six months later, by the summer of 1916, Raymond felt a "distinct change" in morale. Even his fellow officers were now "more tired of the war, more frightened of shells and talk[ed] more constantly about the prospects of peace."

Raymond's own mood darkened too. His stints in the line were longer and bleaker. "An order has just come out that there is to be no cheering in the trenches when peace is declared," he wrote his wife. "No one can say that our Generals don't look ahead."

Soldiers at the front frequently received the *Daily Mail*, published by Lord Northcliffe, a conservative cheerleader for the war, a paper that regularly attacked Raymond's father, the prime minister, so much so that Raymond wrote his wife that he would "rather beat Harmsworth [Northcliffe's name before he acquired his title] than beat the Germans. He seems to me just as aggressively stupid and stupidly aggressive as they are, and much less brave and efficient."[3]

Even before the summer offensive began, a number of Raymond's friends had already been killed. The offensive struck down more. Hearing of another casualty, he replied to a friend, "A blind God butts about the world with a pair of delicately malignant antennae to detect whatever is fit to live and an iron hoof to stamp it into the dust when found." But, he added, "out here I believe one feels these disasters less than one would at home. If one thinks at all (which rarely happens) one feels that we are all living so entirely on the edge of doom, so liable at any moment to fall in with the main procession, that the order of going seems less important."[4]

In August, Raymond was almost killed by a trench mortar shell. It hurt his eardrums and put "quite a big dent" in his helmet but left him, he wrote, "not much the worse."

Raymond did not regard the war as an ennobling experience. He agreed with his wife "about the utter senselessness of war.... It extends the circle of one's acquaintance, but beyond that I cannot see that it has a single redeeming feature. The suggestion that it elevates the character is hideous. Burglary [and] assassination... would do as much for anyone."

Raymond was a good friend of Churchill, whom he saw several times during 1916. He was aware of Churchill's misgivings about the offensive. He was neither surprised nor resentful to hear, from a well-placed friend in Whitehall, about Churchill's memo pronouncing the offensive "to be a murderous failure."

Raymond had just observed an attack on a part of the line he knew well, "a great disaster. Entirely owing to the folly of generals who, I fear, have not suffered for it." Instead, the official communiqué "was allowed to pass it off as a moderately successful trench raid instead of an utter failure by 2 divisions." Some he knew at headquarters thought the offensive was working. As for himself, he wrote, "I wish one could form any idea as to whether our offensive is being a success or not."[5]

## The War Committee Goes Back to Work on the Peace Road

In London, Britain's leaders were quietly returning to the issue of how to bring the war to an end. Remembering very well that in May the issue had been put off until after the summer offensive, a strong group was determined to keep the American peace option open. It was led by Foreign Secretary Edward Grey, his parliamentary deputy, Robert Cecil, First Lord of the Admiralty Arthur Balfour, and Treasury Secretary Reginald McKenna. Cecil—an exceptionally talented lawyer who was also Balfour's cousin—played an active role in leading the staff work for the Foreign Office.

Early in August, the Foreign Office circulated a lengthy "suggested basis for a territorial settlement in Europe." This background memo presented essentially moderate aims, to "give full scope to national aspirations as far as practicable," though the writers acknowledged that, if Germany and its allies were decisively defeated, Britain's allies might have much more ambitious aims.

The diplomats presumed that the Germans might restore Belgium, since Britain would make this "a sine qua non for consenting to any kind of peace." For anything beyond Belgium, though, the Foreign Office thought any concessions from the Germans "would have to be bought," either with money or lands controlled by Britain. If there was peace as "the result of a draw," the diplomats expected the Germans to insist on getting at least enough "to justify themselves to their people."[6]

On August 10, the question of peace planning was raised at the very top of the government, in the War Committee, for the first time since Wilson's offer had been put off at the end of May. Asquith was a bit surprised that the matter was on the agenda, but Cecil and Balfour stressed that it was essential to start getting prepared.

Wars can end in two stages. First, the parties can agree to just stop fighting. This may be a negotiated, preliminary cease-fire agreement, called an armistice. Second, the warring sides can agree on a treaty of peace.

To get ready, Cecil and Balfour wanted everyone to understand that governments had to consider both armistice terms and peace terms. Should the fighting stop while peace talks went on, possibly for months? If so, what would be the terms for this cease-fire, this armistice?

Cecil and Balfour foresaw a crucial question: Should Britain lift the blockade of Germany during the armistice, as no doubt the Germans would ask them to? The War Committee debated this point, analyzing what the United States might accept.

During this debate, the Conservative leader, Bonar Law, twice butted in to say that all this talk of peace preparation seemed "premature." Both times his comment was ignored by the others; the discussion continued.

Finally, Balfour suggested that everyone should "thrash over" the issues some more on their own. Asquith could not believe the Germans would ask for an armistice, since British terms for a cease-fire might be "practically an admission of defeat by Germany." But he agreed with Balfour that the committee should "ruminate over the matter."[7]

This they did in the following days, speculating about notional terms either for a temporary armistice or for a permanent peace. Interestingly, General Robertson told War Committee secretary Maurice Hankey that he was "very anxious for us to consider terms of peace." Managing the process, Hankey encouraged Balfour to keep working on possible peace terms.[8]

———

ON THE day of the August debate renewing discussion of armistice or peace terms, Baron Francis Bertie visited London from his post as the British ambassador to Paris. He ardently lobbied Asquith and Grey to wave away any American peace move. Bertie insisted that the French were not interested in peace. Grey had stubbornly replied that the American option had to be kept open.[9]

A week later, on August 17, Bertie received the riveting news from the king that French president Raymond Poincaré wished to make peace "as soon as possible," with Wilson's aid. Startled, then angered, by this revelation, which belied the claims he had just made to his government's leaders, at first Bertie kept the king's report to himself. He said nothing about it to Grey or the Foreign Office.

Instead, looking for a way to shape this news, Bertie returned to Paris. On August 21, he privately confronted the French prime minister, Aristide Briand, about what Poincaré had told the king.

Briand did not deny it. In Bertie's own, not very objective account, Briand shrugged that Poincaré was "not in touch with public opinion." Briand dutifully promised that the French people were determined to go all the way (*aller jusqu'au bout*). (Poincaré had told the king that the French public was too optimistic, because it did not know all the facts.)

Pressed on how France would react to an American peace move, Briand chose his words carefully. London, he said, seemed to think that such an American move "could not be rejected." Britain should promise to consult allies and learn more about the terms that Germany was proposing. If the German terms were unacceptable, then perhaps they would "not be good enough for the Americans" and "the mediation would fail without our having rejected it." Briand did not comment on what might happen if there seemed to be a reasonable basis for negotiation.

Now that he could frame his report with Briand's guarded comments, Bertie told the Foreign Office what Poincaré had confided to the king about his readiness for an American peace move. Bertie did inject his own opinion, which was that anything Wilson did would be nothing more than "a Presidential Electoral manoeuvre solicited by Germany." To Bertie, the only issue was that Germany had not yet "been sufficiently defeated," not yet "properly beaten, starved of food...and brought to her knees."[10]

The War Committee studied Bertie's report. As foreign secretary, Grey answered by inviting the French to join the British in thinking about just what answer to give to an American move. It could not be a blunt no. The French leadership too should consider (as the British leaders were) possible terms of at least the initial cease-fire, of an armistice, while peace talks were held.[11]

Asquith had a chance to discuss the future directly with Prime Minister Briand just a few days later. The British prime minister went to Calais, mainly to work on coordination of the ever difficult financial challenge of funding the war. Again, Briand was careful.

"At this time," he emphasized, the French were for *guerre à outrance*, all-out war. The Allies should provide for enough finances to fight on to get the best possible peace. He then suggested that this meant enough money to make it to March 15, 1917.

McKenna and the head of the Bank of England both thought Briand was saying that the French could not go on after that. Maurice Hankey, who was also there, thought it just meant Briand did not wish to speculate what would happen after that date.[12]

———

THE FOLLOWING week, at the end of August, the secret discussion of peace possibilities gathered more weight. The peace talk was spurred on by two notable developments, one public and one very secret. The public development was Romania's entry into the war on the Allied side. The very secret news, known to very few, was that the British government had learned of the German peace overture to Wilson, Chancellor Bethmann Hollweg's August 18 message to Ambassador Bernstorff.

The Admiralty's codebreaking unit had discovered one of the round-abouts, through Stockholm, that the Germans were using to send messages to and from their embassy in Washington. Since the relevant coded cables to and from Sweden passed through wires that the British could access, they could extract the German encryptions, buried within the Swedish traffic. The Admiralty's unit, called Room 40, had broken the German diplomatic code then in use.

The head of Room 40, an officer named Reginald "Blinker" Hall, was one of the strangest officers in the Royal Navy. He had suffered an illness that disabled him from sea duty. The American ambassador in London, Walter Hines Page, would later memorably describe Hall as a man who "hasn't a hair on his head nor a tooth in his mouth. Some dreadful illness once all but killed him and left him—a man of genius,—a freak if you will, as I dare say all men of genius are.—My Lord!"[13]

Instead of going to sea, Hall had placed himself at the influential center of a web of secrets. An extreme conservative and hard-liner on the war,

Hall distributed intelligence material selectively for maximum, secret, political impact. Depending on the content, he distributed some intercepts and buried others in his files.[14]

Hall passed the news of the codebreaking breakthrough and the German interest in American mediation to his chief at the Admiralty, Arthur Balfour. Balfour passed the information on to Hankey, the War Committee's secretary, and presumably to his friend Grey.[15]

On August 28, Grey reached out to House to send a caution probably prompted by learning of the intercepted German message. Grey wrote that he had heard of Bethmann's saying in Berlin that "in October Germany will have to ask for an armistice and that by that time President Wilson will be ready to arrange one for them." Grey wanted to be sure House knew that "England will not contemplate peace till the Allies consider the moment has come to make it." They were not likely "to consider peace as long as the military situation continues to improve in their favour, or there is good prospect of its doing so"—"*unless* of course Germany is prepared to give terms satisfactory to the Allies." Grey assumed the German public "still expect terms satisfactory to her and humiliating or onerous to the Allies."

Grey did not explain what terms would be "satisfactory to the Allies."[16]

———

Two DAYS after Grey sent this letter to House, on August 30, Prime Minister Asquith settled into his chair in the conference room at Number Ten Downing Street for another meeting of the War Committee. Such meetings usually began with a general review of the military situation. This time, Asquith started off quite differently. He announced that "the time had come where it was very desirable to formulate clear ideas on proposals for peace."

The membership of the War Committee had changed during the summer. Horatio Kitchener had drowned in June. The ship carrying him on a mission to Russia hit a mine just after departing and immediately sank. Lloyd George had taken over the War Office. Replacing Lloyd George at the Ministry of Munitions was one of Asquith's close allies, Edwin Montagu.

Everything, Asquith said, including what he had heard from his French counterpart, Briand, indicated that they "would be face to face with the question [of peace] before the end of the autumn." He then asked each member of the War Committee to put his ideas about peace on paper. It was time to create a "common stock of ideas" to be ready when the time arrived for decisions. Balfour strongly seconded this.

Then the group turned to the usual military update. Robertson reported that Haig was optimistic. The civilian members of the War Committee were not so confident, but their mood at this time, right after Romania had joined the war on their side, was cautiously upbeat.[17]

Montagu sent around a memo that urged immediate consideration of peace terms. An American peace option might be distasteful. All American politicians, of either party, were "contemptible and untrustworthy." Nevertheless, Britain would have trouble explaining a refusal if Wilson offered mediation or called for an armistice.

Montagu hated the Germans. But he made the case for ending the war, asking, "What does unqualified victory pushed to its final length mean?" "There is," he admitted, "no community of aim" among Britain's allies "except detestation of Germany and a determination to avoid a repetition of her menace." "What," he asked, "does France really care about Belgium, or what do we care about Alsace Lorraine? What does Russia care about either Belgium or Alsace Lorraine? What do we really care about Constantinople or Poland?"

Britain herself, Montagu pointed out, had "no material objects" except for three points. These were "the maintenance of our sea-power, the security of peace and the restoration of Belgium."[18]

———

THE NEXT week, Asquith and Hankey went back over to France to visit the troops and meet with Haig. On September 6, Asquith had a chance to visit his son Raymond.

Raymond had been in a training exercise. He rode his horse over to meet his father near the destroyed village of Fricourt. It was a "glorious hot day," Hankey recalled. Raymond and his father talked and wandered around the rubble of Fricourt, where "literally not one stone [was] left on another." They went to look at some captured German dugouts.

The dugouts came in handy. Some large German shells started falling nearby. Raymond's father "was not discomposed by this," but his chauffeur, who was holding Raymond's horse, "flung the reins into the air and himself flat on his belly in the mud." Raymond found it "funny." The group then went down into one of the old German dugouts, an enormous underground shelter—"wood-lined, 3 storeys, and electric light," as "safe as the bottom of the sea," Raymond noted to his wife.

They waited out the shelling, then said their good-byes. The prime minister drove on to lunch with an army commander. Raymond rode back to his unit. The weather, Raymond thought, had indeed "become lovely again—bright sun with a touch of autumnal crispness in the air."

His father, the prime minister, was greatly heartened by the visit. Haig was full of optimism, confident the Germans were running out of reserves. Most of all his son seemed "so radiantly strong and confident that I came away from France with an easier mind."[19]

---

As the autumn leaves fell, the illusions of summer faded too. On September 12, Asquith opened another meeting of the War Committee at its usual 11:30 time.

The news from Romania was bad. The Germans, Bulgarians, and Austro-Hungarians were gathering to invade Britain's newest ally. Little could be done to help them.

Asquith reported positively on his trip to France, noting that he had found Haig's headquarters to be "in the highest spirits." Still, overall progress was arduous: it was all just "push, push, push, and must necessarily be slow work."

Lord Curzon asked, Could the Army "push through" before Christmas? Asquith did not think so.

In that case, Grey said, "the situation was not much affected." Of course, they should "keep going." But he wanted to know what it would all lead to.

General Robertson's only answer was that "there was nothing else to be done."

From that grim moment, for the rest of 1916 and on into 1917, the war news for Britain would only get worse.[20]

---

Three days after that meeting, Haig's forces launched another large local attack. Leading his soldiers into no-man's-land in the first wave of a major assault on September 15, Raymond Asquith took a bullet in the chest. He was dead before he reached the casualty clearing station.

His soldiers mourned. One private wrote to his old schoolmaster, "There is not one of us who would not have changed places with him if we had thought that he would have lived, for he was one of the finest men who ever wore the King's uniform, and he did not know what fear was." A sergeant in his regiment told a fellow soldier, "He was the finest officer I ever served under."[21]

At Asquith's home in London, his wife, Margot, received the phone call. "I pulled myself together," she wrote in her diary, "got my handkerchief out of my coat pocket in the hall." She then called her husband out of his dinner.

> He saw my miserable, thin, wet face, and put his arm round me.
>
> "My own darling—Terrible news"—he stopped me. "I know, I've known it—Raymond has been killed."
>
> I nodded.... We walked back into the bridge room. Henry sat down on the Chinese red arm-chair; put his head on his arms on the table, and sobbed passionately.

Asquith "never fully recovered" from the death of Raymond, "a symbol of a talented generation." The next month, another of Asquith's sons was wounded.

More and more that autumn, the prime minister seemed withdrawn, distant, and distracted. His hands were shaky; his face sagged. He was drinking too much. He began missing cabinet meetings and became reluctant to offer opinions. To one of his closest friends, Asquith confided, "I feel, for the first time at any rate, bankrupt in pride and life."[22]

## David Lloyd George Launches His Thunderbolt

On September 28, the War Committee met as usual. Asquith was there. As usual, Robertson reviewed the military situation. He turned to the situation on the western front. Bonar Law asked "what [their] casualties had been."

Not counting an attack on Thiepval, Robertson replied, "they had been 125,000 from September 19 to September 26." Lloyd George thought Thiepval would add another 7,000 to 8,000 to that number.

Bonar Law asked what the next move would be. Robertson talked of an attack on Bapaume, where there was a road junction.

Then, seemingly out of the blue, General Robertson turned the discussion to the issue of how to make peace. (Hankey, taking notes, put a little exclamation mark in the margin.) Robertson raised the possibility of an armistice. Robertson told the group that he had promptly responded to Asquith's August 30 request for papers on armistice and peace terms.

Asquith said they were indeed preparing for "proposals by the President of the United States." Perhaps because the American election was so close, Asquith guessed that Wilson was less likely to make a peace move at the moment.

Grey spoke up. For now, he said, "the best thing to do was to lie low."[23]

---

"Lie low" is not what happened next. The day after this discussion, on September 29, 1916, newspapers around the world carried a remarkable story by Roy Howard, head of the United Press news service, that grabbed attention everywhere. Howard had just been in Europe, and this story helped make his reputation as a journalist.

"There is no end of the war in sight," Howard began. "Any step at this time by the United States or any other neutral in the direction of peace would be construed by England as an unneutral, pro-German move."

As authority for this remarkable statement denouncing any move to make peace, Howard cited "no less authority than that of the British man of the hour, David Lloyd George, secretary of state for war." The British people did not want a compromise peace. Howard quoted Lloyd George as declaring, "Britain has only begun to fight."

Howard had asked Lloyd George to comment on talk of an American peace move. " 'Sporting terms are pretty well understood wherever English is spoken,' he replied with a half smile. 'I am quite sure they will be understood in America.'" For two years the British had a bad time, and "now that the fortunes of the game have turned a bit, [they] are not disposed to stop because of squealing done by the Germans, or for the Germans, by probably well meaning, but misguided, sympathizers and humanitarians."

Britain, France, Russia—all, he said, were willing to fight for twenty years if needed, until they achieved victory. "The fight must be to the finish—to a knockout." Any peace before that was "unthinkable."[24]

Lord Northcliffe, the Robertson and Haig ally who published the London *Times* and the *Daily Mail*, among others, had arranged for Lloyd George to see Howard. Howard admired Northcliffe, calling the press lord "the biggest man and…the most powerful man in the British Empire today."[25]

In fact, Lloyd George had carefully scripted this "interview." Lloyd George had a lively conversation with Howard, which he and Northcliffe had set up in order to knock down an American peace move. After Howard wrote up a version of their interview, Lloyd George went over the draft, revising it until he was ready to approve the piece that would appear under Howard's byline.[26]

———

WHY DID Lloyd George launch this thunderbolt?

Since the beginning of 1916, Lloyd George had *been a principal architect of the American peace option*. He had consistently held that such a move would be essential, that otherwise the war might continue indefinitely. The American option should be developed and held in reserve until after the summer offensives had been tried, Lloyd George had said. He had specifically, repeatedly mentioned September 1916 as the time when such a peace move would be ripe. House leaned on what Lloyd George had told him, referring to it time and again in his meetings, his diary, and his correspondence.

So, why, when September arrived, did Lloyd George utterly reverse this position, and in such an ostentatious way?

Outsiders, reading the interview, might reasonably assume that Lloyd George sounded so tough because he felt good about Allied military prospects. Even more than sixty years later, an outsider who should have known better, prominent British historian A. J. P. Taylor, argued that Lloyd George "committed himself to the knock-out blow in the belief that, as secretary for war, he was about to deliver it."[27]

Lloyd George knew better. In private, he was anything but confident. By the middle of September, he thought "the failure on the Somme was clear." "The public know only half the story," he told another friend. "They read of the victories. The cost is concealed." To others, he acknowledged that the other fronts were also going badly. "Britain was no longer winning." He bitterly complained that no knockout blow was coming or even in prospect.[28]

To solve the puzzle of Lloyd George's turnabout, the first step is to notice how his position in government had changed since House last saw him. Since July, after Kitchener's death, he had been leading the War Office. In the public eye, he was now perhaps the most visible government minister associated with the war. Robertson dominated war strategy; Montagu, now minister for munitions, dominated war production. But Lloyd George, as war minister, had become the symbolic, public presence. The combative Welshman was Britain's Mars.

Back in June, Margot Asquith had argued and schemed to keep Lloyd George out of the War Office. She predicted that if he got that job, Lloyd George would "take good care to cut Henry [Asquith] out—to pose as the saviour of the soldiers.... Northcliffe and [London *Times* editor] Robinson will share the victory."[29]

As she had predicted, following his appointment Lloyd George began reaching out more and more to Conservatives, to Northcliffe, and to Northcliffe's circle. With his old Liberal friends at the end of July, Lloyd George was now talking up the idea of a general election "in which the issue would be the more vigorous prosecution of the war."

Personal animosities also fueled the Liberal divide. Lloyd George and McKenna especially disliked each other. They had clashed again during the summer. Lloyd George made an ill-founded argument that the Americans were so dependent on British war orders, they were bound to supply the dollar credits. McKenna had conclusively refuted this.

Another catalyst might have been a message from the British ambassador in Washington, Cecil Spring-Rice, who derided Wilson's possible peace move as a ploy to win Irish American and German American votes. In September, Spring-Rice sent a cable urging that someone in London should speak out to head Wilson off.[30]

There was also another, more proximate, reason for Lloyd George's interview. He had just read a decrypted intercept of another message between Berlin and Washington. This one had been decrypted by the army's codebreaking unit in the War Office, called MI1b, which had broken the *American* diplomatic code (the navy's Room 40 had broken the German diplomatic code). Thus they read the message sent by the US embassy in Berlin back to Washington on September 25.

This was the message in which Ambassador James Gerard reported that Germany was "anxious to make peace" and would accept a presidential offer of mediation of the kind Theodore Roosevelt had made in 1905 to end the Russo-Japanese War. The decrypted cable said that Germany demanded the "utmost secrecy"; if there was "any hint" that the suggestion originated with Berlin and was not "the spontaneous act of the President," "the whole matter will fail and be denied."

MI1b sent this particular intercept to Lloyd George, as head of the War Office. Blinker Hall, in the Admiralty's Room 40 codebreaking unit, knew from the decrypted German diplomatic messages that Wilson was in fact *not* planning to make any move before the election. But Hall chose not to distribute those messages. Lloyd George read the decrypted American message early in the day on which he would later have his first meeting with the American journalist Roy Howard.[31]

It is possible that Lloyd George had another motive. There were decrypts in which Berlin reminded Bernstorff of the pressure on Bethmann from the U-boat advocates. If Lloyd George thought about those, he might have believed that, if the Americans could be deflected from a peace move, Berlin might then resume unrestricted submarine warfare and bring America into the war as an ally of Britain and France.

There is no direct evidence to prove that such a clever scheme was in Lloyd George's mind. He makes no such argument in any record. If this had been a motive, he would have been reluctant to acknowledge it, and he could not have discussed the secret intelligence intercepts. Nor would he have wished to admit that he had sabotaged peace talks in order to manipulate America into joining the war.

The simplest explanation is that Lloyd George made his move, sparked perhaps by Spring-Rice's plea to shoot down Wilson's plan and by the intercepted American cable, in order to dramatize his public image. He was acting, characteristically, with a quick, impulsive, bold opportunism to redefine himself in British politics.

Lloyd George was presenting himself to his country as the all-out war leader. Perhaps recognizing that Asquith's weakness would require a change in political leadership, he had taken a bold but easily recognizable platform position: he would wage the war fiercely and keep going until it was won. He would defy the worrywarts like McKenna, whom he hated. He would be Mister "Fight-to-the-Finish."

Although he was a member of the Liberal Party, Lloyd George's positions and behavior had gradually alienated him from most of his base. He would never become that party's leader. More and more, his political allies were to be found among Conservatives. His political future was now tied to his role in the war and to the coalition "unity" governments that were a creature of the conflict.[32]

Yet Lloyd George's new identity created a kind of split personality. In public, he was Mister "Fight-to-the-Finish"; in private, he was a fierce, outspoken critic of the conduct of the war. He was as disgusted with the generals as they were with him. He was scornful of their calls for fresh assaults on the western front. He was pessimistic about Britain's prospects.

Lloyd George solved this internal division, intellectually and psychologically, by becoming a constant advocate of panacea solutions to win the war somehow without gigantic British ground assaults. These were usually schemes in the Balkans that involved Russia or relied on Italy—places Lloyd George had not seen, foreign armies he did not know.

His plans were impractical. Robertson and other generals understandably resisted them tooth and nail. When confronted with their infeasibility, Lloyd George usually declaimed about lost opportunities and then, but only then, grudgingly went along with what the generals wanted to do.

In truth, no visible plans offered much prospect for British and French victory. The various offensives could only grind away, in the hope that one or more of the Central Powers would quit before one or more of the Allied Powers did.

Lloyd George's "knockout" interview was therefore, in part, a big bluff. It was a bold front to camouflage the fraying Allied options. And it was good domestic politics.

————

Lloyd George's interview, denouncing any peace move, hit Foreign Secretary Edward Grey like a "bolt from the blue." The government had not approved any such statement. Lloyd George had been sitting in the War Committee meeting the day before when Grey had urged all to "lie low." No one had disagreed.

But how could the government denounce Lloyd George's public stance? If Asquith revealed that Lloyd George did not represent the government, he would set off an explosive debate about the government's divisions, the prospects for peace, and the prospects for victory, a debate for which he, mourning a son not two weeks dead, was entirely unready. Such a debate would also probably bring down the government.

Grey was not prepared to stay silent, however. He immediately wrote to Lloyd George. The interview, Grey told him, had been "unnecessary" and unwise. "It has always been my view that until the Allies were sure of victory the door should be kept open for Wilson's mediation. It is now closed for ever as far as we are concerned." Lloyd George need not answer him, Grey wrote, adding, "Nothing more can be done till we see the effect."

Lloyd George did answer him. He sent Grey the intercepted American message. "Any cessation of hostilities now would be a disaster," he argued. "Although we could always refuse or put up impossible terms, it is much better that we should not be placed in that predicament. You could not have warned off the United States without doing it formally. I could commit a serviceable indiscretion." In other words, Lloyd George was saying that he had protected Grey by taking on the job of breaking ranks and striking out at Wilson.

Grey should not worry, Lloyd George wrote. "It will work out all right. I know the American politician. He has no international conscience. He thinks of nothing but the ticket, and he has not given the least thought to the effect of his action upon European affairs."[33]

Lloyd George did not seem to know, or he knew but dissembled, about the fact that his government knew Wilson was *not* planning to use a peace move as a ploy to win votes. Hall had the decrypt of Bernstorff's report that Wilson would act only *after* the election was over.

Lloyd George gave another version of the story to his mistress and secretary Frances Stevenson. He told her about the intercepted American message. If he had not made his statement, "Wilson would most probably have made the proposal to us, & it would have been difficult for us to refuse to discuss terms."

To her, he said that peace talks "would spoil all chances of a great decisive victory for us." Lloyd George did not add in the part about how Lord Northcliffe had arranged the whole affair. Nor does the reference to a "great decisive victory" even line up with what Lloyd George would later tell Stevenson. The next month he told her (again) that "the Somme offensive is a ghastly failure" and that he had no confidence in Robertson's war strategy.[34]

––––––––

DESPITE LLOYD GEORGE's best efforts to derail a peace process, the bluff did not work on Wilson. Wilson was not deflected. In October, he personally reaffirmed his interest in the peace move when he saw Bernstorff. House assured Bernstorff that Wilson planned to launch the peace move as soon as he was reelected.[35]

The bluff did not quite work in London either. Although the government chose not to publicly contradict Lloyd George when he falsely assured Parliament that he had consulted with his colleagues before giving his interview, his reckless talk did not blow up the case for peace.[36]

In private, Foreign Secretary Grey upbraided Lloyd George. The Treasury secretary, McKenna, did not think Lloyd George's jingoism would appeal to soldiers or their families. "They don't want an indefinite war," McKenna explained to the editor of the Liberal *Guardian*. They want "a reasonable peace."

McKenna added another point to the editor. The "affront to America" was "sheer lunacy" from a financial point of view. That point loomed larger and larger in October and November, as the whole British debate on the future of the war reached a climax.[37] All the options remained—just—on the table, which was being rocked on all sides.

## "How Then, Is the War to Be Brought to an End?"

McKenna's outburst, about Lloyd George's "sheer lunacy," may seem intemperate, but not if seen through the eyes of the head of the British Treasury that autumn.

With the desperate expedients adopted in May and June, the Treasury and the Bank of England had gotten through the summer. But Allied finance in the United States reached its "most critical stage" during the last months of 1916. "This was the period, it may be recalled," a Morgan banker wrote for the firm's internal history just after the war, "in which arose the most insistent demand for all the shell, shell steel, and copper which America could muster." On top of this were purchases of manufactured goods like rifles and necessities like food. The Bank of England was also trying to maintain the value of the pound, in order to keep the situation from deteriorating even more rapidly. "It was a heartbreaking task."[38]

In September, McKenna asked J. P. Morgan & Co. to meet dollar requirements of at least $50 million a week. Jack Morgan cabled back to his partner in London, Henry Pomeroy Davison, that "this sum is so enormous" that he was sure "there must be some mistake." After all, total American exports of all kinds so far in 1916, to all countries in the world, stood at about $60 million a week.

There was no mistake. In fact, McKenna soon realized that his September number was too low. By October, it had risen to an Allied dollar requirement of $75 million a week.[39]

The Allies did not have the money. What ensued in the autumn of 1916 was a complicated set of improvisations, best understood as what would happen if a great estate realized it was out of cash and could no longer pay its staggering monthly bills. The estate owners might first gather all the valuables that could be sold or pawned. Meanwhile they would take out a series of loans—secured by these valuables—to make the finite hoard last as long as possible.

This is what the British government's leaders did, with some help from France and Russia. They gathered up their gold reserves, shipping them to Canada, from where they could be transported to New York as needed. They gathered, or extracted, all the marketable securities (stocks and bonds) in American companies. Those exhausted, by autumn they were doing the same with all the other marketable securities they could scrape up—such as the securities for the great railroads of Britain, Canada, India, and Argentina. Meanwhile, Morgan constructed the loans to spread out how fast the stock of valuables would be handed over to buyers or lenders, ideally just as collateral, in order to make them last.

As one might imagine, practically every month brought little emergencies to connect these new loans to the cash to pay that month's bills. Morgan advanced some of this cash, as needed, from its own resources. The British had to be careful, though, to keep Morgan safely afloat, ready and able to cope with these emergencies.

By October, it was already clear to the Treasury, and to Morgan, that these measures would not be enough. They first had to deal with an ominous "rifles crisis." The British were angry because American companies making rifles were doing a shoddy job. The British government withheld payments. The American companies and their banks retaliated. They were quite happy to threaten to cut off doing any business with Britain. Such a break, especially with the other banks, threatened to knock down the whole fragile edifice of Anglo-American finance.

Asquith called a meeting of the War Committee in his private rooms at the House of Commons. The Morgan partner in London, Davison, was invited to attend. The government, very grudgingly, realized that it had to give in to the American companies.

The episode confirmed, as McKenna had already warned, that the American companies and their banks were doing so much business at home that they did not rely on the British market. They were not willing to lose too much money in order to make the British happy or keep the British business.[40]

That morning, October 18, over breakfast, Davison had a wide-ranging conversation with Asquith, Lloyd George, and others. "In a state of great anxiety," Asquith told Davison that "the whole British war programme was at stake" unless Britain could raise a further $1.5 billion (an amount equivalent to more than 10 percent of Britain's whole gross domestic product that year) in the next five months.

Davison advised keeping up a brave front. "Proceed as though you are going to get it."[41]

Working with the British, the Morgan firm came up with a gambler's plan. The British, through Morgan, would start borrowing the vast sums with short-term, unsecured loans from other American banks—payable with good interest over periods as short as thirty days. The British government would use the next short-term loan to pay off the previous one.

Even this daring plan could not provide an indefinite solution. But in this way, the British hoped to keep the Allied war program afloat at least into early 1917. Then they might try again to sell bonds on the open market. After the bond failure in 1915, they dared not try again until early in 1917. They were not confident that this interim scheme, this chain of giant unsecured short-term loans, would work. But it was the best they could do.

Davison traveled to New York in mid-November. His job was to persuade American banks and the US government, in the form of the Federal Reserve Board, to support this risky chain of large and unsecured short-term loans.[42]

This context, then, perhaps helps to explain why McKenna regarded Lloyd George's "affront to America" as "sheer lunacy." As members of the War Committee responded to Asquith's call for views on peace terms, the Treasury sent in its paper. The Treasury formally explained that Britain was running out of money to continue the war.

Britain would soon have to try to borrow dollars without being able to offer collateral. The US government could easily undercut such loans by warning banks away from the risk (and Wilson and the Federal Reserve Board would in fact do exactly that, a month later). British Treasury officials made the point as clearly as they could: "Out of the 5,000,000 [pounds] which the Treasury have to find daily for the prosecution of the war, nearly 2,000,000 has to be found in America."

American firms wanted British business, true. But, as McKenna put it, "we cannot expect that these [commercial] influences will induce the United States to finance anything approaching the total requirements of ourselves and our Allies." The bottom line: "If things go on as at present, I venture to say with certainty that by next June or earlier the President of the American Republic will be in a position, if he wishes, to dictate his own terms to us." Another Treasury expert, John Maynard Keynes, added that it was "hardly an exaggeration" to say that the Americans would have this power to set the peace "in a few months' time."[43]

———

AT THE end of August, Asquith had asked all the War Committee members to offer their thoughts on peace terms. Treasury had emphasized that Britain was running out of the dollars to continue the war. The other papers on peace terms had also come in.

General Robertson and the Imperial General Staff had worked through the details. On the substance, their paper's approach seemed moderate, mindful of only a couple of principles: "to leave Germany reasonably strong on land," to maintain the balance of power in Europe, "but to weaken her at sea."

Yet at the end of the paper, Robertson set the bar very high for any cessation of the fighting. Before any cease-fire, any armistice, he argued, the Germans must withdraw all their troops home, release all their prisoners, and surrender part of their fleet.[44]

A Conservative member of the cabinet, the minister in charge of food and agriculture, Lord Crawford, circulated a paper objecting to Robertson's extreme position on terms for an armistice. Crawford shared the usual Tory scorn for Wilson. But Robertson's terms were "a refusal to enter upon negotiations." That would be an error, Crawford argued. This minister then offered a specific illustration of how to draw possible cease-fire lines close to the prewar border of France.[45]

From the Admiralty, Balfour circulated his views in a paper titled "The Peace Settlement in Europe." If the Allies could dictate terms, they might want to restore European balance by "rearranging the map of Europe in closer agreement with what we rather vaguely call 'the principle of nationality.'" But he argued for relatively limited war aims, aims that would not meddle in the internal governance of either Germany or Austria-Hungary.[46]

---

As September turned into October, the military outlook for the Allies grew darker still. In addition to the bad news from Romania, the British fleet commander, joined by the trade minister, warned Asquith that the shipping situation was unsustainable. Even though U-boats were obliged to give warning before attacking civilian ships, losses at the October rate might alone force the Allies to make peace by the early summer of 1917, if not sooner. It was getting hard to maintain supplies of food.[47]

At the end of October, Hankey put together a general review of the war. British casualties alone amounted to "a wastage" of, on average, about 120,000 men a month. Manpower everywhere was in short supply. Such losses could not be replaced while also maintaining production in vital sectors like shipbuilding or food.

Hankey's dispassionate sums masked his personal grief. A couple of weeks earlier, his younger brother had been killed in France.

In private, Asquith, Lloyd George, and others were talking at length about how poorly the war was going and about the complacency of the General Staff. "They are bleeding us to death," Hankey noted in his diary. Lloyd George and Robertson were so fed up with each other that both were threatening to resign.[48]

Hankey's summary made it clear that the "most urgent" problem was simply "staying power." The problem of dependence on the United States was insoluble. The financial situation was so grave that "within the next few months," the Allies would be "entirely dependent upon the goodwill of the President of the United States of America for their power to continue the war."[49]

As one historian has pointed out, "The moral of these...reports was plain. In the short term it was the Entente, whose entire policy since 1915 had rested on the assumption that in a long war they possessed the greater staying power, who were the more vulnerable to economic pressure."[50]

———

ALL THESE doubts and arguments came out into the open at an extraordinary War Committee meeting on November 3, just four days before the US presidential election. There was no formal agenda. Attendance was strictly limited. No one but cabinet-level civilians were allowed in the room. With Asquith chairing, the others present were Grey, McKenna, Balfour, Lloyd George, Curzon, Montagu, and Law.

Lloyd George was the star. He read a paper prepared for the meeting by General Robertson, who was not in the room, about "the probable duration of the war." Robertson's paper was careful and balanced. He opened with a list of key factors, like the solidarity of the Allies, hardly any of which were really matters of military judgment. He presented a fair assessment of the pros and cons of the military position.

Robertson admitted that he could not estimate when the war might end. If all the political assumptions remained constant, the war was bound to last, he wrote, *at least* through the summer of 1918. "How long it may go on afterwards I cannot even guess."

At a minimum, Robertson called for full government conscription or mandated work from every man and woman in Britain (raising the maximum military age from forty-one to fifty-five). There would have to be all possible use of foreign labor, a clear statement to the nation about the gravity of the task, and stronger central control over all aspects of the war effort.

This was, Lloyd George said, "one of the most serious documents on the war that he had read." They "were not getting on with the war....At no point had the Allies achieved a definite, clean success." "How then," Lloyd George posed the question, was "the war to be brought to an end?"

Robertson's approach amounted, he said, to hammer, hammer, hammer away at the main German forces until they wore down. For that sort of plan, though, it was "essential that the anvil should be more damaged than the hammer." Just the opposite was happening. Lloyd George then detailed, at length, how the Allied side was being more worn down. He noted the fractures among the Entente.

The public did not know how bad things were. But the people "will forgive anything except inaction and drift." The principal Allied leaders needed to meet "to take stock of the situation," as they made their plans for 1917.

The group concurred with Lloyd George's dismal picture. Some members (perhaps Curzon and Law) groused that he was "unduly pessimistic." No one at that meeting called out Lloyd George on the utter contradiction between what he had said publicly in his famous "fight to the finish" interview and the bleak outlook he now offered in secret just five weeks later. All agreed that continued assaults in France were unlikely to lead to decisive results.[51]

Asquith told Hankey that Lloyd George's summary of the situation was one of the most concise and logical he had ever heard—"not a word wasted." Lloyd George was proud of his "damning" indictment. He believed he had shown "how [Britain's] conduct of the war had met with failure at every turn."[52]

As for what to do, though, Lloyd George had less to say. He could call only for conferences of Allied leaders to develop some better strategy. He plainly wanted to shift the main strategic focus from France to the Balkans. But he presented no plan as to how to do so. Hardly anyone else—and certainly not Robertson—saw any merit in it.

Very privately, Hankey offered Asquith a different answer, another way to bring the war to an end. Prepare for a negotiated peace. If "the unlimited objects can no longer be hoped for," he advised, "the statesmen should set to work to define the limited objects which we should seek to attain."[53]

Neither Asquith nor Grey saw how they could act on Hankey's advice. Given Lloyd George's public position denouncing American peace moves, how could they now launch an American peace option without bringing down the government?

Finally, an elder statesman in the cabinet decided that he had to speak out (in secret) and catalyze a coalition to end the war. It was time for someone to say, in writing, before the whole cabinet, what others were thinking. This man was Henry Charles Keith Petty-Fitzmaurice, fifth Marquess of Lansdowne.

## The Cabinet Confronts the Two Roads, War or Peace

Lord Lansdowne was a leading figure in the Conservative and Unionist Party. Earlier in 1916, he had joined Austen Chamberlain as one of the two Conservative members of the cabinet's select Military-Finance Committee tasked with examining how to balance ends and means. He was a leader for the coalition government in the House of Lords.

Seventy-one years old, Lansdowne had immense experience. One of the great Conservative statesmen of the Victorian and Edwardian eras,

*Lansdowne*

he had served as governor-general of Canada, as viceroy of India, and as head of the War Office (Lloyd George's current job). He had been Grey's predecessor as foreign secretary. His style in office had been reserved and cautious, but "decisive at critical moments." His judgment was long respected.

Lansdowne was no pacifist. He had done much to help prepare the country for war. He had good access to intelligence reports. Until the autumn of 1916, Lansdowne had supported a "fight to the finish." After the summer bloodbaths, he decided it was time for a change of course.

When Asquith had sent around his secret request for proposals about peace terms, Lansdowne watched the way others were responding. He saw the paralyzed reaction to Lloyd George's sensational interview, appearing to rule out the American peace option. He decided that he would shoulder the burden of trying to force the issue.

On November 13, Lansdowne secretly circulated a memo to the full cabinet. In it, he elaborated his argument fully and concisely, "with his usual quiet ruthlessness."

He questioned the premise of the "fight to the finish." What prospects were there to dictate peace to a defeated enemy? Was the war really to be prolonged for at least another year? "What will that year have cost us? How much better will our position be at the end of it? Shall we even then be strong enough to 'dictate' terms?" He deemed it "almost impossible to overrate the importance of these considerations."

Reviewing the secret papers that had been circulated, Lansdowne laid out the full, ominous picture. Yes, he granted, some people said the Central Powers were even worse off. Yet even so, he wrote, "it is none the less our duty to consider, after a careful review of the facts, what our plight, and the plight of the civilized world will be after another year, or, as we are sometimes told, two or three more years of a struggle so exhausting as that in which we are engaged."

The casualties would mount at the same numbing rate. "We are slowly but surely killing off the best of the male population of these islands. The figures representing the casualties of our Allies are not before me. The total must be appalling."

The casualty numbers were not impersonal to Lansdowne. Both of his sons had gone to fight in France. One had already been killed, in 1914, near Ypres.

The costs, he wrote, had achieved a monumental scale. "Generations will have to come and go before the country recovers from the loss which it has sustained in human beings, and from the financial ruin and the destruction of the means of production which are taking place."

Lansdowne was clear about the moral question the government faced: "The responsibility of those who needlessly prolong such a war is not less than that of those who needlessly provoked it."

Lansdowne then pointed his analytical searchlight at Lloyd George and the "fight to the finish" argument. What was his theory of victory? From those who wanted to fight until Germany was beaten to the ground, "we ought to know something of the data upon which this conclusion has been reached. To many of us it seems as if the prospect of a 'knock out' was, to say the least of it, remote."

What about Britain's allies? Lansdowne noted war weariness in France and in Italy. "The domestic situation in Russia is far from reassuring. There have been alarming disorders both at Moscow and in Petrograd."

He therefore deplored Lloyd George's September interview. Britain should, he stated plainly, be ready to consider some neutral effort to bring peace. British leaders should not "regard as unfriendly any attempt, however sincere, to extricate us from the impasse."[54]

Lansdowne's memo was direct and forceful. Its assessment of the situation was accurate; its future predictions—for instance, about the ominous situation in Russia—equally on target. At the time he wrote, czarist rule in Russia would only survive for four more months.

His memo made a memorable impression on everyone who received it. Some derided it. Lloyd George, although the target of some of Lansdowne's conclusions, regarded the paper as courageous. Years later, he reprinted the memo in full in his memoirs. As another mark of unusual respect, Asquith fully reprinted Lansdowne's memo in his memoir too.

Another Conservative in the cabinet, Lord Crawford, promptly wrote to Lansdowne to agree with him. Crawford was not a member of the War Committee, but he had been drawn in more and more because of his responsibility for food and agriculture. "The submarine danger menaces our whole position, Russia is still unprepared, France exhausted, Italy fatigued—Germany increasing her strength internally," Crawford wrote. "How long can we last?" The main thing, Crawford said, was to open talks.

"It would be folly to impose [armistice] terms so impossible of achievement that no discussion could ensue."[55]

---

ASQUITH AND LLOYD GEORGE went to an Allied strategy conference at Chantilly, in France, just as Lansdowne's memo was being circulated and read. Just before he left, Lloyd George told his mistress that he saw "no way out of it. It is too late to do anything. The Germans are cleverer than us... and they deserve to win." The next day, he was filled with dire foreboding: "There is nothing but disaster ahead."[56]

In France, the political leaders were not very optimistic either. All year long, civilian legislators in secret sessions had criticized the conduct of the war. The French commander, Joseph Joffre, was also committed to endless offensives. In the civilian politicians' view, "the commander is not up to the task, and the government does not know how to impose its will on the command. It is necessary to change one or the other."

French postal authorities, analyzing soldiers' letters home, concluded in late 1916 that morale was in "crisis." "Soldiers had concluded, postal authorities reported, that the costs of the war greatly exceeded any potential gains. They wanted Britain and Italy to make an effort 'proportional' to that of France, and they believed Britain had 'duped' France. Many wanted an immediate end to the war or a 'partial' victory in which 'appearances' could be maintained. Many also were saying, 'we do not want responsibility for continuing the slaughter; we want peace, nothing more.'"[57]

Yet, at the Chantilly conference, "intimidated by the surly scowl" of the generals, the political leaders felt unable to do anything about the military plans for more offensives along the usual lines. General Haig was pleased by the result. He thought he had "crushed" Lloyd George at the conference.

Lacking any practical alternative, Asquith and Lloyd George returned, deflated, to England. Lloyd George told a close friend, "I am very depressed about the war. Perhaps it is because I am tired. I have not felt so depressed before. I want to go away for a week alone, so that I may think quietly by myself. Things look bad."[58]

Lansdowne's memo was put on the agenda for discussion by the full British cabinet, not just the War Committee. The cabinet would discuss it the following week, on Wednesday, November 22, 1916.

———

PREPARING FOR these profound debates, no one in London knew much about the parallel series of arguments going on in Berlin. None knew about Bethmann's argument for Germany to now settle for a defensive Hubertusburg peace.

No one in London knew that, having been reelected on November 7, President Woodrow Wilson had already decided to make his peace move as soon as possible. The very day that Lansdowne circulated his memo was Wilson's first day back in his office at the White House. He cleared his calendar to work on his peace initiative. He summoned House to come to Washington to help.

Wilson knew of Germany's urgent wish to end the war. He had no idea what was happening in London. Had he known, he would have realized that his timing could not have been more opportune.

On all sides, the conditions making it possible to end the war were in place. And at last, after months of impatient restraint, Woodrow Wilson, reelected, returned to the White House determined to launch his peace mediation as soon as possible, as his highest priority and first item of business. The catalyst that could end the war was at hand.

# CHAPTER 5

# How to End a Great War

## Peace Without Victory Beckons

By the autumn of 1916, the prospects for a decisive military conclusion to the war seemed poor. Neither Woodrow Wilson nor Edward House believed that either side had a good chance of ending the war with a military victory anytime soon; the military experts in Washington predicted a draw.

In secret, most leaders of the warring powers had given up on their old victory illusions, if they had ever had them. Their private appraisals of what was possible were bleakly realistic.

The Germans and Austro-Hungarian allies were suffering from hunger and the blockade. But as Secretary of State Robert Lansing's deputy, Frank Polk, pointed out to the overoptimistic US ambassador in London, "Some say [the Germans] can go on indefinitely." Then there was another factor, Polk stressed. "Confidentially," he added, "my own feeling is that the Allies have to fear Russia making a separate peace."[1]

By the autumn of 1916, after a last great offensive effort had failed, Russia was so drained and exhausted that it could no longer mount major offensive operations. Allied arms supplies to Russia were limited, and there was no easy way to ship arms to Russia anyway, since the land routes were gone, and the best sea routes, through either the Baltic or the Mediterranean/Black Sea route, had both been cut.

The Germans had tried, and failed, to persuade the czar to quit the war. The Germans had offered to return to the prewar status quo. The czar had repeatedly refused. Because of those Russian refusals, Germany, in the autumn of 1916, granted independence to a Polish state created out of Russian Poland.

The imminent danger to the Allies was that Russia might collapse from within. In the major Russian cities, food was short, prices were shooting skyward, and workers were striking. The czar's government had become incompetent and corrupt. In the autumn of 1916, more representative Russian political leaders (and foreign diplomatic observers) "felt they were racing against the clock: the question was no longer whether a revolution would occur, but when and in what form," from above or below. By the first week of November 1916, Russian parliamentarians exhibited a "revolutionary psychosis: an intensely felt, irrational desire to pull down the entire edifice of monarchic Russia. This psychosis, long prevalent among radical intellectuals, now seized the liberal center and even spilled into conservative ranks."[2]

Austria-Hungary too was profoundly weakened. It too could no longer conduct large offensives. The Germans were leading the invasion of Romania, but they too had given up on planning any other large ground offensives for the foreseeable future.

Only the French and British were still putting together such enormous plans (and spurring the Italians to keep charging against the Austrians). It was already doubtful, though, how much longer France, at least, could mount these sorts of giant assaults.

By the autumn of 1916, the prospects for a negotiated peace were ripe, precisely because the prospects for decisive military victory were not. And many (if not all) leaders on both sides understood this, even if those leaders were not yet ready to disillusion their hard-pressed people.

---

THE IDEA of a compromise peace was not strange; it had been the usual practice in European politics. Peacemakers could draw on "a longstanding European tradition of intra-war diplomacy" to find negotiated settlements. Yet it is easier to start wars than to end them. In this great war, in particular, the fires seemed to be raging almost beyond human control. Whole nations were preoccupied with the daily tasks of waging war. The forces in motion were gigantic.[3]

It might seem paradoxical, but during 1916, "the high death toll actually reinforced the [military's] doctrine of the offensive: the war continued because any yielding, any compromise, any renunciation of unconditional victory, would devalue all the past sacrifices and call into question the legitimacy of the nations at war. The war fed on itself, as it were. Each new sacrifice prolonged the conflict by hardening the resolve on all sides to win the victory that would give sense to the sacrifice. None of the military commanders could free themselves from this logic."[4] The German chancellor, Theobald von Bethmann Hollweg, sometimes referred to this as "the machine of war passion." It set the grinding rhythm of everyday life.

People were just getting on with it. They might feel resigned that, as with some awful volcanic eruption or avalanche, this terrible cataclysm would just have to run its course. *Unless someone offered an alternative.*

If reelected, the American president was determined to offer just that. He was, in fact, determined to act as soon as he possibly could, even though he knew that trying to end the war would be the most challenging task he had ever faced.

All the leaders seemed to know that the Germans and their allies were ready for a peace conference. Foreign Secretary Edward Grey had even told House (in his letter of August 28) that the British had heard this, careful not to say how he knew.

Wilson had a fair understanding of the situation in Berlin. On October 24, Ambassador James Gerard and Wilson spent about four hours together at Wilson's New Jersey home. This was the first time Wilson could talk directly to someone, other than House, who had spent time with the German leaders (and House's last visit to Berlin had been much earlier, back in January).

According to Gerard, Wilson "extracted every bit of information I possessed." The ambassador recalled later how Wilson was "devoted above all things both to keep and to make peace." Gerard also remembered how worried Wilson was that "if he could not force an early peace, he would have to face a war."[5]

---

WILSON AND his team had been thinking about the problem for months. Wilson and House conveyed their most recent assurances of action to the anxious German ambassador, Count Johann von Bernstorff, in early October. From then until after the election, there was another month to get more prepared, to analyze what to do.

Many ordinary soldiers also assumed that the politicians would soon end the war. But how? David Lloyd George had put the question starkly to his War Committee colleagues, sitting across the table from him at Number Ten Downing Street, on November 3, 1916: "How, then, is the war to be brought to an end?"

All the statesmen remembered the recent precedent for a negotiated peace in a war among great powers. This was the settlement, in 1905, of the war between Russia and Japan. The peace talks had been arranged and mediated by the US president at the time, Theodore Roosevelt. In its September message renewing Bethmann's mediation request, the American embassy in Berlin had called out this very example as a model.

If Wilson and his advisers looked at that model, the Russo-Japanese peace mediation, they would have gleaned some interesting insights:

- The Japanese had requested President Theodore Roosevelt's mediation, much as the Germans had requested Wilson's mediation this time. The Japanese had felt their position in the war was pretty good at the moment but might well get worse. The German motives were similar.

- The big initial problem was to get the other side (the Russians) to participate. Roosevelt worked that problem directly and indirectly. He argued the case himself. He enlisted the help of other powers to join in persuading the czar.

- The Americans had not dictated the actual peace terms. Formally, they just convened the talks. The United States did not even participate directly in the negotiations. Informally, though, Roosevelt outlined his ideas for a moderate solution. Those turned out to be close to the final result.

- Roosevelt had little direct leverage over either side. There, Wilson had an advantage. He had much more leverage, especially over the Allies, the side that had to be persuaded to talk peace.

- In Russia and in Japan, domestic opponents denounced the peace talks and argued for continuing the war. In both countries, pro-war factions denounced the resulting treaty. But peace had been made, all the same.[6]

Wilson and House had already talked through how a peace conference could work. They agreed the conference should be held in Europe, not in America, so that most of the belligerents could easily attend. The best site would be in the neutral Dutch capital, The Hague. The Dutch would gladly serve as hosts, having already established The Hague as a setting for earlier talks about issues of international peace (in 1899 and 1907). Wilson planned to go to The Hague to play his part, probably for months, something no American president had ever done.

The Americans were not going to dictate peace terms to the warring powers. They would not even participate, directly, in that part of the peace conference. Wilson had acknowledged this, publicly, in his May 27 speech.

But to steer both sides toward a compromise peace, the Americans had five powerful instruments of leverage:

1. Wilson planned to call for the peace conference. He would therefore have to lead the negotiation of the preliminary agreement to hold it, setting whatever conditions could be attached to that (like a German pledge to restore Belgium).

2. Wilson could help arrange an armistice, a cease-fire agreement, to suspend some or all of the fighting while the peace conference was going on. The United States could be the indispensable go-between to see if an armistice was possible. That agreement could set cease-fire lines, including German withdrawals out of some occupied territory. An armistice agreement could also address whether each side's blockades (by surface ship or U-boat) would continue during the peace talks, which could be part of a trade for German preliminary withdrawals.

3. Wilson could, informally, influence the peace conference negotiations among the warring powers about the terms in territory or compensation to end the war.

4. Wilson could, as he was about to realize, control the availability of funds to sustain the Allied side. Wilson could promise American assistance for humanitarian relief. This was already under way on a nongovernmental basis in Belgium and northern France. Wilson was trying hard to extend these efforts into occupied Poland.[7]

Wilson also could promise American assistance in broader reconstruction of war-damaged societies, to ease the inevitable controver-
sies about indemnities. This too was an idea that Wilson and House
had on their minds in 1916–1917.[8]

5. As all understood, Wilson would be a formal, central participant in
the other set of peace conference negotiations, about the postwar
measures needed to preserve the peace, to keep it from being a mere
"truce." Wilson might also press for this conference to occur alongside the one that only involved the belligerents, so that the work of
the two conferences could interact—and maximize Wilson's opportunities to influence both.

In other words, Wilson had plenty of tools in his box for informal
influence on the terms of a compromise peace—if he chose to use them.

In their last talks, back in February 1916, House and Grey had not
gotten into the details of the first two points. They did not discuss possible
terms for a preliminary agreement to hold the conference; nor did they discuss a possible armistice or the terms for that. But the British government
was already debating just such preliminaries.[9]

## How Wilson Could Make His Case

As he planned his peace move, Wilson knew that a moderate peace would
be one with few or no annexations. It would be a peace of self-defense.
The fundamental political fact was that every one of the warring countries
justified the war to itself as a war of self-defense. In every country, citizens
believed that their country was a victim of aggression, that it had been
forced to protect itself.

Therefore, the Allied leaders, like the leaders of the Central Powers,
needed to be able to say that the homelands had been successfully defended, the immediate threat removed, and the aggressor stopped. If the
peace terms were moderate, Wilson could try to help Asquith or France's
president Raymond Poincaré and prime minister Aristide Briand plausibly
tell that story.

The Germans, Austrians, Hungarians, Bulgarians—and even the
Turks—could have that narrative too. To most citizens in Germany and

Austria-Hungary, the invader threat that rallied publics to the flag came from Russia. They were angry at Britain and France for having joined with Russia.

While waiting for Wilson, Bethmann had already previewed this self-defense narrative to the key civilian politicians in Berlin. They would say that they had "vanquished" the attacks of the encircling Allies. In a letter to a scholar who studied his famous predecessor, Bismarck, Bethmann explained that, in his place, Bismarck "would have maintained the thesis of self-defense which is the deepest truth." Bethmann went on to explain, "In his secret actions, I believe [Bismarck] would have set as his goal: laying a foundation for a strong center as focus for European development, a center that protects [other European countries] but does not rape them.... [I]t is an immense achievement if we defend ourselves successfully against the dangers threatening us in past and present."[10]

The Germans and their allies set no preconditions for the peace conference. Bernstorff simply "always regarded American mediation as the only possible way out of the war." Once "the American Government established a peace conference, this would be sure to lead to peace itself. It could not be imagined that, in view of the nations' need of peace, such a conference could break up without having reached any result."

Also, from the German point of view, as soon as America convened such a peace conference, American entry into the war as a combatant was practically inconceivable. Since "without the help of the United States, the Entente could not win," Bernstorff regarded an American-organized peace conference as very much in his country's interest.

At the conference, Bernstorff was also optimistic about German ability "to ensure a tolerable peace for us." The Germans and their allies would go in with a reasonably good hand. "Diplomatic negotiations have a way of ending owing to general weariness," Bernstorff observed, "in which case the party which holds the best cards secures the greatest advantages. If this happened, we should have the advantage of the position as our military gains would give us a strong lever in the negotiations."[11]

It is therefore a measure of how anxious Bethmann was for America to act that, *even though neither Wilson nor House had said anything about terms or preconditions*, Bethmann had *volunteered*—as a token of good faith— German readiness to restore Belgium. He had offered this concession without requiring any compensation. Ambassador Bernstorff affirmed to Berlin that Belgium would indeed be *the* key issue to Americans (as it would be to the British people). Bernstorff believed that, without a doubt, the Americans would not undertake a peace mediation unless they could count on "the complete restoration of Belgium." He thought Wilson was satisfied with "our announcement that we did not desire to annex Belgium, as sufficient at least to justify him in starting a mediation in the cause of peace."[12]

Since the Germans were anxious to have a peace conference start as soon as possible, and since they had volunteered to restore Belgium, Wilson could present the German offer to withdraw from Belgium as a deliberate effort to create the environment for peace. As a look at a map would show, a German withdrawal from Belgium would necessarily also force all German forces to withdraw from occupied areas in northern France, on the other side of the Belgian border, as well.

If this announcement were paired with a call for a peace conference, the news would be sensational. Such news would instantly transform the domestic political situation in Britain and in France. If Wilson made any kind of peace conference offer that included German withdrawal from Belgium, refusal would be practically impossible for the Allies. In December 1916 top officials in the Foreign Office restated what to them was obvious: that the German occupation of Belgium was "the one rock on which all attempts at pro-German and peace propaganda had shattered." Take away that "one rock" and the political situation in Britain would be very different indeed.[13]

————

DURING THE summer of 1916, aware of Wilson's impatience to move, House was inclined to quit asking for an invitation from London and just force the issue. Since he expected the Allied offensives to fail, House thought there was "a strong probability of the Allies being willing to accept mediation," he wrote to Polk, Lansing's deputy (and House's friend), at the end of July. If the Allies were not willing, he believed "the President should take some action regardless of their wishes."

"There is a strong peace sentiment in both England and France," House explained. He put the matter in blunt political terms. "It only needs to be properly reached in order to become so active as to be a menace to the governments of those countries. If the people of England and France understood what we have been willing to do, they would not permit their governments to refuse our good offices."[14]

Since May 1916, when Germany had given in to Wilson's restrictions on submarine warfare, American leaders, including opinion leaders, were more willing to pressure the Allied side. The British executions of Irish rebels had offended some; others were angered by more vigorous British blockade rules, including a "blacklist" to prohibit trade with American firms that did any business with Britain's enemies. In early October, Polk wrote to a friend who was the American lawyer for the French government, warning him that his other pro-Ally friends "resented, as they put it, being treated as the United States was in 1812" (when it went to war against Britain in part because of outrages against neutral rights).[15]

During the summer of 1916, American anger toward Britain ran so high, including in Congress, that leaders considered new laws that would at least partially embargo Britain (a precedent recalled from those older American efforts to protect neutral rights). Wilson secured authority from Congress to prohibit loans to the warring powers—meaning Britain and France—or restrict American exports to them.[16]

All this was before Wilson fully informed himself about the desperate condition of Allied war finance. The president got a lot of that added information in November, just after his reelection, at which point he began to realize that he would not need to go to Congress in order to wield America's financial power over the Allies.

The Americans believed that the British held the key because of their dominant role in Allied war finance. "Of course," Polk told House, the French "realize that as soon as England goes into a [peace] conference, the game is up."[17]

The Allies needed Wilson to take the lead though. This was a political necessity in Britain and France. Even if some Allied officials were privately ready to admit the fact of a stalemate, to stand up publicly and say so was politically very difficult. Both Britain and France were governed by coalitions. To initiate action, the key figures in the coalition would need to agree to act.

The French government was, for instance, locked in, above all, to demanding recovery of the provinces of Alsace and Lorraine (actually about a quarter of historic Lorraine), which France had ceded to Germany in 1871. There was no visible prospect that France could achieve that war aim on the battlefield. Yet for the French to initiate a conference that might defer this hope was politically and emotionally impossible. Someone else would have to propose that. If Wilson took the lead, he could shoulder that burden. He could arrange at least the preliminary agreement to talk.

Later, in December, the Germans and their allies made a public offer to talk peace. They were challenged in the press to also commit, publicly, to good-faith measures like an unconditional restoration of Belgium and/ or Serbia. But, as the Germans explained privately to others at the time, they could not just give away such concessions in advance, with no assurance that the other side would even agree to talk. As one of their officials pointed out to the European neutral powers, "No negotiation can be properly carried out if one party is in a free and untrammeled position to take up matters with an opponent who is bound by a restricted program publicly announced. These are matters of course."[18]

## The Peculiar Position of Britain

Britain's was the only government that seemed to favor a long war. In public, the voices calling for peace seemed marginal. The private arguments in favor of the American peace option, inside the British cabinet, were conducted in secret, not yet ready for public airing. So, on the surface, in Lloyd George's "fight-to-the-finish" interview, in the pro-war Northcliffe press, it seemed that Britain was stoically resolved to win the long war, as long as it might take.

All of the other warring powers might still desperately want to win. But by the autumn of 1916, France, Italy, Russia, Austria-Hungary, Bulgaria, Serbia, Romania, and the Ottoman Empire had already suffered unbearable losses of life, proportionately larger than Britain's so far. All of them were exhausted, if not played out.

In Saint Petersburg, the autocratic rulers could remember plenty of examples of compromise peaces in the past. They had to wonder if matters could get even worse than they were in 1916. At least the dynasty was still in power. Neither the Germans nor the Austro-Hungarians had entered the Russian core of the empire.

The Germans, very much including the high command of the military, actually *under*estimated their power to continue, because they were so anxious to find some way to end the war soon. In Berlin, many were recalling the Prussian memory of the defensive peace of survival in 1763, the Hubertusburg peace after the Seven Years War. The French and the Austrians all had their own memories of compromise or "inconclusive" settlements.

None of the warring powers, save possibly some people in Austria-Hungary or Serbia, had originally gone to war in 1914 for what their governments or their publics deemed existential reasons. By the autumn of 1916, there was plenty of hatred of the enemy. But there was also plenty of hatred of the war. Privately a great many people on all sides were fed up with it, tired of its hardships, and worried about what new shocks the next day's news might bring. The usual stance was at least to pretend to be loyal, to try to do the job.

Therefore, only the British seemed relatively relaxed about the prospect of the war going on for years longer. An American lawyer, Frederic Coudert, en route to meet his French government clients, passed through London in September 1916. He painted a picture of confident resolve and jaunty spirit. "London is one great military camp and the country teems with munition factories. The Englishman has settled down to make war a business, and to see it through. While everyone one meets has lost somebody, they feel that the ultimate result is certain, and that the rest of the Empire has never been morally or materially so strong. Australians, Canadians, and all the rest of them mingled in the streets, and the whole thing is really exceedingly impressive."[19]

There was a uniquely British aspect to this "long war" resolve. In Britain, the national memory of the country's long wars against Napoleon Bonaparte (1792–1815) was very, very strong. Every schoolchild had grown up with it. On top of that, they had confidence in a great empire, based in a country that, for centuries, had seemed immune to foreign invasion. In British memory, the wars against Napoleon had only ended when Allied armies occupied Paris and Napoleon was irrevocably overthrown.

Part of this history was that the British had tried a compromise peace with Napoleon, the Peace of Amiens, negotiated in 1801–1802 to end nearly ten years of war against France. That peace had been very popular in England at the time. But it proved short-lived, little more than a brief truce. Bonaparte had resumed his restless quest for even greater European dominion. War had returned in 1803 and lasted until 1814, with various allies. Then Bonaparte had been sent off to the island of Elba, near Italy. That had not worked either; he came back to France in 1815. He had to be beaten again at Waterloo and sent far away, for good.[20]

---

THE BRITISH knew the German kaiser was no Napoleon (indeed he was a first cousin of their king). Instead, they usually looked past him and described their enemy as "Prussian militarism." To overthrow that enemy, the British war goal seemed to imply some complete defeat of Germany and an overhaul of its entire system of government, perhaps coupled with large territorial amputations. Britain's allies might want that too and throw in the breakup and parceling out of the Austro-Hungarian and Ottoman Empires. But only Britain seemed ready to fight on for some number of years in order to accomplish this.

But a good case could be made—and was made at the time in London (and even inside Germany)—that a compromise peace, giving up much, if not most, of the occupied territory, would irrevocably damage the traditional prestige and power of the Prussian elite and induce some of the desired political change. The substance of the draft peace terms being circulated in the British cabinet was relatively moderate, concerned with preserving national aspirations. Some British leaders—including both Arthur Balfour and even General William Robertson—secretly explained to their colleagues that it was actually in Britain's interest to preserve some significant German power, or even Austro-Hungarian power, in the heart of Europe in order to sustain a peaceful balance on the continent.

To fight on for years and years, the British in the Napoleonic Wars had relied mainly on sea power and finance, with a relatively small continental land commitment, a practice that could be sustained for a long time. This was still the dominant grand strategic tradition for a Royal Marine officer like Maurice Hankey, who was now at the very center of decision making. It was part of the reason Hankey had been so uneasy about the whole series of choices during 1916.

But in 1915–1916, Britain had abandoned its grand strategic tradition. The alarming gap that had opened between ends and means had spurred bureaucratic creations like the Military-Finance Committee. Britain had committed to a giant continental land army too, in addition to sustaining sea power and financing her allies. The outward image, what Coudert saw, was that the British Empire could do it all.

But the image was a sham. The "all" was being done with American food and munitions, and the dollars to pay for them were about to run out. The British were running low on shipping and manpower too. Those shortages would soon constrain every other part of the economy, including food supplies, unless even more resources could be bought from others with money Britain did not have.

## Belgium—and the Rest

As Wilson prepared for his peace move, he knew the issue of Belgium was disproportionately important to Britain and that Britain was disproportionately important to the Entente Alliance. The violation of Belgian neutrality, along with the danger this posed to France, had been the principal reason Britain entered the war in August 1914, perhaps because the Belgian coastline was uncomfortably close to Kent, Essex, and, between them, the River Thames and London. The British position on Belgium was clear: the Germans should get out, and they should pay for the damage they had done.

If set against the much larger scale of territory up for negotiation on the eastern front, where a war of movement had brought all of central Europe and almost all of the Balkans except Greece under the control of the Central Powers, the issue of Belgium may seem relatively minor. But to get to the peace table, Belgium was the great symbolic issue on both sides of the Atlantic world.

When Belgium was brought into existence in the 1830s, following a revolution against the Netherlands, such a country was a new idea in international politics. There was no such thing as a traditional "Belgian" nation.

Belgium was a state defined more by what it was not. It was no longer part of the Duchy of Burgundy, nor part of the Spanish Netherlands, nor under the thumb of France or Holland. It was a multiethnic compound of French and Flemish speakers. The British were traditionally anxious to keep the Scheldt estuary, and the Low Countries generally, clear of French control. The delicate compromise, in an 1839 treaty, was to guarantee the neutrality of the new state, Belgium.

The Germans had invaded Belgium, violating that 1839 treaty, in order to get at France. If they left Belgium, they wanted to be sure Belgium did not fall back under French or other enemy control. Such an enemy could then deny Germany access to Antwerp and its commercial links to the world. An enemy controlling Belgium could amass an army on Belgium's eastern frontier, right next to Germany's industrial heartland in the Ruhr. So, in a gigantic irony, in 1916, Germany's main concern was with how to reguarantee Belgian neutrality.[21]

The German annexationists and military leaders barreled through that dilemma by preferring to take effective control of Belgium and its Flanders coast. Bethmann knew that such a position would make a negotiated peace impossible.

So, directing the civilian government and the diplomacy, including Germany's secret talks with Belgium's King Albert, throughout 1916 Bethmann instead sought "guarantees" of Belgian military and economic neutrality, to be worked out directly with the Belgian government. Most of the Belgian government, and especially the king, wanted to return to true independence. That meant getting the Germans out without the country being turned into ruins. It also meant getting the Germans out *without* becoming a satellite of their French or British rescuers.

Such a German-Belgian understanding was quite possible. If no such understanding could be reached, Bethmann's inclination was to seek to annex just the border fortress of Liège (in German, *Lüttich*) "to protect our western industrial area."[22]

As far as Wilson and House knew, from Bernstorff and other reports, the Germans were prepared to withdraw from Belgium and restore it unconditionally. The Americans could attempt to nail down Bernstorff's promise in a preliminary agreement. If the prize was the peace conference that Germany sought, the Americans might well succeed.

Or the Americans might find themselves involved in the details of how to restore guarantees of Belgian neutrality. If so, American involvement in Belgian humanitarian relief and willingness to contribute to Belgian reconstruction could play a huge role in facilitating the restoration of that country without negotiations breaking down over issues of fault and indemnities for damage.

The belligerent countries would have to sort out the other territorial issues mainly among themselves. Wilson might want to make suggestions, but neither he nor House took an interest in most of these issues.

The French would press for German cession of Alsace and Lorraine, German-ruled since 1871. In exchange for some cession of a portion of this territory back to France, Bethmann would bargain for access to the iron ore from the valuable Briey-Longwy fields that German forces currently occupied in eastern France. By December 1916, both the French and the Germans were, through secret intermediaries, beginning to puzzle over ways to defuse the old controversy over Alsace and Lorraine.[23]

In November 1916, the Germans restored an independent kingdom of Poland, fashioned out of conquered Russian Poland. For Russia, the issue of Russian Poland would be difficult. But Poland had already been lost.

In general, the British and the Americans were not very interested in how matters were settled in the East, which is where the Germans and Austrians focused more of their ambitions.[24] Russia could insist on the restoration of Serbia, which the Germans and Austrians had secretly agreed to accept in some form. Russia could ask for guarantees of access to the Mediterranean, through the Dardanelles, and would probably get them. There would be claims for indemnities to compensate for damage, arguments about lost colonies, and much more. But the details and trade-offs among all these interests were not interesting to the Americans, who would, in any case, not be sitting at that table for those discussions.

———

ON AUGUST 30, Wilson had sat down with leaders of a citizen antiwar group, the American Neutral Conference Committee. They wanted the president to call a peace conference of the neutral nations to combine their neutral pleas for peace.

Wilson heard them out. He explained that their particular conference idea would not work because it would inhibit the ability of the United States to use its own influence.

"The influences that are making for peace" were "growing every day," he promised. This "tide is rising." "I believe that a psychological moment will come," he continued. "I am praying that it will come very soon, when some suggestion made out loud by somebody that they have to listen to will be irresistible, that they will have to begin to parley."

Wilson was certain of one thing: "If they once stop fighting and begin to parley, they will never begin fighting again." He predicted, "The minute that happens, the war is over. They will never go back to it. They will never revive the forces that will sustain them in it."[25] Everything depended on getting the talks started.

That was also how an astute German professional, Moritz Julius Bonn, saw things just after the war. Bonn had been summoned by the left/center-dominated new German Reichstag to evaluate the German peace efforts during 1916–1917.

We Germans, Bonn concluded, "were unwilling to announce outright our peace conditions, because we proceeded on the fundamentally correct theory that once we sat about the conference table a way would be found for everything." At the conference table the military authorities on both sides would lose much of their clout. They "would then no longer be in a position to go beyond the modest demands which a peace of understanding held out."

The Entente Allies understood this and were "just as clear on this point." "The Entente knew that from the moment when we should have taken our seats at the conference table, no power on earth could have brought its peoples out into the trenches again, any more than our people."

Knowing nothing of the secret debates that tormented leaders in London and Paris, Bonn assumed that the Allied Powers "did not wish to take their place at the conference table." In that case, he said, "it was Wilson's task to direct them there."[26]

As soon as he was reelected, Wilson turned his full attention to the job of doing exactly that.

CHAPTER 6

# "Peace Is on the Floor Waiting to Be Picked Up!"

## "Unless We Do This Now, We Must Inevitably Drift into War"

On Tuesday, November 7, 1916, Woodrow Wilson was reelected to a second term as president of the United States. The election was extremely close. In the more than thirty years from 1896 to 1928, the 1916 election was the only one in which a Democratic presidential candidate defeated a candidate backed by a united Republican Party. Wilson's carefully judged stance on the war had struck the right balance and probably tipped the scales.

The following Sunday night, November 12, Wilson took the train south to Washington from his home in New Jersey. He had been away for two months, during the climax of the campaign. The weather was gray and cold, with a drizzling rain. That did not deter about five thousand Wilson supporters from turning out to greet him. They warmly cheered the returning president as he disembarked at Union Station.[1]

Wilson's first day back in the White House was Monday, November 13. On that day in 1916, thousands more men were killed and maimed at the war's various battlefronts. It was not an unusual day. The cost was routine.

That Monday, British, Australian, and Canadian troops began a set of assaults, lasting about a week, to capture a ridgeline and a few fortified villages that had originally been British objectives for the very first day of the Somme campaign, four and a half months earlier. The weather was cold, wet, and miserable. By the end of the week, snow and sleet "added to the intense suffering of the infantry" as they attacked through a "near featureless bog" with a layer of ice forming along the top. In just that week of November 13, in just that one set of assaults, casualties just for the British Empire's forces topped twenty-two thousand—about a third of whom were killed.

One of those killed on November 13 was Britain's wittiest short story writer and satirist, H. H. Munro, better known by his pen name, "Saki." Stuck in a shell hole that night, cautioning another soldier, Munro snapped, "Put out that bloody cigarette!" A German sniper shot him.[2]

Also, on that same Monday, November 13, Lord Lansdowne circulated his devastating memo to his fellow cabinet members, rallying a coalition to end the war. That Monday, back at work for the first time as a reelected president, Wilson gathered all the paperwork about peacemaking, knowing it was the most important project of his political life.

"Please say to *all* that the President is so engrossed just now with business of the most pressing sort," Wilson penciled in a note to his secretary and office manager, Joe Tumulty. Tell visitors "that it is not possible for him to make appointments unless the matter *cannot* be postponed."

Wilson had been waiting for this moment like a coiled spring. He was "convinced that we were now approaching a real crisis in our relations with Germany," Tumulty observed. "Unless peace could be quickly obtained, the European struggle would soon enter upon a phase more terrible than any in the preceding two years, with consequences highly dangerous to the interests of our country."[3]

––––––––––

WILSON WAS already pushing past a warning from his adviser, House. The previous week, House had written to Wilson to tell him that the British government did not want his mediation. As evidence, there was Lloyd George's September "interview" with Roy Howard. Wilson had read that the day it was published and ignored it.

In October, House had sent along a further off-the-record summary provided by Howard, asserting that Lloyd George "not only voiced the official but the popular British attitude" and that "any peace proposals at this time would be fore-doomed to certain British rebuff." House had immediately relayed this to Wilson, who ignored that too.

House met with Howard in person on Monday, November 6. This particular meeting with Howard appears to have had a strong impact on House. It provoked him to take the time, on the incredibly hectic day before the election, to write about it to Wilson. It is perhaps indirect evidence of how much turmoil this meeting caused him that House decided not to dictate anything about the meeting to his diary.

House's letter about it to Wilson was also very odd. House wrote that, according to Howard, the Germans all hoped Wilson would lose the election and that the French and English, "almost to a man," wished for Wilson's success. "Lloyd George, Northcliffe and others are particularly keen to have you win."

This was a strange lie, an obvious effort to touch Wilson's vanity. These men, especially the Conservative press lord Northcliffe and his circle, regarded Wilson as weak and contemptible. Anyone familiar with the London political world, as House was, knew this.

To this untruth, House added another. Lloyd George, House claimed, had really given his interview to *help* Wilson. Lloyd George was just trying to give Wilson an excuse so that the president could fend off unwanted German requests for American mediation.

Then, House added that, having "kept in close touch with the European situation," he found "indisputable evidence that Germany is not yet willing to agree to peace terms that this country could recommend to the Allies." The Germans "sneer" at ideas like a league to keep the postwar peace. (Two days later, German chancellor Bethmann Hollweg gave his Reichstag speech, publicly welcoming a postwar league of nations to keep the peace.)

There was only one solution, House concluded. That was to go back to the spring proposal to "bring the full weight of this government on the side of a plan for a lasting peace." This would be a demand for peace, on terms "not unfavourable" to the Allies, which, if rejected, would "probably" (as Wilson had inserted) lead America to join the war on the Allied side.[4]

Wilson did not answer this strange letter from House. Instead, he proceeded, as soon as he returned to the office, to clear his schedule to work on his peace move.

---

BACK IN the White House, Wilson sent a telegram to New York City summoning House to "come down in time for dinner tomorrow" to "spend a little time with us."

Receiving Wilson's wire, House and his secretary packed their things. The next day, Tuesday, November 14, they took the train to Washington. Arriving that afternoon, House made his way to his usual room on the second floor of the Executive Residence in the White House.

No sooner had House put down his bags than Wilson came to his room. Later that night, as was his usual habit, House quietly dictated his diary entry about what ensued: the start of one of the most consequential foreign policy discussions between two people to be found in the records of American history. The only evidence for the conversation is what House set down in his diary that night and the next.

Wilson "at once" explained his desire to compose the note to the warring powers that the Germans had been pleading for since August. This would be a note "demanding that the war cease." Wilson insisted "that unless we do this now, we must inevitably drift into war with Germany upon the submarine issue."

House was against it. Though he left no record of his own, Wilson must have been surprised by House's blunt opposition.

The Allies would think such a call for a peace conference "an unfriendly act," House declared. The Allies would resent such a proposal coming just "at a time when they are beginning to be successful after two years of war."

This last claim was conspicuously inaccurate. Even the publicly known war news at the time was not very encouraging to supporters of the Allies. Nor had House ever before expressed optimism about Allied military prospects—just the opposite. But this was the upbeat line now being voiced (in public, not in private) by Lloyd George, relayed via Roy Howard.

Wilson brushed this off. He pressed his argument to move and call for a peace conference, and to do so immediately.

House firmly resisted. The British could not possibly agree, he insisted.

As the shadows lengthened on that Tuesday afternoon, a week after the election, the argument went on. Wilson had to leave to attend an event. As soon as he returned, they resumed their debate. The back-and-forth between the two men continued into the night.

House adamantly opposed pushing for peace.

Wilson heard him out. Very well then, Wilson answered. House should once more go to London as his envoy. There, House could try to work out an approach that the British could support.

But House did not want to do that either. He said he would prefer to be sent to the underworld, to "Hades," rather than to present such a peace proposal to the British or French.

Wilson did not give up. The two men "then argued over and over again the question of what was best to do."

House wanted to "sit tight and await further developments."

Wilson disagreed. He worried about waiting much longer. "The submarine situation would not permit of delay and it was worthwhile to try mediation before breaking off with Germany."

House argued "again and again" that America "should not pull Germany's chestnuts out of the fire" and reward that country's bad behavior.

Wilson had thought about that. He introduced the idea of setting conditions on his mediation, conditions the Allies might welcome. He did not dwell on the distinction between preliminary terms to talk, or armistice terms while talks went on, or final peace terms. Nor did House.

Wilson also argued that the United States could make a deal "by which we would agree to throw our weight in [the Allies'] favor in any peace settlement brought about by their consent to mediation." Yet House was against that too. He told Wilson that discussion of peace terms "would soon get into a hopeless tangle."

This was another contradictory stance for House to take. Just the previous week, in his preelection letter to Wilson, House had recommended going back to the assurances given to the British in February and March. Back then, House had spent hours hashing out just these sorts of details about terms. Yet, in this conversation with Wilson a week later, House said that working out preferred peace terms would be too hard. Calling for the evacuation of France and Belgium would be easy, he said. But then he threw at Wilson all the challenges of sorting out the Alsace and Lorraine dispute, "Poland, Serbia, the Balkans, Constantinople etc. etc."

Finally, at about 11:00 p.m., Wilson suggested they get some sleep. House "could see that [Wilson] was deeply disturbed."[5]

———

THE NEXT morning, Wednesday, November 15, the argument resumed. They were "hard at it again." The president seemed to have had a bad night.

The morning featured a distraction, an unauthorized move by Secretary of State Robert Lansing that infuriated the president. German occupation authorities had been deporting Belgians to serve as forced laborers. Wilson discovered, reading the lead item in the morning papers, that Lansing had sent a protest to Berlin about this. Lansing had not cleared this protest with President Wilson. The press described the incident as a new source of hostility between America and Germany.[6]

The deportations were being organized by the German military, by Paul von Hindenburg and Erich von Ludendorff, as one more aspect of the new "Hindenburg program" for complete mobilization of all possible manpower into the war effort as a matter of "military necessity." In fact, the Belgian deportations were so ill conceived that even Ludendorff recognized that the experiment was a disaster, and the program would be shut down in February 1917.[7]

Wilson did not understand all this. But he lost his temper, a rarity for him. He was furious at Lansing; perhaps he was also displacing some of the frustration he felt with House. Both the president and his wife were angry that Lansing had roiled the waters at this delicate moment of possible peacemaking without first consulting the president. Wilson called Lansing and scolded him.[8]

House disagreed with that too. He told the president he thought Lansing had done the right thing.

Wilson argued back. Rather than complain about the deportations, why not just try to solve the fundamental issue? That was Germany's occupation of Belgium, which the Germans might undo as part of the move to make peace.

House instead seized on these labor deportations as one more "argument against making a peace move at present."

Impatient to get going and seeing that House was disinclined to help him, Wilson said he would go ahead and draft his peace move himself. Once he had put it down on paper, in concrete form, they could then review it, Wilson said, "with more intelligence."

House recorded that he "did not yield a point." Nor, House noted, did Wilson "yield in his argument that [a peace note] might be effective."

House threw up a nightmare scenario. What if Germany accepted the mediation and the Allies refused? In that case, House claimed, Britain *might go to war against America.*

Wilson tried to shrug this off.

House elaborated. Britain, at war with America, might destroy the American fleet. Britain might then land legions of troops from Japan, Britain's ally, to invade the United States, marching through North America. He conjured an image of British warships sailing into America's harbors and hundreds of thousands of Japanese soldiers marching into America's cities.

Wilson seemed to hardly know what to say in response to this startling argument.

House had now been arguing almost continuously with the president for an entire evening and the following morning.

Wilson finally gave House a direct order. Go and see the German ambassador, Count Bernstorff. Tell Bernstorff that he, Wilson, would keep his promise. He would make a peace move as soon as possible.

Wilson did not apparently reflect on whether House was still a reliable messenger, but he had no other option, unless he handled this with Bernstorff himself. His predecessors would have done that, but that was not Wilson's way.

———

WHILE WILSON moved on to other business, House asked his man at the State Department, Lansing's deputy, Frank Polk, to come see him in his room at the White House.

Polk and House commiserated over Wilson's peace move. They rehashed House's otherworldly scenario about the British-Japanese invasion of America. Polk suggested that the Japanese invaders might end up at the Gulf of Mexico.

The two of them then walked across the gardened concourse from the Executive Residence to the State Department next door. The secretary of state worked in the beautiful, grand, thirty-year-old baroque building then called the State, War, and Navy Building (today called the Eisenhower Executive Office Building). The two men went upstairs to see Lansing.

All three then mused about Wilson's idea to make an immediate peace move, which they concurred was "awful." Led by House, they again voiced the argument that Wilson's "peace demand" could lead to the "stupendous folly" of America finding itself at war with Britain and France.

This was now at least the third time that day that House had repeated this scenario of such a war, enlivened by the bizarre notion of a British and Japanese invasion of America. The politics and economics of the scenario were otherworldly enough. At that moment, Britain and its allies were *utterly* dependent on colossal flows of American supplies just to feed their people and continue the war that already consumed them. Also, for anyone who had any knowledge of actual military affairs at the time, of what would be involved in actually shipping, landing, or supplying such vast forces in North America, this nightmare would seem as realistic as the Martian invasion that H. G. Wells had conjured up to thrill readers in his serialized novel *The War of the Worlds*.

Reading this passage of House's diary, the diary of a man who prided himself on his urbane, cosmopolitan worldliness, is like walking along the smooth, polished surface of a marble floor, then jumping back as the earth shakes, the marble cracks, and the earth's crust yawns open. This British-Japanese "invasion" fantasy was not a momentary flight of fancy. Nor was this the last time House would invoke it. What comes to mind is Walter Lippmann's bewildered comment, from reviewing House's 1912 fantasy novel (which Lippmann did not know House had written) that whoever wrote the book apparently had the imagination of a "boy of 14."

––––––––––

IN THESE last weeks of 1916, Wilson faced what he knew to be the supreme test of his statecraft, at a pivotal moment in the history of the world, largely alone.

House was a discreet messenger and gifted manipulator. He was a good judge of people and social situations and well practiced in the art of vetting and wielding patronage—a prime skill in American politics. Lansing and Polk were good lawyers. They could analyze the law, take instructions, and represent their clients. They could write protests and answer them. But none was an original policy thinker. None had ever crafted a major solution to a public problem, foreign or domestic. None had ever developed a diplomatic strategy or choreographed the execution of one. They had no experience in and did no written policy staff work. And none of them fundamentally agreed with the direction Wilson wanted to take.

This was the situation as the president set about preparing the most important policy initiative of his life. A British student of Wilson's decisions, Patrick Devlin, accustomed to Whitehall's staffing methods, came away astonished, as it dawned on him that there was "no body of men to prepare the issues for [Wilson's] decision." Wilson "might almost have been running a parish with the help of his wife and a curate and a portable typewriter."

For months, House, Lansing, and Polk had known that Wilson hoped to make a major peace move. Yet none of these men had prepared any analysis for Wilson about how he might proceed—not one page.

No one, for example, bothered to examine the Russo-Japanese precedent. None seemed aware of how to break down the issues of preliminary conditions to talks or conditions for a cease-fire or armistice before the peace conference itself. In other words, Wilson was given nothing to spotlight any of the choices or bargaining opportunities mentioned in the previous chapter, issues already being analyzed and debated at the highest levels in London and in Berlin.

Wilson's top aides were not bothered, however, by a lack of preparation. As they conferred together in Lansing's handsome second-floor office overlooking the White House grounds, they were bothered by their president's fundamental policy direction. How could they stop or deflect his peace move to end the Great War?

We must all, House told them, "drift for awhile until we [can] get our bearings."[9]

## The Puzzle of Edward House

Why, in November, did Edward House choose to follow Lloyd George's lead in speaking forcibly against peace talks? Never, in the five years that House and Wilson had worked together, had House opposed the president on any issue so openly, so directly, and in such a sustained way.

The puzzle deepens. Ever since March 1916, when House had returned from Europe, all through the summer, Wilson's and House's views were well aligned. House readily echoed Wilson's plan to move for peace after the election, *even if the Allies did not agree*. House had confided to Polk that Wilson could overcome the Allied resistance by igniting the growing mood for peace in the Allied countries.

House had been perfectly aware that Wilson planned to move after the election. He had said so to Bernstorff, and the ambassador had dutifully reported this to Berlin. Until November 6, House had given no sign that he was opposed to such a move. So what happened?

When House wrote to Wilson on November 6, he was unquestionably reacting to the meeting he had just had with Roy Howard. Even so, House had evidence that Howard's assertions that the British would oppose a US peace move might be untrue. House had a young friend on the staff of the American embassy in London who had found out, and written to House, that Lloyd George had released his interview "quite independently" and "without the sanction or approval of the Cabinet in any manner." House's friend added, "In fact several members of the Government with whom I have discussed it have not considered it in the least expressive of public feeling and in some cases have frankly regretted it."[10]

Any explanation must start with the attitude of Lloyd George. For more than a year, all of House's work on the peace move had involved Lloyd George. Lloyd George had become a principal source of encouragement, more important than anyone else except British foreign secretary Edward Grey. When House was strongly, personally (albeit wrongly) assured by Howard not only that Lloyd George had turned adamantly against the peace move but that the rest of the British government joined him, House's own convictions about the future of the war were unmoored.

Always, always, House had wanted America to work in concert with the British. This was not just a view of the US national interest. This preference had a personal, social dimension for House. He held no public office. His whole stature depended on his informal place. For years, outside America, his social stature was defined by the way he was received and treated in London official society. That was what validated his whole sense of himself, his stature as a gentleman and a statesman.

It was one thing to talk in letters of defying the British, echoing Wilson. But when he realized Wilson really meant to do it, defying not just the Conservatives but also Lloyd George and London official opinion, House could not stand it. He could not stand even to go back to London carrying an unwelcome message.

House had a bottom line: Though he found the Entente Allies' behavior "irritating almost beyond endurance," he feared that Wilson's "tendency to offend the Allies in order to keep clear of war with Germany" would likely lead the United States into trouble with the Allied nations. "If we are to have war," he wrote, "let it be with Germany by all means." Note that the alternative, his nightmarish fantasy of a war with the Allies, still seemed to be in the back of his mind.[11]

House did not know what to do. He could have worked with the British and French on preliminary conditions, like Belgium. He could have worked on possible armistice terms, too, to make it easier for them to accept Wilson's peace conference and end the war. But, although Wilson alluded to this, House did not appear to comprehend such preliminary processes.

Instead, as the days passed, House and his allies, Polk and Lansing, were filled with self-pity and condescension. It was difficult enough to have to deal with foreign countries. Now, Wilson too was quite a burden, since "the President must be guided, for he has no background of the European situation." To his diary, House described Wilson as a not-too-diligent pupil more interested in domestic affairs, a man who would not study enough "to act intelligently."

The president, House complained, was "not a man of action and seems incapable of delegating work to others."[12]

## Wilson Drafts America's Peace Proposal

Following Wilson's order, House met Count Bernstorff on Monday, November 20. For the German ambassador, this was a crucial, long-awaited meeting. For months, Bernstorff had been waiting for the election to be over so the American peace move could begin.

Berlin was waiting too. The week after the election, having heard nothing, Bethmann's deputy, Gottlieb von Jagow, urged Bernstorff to go find out "whether the President is going to take peace mediation steps, and, if so, what steps and when."[13]

The chancellor, Bethmann, was under fresh pressure to expand submarine warfare. His Austro-Hungarian allies, in contrast, were urging him to quit relying on Wilson. The leaders in Vienna wanted the Central Powers to go ahead and make a public peace call of their own, once they could pair this with some signal military victory (the campaign to finish off Romania was nearing its close).

The submarine issue was back in the news. In November, there had been a couple of incidents in which civilian ships had been torpedoed without warning. Berlin asked Ambassador Bernstorff whether Germany could at least start torpedoing without warning those merchantmen who were visibly armed with a gun battery to destroy any submarine that surfaced to stop them.

Don't make any change in the submarine program, Bernstorff advised, "until it is decided whether Wilson will come out with his peace mediation." The Germans expected they would not have long to wait. "I consider this will occur in the near future," Bernstorff cabled, just before he went over to House's Manhattan apartment.[14]

---

HOUSE ADMIRED how Bernstorff handled himself at their November 20 meeting. "We can count upon his doing everything possible to prevent" war with America, House reported to Wilson later that day. The two men smoothed over the recent submarine incidents. Bernstorff predicted, correctly, that Germany would admit fault in the main cases and offer to pay damages.[15]

House, as ordered, relayed Wilson's message that the president would move for peace "as soon as possible." This would happen before the end of the year, House promised.

Yet House undermined the promise. Bernstorff reported to Berlin that, according to House, "Wilson still hesitates to enter into peace negotiations, because the State Department expects a refusal on the part of [Britain and France], while House is pressing hard and full of hope." Bernstorff advised his government to avoid further incidents because, "above all things, Wilson feared the humiliation of a rejection" of his peace move by London and Paris.

Spinning this story to Bernstorff, House had exactly reversed his and Wilson's actual positions.[16] Misrepresentations like these, reported to a

German government that hung on every word of these precious reports from Bernstorff, would eventually have fateful consequences.

The British did not know of these November exchanges between Berlin and Bernstorff. An unarmed German cargo submarine, arriving in New London, Connecticut, had just delivered new codebooks for its Washington embassy's use. It would take the British experts about two months before they could break the new code.[17]

Bernstorff pleaded with House for America to act—immediately. "Peace was on the floor waiting to be picked up!" he said, House reported to Wilson. The Allies would surely have to talk, the German ambassador explained, "particularly since Germany is willing to evacuate both France and Belgium." Since Germany was willing to do that, "any refusal to negotiate would be an admission that [the Allies] were continuing the war for conquest."[18]

If Wilson or House had any doubt about Germany's willingness to restore Belgium and withdraw from occupied France, Bernstorff had now dispelled it. In addition to this news from Bernstorff, information was now flowing into Wilson every day about a growing interest in peace, including in Britain and among the soldiers. On November 21, as soon as he had read House's report on his meeting with Bernstorff, Wilson wrote back to his adviser that he was convinced. "This is very nearly the time, if not the time itself, for our move for peace."

Wilson informed House he was now drafting the move himself. The president promised that once his draft was elaborate enough to constitute "a real proposal," "we will get at the business in real earnest." Wilson promised, "I will make the best haste I can, consistent with my desire to make it the strongest and most convincing thing I ever penned."[19]

Wilson's passion was impressive; his language was revealing. He envisioned a note, a proposal, worded persuasively. But a major part of his challenge would be practical, not rhetorical. He himself had defined the challenge only six weeks earlier, talking to journalist Ida Tarbell, about some way to settle the war. "What I want to know," he had told her, "is how it is to be done.... I am not interested until a practical method is proposed—that is, I suppose that in government I am a pragmatist: my first thought is, will it work?"[20]

ALTHOUGH HE was slowed, floored by "a really overwhelming cold" that had "sadly thrown [his] plans out," Wilson continued to work on drafting his peace proposal amid a stream of more news about peace possibilities. The State Department learned (as had the British government) of a substantial Austrian peace feeler. This too signaled important possible concessions: Vienna indicated that the Central Powers were willing to evacuate Belgium and northern France, restore Serbia, form a general peace league, and take up other questions relating to Italy, Russia, and Alsace-Lorraine.[21]

Meanwhile, the American diplomat in charge in Berlin, Joseph Grew, went to Wilhelmstrasse to present directly to the chancellor the American complaint about the Belgian labor deportations (carrying out the Lansing instruction that had infuriated Wilson on November 15). On November 22, Grew made a long, carefully prepared presentation. The chancellor listened patiently.

As soon as Grew was done, Bethmann turned the conversation to a discussion of peace. "If his suggestions that Germany wanted peace should be continually ignored, Germany would be forced in self-defense to adopt hard measures," Bethmann pointed out to Grew. "But this would not be Germany's fault." Germany would not be guilty of the continued slaughter. "This he repeated several times in different words."

Bethmann sat at his desk, "speaking slowly, deliberately and sadly of the horrors of war." He reminded Grew that he was facing great opposition from the right-wing newspapers and politicians in Germany due to observance of the pledge not to use submarines against merchant vessels without warning.

"What do these difficulties [with the deportations] in Belgium matter," Bethmann asked, "compared to the hecatomb of lives lost on the Somme since last July?" The chancellor "gave an impression of great weariness and sadness and discouragement at the failure of his peace suggestions to bear fruit," the American diplomat observed. "I could not fail to feel, although not directly expressed, his clearly intimated disappointment that the United States had not taken steps leading towards peace."

Reiterating what Bethmann had said in his November 8 speech, Grew also reported that Bethmann promised that "the retention of Belgium" was not a principle of German policy. Germany also was willing to join a postwar "tribunal" to enforce peace. Wilson, House, and Lansing all read and referred to this report.

Grew was not particularly pro-German. But in November 1916, he found Bethmann "impressive beyond description." He wrote that the chancellor "seemed to me like a man broken in spirit, his face deeply furrowed, his manner sad beyond words."[22]

---

GETTING OVER his cold, Wilson began a series of moves, all done within the space of one week, the last week of November. First was a strong message to the British government. Second, he finished drafting his peace note. Third, he found a way to wield his full leverage over Allied finances.

His first concrete move: to put more pressure on the British to consider an end to the war. He instructed House to send a letter to the British government, specifically to Grey. Since the head of British military intelligence in the United States was on his way back home by ship, there was an opportunity to have him hand-deliver a very secret message.

Wilson wanted the letter to Grey to convey two messages, loud and clear. One was that "the United States would go any length in promoting and lending her full might to a League for Peace."

The other message was that the American people "were growing more and more impatient with the intolerable conditions of neutrality, their feeling as hot against Great Britain as it was at first against Germany." Wilson warned that this hostility was "likely to grow hotter still against an indefinite continuation of the war if no gre[a]ter progress could be shown than now appears, either for the Allies or the Central Powers."

House obediently wrote this letter to Grey with these two messages. In this letter to Grey, without revealing Bernstorff as a source, House added that there was "a feeling that Germany is now ready to largely meet the conditions laid down by Mr. Asquith" (referring to the kind of minimum territorial peace terms House had heard from Asquith in February). Therefore, House argued that Britain could get what it wanted: a fair peace. "With the weight of this Government thrown into the scales on the right side (and every other neutral would probably join us) Germany would yield everything that could properly be demanded of her."[23]

House entrusted this letter to the courier, the British naval officer who had been heading British intelligence work in the United States. That officer carried these important messages across the Atlantic. Wilson's plea to London would arrive early in December.[24]

MEANWHILE, AS he directed House to write to the British, Wilson worked on the substance of his peace proposal, looking for ideas about what to say. He thumbed through more letters and press clippings about possible peace moves. One set of these caught his eye, passed to him both by Tumulty and by House. It was a clipping from the pro-Allied *New York Times* and included the first installments in a series of opinion pieces written by "a prominent publicist" and signed under the pseudonym "Cosmos."

"Cosmos" was Columbia University president Nicholas Murray Butler. Wilson disliked Butler, so the pseudonym, by disguising the author, probably helped in getting Wilson to read the essays. Both "Cosmos" and the *Times* editorial page were sympathetic to the Allies, denouncing Prussian militarism. But both now emphasized the futility of further fighting.

"Cosmos" picked up on the exchange of speeches—Grey's October 23 speech praising the idea of a postwar league and Bethmann's November 8 Reichstag speech answering Grey and welcoming such a league. "Cosmos" was quite impressed with Bethmann's speech, calling it "much the most significant statement that has been made in German official life in the memory of any man now living."

It seemed, "Cosmos" (Butler) observed, that both sides now accepted "the free development of all nations, of small as well as great nations." "Cosmos" quoted Bethmann's statement that, after the war, "through the whole of humanity there will ring out a cry for peaceful arrangements and understandings which, as far as they are within human power, will prevent the return of such a monstrous catastrophe." Now was the time, "Cosmos" argued, to seize on this convergence of views.[25]

WILSON'S WRITING style was to sit down and type out his main ideas in organized sequence. Then he would review his typed draft and make handwritten corrections in shorthand.[26]

With great eloquence, Wilson explained that any of the war's former glamor was now gone. "The big striking thing for the imagination to respond to was the untold human suffering." If the war continued, it could only end with "the attrition of human suffering, in which the victor suffers hardly less than the vanquished. This may require one year, maybe two." Better to end "the mechanical game of slaughter of today" with its "trench warfare and poisonous gases."

Wilson asked, "Must the contest be decided by slow attrition and ultimate exhaustion, the slow expenditure [of] millions of human lives until there are no more to offer up on one side or the other? Triumph so gained might defeat the very ends for which it had been desired."

If peace should be made now, how, then, to make peace last? A peace based on a decisive victory would not last, he wrote. Such a peace would so embolden the victor and so embitter the defeated that it would only lead to the next war. The horror of this war presented "an unparalleled opportunity" for a different kind of peace.

Apparently inspired by the "Cosmos" essays, Wilson noticed the seemingly common desire, on both sides, to forswear wars of conquest and aggression and to cooperate in measures like a league of nations to prevent them. Wilson's note therefore proposed that the warring powers define the terms on which they would end the war.

"The simplest means" for them to define their terms, he wrote, would be a conference of the warring powers and the most relevant neutral powers. Wilson's draft note called for such a conference "whatever its outcome may be." If a conference was not feasible, perhaps some other way could be found to define the terms.

Wilson wanted the peace conference to be "very simple" and "very practical." It was time not for vague, abstract goals but for "a concrete definition" of the guarantees the warring powers would need for "practical satisfaction" of their objects. Those terms could then be combined with "the very great and substantial guarantee" that, Wilson felt "perfectly confident," would "be supplied by a league of nations."

Wilson's draft note did not, however, discuss any possible preliminary preconditions for holding a conference. Nor did it discuss the possibility of a cease-fire or the terms for an armistice.

This draft complete on Saturday, November 25, Wilson wrote to House and asked him to come down on Monday, November 27, "to talk it over." There was no time to lose. "I think things are thickening and we should choose our course at once."[27]

## Wilson Gives the Allies a Financial Heart Attack

As he dispatched his letter to pressure the British government (the House-Grey letter being carried across the Atlantic), and as he also completed his draft peace note, Wilson took another big step. He showed the British and French that he knew just how financially vulnerable they were. Before his reelection, Wilson voiced his realization that Americans were now the "creditors of the world." They could "determine to a large extent who [was] to be financed and who [was] not to be financed." Wilson would now use that leverage.[28]

As a Morgan executive observed in the company's internal history prepared right after the war, "The stupendous financial requirements of the British Government now dominated the whole situation."[29] Back in September and October, London decided to embark on a huge, desperate credit scheme built around a novel group of short-term, unsecured government loans, or Treasury bills, due in as little as thirty to sixty days. As each set of loans came due, fresh short-term loans would be used to pay off the last set. The British leaders and their American financiers hoped this plan could get them through the next six months so that their gold and securities could last that much longer. The scale of the credit scheme was at least $1 billion, then equivalent to about 6 percent of the entire British gross domestic product.

Having seen the Federal Reserve Board already take action to warn banks about some French loans in October, the key Morgan partner in London, Henry Pomeroy Davison, decided to go back to the United States and make the pitch in person to convince the Fed board to support the firm's large short-term, unsecured Treasury bill plan before it was made public. Davison made his presentation on November 18. It did not go well. Board members were extremely anxious. Davison pushed ahead. He announced the planned bond offering on November 22.[30]

The Federal Reserve Board was worried about the exposure of the large city banks that planned to buy the T-bills. But politics were also a factor. The vice chairman of the board, Paul Warburg, came from a German Jewish banking family and had himself been a leading banker in Germany before the war. His brother ran an important bank in Hamburg. Warburg did not like Prussian militarism, but he retained sympathy for Germany, and he did not want America to join in the war on the Allied side.

The board's chair was an Alabama banker, William Proctor Gould Harding. He too was uneasy about the politics of this Morgan loan plan. "I cannot escape the conclusion," he wrote to the powerful head of the Federal Reserve Bank of New York, then convalescing out west, "that the United States has in its power to shorten or prolong the war by the attitude it assumes as a banker. If we decide to finance one group of belligerent powers by giving it unsecured credits, we assume in large part a burden which another group of belligerents is carrying on its own account [paying on its own], and the possible complications which may come from this policy are fearful to contemplate."[31]

Harding, Warburg, and the rest of the board wanted to issue a public statement, to caution banks about these new, short-term, unsecured British and French Treasury bills. The issue was so sensitive that Harding went to see President Wilson about it on Saturday, November 25. He wanted Wilson's advice.

As he received Harding in the White House that Saturday, Wilson had his peace move in front of mind. He had just instructed House to send that tough letter to Grey. He had just finished drafting his peace proposal.

Wilson gave Harding a plain message. He gave it to him in person, and he gave it to him in writing. In person, he told the board chairman that US relations with Great Britain "were more strained" than with Germany. In writing, he asked that the board's warning about British and French loans "be made a little stronger and more pointed and be made to carry rather explicit advice against these investments."

The Fed's warning should not be just a "mere caution," Wilson went on. Members of the Federal Reserve Board should not endorse large further loans to Britain without adequate reserves or security. Such loans, Wilson hinted, "might at any time be radically affected by a change in the foreign policy of our government."[32]

Wilson developed this financial maneuver entirely on his own. No one in his government had suggested it. When he first learned of the board's warning, House was entirely uncomprehending. He did not know of Wilson's relation to it, and he noted in his diary that such a warning certainly should not be used to hurt credits to the Allies. Yet this was exactly what Wilson had intended to do.

The board published its warning on Tuesday, November 28. The effect was instantaneous and lasting.

There was a general panic related to British and French securities of all kinds and the companies that relied on them (like Bethlehem Steel). Morgan quickly had to withdraw the entire T-bill offering for both Britain and France. The British and French stemmed the panic only by rushing some of their dwindling reserves of gold to New York to maintain the exchange rate and calm the markets.

If Wilson had wanted to test American financial influence, the test worked. London felt Wilson's move as an elderly man, warned repeatedly by his doctors about his heart condition, might if he felt a sharp, paralyzing pain on the left side of the chest.

The effect did not go away. The board's action, Davison told his partners, was "the most serious financial development in [the United States] since the outbreak of the War, and one likely to be of far reaching consequence." The outlook for Allied financing efforts was now "very very dark."

The British and French had to abandon their hope to stretch out their gold and securities with the string of short-term credits. British financial officials believed the "mischief done was irreparable." The sands of the hourglass were now running out for how much longer British and French reserves could sustain the current level of Allied war effort.

Months earlier, the British had cast about for alternative sources of supply in order to retaliate against difficult Americans. As they had discovered before, however, "there was really nothing to deliberate about because our dependence was so vital and complete in every respect that it was folly even to consider reprisals." They could not sustain the present war effort for more than another few months.[33]

More knowledgeable British leaders had long feared this day. Some British officials (and Jack Morgan) were inclined to blame German Jews on Wall Street for their trouble. Morgan cabled Davison, "It may be necessary to come out in public attack on German Jews and their influence with Government." Davison quickly cautioned Morgan against any such anti-Semitic attack, saying it would be "futile as well as harmful."

Davison guessed (rightly) that the real issue was policy. He guessed (rightly) that the real source of the trouble was President Wilson. He sensed "there was something in the air" about "an important Peace movement."

At the German embassy in Washington, Bernstorff also correctly surmised, as he cabled Berlin, that this warning was "the first indication that this Government proposes to exert pressure upon our enemies in the cause of peace." To the British ambassador in Washington, the situation was equally obvious. "The object of course is to force us to accept President's mediation by cutting off supplies."[34]

## House and Lansing Deflect and Delay

Learning that the president had completed his draft peace note, House's first reaction was dismay. "I am fearful of its effect," he confided to his diary.[35]

The next day, Sunday, November 26, House made his way to the still-new Penn Station, then a beautiful beaux arts structure, for his train to Washington. He was met at Union Station by Polk, who updated him on the latest diplomatic cables, and they rode over to the White House, Polk getting out at the State Department next door. House dropped his bags as usual in his room in the Executive Residence. After tea with Mrs. Wilson and the wife of Ambassador James Gerard (whose husband had not yet returned to his post in Germany), he dressed for dinner and light conversation. Afterward, he and Wilson retired to the study.

Wilson's study was a pleasant room. It had tall ceilings and a fireplace in the center, above which hung a large, full-length portrait of George Washington. Waist-high bookshelves lined the room. Above the books there were many little pictures, including of other presidents, like Abraham Lincoln. Wilson's desk was angled diagonally in a corner of the study, to the right of the fireplace, so that he could easily look up from his work and see anyone coming in. The two men settled into leather-upholstered chairs and got to work.

House read through Wilson's draft peace note. He made some minor suggestions about ways to avoid giving needless offense to the Allies. He then proposed an absolutely vital change, a revision that changed Wilson's whole strategy for ending the war.

In his original draft, Wilson had called for a peace conference. The conference was, he had written, the simple and direct way for the warring powers to state their terms. It would also have been the galvanizing, concrete event that would have riveted the world and probably stopped the fighting.

House argued that Wilson should stick to the conceptual core—just ask each side to state their terms. Take out the call for a conference.

Wilson went along with this. Instead, at House's suggestion, Wilson wrote, "The President is not proposing peace; he is not even offering mediation." He was merely taking "soundings" to learn the terms for ending the war.

That done, Wilson again asked House to go to England so that he would be in London when the note was delivered. House still did not want to go. He thought the peace move might "be received with great indignation and construed as a move in favor of Germany." The time was just not right. Wilson needed to prepare the way for reception of the note, "particularly in the Allied countries."

How, then, should Wilson prepare the way? House had no idea. So he just urged Wilson to make another, firmer protest about the Belgian deportations. This, he thought, might make a good impression with the Allies.

House was unaware, and Wilson did not explain, how Wilson had worked with the Federal Reserve Board's chairman, Harding, earlier that same day. That financial action was about to make a very large impression on the Allied Powers indeed, though not the one House had in mind.

Nevertheless, when House returned to New York a few days later, he was "pleased that he had persuaded Wilson to alter the character of the note so that it no longer represented an insistent offer of mediation, but was merely a suggestion that both state clearly the terms upon which they were ready to discuss peace." Even that mild note, though, seemed premature to House, since he thought "the Allies were determined to listen to no hint of peace."[36]

———

FOR THE rest of his week in Washington, House—coordinating with Lansing—had pressed the theme of delay, to get time to somehow soften Allied opinion. House, coordinating with Lansing, also mounted a redoubled effort to persuade Wilson not to send him to Europe, arguing that since such a journey would be seen as a peace mission, it would generate too much attention.

Lansing's own views were clear enough. In private, he recorded how strongly he opposed Wilson's peace plan. Its collapse would lead, in Lansing's view, to the United States being drawn into the war on the side of the Allies. This is what Lansing wanted.

Additionally, he thought that only democracies were fit to join a postwar league. In his view, Germany was not a democracy; it was a "military despotism." Back in September, Lansing had noted his opposition to any "compromise peace" with the Germans. He pledged to himself, "I will never sign an ultimatum to Great Britain."[37]

Along with the earlier protest note about Belgian deportations that had been leaked to the American press, Lansing and House persuaded Wilson to send a confidential message to Bethmann. In it, Wilson answered Grew's report about his November 22 meeting with Bethmann, addressing the "distress and disappointment of the Chancellor that nothing had come of his intimations about peace."

Wilson noted the recent problems with submarine incidents and the Belgian deportations. He asked for "practical cooperation on the part of the German authorities in creating a favorable opportunity for some affirmative action by him in the interest of an early restoration of peace." Other than avoidance of new submarine incidents, a condition Berlin already understood, the message did not explain what "practical cooperation" Wilson had in mind.[38]

House returned to New York, still telling Wilson, as he wrote on Thursday, November 30, that the peace move should be delayed, that it needed more work. He claimed that none of his many contacts thought the time was right. For instance, House wrote, he had just met with a pacifist member of the British parliament. This MP naturally favored peace but said Wilson's demand would not meet with a favorable response.

House had misrepresented what was said. According to the MP's diary, he had said just the opposite. He had told House that Wilson "should offer mediation. Christmas was now coming and people's thoughts would be turned toward peace. This was the right time to strike." Even if the offer was not immediately successful, "its ultimate success was certain."

That was not what House told Wilson. "The Germans," he wrote, "are the only ones that believe it can be done now." He warned that if the president acted hastily, he did not see "one chance in ten of success."[39]

House had summarized his plan for his diary while at the White House, on November 26. "My whole idea is to delay until the time seems propitious. It is too important a matter to bungle, and if [Wilson] is not careful, that is what he will do."

WILSON DID not want a delay. He was more and more anxious that his moment was slipping away. On December 3, he wrote to House, arguing for action. "The situation is developing very fast, and if we are going to do the proposed thing effectively we must do it very soon."

Wilson was impatient. He quoted back to House his own words about how the "background" needed to be prepared for the Allies to receive Wilson's peace note. Very well, how? "I wish you would expand that suggestion into concrete items and let me know just what sort of a programme, with what steps in it, you have in mind."[40]

House had no "programme" to suggest. He lamely replied that Wilson should keep doing what he was doing, like protesting Belgian deportations and making good speeches about his love of liberty.

House added a report to Wilson about his visit with the French ambassador, Jules Jusserand. Jusserand had many complaints, especially over the Fed's financial warning. After hearing him out, House then asked about how the war might proceed.

Jusserand admitted "that it was probable that no material change in the western line could be made at least for a year or more."

Why then, House asked, not accept the offer of American peace mediation?

Jusserand, House reported, "seemed to concur in this." But then, "at the last moment upon leaving," the ambassador "veered away into the high-flown foolish declaration that France would fight to the last man."

HOUSE HAD once been useful to Wilson in many ways, suiting Wilson's aloof and reflective personal style. In the only recorded explanation by Wilson of how he saw House, in August 1915, he confided to his future wife that House was a source of "prudent and far-seeing counsel," that he was "disinterested and unafraid and incorruptible." But, Wilson added, "his mind is not of the first class. He is a counsellor, not a statesman."[41]

In his plea for House to give him a "programme," the president seems to have partly understood what was happening. But Wilson did not quite know how to get diplomatic negotiations for a peace conference under way. Neither House nor Wilson started a practical negotiation about preliminary conditions for a peace conference. Even initial probes to start such practical discussions would have had an electric effect, galvanizing officials in London, Paris, and Berlin.

Instead, House kept spinning his various conversation partners around, slowing Wilson just enough to delay him without another blunt confrontation like the one they had in mid-November. He told Wilson some of what he wanted to hear, always pushing and edging him around the dance floor, just enough to deflect him from any concrete action.

Nor had House abandoned his own feverish delusion about the possibility of a British-Japanese invasion of America. At a December cabinet dinner at the White House, House pulled aside the secretary of the navy, a former North Carolina newspaper editor, Josephus Daniels, to ask how well the coast was defended by mines.

Daniels said the United States had some mines and was building more.

House then asked if America was prepared for war if it started tomorrow.

Daniels must have been a bit taken aback. "War with whom?" he asked.

War with Great Britain, House answered. To his diary, House simply noted, "There was no need to await a reply since his face told the story."

House went on to repeat in his nightly diary his dark invasion fantasy, the one he had been voicing for a month, of how Japan and Britain "could put us out of business just as rapidly as they could march through the country." They would bring their armies to Canada. What with censorship and troop movements, no one would know. Then they would attack. As their armies marched south, "we should be so helpless to resist them as Belgium and Serbia were to resist the Germans."[42]

House did not want Wilson to challenge the British with a peace move he thought they did not want. He had no plan to persuade them to go along with one. All that was left for him was to watch and wait.

On December 3, House read news of a major cabinet struggle in Britain. He wrote to Wilson, "If the Lloyd-George-Northcliffe-Carson combination succeed in overthrowing the Government and getting control, there will be no chance for peace until they run their course. England will then be under the military dictatorship."

On December 7, House must have wondered whether his November letter to the British foreign secretary, Grey, had been delivered by the courier. This was the very secret letter Wilson had told him to write to put pressure on Britain to act, the one that had assured the British they could get a fair peace. By this time, of course, Britain had also experienced the financial shock from the Federal Reserve Board's warning. House cabled Grey, "These are anxious days. Is there anything you can say to guide us here?"[43]

———

WHILE HOUSE waited on Britain, Germany waited on Wilson. Wilson studied another report, from Joseph Grew in Berlin, that the army was mobilizing labor (including in Belgium) to release more men to prepare for the 1917 campaigns. The navy was still eager to expand submarine warfare. Food was short.

"The Chancellor, however, is to all appearances sincerely in favor of any steps which might lead to peace." The German civilian leaders, Grew wrote, "feel...that the war can now only result in a draw, that the continued loss of life is and will be futile and that although Germany is able to maintain the present situation indefinitely, if not to [the] end, humanity calls for an end."

The American embassy in Berlin, reflecting the views of both Grew and the military attaché, believed Bethmann could still manage the domestic politics of peacemaking. The Germans, they explained, were reluctant to call publicly for peace because of "the fear of a confession of weakness," not because there was "any lack of desire for peace among the people, officials and politicians of Germany as a whole."[44]

The embassy's assessment of Bethmann's sincerity was more accurate than Grew knew. The day after Grew sent in that appraisal, on December 2, Bethmann personally went to the kaiser. He asked him to approve a special imperial order instructing submarine commanders to avoid any action that might complicate matters with America. Bethmann "stressed that we must avoid a conflict with America at all costs at least until the outcome of [Wilson's] peace action was decided, which should be by the end of the month."[45]

Back in Washington, though, House had little news for Bernstorff. House still regarded the German "as the only Ambassador of the belligerent countries that seems to have any sense of proportion." Yet, having little new to say, House explained Wilson's inaction in a way that made matters much worse.

He told Bernstorff, correctly, that the president was drafting something. But, as he had before, House told Bernstorff that it was Wilson who was delaying action. Bernstorff reported, echoing what House had told him, "Everything is prepared for a peace move, but with the vacillating Mr. Wilson it is always a matter of doubt as to when he will come out with it."

"All the authorities here have now been won over to the move," Bernstorff passed to Berlin. The move could come "overnight," House claimed, if something could be done about the Belgian deportations. But, Bernstorff explained, again parroting House, Wilson feared he was so hated in England "that people would simply refuse to listen to him over there." None of this was true.

As before, House lied to Bernstorff, reversing the truth about himself and Wilson, telling the German ambassador that he, House, was the one "constantly urging Mr. Wilson on to action." Perhaps, Bernstorff reported, if the US Congress demanded peace, Wilson might then "reach a decision once and for all."[46]

This further report from Bernstorff began to have a real impact on the thinking in Berlin. Bethmann received it on December 7. For months, Bethmann had been leaning on Wilson as the best vehicle for a peace option.

For months, others, distrusting Wilson, had argued that it was better for the Central Powers to go ahead and act on their own. They should make their own public peace move, once they could crow about fresh victories and not look weak. That German and Austrian choice was imminent.

CHAPTER 7

# What Is Wilson Trying to Do?

## The British Reach a Turning Point

All through the autumn of 1916, most of the men leading Britain's war effort shared growing doubts about the way forward. At the beginning of November these doubts had finally burst into a full crisis over Britain's future in the war, a crisis summarized by Lloyd George's dismal presentation on November 3 and capped by his question, "How, then, is the war to be brought to an end?"

On November 13, Lord Lansdowne had broadened that debate beyond just the War Committee to include the entire governing cabinet. He dissected each premise of the British war effort. He saw no evidence for a coming "knockout blow" that would make things better. He pointedly challenged whether another year of such fighting could possibly be worth what it would cost.

Never, since the beginning of the war, had Britain's leaders engaged in such a fundamental debate about the whole future of the British and Allied war effort. Lansdowne had helped lead the challenge, but he was not alone. The ministers responsible for the economy—for finance, for trade and industry, and for food and agriculture—were all sympathetic to his argument. The War Committee's secretary, Maurice Hankey, privately counseled Asquith to reconsider the peace option. At the Foreign Office, after Lansdowne circulated his memo, Edward Grey began preparing his own version of the argument, coordinating his effort with Lansdowne.[1]

———

ON WEDNESDAY, November 22, the full cabinet had its first discussion of Lansdowne's challenge. Prime Minister Asquith and War Secretary Lloyd George were very clear: the Lansdowne argument for the peace road meant looking at the "overtures for peace in the air, certainly from Germany via President Wilson."

The lord chancellor (minister for justice), Lord Buckmaster, said Lansdowne's argument was of "capital importance." It "could not be ignored."

Lloyd George agreed. He granted that Lansdowne's memo "was a state document of the greatest importance." He differed from Lansdowne, however, in that he thought "a knock-out blow [was] possible." But, he said, "we must clear our minds as to what we mean." He "begged to record his admiration of [Lord Lansdowne's] courage in putting his thoughts to paper. Anyhow we must make up our minds."

"Can we strike a knockout blow?" Lloyd George put the question. "If we don't settle our policy there will be hesitating counsels, divergence of aim—increased nervousness of neutrals." The subject was so "great and far-reaching" that Lloyd George proposed holding another "special Cabinet" meeting, devoted only to Lansdowne's paper. The cabinet readily agreed to this.

With the subject opened, ministers voiced more of their worries. Grey said he was most bothered about the submarine menace. Walter Runciman, the minister for trade and industry, predicted a "shipping breakdown" by June 1917 from a shortage of both ships and the labor to build them. Food and agriculture minister Lord Crawford noted the growing shortage of food: "We are a besieged country." Treasury Secretary Reginald McKenna emphasized the financial crisis. "To conduct war for six months on our present financial powers will be difficult," he said, "for 12 months almost impossible." And "quite apart from our willingness," the United States would be able "to call a halt next summer or autumn." (McKenna was being optimistic. This was still a week before the Federal Reserve Board issued its crushing warning against making unsecured loans to the Allies.)

Lloyd George conceded that if the cabinet concluded that a knockout blow was not possible, "we ought to consider what terms of peace we could offer or accept."

The cabinet agreed to schedule this further discussion. To prepare, the ministers asked General William Robertson, as chief of the Imperial General Staff, to provide a written assessment of "the probabilities of a knock-out."[2] The minsters would also have to judge Britain's capacity, in any case, to sustain the current war effort.

Britain was entering in on the kind of soul-searching crisis that the Germans had been engaged in since the summer. In a situation now even more dire than the one it had faced in the spring, the British government confronted the stark choice between war and peace.

———

LLOYD GEORGE, less than three weeks earlier, in a memorable meeting of the cabinet's War Committee, had been the very voice of eloquent despair. For practically an hour, he had devastatingly indicted Britain's military prospects—a stance very far from the bellicose public face he had worn in his sensational September interview with Roy Howard, bragging how eagerly Britain wanted a fight to the finish. So why, on November 22, amid all the evidence that Britain could not afford to continue the war, was Lloyd George saying he believed in a "knockout blow"? What was he thinking?

That day, Lloyd George confided to Hankey. His reasoning was straightforward and very egotistical: he, Lloyd George, had to take charge of Britain's war effort, whereupon he could somehow set it right.

Only he could force a change to an "eastern" strategy, with campaigns in the Balkans or in Italy, that he hoped would break the stalemate. He would appoint civilian dictators to take charge of all food, all shipping, and all industrial manpower. Under his leadership, Britain could mobilize completely for war, just as the Germans were doing.

To force the crisis that would put him in charge, Lloyd George welcomed a polarized debate that would inevitably devolve into two factions—those determined to "fight on to victory," led by himself, and those who wanted to make peace, whom the Northcliffe press would mock as "defeatists." In such a public debate, absent some outside peace move by Wilson, the peace advocates in Britain would be at a disadvantage. None of Britain's leaders felt they could safely reveal the full truth about the war issues to the wider public. There thus would be no airing of Lloyd George's indictment of the military strategy, no revelation of the desperate financial situation, no announcement of the impending crises in shipping, in manpower, and in food. The public would not know how dire the situation was. But this one-sided imbalance of knowledge favored the war camp.

The public debate would instead be vague about the underlying substance, foaming on the surface about quarrels over process and people. To force the action, Lloyd George proposed to reorganize the cabinet's War Committee, supposedly to make it work better, with himself at its head. He would then rid the War Committee of all of his enemies, like McKenna, and those most open to the peace option.

Initially, Lloyd George planned to leave Asquith as the prime minister but not a member of the new War Cabinet. Asquith would become a figurehead to hold the government coalition together, while Lloyd George ran the war. Lloyd George hoped to bring along just enough "win the war" Conservatives, throw in a few men from the Labour Party, and form a new kind of coalition to back him in Parliament.

When Lloyd George confided his reorganization plan to Hankey, the War Committee secretary saw through the maneuver, noting in his diary that the "net result would be to put absolute power in [Lloyd George's] hands." Hankey, who was not a politician, kept his feelings about that to himself. But he was outraged at the way Lloyd George was using the war crisis, with these "really ridiculous" personnel choices, as a "mere political expedient" to make himself "virtually 'dictator.' "[3]

---

As Lloyd George and his allies began preparing to set up the political crisis on their terms, the cabinet went forward with its plan (the plan Lloyd George had proposed!) for the full debate about Lansdowne's memo and Britain's future in the war. The onus was on General William Robertson to assess, in writing, if the military could in fact deliver a knockout blow.

The question certainly put Robertson on the spot. He had no such "knockout blow" to promise or suggest.

In his view, as he had explained before, there was nothing to do but keep hammering away at the Germans, mainly on the western front, to wear them down and eventually break them. This strategy, combined with a blockade, would likely take at least two more years of campaigns, as he had acknowledged only a few weeks earlier.

Robertson also was contemptuous of Lloyd George's panacea of an "eastern" strategy in the Balkans. Three such "eastern" strategies had already been tried. The campaign in the Dardanelles (best known now as "Gallipoli") had been a disaster. The campaign in the Balkans had failed too, with French, British, and Serbian remnants still maintaining a futile beachhead at great political and military cost at Salonika in Greece. A campaign in Mesopotamia (modern-day Iraq) had turned into a minor catastrophe. Now a fourth such attempt, the new Balkan front in Romania, was in the process of collapsing too. Nor were the prospects in Italy very interesting.

Knowing Robertson's unwillingness to endorse his preferred "eastern" strategy, Lloyd George was scheming to get him out of the way by sending him off, for months, on a military mission to Russia—chillingly similar to the one Lord Kitchener had embarked on in June, only to go down with his ship and its crew when they hit a mine. Robertson was not taken in by what he called the "Lord K dodge."

Although they detested Lloyd George, Robertson and Douglas Haig, the British commanding general in France, stoutly cheered the policy of a "fight to the finish." But Robertson did not envisage a quick finish, much less a knockout.

The other great issue posed by Lansdowne, and now by the whole cabinet, was whether the war effort could be sustained. Which would break first, the hammer or the anvil? On November 22, Robertson told his favorite pro-military journalist that the government "might succumb to any opportunity of an early peace."[4]

With all these irritations and frustrations bubbling in the background, Robertson lost his temper when he received the cabinet's blunt question about whether the armed forces could administer a knockout blow. In his written reply, he was outraged and defiant.

"I am surprised that the question should be asked," he wrote. The army, Robertson thundered, had never had any doubts. "I thought that I had made it clear that we could win it only if we did the right thing and did it in time."

He had promised only "harder and more protracted fighting and a much greater strain on our general resources than any yet experienced." That was the only way to "wring from the enemy that peace which we have said we mean to have." About that peace, he said only that it should not leave the "military domination of Prussia intact."

Everyone should just do their job for the years of fighting that lay ahead. Robertson felt sure (just as Erich von Ludendorff did in Germany) that Britain could do much more. The people and resources could be mobilized more completely, more rigorously, for total military service. As for other "nonmilitary" issues, like the vital crisis in finance, Robertson airily waved at them and commented that such difficulties were usually exaggerated.

Robertson then lashed out at the weak-kneed civilians who dared to even ask such questions. There were, he added, "amongst us, as in all communities, a certain number of cranks, cowards, and philosophers, some of whom are afraid of their own skins being hurt," who might argue "that we stand to gain more by losing the war than by winning it."

"In short," Robertson concluded, "we need to have the same courage in London as have our leaders in the North Sea and in France. The whole art of making war may be summed up in three words—courage, action, and determination.... We must make up our minds to fight or to make peace.... We shall win if we deserve to win."[5]

---

A MORE MODERATE, civilian voice in the cabinet took Robertson's side. This was the Conservative minister working with Grey at the Foreign Office, Robert Cecil. Cecil worked closely with Arthur Balfour (his cousin). He was close to Grey. He had been analyzing the peace option possibilities at least since August.

"Our situation is grave," Cecil admitted. "It is certain that unless the utmost national effort is made it may become desperate, particularly in the matter of shipping." "The position in Allied countries is even more serious," he also conceded. "France is within measurable distance of exhaustion." Ambassador Francis Bertie had just separately reported on growing "restlessness and disquiet" in French public opinion, given "the fact that the end of the war, in spite of the enormous sacrifices which France has made, is not in sight."

Cecil went on. "The political outlook in Italy is menacing. Her finance is tottering. In Russia there is great discouragement. She has long been on the verge of revolution."

But, deferring to Robertson and Haig, Cecil argued for one more year of great ground offensives on the western front. Cecil wrote hopefully, "If therefore we can carry on for another year, we have a reasonable prospect of victory."

The peace option was not yet attractive enough, as far as Cecil could see, because under current circumstances, with no compromise on the German side, nothing done to alter the current German position on the ground, "a peace now could only be disastrous. At the best we could not hope for more than the *status quo* with a great increase in the German power in Eastern Europe."

In that case, Cecil preferred to make "drastic changes in [Britain's] civil life." "The Germans are putting their whole civilian organization on a war footing, and we must do the same." This meant government takeover of industry and labor.[6]

Cecil reflected an emerging consensus about the need for more civilian exertions. On November 30, the War Committee agreed that all men up to the age of sixty should be subject to compulsory national service.

One small irony, since many in America were so angry about German deportations of Belgian laborers, was that Britain was expanding its own larger levies to include available low-wage foreign labor. Britain focused on importing many thousands of laborers from China, India, Egypt, and South Africa.[7]

---

SETTING UP the expected special cabinet discussion, Lansdowne and Grey replied to Robertson's angry paper. The general, Lansdowne coolly observed, had not offered "a very helpful contribution." The problem could not "be disposed of by confident assertions as to the temper of the Army, which no one ever doubted."

Lansdowne assumed, in his gentlemanly way, that the remarks in Robertson's paper about "cranks, cowards, and philosophers" were surely not directed at him. Lansdowne did not have to mention that his oldest son had been killed in France. Everyone knew it. The king himself had visited the gravesite.

Staying coldly analytical, Lansdowne zeroed in on the military prospects and the broader weaknesses that Britain and her allies faced. Weighing those factors, Lansdowne concluded, "we ought at any rate not to discourage any movement, no matter where originating, in favour of [peace talks]."

Britain might fare well in such negotiations, especially since her goals were not yet well defined. Lansdowne reminded his colleagues that the cabinet had "authorized a full enquiry into the whole of the many-sided and complex problem." And "those who ask questions which the Cabinet think worthy of a respectful answer will not consider that they are answered when they are told that such questions are an 'insult' to the fighting man."

The day after Lansdowne sent around this reply, Prime Minister Asquith sent him a note. "I write at once to assure you of my complete concurrence in what you say."[8]

Grey's reply to Robertson took a different tack but ended in the same place. To Grey, the issue of peace was "a question, not of sentiment, nor of rhetoric, but of cold, hard fact. It should be examined as far as possible without emotion, certainly without sentiment, and without rhetoric." That, Grey added, was just the way Lansdowne had examined it.

The analytical problem was straightforward. If the position of the Allies is "likely to improve...it is premature to make peace."

If the position is not likely to improve—if "a year hence we should be able to secure terms of peace not more favourable than at present"—it is obviously "better to wind up the war on the best terms now obtainable."

There was also another possibility. Suppose the position of the Allies might get worse? In that case, the Allies should "wind up the war at once on the best terms obtainable, presumably through the medium of not unsympathetic mediation [meaning Wilson]." If the Allied governments did not do this, "they would be responsible for future disaster to their countries."

Grey presented, then, the analytical question: How did the government assess these three possibilities? He had to defer to Robertson and Haig's view that the prospects were good for improving the position with another year of fighting. But all this was "provided the Allies can continue the war with full vigour." To Grey, that was doubtful.[9]

———

IT WAS as if Lansdowne and Grey had scripted the next scene in a melodrama. One day after they circulated their assessments of Allied resources came the shock on November 28. That was the US Federal Reserve Board's warning (instigated by Wilson) against more loan financing from the United States.

As markets panicked, Prime Minister Asquith quickly summoned a small group of the War Committee to gather at Number Ten Downing Street for an unusual evening meeting. They settled into their familiar chairs at 6:00 p.m. to discuss the Fed's warning about loans to the Allies.

McKenna outlined the "very serious situation." Balfour, who was recovering from an illness, called this news "the most serious matter which had come up for consideration before the War Committee." It was, he said, "infinitely more serious than the submarine menace."

Bonar Law was not so worried. Surely the Americans would keep lending to make a profit. Others ignored him. That argument had been made before and refuted convincingly, underscored by how the British had been forced to back down in their confrontation with American arms sellers in the October "rifles" crisis.

Grey, also noting the existing shipping problems, concluded, "We might have to consider the question of [peace] terms."

McKenna agreed. The Allied finance issues would effectively start winding up the war. There was no way to continue if they "were unable to purchase wheat and munitions." At the present rate of consumption of materials, they "should very shortly have to close down, possibly within a month," Edwin Montagu, the minister of munitions, put in, "if the American supplies were shut down."

After a long discussion about what might be possible, the group confronted not only what the British could sustain but how much they could continue to support their French and Russian allies. McKenna and Balfour agreed that "the scale must be reduced."

Grey pointed out that the Federal Reserve Board's action was no random event. President Wilson, Grey explained, had long believed "that the War could be wound up now on reasonable terms." The British might regard such terms "as unsatisfactory and inconclusive," but Grey expected Wilson to pressure both sides to end the war. Germany could not win, and the Allies "now could not achieve a decisive result."[10]

The financial alarm carried over into a regularly scheduled full cabinet meeting the next morning, November 29. McKenna and then Asquith were called out of the room and returned with news that the markets were in full flight. The group of officials managing Britain's foreign exchange recommended that Britain should "go off the gold standard" and refuse to exchange sterling for gold and that the move should be made that very afternoon, by 3:00 p.m.—just a few hours away—before the markets opened in New York.

McKenna disagreed. Such a surrender would make things even worse. If Britain abandoned gold, she would "gravely damage [her] credit" and would be unable to "finance the Allies after March [1917]."

Asquith was persuaded. He, McKenna, Grey, Lloyd George, Law, and Austen Chamberlain left Downing Street and trooped over to the Treasury Building, where they told the exchange group to hold the line and stay on the gold standard, dispensing whatever gold was needed to get through the immediate panic.[11]

---

GREY'S GUESS about Wilson's role and his purposes was right on the mark. The Federal Reserve Board's warning had made all the impact Wilson could have wanted.

Yet Wilson's financial move was not coupled with any political move. At the moment when he had maximum leverage to move events, Wilson seemed to be doing nothing. There was no call for a peace conference. Most of all, there was no American suggestion that such a conference might be paired with some preliminary understanding in which the Germans agreed to give up ground, above all on the pivotal symbol of Belgium.

Wilson had thus done nothing at all to help Grey or any other British peacemakers find the face-saving exit from this terrible war. At this delicate moment in Britain's war crisis, weeks after his reelection, Wilson had still not thrown any sort of lifeline to these men. He had simply created a panic.

In the view of the British ambassador in Washington, Cecil Spring-Rice, the American government seemed "entirely indifferent to the opinion of the outside world." Spring-Rice's assessment, passed around the cabinet at the end of November, found the Americans "perfectly satisfied with the present condition of affairs and their superabundant prosperity." Nothing, at least nothing good, was to be expected from Wilson, the ambassador suggested.[12]

Grey understood what Wilson needed to do. During the London debates, on November 26, Grey wrote to Spring-Rice. "We cannot encourage [Wilson's] mediation without being prepared to accept it." But suppose Wilson took the initiative and made the first move? In that case, Grey wrote, "I would personally advise His Majesty's Government to suggest to the Allies that they should state the minimum conditions to be laid down on which they would accept mediation or begin discussion of peace terms."[13]

Grey was not talking about getting assurances about the final outcome of the peace treaty. Those sorts of assurances would come well down the road and would be hard to deliver. Instead he was talking about preliminary preconditions to the peace talks themselves. There is no great mystery about what kind of preconditions mattered most to Grey. Since 1915, his top priorities were simple: the restoration of Belgium and the preservation of France.

Through various sources, including earlier intercepted decrypts of German and American cables, including the Austrian peace feelers, the British government had evidence that the Germans were willing to withdraw from Belgium, even if Grey did not know about the express assurances that Chancellor Bethmann Hollweg and Ambassador Bernstorff had already conveyed to the Americans.

Britain had gone to war to sustain the balance of power, respond to the violation of Belgian neutrality, and defeat Prussian militarism. If Germany had to disgorge most or all its gains in the West, a British government could plausibly argue that the Allied shield had stopped the German spear. The Allies had swept German ships and shipping from the seas. They had defeated and discredited the supposed Prussian militarist dreams of conquest.

If the Americans had even started work on such possible preconditions, Grey was obviously ready to play. Just the beginning of such a conversation would have riveted government attention. Any material guarantees, and certainly an assurance about Belgium alone, would have transformed the politics of a debate already so finely balanced. The would-be peacemakers could then demand of Lloyd George whether he could credibly promise to do better.

But from Washington and New York there was silence.

————

GREY COULD *not make the first move.* His coalition government had not authorized that. Nor did he have an informal way to help the Americans see how to use their leverage—House had not come to London, and there was no good American representative with whom Grey could explore this.

In public, all of Britain's allies might breathe defiance. That too could change. "What I fear most," Grey wrote, "is that one of the Great Allies, when told, *as they ought to be told now*, that our support in shipping and finance, one or both, has to be curtailed in a few months, will abandon hope of ultimate victory."

At that point, he predicted, that ally would "demand that the war be wound up on the best terms available." The Allied diplomatic unity would visibly fracture. The Germans would then have even more of an advantage. At that point, the British would wish that they had sought "the intervention of President Wilson—(if it is still available in the spirit described)."[14]

As Grey was writing those words, at the end of November, a courier was still crossing the Atlantic with House's letter, written on Wilson's order, explaining that "Germany is now ready to largely meet the [peace] conditions laid down [earlier in 1916] by Mr. Asquith" and that, at a peace conference, the United States would help make sure that "Germany would yield everything that could properly be demanded of her."

But by the time that American letter was delivered, in early December, when House followed up by cabling Grey, pleading for some "guidance," Grey was no longer in office.

––––––––

THE BRITISH cabinet never held that follow-on special session to complete the discussion of Lansdowne's memo about the choice between war and peace. It never had the debate about General Robertson's paper and the replies to it. It never concluded the discussion it began on November 22. When something doesn't happen, historians rarely stop and notice.

Instead, during the first week of December, Lloyd George launched his public attack. His public demand was for a supposedly more effective reorganization of the government. If his proposals were turned down, he threatened to resign. This would pull down the government. He would go to the country, leading the cause of making an all-out effort to win the war.

Given the constraints of what could be said publicly, Asquith tried, and failed, to mollify Lloyd George with various reorganization schemes. After their rejection, Asquith resigned. To the surprise of many, Lloyd George was able to form a new coalition government dominated by Conservatives and a few remaining Liberal allies.

He ruled as prime minister on a base of mainly Conservative support. The new coalition took office in the second week of December 1916. All the principal figures in the cabinet open to peace were thrown out: Grey, McKenna, and Lansdowne.

The new "War Cabinet" of December 1916

The new foreign secretary was Balfour. He moved across the street on Whitehall, transferring from the Admiralty to take Grey's place at the Foreign Office.

The Northcliffe press, in *The Times*, glorified the heart of the new government.

## The Germans Call for Peace Talks

During the second week of December 1916, the German government publicly announced that the Central Powers were ready to talk peace. Since October, Germany and Austria-Hungary had been talking about making a public peace offer of their own. Vienna had no confidence in Wilson and wanted to try to get something going. Even if such a move failed, it would at least show publics at home that it was the Entente Allies who did not want peace.

Bethmann had put off the Austrians. He realized any peace offer made by the Central Powers would inspire distrust. He still wanted Wilson to take the initiative. The Germans also wanted to wait until they and their allies had completed their victory over Romania.

On November 25, Bethmann had reiterated to Bernstorff, "It is our urgent wish that Wilson will decide to take early steps in this matter." If the issue was still in the air by the new year, war planning for 1917 would start pushing any talk of peace out of the way.

The new command team, Paul von Hindenburg and Erich von Ludendorff, felt firmly in charge of reorganizing the war effort. They were scornful of American weakness and sympathetic to the navy's itch to go all-out with the U-boat war.

The U-boat issue was an emotional one in Germany. People were hungry. A potato famine was yielding a hungry winter in Germany and Austria-Hungary. Hungry people wanted revenge. They wanted their submarines to starve the British too.

There was plenty of German hostility toward America. In 1915, troops in France built a work of art. They called it "Wilson, the Neutral," with a chalk bust of the American president, smiling, set on top of a pedestal made entirely of unexploded shells that the troops had recovered, all of them made in the USA.[15]

Scheming against Bethmann, the German military helped oust his longtime deputy at the Foreign Office, Gottlieb von Jagow, who resigned at the end of November, pleading illness. Bethmann's new secretary leading the Foreign Office was Arthur Zimmermann. Zimmermann was a vigorous, talkative, opinionated, and thoroughly shortsighted person. He had long voiced his doubts about Wilson, insisting that the American president was just a tool of the Allies.[16]

Bethmann's views on the substance of a compromise peace had not changed. In late November, his adviser, Kurt Riezler, confided to his diary that if, in the West, Germany got about "zero," and if Poland remained free and Germany got "Suwalki [a small region today on the Polish-Lithuanian border] and a few colonies, the peace would be more than brilliant."[17]

As for how to achieve peace, Bethmann still clung to the Wilson option. On December 2, the chancellor made the daylong journey to General Headquarters in Pless and took his concern to the monarch himself. He persuaded Wilhelm to issue a formal imperial order that warned submarine commanders to avoid any action that might lead to complications with America. Making his case to Wilhelm that December day, in front of the uniformed and beribboned staff, an admiral noted, the chancellor "stressed once again that he must avoid a conflict with America at all costs until the peace move, which both we and America are planning, had come off."

House had told Bernstorff that Wilson was delaying, hesitant, fearing Allied rejection, anxious about press reports of German misbehavior. Relying on this report, Bethmann admitted to Hindenburg, "Whether [Wilson] will really carry out this [peace move] intention remains completely uncertain." Wilson, he said, was "undecided and afraid of a rejection." This was a description of House's views, not Wilson's. But the German government did not know that.[18]

On December 2, Bethmann pushed his worries about Wilson to the side. He wondered whether he should ask for even stronger restrictions on the submariners, "at least until the outcome of his peace action...was decided."[19]

———

ON DECEMBER 7, Bethmann got another report from Bernstorff relaying more misleading information (from House) about Wilson's supposed vacillation.[20] Two days later, the Germans made the decision to go along with the desires of their allies and publicly announce the Central Powers' offer to talk peace. Bethmann was not trying to discard the Wilson option. He hoped to put, as he said, "two irons in the fire."[21]

Before the German announcement, Bethmann met secretly with representatives of the states in the German federation. He briefed the civilian leaders on the upcoming offer of peace talks, an "infinitely serious decision." He wanted them to set the right tone for whatever discussions might come.

They all had a duty, he said, to say to the people and the army, "who have been doing their utmost for two and a half years," "We do not want, for the sake of wild conquest, to let this war last one day longer than necessary."

"Who can see into the future?" Bethmann continued. If the war went on, they would do the best they could. But who knew what might happen? "Who could challenge fate in such world events? Give us the possibility, that peace returns, so that our consciences are clear before God and our people."[22]

On December 12, the Central Powers announced their offer to open peace talks. The proclamation said nothing about peace terms. The German announcement's tone, on behalf of the Central Powers, was confident and defiant.

Predictably, the Allied Powers rejected the overture as an offer of a victor's peace. When the German peace note came out, Robert Cecil, who was still at the Foreign Office and now working with the new foreign secretary, his cousin, Balfour, prepared the reply. The first line of his paper read, "It is assumed that the policy of this country is to avoid being forced into peace negotiations at the present time." Unless one of their allies defected, the only thing that "could defeat this policy" was "the active intervention of the United States by cutting off supplies of money and munitions."[23]

Lloyd George explained it this way to the House of Commons: "What are the [German] proposals? There are none." Britain and its allies would not walk into such talks with no terms and no preconditions. That would just "put our head into a noose," he said.[24]

## Wilson Finally Makes His Peace Move

Wilson was at last finishing the draft of his own peace note. The German announcement had disappointed him momentarily because it seemed to eclipse him.

But the day after the Germans and the Austrians announced their joint offer of peace talks, Bethmann reassured Wilson. Ambassador Bernstorff wrote to House to tell him Bethmann was doing all he could to provide "practical cooperation" to avoid further submarine incidents. (This was true.) Bethmann still hoped Wilson would collaborate in finding a way to end the war, Bernstorff said.

Also, at the time of the public announcement, Bethmann reassured the Americans that he and Wilson had a common purpose. He explained his thinking to chargé Joseph Grew, at the American embassy. Germany, Bethmann said, had "never aimed at the destruction of her enemies," and "larger streams of blood will not bring about lasting peace." Only "the common endeavor of all nations" would bring a lasting peace, with "mutual respect and the recognition of their several rights."

This was the kind of language Wilson wanted to hear. Bethmann hoped Germany's offer to open peace talks would "coincide with the wishes of the President of the United States."[25]

———

ENCOURAGED, WILSON polished his draft peace note. By early December, House was no longer trying to discourage him.

House's own views had shifted again. He had already persuaded Wilson to take the call for a peace conference out of the note and step back from an offer to mediate. He was also seeing more evidence that he had misread the state of British opinion. He now agreed with an antiwar British MP that Wilson's planned peace note might set off "such a discussion in Parliament and in England that within a short time they would have to accept mediation."[26]

It might have helped that House (and Wilson) were beginning to get more balanced news about the situation in Britain. Given the general distrust of anything from their ambassador, Walter Hines Page, House had reached out to another American diplomat attached to the London embassy, William Hepburn Buckler.

Buckler was an unusual character. Born in Paris and educated at Cambridge, he had returned to the United States to practice law in Baltimore and was also a gifted economist. He had joined the newly established US Foreign Service almost as a lark in 1906. In 1914, Buckler was set up as a "special agent" at the American embassy. Already a noted lawyer and archaeologist (his main postwar fame was in archaeology), Buckler nominally dealt with Austro-Hungarian and Turkish affairs. But he had a writ to talk to all the British political parties and a channel directly to House.[27]

To House, Buckler was blunt about the dismal military situation that Britain really faced, along with the dire shipping shortage. And, unlike others at the embassy, Buckler supported an American peace move. "Perhaps this country [Britain]," he wrote, "will at last have the sense to see that the price of peace is going higher, and that she would do well to join the bidding before it is prohibitive." That notion, he thought, must "ere long penetrate even the ignorance and complacency of the ruling class here." He hoped for peace, frankly, "because I dislike to see the drubbing of the Entente become more severe, as it is bound to be if peace is long postponed."

Buckler did not think Lloyd George would solve Britain's war crisis. Lloyd George, he wrote, "was bound to be tried as a strong well advertised quack medicine." That medicine was, he thought, "unlikely to cure the patient."[28]

---

ADJUSTING TO the new British prime minister, House urged Wilson to write to Lloyd George and remind him that he had once supported American mediation to end the war. The president could perhaps allude to possible peace terms.

Wilson agreed with House on the need to move. "The time is near at hand for *something!*"

"But," Wilson explained, "that something is not mediation such as we were proposing when you were last on the other side of the water." Wilson added, "We cannot go back to those old plans. We must shape new ones."[29]

It is not clear what Wilson meant by this. He certainly did not intend to dictate terms of the treaty to end the war. His draft note, inspired by the rather abstract suggestions "Cosmos" had made in the *New York Times* the previous month, was now only going to ask them to state their war aims.

As Wilson polished his peace note in December, he still made the hard-headed, realistic argument that a fight to the finish would produce a poor peace. "If the contest must continue to proceed towards undefined ends by slow attrition until the one group of belligerents or the other is exhausted, if million after million of human lives must continue to be offered up . . . , if resentments must be kindled that can never cool and despairs engendered from which there can be no recovery, hopes of peace and of the willing concert of free peoples will be rendered vain and idle."

But at House's suggestion, Wilson wrote, "The President is not proposing peace; he is not even offering mediation." He was merely taking "soundings" to learn the terms for ending the war. These changes drained his peace note of any really actionable content.

The draft was further delayed as Lansing picked over it, then House looked over it some more. House thought even this mild note would still prove objectionable to the British. "I find," he confided dramatically to his diary, "the President has nearly destroyed all the work I have done in Europe" to persuade the Allies that Wilson was on their side.

House's complaint was not that the note took no concrete action. He was proud that he had stripped the conference call out of the note. House was annoyed that the tone of the note was so balanced. House thought such evenhandedness was bound to offend the British since they so strongly believed in the righteousness of their cause.[30]

———

WILSON CIRCULATED his note on December 18, six days after the Germans had issued their public offer to talk peace. The American intervention for peace was a news sensation. It put Wilson on the world stage as a possible peacemaker.

But most of the commentary was superficial, simply touching on the fact of Wilson's intervention. It divided in predictable, reflexive ways. Partisans of one side or the other thought the note should have taken their side. Or they thought that Wilson should not try to interfere at all.

In America, most commentary was positive. Most American politicians and opinion leaders shared the view of William Jennings Bryan's antiwar ally, the chairman of the Senate Foreign Relations Committee, Senator William Stone of Missouri. Stone thought Wilson's note was "timely," that the president was "to be heartily commended for his courage, and to be congratulated for having seized the logical moment to urge the substitution of discussion for the carnage of the battlefield."[31]

Beyond that surface reaction, the governments of the warring countries were confused. They were confused about what the note did *not* say. What was the substance? There was no call for a peace conference. The note seemed vague and patronizing. What was Wilson trying to do? Their reactions were generally negative—on both sides.

It was as if a big gun had slowly been wheeled into position, watched with great anticipation. The lanyard was pulled. There was a great exhalation...of air. It was a misfire.

To make matters worse, right after the note went out, Secretary of State Robert Lansing issued a press statement to explain it, without having first cleared what he planned to say with the president. Lansing tried to rationalize Wilson's note by writing, "We are drawing nearer the verge of war ourselves, and, therefore, we are entitled to know exactly what each belligerent seeks, in order that we may regulate our conduct in the future."

"Verge of war"? What on earth did Lansing mean? The only possible war the United States might imminently be forced into was one on the side of the Allies, against Germany. Wilson had nothing of the kind in mind. He was livid.

In fact, Wilson was so angry that he almost fired Lansing that very day. Rather than dismiss him, Wilson coldly instructed him, first in writing, then in person, to issue another statement. He would have to say that his statement was being "radically misinterpreted," that there was no change whatsoever in the US policy of neutrality. In other words, Lansing had to humiliatingly reverse himself.

In his private meetings with the British and French ambassadors to explain Wilson's note, Lansing had gone further. He was anxious to reassure the Allies that America had not colluded in the German peace offer. He encouraged the Allies to state terms, even maximum terms, which Lansing said—speaking for himself—he was willing to support.

Some historians, like renowned Wilson expert Arthur Link, have argued that Wilson issued an otherwise commendable peace note, yet was betrayed by Lansing's unneutral interpretation of it. Link was right to criticize Lansing.[32] But Lansing's foolish statements had no important impact on the actions of the British or the French.

Lansing's press statement did have an impact, however, on some significant figures in Berlin, Pless, and Vienna. Those who were already distrustful of Wilson saw this as confirmation of their suspicions.

The kaiser, reading a report on Lansing's statements, jotted one of his frequent, impulsive marginal comments, in this instance remarking that Wilson's peace note was meant to "support England." The state secretary at the Foreign Office, Zimmermann, described Wilson's note as "in accord with English agreement," to deflect attention from the Central Powers' offer to talk peace.[33] To Germany, Wilson's note did not feel at all neutral.

## All Sides Struggle to Interpret Wilson's Note

Among most of the civilian authorities in Germany, even those more sympathetic to Wilson, there was, Swedish scholar Karl Birnbaum observed, a sense of "profound disappointment" in Wilson's note. It had said nothing about a peace conference. The Germans had hoped that Wilson would follow Theodore Roosevelt's example in the Russo-Japanese War. They had expected him to call for a conference in a neutral place like The Hague or Copenhagen. They expected those peace negotiations to then be prolonged and difficult. But they hoped that maybe they could come away with a face-saving outcome.

By asking them to announce their peace terms, Wilson had actually made their position more difficult. For months, Bethmann had tried to avoid being pinned down on a minimum position, his bottom line. Using vague assurances, he had managed his military, his allies, and his internal political partners. It was all about getting to the conference. Once there, Bethmann's authority and discretion would then be very great.

If Bethmann seemed ready to accept too little, that would hand ammunition to his many internal enemies. If he seemed to ask for too much, Germany would look like it was not willing to make real compromises.

Bethmann's deputy at the Foreign Office, Zimmermann, explained all this to Grew. Zimmermann "was quite sure Germany's peace terms were more moderate than those of the Entente." But "Germany could not be the first to divulge them, first, because one party to a negotiation could not give its hand away at the start and, secondly, because of the unfavorable effect which this would have on the German public, part of whom would undoubtedly be dissatisfied."[34]

Several days after sending his note, Wilson realized this part of his error. He sent out word that he would be glad to get information about proposed peace terms confidentially, instead. Bernstorff similarly told Lansing that it would be very difficult for any of the powers to discuss their terms, except at a peace conference. Lansing replied that disclosures "could be confidential and might, little by little, lead to a conference."

Bernstorff did not know quite what to make of this. He reported his guess that Wilson at least "would like to serve as a clearing house for further steps toward peace."[35] But what did that mean?

RIGHT AFTER they received Wilson's note, a group of top German officials, including Vice-chancellor Karl Helfferich and Zimmermann, sat down to breakfast together to puzzle over what Wilson was trying to do. They came up with a theory. Perhaps he was trying to gather all the war aims from both sides so that he could then try to dictate final peace terms as a strong mediator (*Vermittler*, in German).

The word "mediator" can mean more than one thing. A mediator can convene talks, as Roosevelt had for the Russians and Japanese. Or, in another role, a mediator can become a judge, dictating the settlement.

Zimmermann guessed that Wilson wanted to make himself the arbiter and to "centralize the peace move in himself"—in which case there would then be no peace conference at all! The breakfast group members all agreed that Wilson should not play this role of judge and preempt a peace conference. The Germans preferred to have direct talks with their enemies, where perhaps they might exploit some of the differences among them.[36]

Their suspicion was mistaken. There is no evidence that Wilson planned to substitute his arbitration for a peace conference. In his May 27 speech about American commitment to a postwar league, Wilson had said explicitly that he did not intend to participate in the negotiations among the warring powers to set the territorial terms for peace. But, unfortunately, Wilson's curious peace note invited such misunderstandings.

The formal German reply to Wilson's peace note, coordinated with Vienna, deflected Wilson's request to disclose peace terms. The Central Powers instead argued there should be a peace conference and that "a direct exchange of views" was best. They suggested a gathering of delegates from the warring powers at a neutral spot in Europe.

Because of their suspicions about Wilson's intentions with this supposed clearinghouse, the German government specifically suggested to the Americans that there should be two peace conferences. One would include the warring powers. A later one, adding key neutrals like the United States, would address the postwar system.[37]

Procedurally, although Wilson had imagined two sets of negotiations, back in the spring he seemed to envision that they would happen at the same time in concurrent, overlapping conferences—one on ending the war and the other on postwar plans—both at The Hague, with Wilson present in person. Concurrent conferences would make it easier for Wilson to have some informal influence on the discussions among the warring powers and also allow him to leverage American offers, for instance on aid for postwar reconstruction, to help with the settlement of the war issues. But Wilson had not begun discussing these important procedural points with any foreign governments.

Instead, the combination of Wilson's delay and then his puzzling note, the reports about him, and Zimmermann's suspicions all started leading Bethmann and the German government to doubt Wilson, and with him the most appealing peace option. But the other German options were dark. Bethmann was reluctant to give up on Wilson entirely. He kept hoping that Bernstorff would cable news of some further opening.

———

OVER IN London and Paris, the British and French professionals were puzzled too, trying to figure out what Wilson was doing. Cecil, receiving Wilson's note, was baffled by this "very unusual" step. He did not understand how the warring powers were supposed to make known their peace terms. The American ambassador, Page, clueless, had no answer, except to cite the president's high ideals.

Privately, some of the more conservative British top officials, the "fight to the finish" group, were spluttering. One, at the Foreign Office, wrote to Spring-Rice that Wilson's note was "a slimy mass of murkiness" and "quite impracticable," a "somewhat clumsy proceeding." But none of this was stated publicly.[38]

Lloyd George's War Cabinet quickly agreed that they had to show restraint—and not fly out angrily at Wilson. The British press was told to stay disciplined, follow the public line, and not attack the American president.

The British paid little heed to Lansing's suggestion (so quickly retracted) that the Americans were on the "verge of war." The British felt sure that Wilson would rather make peace than bring the United States into the conflict. And they were still only too aware of how much financial leverage Wilson had over them. Cecil warned them, "If [Wilson] desired to put a stop to the war, and was prepared to pay the price for doing so, such an achievement is in his power."[39]

After a few days passed, the British government realized, with relief, that, given the abstract way Wilson had designed his note, their short-term problem was not really all that difficult. They could pretend to make a forthcoming reply to Wilson by finding some way of publicly describing their war aims. They could simply put out, for public consumption, whatever idealized phrases the Allies could agree on.

The French and British took their time preparing their formal reply to Wilson, then coordinated it with others, including with Russia. They issued it weeks later. The tone was sweeping.

The Allied reply started with the restoration of all occupied territories "with just reparation." It also called for "the reorganization of Europe." This transformed Europe would be based on "respect of nationalities and full security and liberty [of] economic development." This would include, at least, the liberation of Italians, Slavs, Romanians, and Czechoslovaks from "foreign domination." That implied the breakup of the Austro-Hungarian Empire. "Bloody" Turkish tyranny would end with the expulsion of the Ottoman Empire from Europe.

The Entente had a spot of trouble figuring out what to say about Poland. Secretly, France and Russia had just agreed that Russia would be allowed to carve a larger Russian Poland out of Germany and Austria-Hungary. In return, France would have a free hand to annex German lands west of the Rhine, in addition to regaining the territory lost in 1871. None of this was mentioned in the Allied reply to Wilson. They just alluded to a new Poland, under Russian protection.[40]

The British government never took Wilson's note seriously as an actual diplomatic move. It was seen as a piece of public theater.

One historian of the episode, Sterling Kernek, concluded that Wilson's note "never had a chance of success because of its inherent weakness." "Indeed," Kernek added, "Wilson's note perhaps facilitated Britain's rejection of peace negotiations. In effect, the world's leading candidate for the role of peacemaker had implied that the cause of peace would be served without actual peace negotiations, but merely by a declaration of terms and a kind of negotiation for the benefit of the galleries."[41]

BEYOND THE public theater, though, Lloyd George's government still found it "baffling" to figure out what Wilson was trying to do or why. At one point, Lloyd George entertained the wild theory that Wilson was discharging a pledge made to "pro-German Jews" who had donated to his campaign. At other times he claimed "evidence of German, pacifist and Irish influence...dread of belligerency, and a preference of military stalemate" to explain American interest in mediation. Wilson was "the quintessence of a prig."[42]

Yet, amid all the disdain, all the loud talk of fighting to the finish, a vital core in the Foreign Office, and indeed Lloyd George himself, still wanted to keep the American peace option alive. Because in secret, they had no reason to be more confident about what might happen in 1917.

There was some important continuity in the new government. Balfour was now the foreign secretary. He had been close to Grey. He had been involved in all the arguments about American peace moves from the start. He and his cousin, Robert Cecil, usually had similar views. Both of them had long inclined toward relatively moderate British war aims. Balfour had kept Grey's private secretary, Eric Drummond.

Over at Downing Street, Hankey too had been one of those consistently open to the American peace option. He remained there, now as secretary of Lloyd George's reorganized War Cabinet, which had replaced the War Committee.

After the new government took office, Balfour would have received the secret letter that House had sent to Grey at Wilson's order, the one warning of American impatience and promising that Britain would be able to get the peace terms discussed earlier in the year. With that in mind, and with the added impetus of Wilson's peace note, the War Cabinet decided to recheck: Just how dependent are we on American supplies and official goodwill? The answer was depressingly familiar: the dependence was overwhelming.

Then, to tell the new group what peace terms had been discussed earlier in 1916, the Foreign Office circulated to the new War Cabinet the old House-Grey memorandum, with its minimum, moderate peace terms. Officials wondered whether it was time to revive some plan like that. For the moment, they paused and waited.[43]

What especially irritated Balfour about Wilson's December note was the same thing that had irritated him back in May, when, on behalf of the peace group, he had drafted a British reply to Wilson's mediation offer. Balfour needed a few assurances about the terms, that the Germans would have to compromise, would have to give up something. In his note, Wilson made no reference to any substantive peace terms. To Balfour, the president still seemed infuriatingly indifferent about the terms to end the war—not even mentioning Belgium.

Balfour's interpretation of Wilson's note, that he was agnostic, was thus practically the opposite of the German suspicion, which was that Wilson wanted to dictate terms. The language of Wilson's note was so vague that Berlin and London could interpret it entirely differently.

Balfour and Cecil could not swallow a peace in which the Germans yielded nothing. German aggression had to be knocked back at least enough so that the Prussian militarist faction could not portray the war as a wonderful success. To Balfour, "the mere termination of hostilities would provide no sufficient cure for our ills."[44]

Looking for a way to reactivate diplomacy with Washington, Balfour, aided by his private secretary, Drummond, decided to rely less on their ineffective ambassador, Spring-Rice. They opened, with the help of British intelligence, a new back channel into the Wilson White House. Their channel took the form of a boyish-looking thirty-one-year-old army captain with a neatly trimmed mustache, named William Wiseman.

Wiseman came from an aristocratic family and carried the hereditary title of baronet. His father, grandfather, and great-grandfather had all been naval officers. Wiseman had attended Cambridge, boxing there at the varsity level in the bantamweight class. He tried journalism and then went into business, with modest success in various ventures across North America, from Canada to Mexico.

When war came, Wiseman—married with two children—joined up and became an army officer. He was gassed in Flanders in July 1915. Back home, convalescing, he looked for work at the War Office.

There he talked with one of his father's navy friends, Mansfield Cumming. Cumming headed a War Office branch called MI1c, the predecessor of today's British Secret Service (MI6). Wiseman impressed Cumming, including with his experience in America. In October 1915, Cumming sent Wiseman to the United States as an intelligence officer.

By December 1916, when he first met House, Wiseman was the head of British intelligence in the United States. He communicated directly with Cumming (called "C"). Cumming, in turn, worked closely with Balfour and Drummond at the Foreign Office. On occasion, Wiseman would get communications directly from one of them too.[45]

After the German peace note, before he met House, Wiseman sent London a reasonably educated estimate of possible German terms. Wiseman reminded London that the Germans had been pushing for a peace move since August, that Wilson had been preparing a move for some time, and that Ambassador Bernstorff had hoped the peace talks could have begun before Christmas. All of this was accurate.

As for German terms, Wiseman advised that the "Germans are prepared to evacuate Belgium, France and Poland." They and their allies hoped to get an advantage in the final dispositions in the Balkans. The Germans, he reported, were also willing to work with the League to Enforce Peace movement and hinted at limiting armaments. All of this was reasonably accurate too.

Wiseman recommended that Britain set Belgium as its precondition for talks. "Quit and indemnify Belgium and then we will discuss peace."[46]

A couple of days after dispatching this message, Wiseman first met House. House immediately liked the young, worldly army officer who was so knowledgeable about and sympathetic to America. That night, House noted to his diary that Wiseman "proved to be the most important caller I have had for sometime."

In that first conversation, Wiseman told House that Lloyd George was preparing a public reply to the German peace talks offer. House offered to obtain and pass along whatever he could get from Bernstorff about Germany's desired peace terms. House told Wilson he had agreed to this.[47] (Suspicion of just such leakage was a reason the German Foreign Office did not want to share details about their peace terms with Wilson, even confidentially.)

Balfour then asked Wiseman to find out something else from House. Balfour and Lloyd George wanted to know if the March understandings detailed in the House-Grey memorandum were still valid. Were the Americans still sympathetic to those minimum British terms (Belgium, Alsace-Lorraine, a Russian outlet to the sea, with compensation for Germany)?

Wiseman checked. He cabled back: House said there was no change. The United States would still help obtain those results (reaffirming what House had promised Grey, at Wilson's order, in the letter House had sent a few weeks earlier).[48]

The British were not the only ones nervously checking their peace parachute while presenting a bold face to their publics. The French prime minister, Aristide Briand, established a secret liaison to Bethmann in Berlin. This was done through unofficial emissaries of both men who met in Geneva beginning in December 1916.

"During a series of conversations which continued until March, the two men very delicately discussed the possibility of resolving the Alsace-Lorraine problem, through either autonomy within the Reich or the return of part of the territory to France," with some mutual control over the remainder. In exchange, France would grant Germany certain economic concessions after the war. These were just explorations, which fell apart as circumstances changed during 1917, but they indicate—just as the British had learned from French president Raymond Poincaré's discussion with the king back in August 1916—that France too was considering its peace options, but only in ways that were far out of public view.[49]

———

As 1916 came to an end, all of the warring powers had figured out how to answer Wilson's peace note. Yet none of this did much to resolve their separate war crises. What should they do about the future of the war? It was time to set plans for 1917, which would take months to coordinate and prepare.

The Germans and their allies had to decide whether the peace option was still viable. The military leaders certainly were not counting on it. They were planning to go on the strategic defensive on the ground in the West, shortening their lines. Hindenburg and the navy's commander were finalizing their own proposal to end the war. They were planning to make another big push to at last persuade the kaiser to launch a decisive submarine campaign that might bring victory, even if it widened the war by bringing America in.

In London, the new Lloyd George government still faced the same war crisis that had broken the Asquith government. There was still no evident way to bring the conflict to an end.

Lloyd George spent his first months in office flailing at efforts to develop a new "eastern" strategy aimed at Austria-Hungary, especially from Italy. Predictably, he failed. Robertson and Haig successfully maintained the focus on the western front. The plan was for yet another year of British and French offensives there.[50]

But that was only one half of the British war crisis. Could the gigantic Allied military effort be sustained? The deeper resource problems had not gone away, above all in finance.

Lloyd George might have smiled at the irony that, when he arranged the new government, Bonar Law, of all people, was the one to take McKenna's place in charge at Treasury. No one had been more skeptical about McKenna's alarms. On November 28, Law had boldly told McKenna that "there could be no slackening of the pace.... We must face victory or bankruptcy." Law was now personally in charge of carrying out that advice.

Instead, of course, Bonar Law received a cold shower of reality. A very conservative general, about to go off on the military mission to Russia that Robertson had avoided, found the new chancellor of the Exchequer so worried about the finances that he now seemed "half in love with peace proposals." To the general, Bonar Law conceded, "If America liked to refuse us money and ammunition, then we *must* make peace."[51]

The British financial situation had gone critical. The cabinet papers had long talked of Wilson's ability to cut off supplies. What they did not say, what few officials actually understood, what even Wilson himself did not really understand (because he did not know the secret details of Allied finance) was that, in effect, Wilson *had already cut off Allied supplies.*

The Federal Reserve Board's warning of November 28, the one that Wilson had helped to orchestrate, effectively killed any hope of getting large unsecured loans from US investors. That was that. The hourglass of financial reserves had now been turned over. The final reserves of gold and marketable securities that could be deposited to secure new loans were draining away, foreseeably, inexorably. "Never before was the need for exchange more critical or the task of providing it more difficult than in the months immediately following the Reserve Board's action."

For months, the British Treasury had speculated about when the golden sands in the hourglass would run out. Treasury usually guessed the reserves would last until about the end of March 1917. Based on later events, this estimate was close to the mark.

Right after the Federal Reserve Board's warning, Morgan told the British government it had to order an "immediate curtailment" of Allied purchases in the United States. The Allies wanted to do it. The British government even announced curbs.

It did no good. The government could not implement the restrictions. It could not cut back on American supplies without fundamentally reconsidering the broader British and Allied continuation of the war. American goods constituted 40 percent of British war spending; the American resource flow was larger than the entire war budget of France. Even to cut it in half would substantially constrain the scale of the Allied war effort. That would dash any illusions of wearing the Germans down. It would force Allied governments to demobilize huge numbers of soldiers and send them back into farming or industry.

So, at Treasury, John Maynard Keynes watched as Britain "dragged along with a week or two's cash in hand." Treasury officials who knew how close they were to the bottom of the barrel were afraid to frighten ministers again with the full, alarming details, for fear that this time the cabinet would immediately abandon the gold standard. That would set off a bank run—which had already come so close to happening on the afternoon of November 29.

Keynes's Treasury colleagues "had been brought up in the doctrine that in a run one must pay out one's gold reserves to the last bean." Stoically,

Britain's financial officials were doing just that, standing at the payments window, doling out what was left.[52]

Whether in Berlin or in London or in Paris, as the year 1916 drew to a close, the United States still seemed pivotal to all the thinking about 1917 and the planning for the whole future of the war. So, the question hung: What is Wilson trying to do?

# CHAPTER 8

# Peace Without Victory?

## A Worried President's Shrinking Inner Circle

Wilson had circulated his peace note on December 18. House had shrugged his shoulders. House doubted the Allies were interested at that time in making peace. Since House was resigned to waiting until Britain wanted peace, and since he had no particular ideas about how to get the British there, the adviser had become philosophical. He believed the war would just have to continue for a while longer. He now worried not about danger from Germany but about future trouble with Britain.

Wilson was not so resigned or so philosophical. He had been impatient, with the British in particular, for months. His impatience had sharpened into action: the harsh letter he had ordered House to send to Grey at the end of November and the financial measures the president had orchestrated at the same time. This distance from the Allies, especially from the British, had been growing for more than six months, ever since the high-water mark of pro-Allied feeling back in 1915–1916.[1]

Meanwhile, it was Christmastime in Washington. On Christmas weekend, 1916, the president and his wife, joined by friends and relatives, walked over to the Treasury Building next door to sing Christmas carols. The family came together to unwrap presents, play charades, and celebrate the season.

Amid the revels, Wilson was troubled about the state of his peace effort. Yes, his initial move had gained much press attention. But he quickly realized that, after more than a month of preparation, his note was a bust, having no practical effect. The dispiriting formal German reply had arrived. Though so far they were only informal, stony answers had come in from London as well.[2]

Wilson's theory behind his peace note—that each side would state war aims/peace terms to reveal the potential for compromise—was obviously not proving out. Wilson wasn't sure what to do next.

Still, the president was restless, never having lost sight of the pressure of time and events. For months, German chancellor Bethmann Hollweg's warnings about the pressure he was under had been consistent and clear. Wilson had listened. In November, Wilson had warned House that if his peace move did not succeed, America might be pulled into the war over the submarine issue.

On December 12, Walter Lippmann, one of the editors of the *New Republic*, had attended a gala dinner at the White House to celebrate the season and the president's reelection. He had become a friend to both Wilson and House. At the dinner, Lippmann pulled Wilson aside. He asked him about the German offer of peace talks announced earlier that day.

Wilson gave voice to his worries. He said he was sure the Allies would reject the German offer, given the current situation on the ground in Europe. He feared that Bethmann might have to give way to lifting restrictions on submarine warfare, unless America could do something to help.

"If they don't let me mediate, we'll be drawn into the war," Wilson confided. "We've got to stop it before we're pulled in."[3]

———

As WILSON pondered what to do next, he had no official help. He could not look to his State Department since he had lost all confidence in its chief, Robert Lansing. On their end, House, Lansing, and Frank Polk just complained to each other about Wilson's drift and apparent passivity.[4]

Polk told House he thought Wilson was "for peace almost at any price." In early January, Lansing complained to House that the president "failed to discuss international questions with him." House recorded in his diary, "As far as he [Lansing] is concerned, the State Department is sailing without a chart." The president, according to Lansing, "'sees no one and...his mind is a vacuum during your [House's] absences.'"

Lansing wanted the United States to break relations with Germany immediately, using one or another submarine incident. Wilson would not do it. Quite the contrary: Wilson told Lansing that "he did not believe the people of the United States were willing to go to war because a few Americans were killed" in some sinking of an Allied ship.[5]

House told Wilson that Lansing was unhappy. Wilson did not care. He replied bluntly that "Lansing was not in sympathy with his purpose to keep out of the war." He told House that he "came very near to asking for [Lansing's] resignation when he gave out the ['verge of war'] statement regarding the last note."

As 1917 began, Wilson was more alone than ever before. He had no use for his secretary of state. He had no use either for his ambassadors to Britain or to Germany. "The little circle close to the President," House noted in his diary, "seems to have dwindled down to the two of us: Mrs. Wilson and myself."[6] Neither Mrs. Wilson nor Mr. House had any ideas to offer about what the president should do next.

## The Bernstorff-House Peace Plan

Absent any analysis from anyone in the government, Wilson and House leaned more and more on outside thinkers for fresh ideas. During these weeks in December 1916, none were more important than a pair of editors at the *New Republic*, Walter Lippmann and Herbert Croly.

The new magazine, based in New York City and created in 1914 with an endowment from a wealthy couple, had become the leading voice for practical Progressivism. Croly was already a well-known thinker and had recruited the young Lippmann to join him. Almost instantly the magazine became "a forum for the most serious and original minds writing in English" on both sides of the Atlantic (including the newly famous poet Robert Frost).

At first, the magazine and its editors had been close to Theodore Roosevelt. During 1916, alienated by TR's pro-war talk, the editors shifted toward Wilson. They became friends of House too.

The closeness with Wilson and House ran both ways. Twice during 1916, Wilson invited Lippmann, then only twenty-seven years old, to spend time with him. "Let me show you the inside of my mind," Wilson had said. He did and turned Lippmann from skeptic to convert.

The magazine actively supported Wilson's reelection. By the winter of 1916–1917, both Lippmann and Croly were insiders, meeting frequently with House, their weekly editorials avidly followed by the White House.[7]

Lippmann and Croly entirely supported Wilson's efforts to make peace. On December 29, after Wilson's peace note, Croly wrote to House (who relayed the letter to Wilson) that both he and Lippmann were devoted to backing up the president's peace work more "than in anything else we have ever tried to do through the New Republic." They thought Wilson's peace effort was "one of the greatest enterprises ever undertaken by an American president."

Wilson reciprocated this warm support. After an informal press conference on January 8, the president pulled aside the magazine's Washington correspondent. "Write Mr. Croly and Mr. Lippmann," the president instructed. "Tell them that I appreciate the work they are doing and that I am in entire agreement with their articles on peace."[8]

The articles the president was referring to, with which he was "in entire agreement," had been outlining a peace program. Since Wilson was getting no policy analysis from his government, Lippmann and Croly, for a vital few weeks, became the most influential American source of ideas guiding Wilson and House's next moves. It is therefore worth paying close attention, as Wilson and House did, to what they wrote.

————

KNOWING NOTHING of the secret German requests for American mediation that had begun in August, the editors had welcomed the public German offer to begin peace talks, announced on December 12. "The real negotiation," the editors wrote, "if there is to be any real negotiation, will now begin." The point now was to "bring about a conference."

What should the Germans do to provide a "basis of further negotiation"? the editors asked in their issue of December 23. Their answer: the Germans should be willing to join in "an international league organized expressly for the purpose of guaranteeing security to all its members."

Then, in an essay they titled "Peace Without Victory," Lippmann and Croly turned their critical eye on Lloyd George and the British. They scoffed at the extreme war aims voiced by the "Britain of [the press baron] Northcliffe."

" 'Prussian militarism' and 'crushing Germany' might do as recruiting formulas." They "might serve to keep the nation in fighting trim, but as a guide to statesmanship they were futile. They meant everything and nothing." The editors mocked the "company of Englishmen," several of whom they named, for whom "these battle cries would mean among other things a successful offensive to the Rhine, a parade of victorious Cossacks in Berlin, weird and wonderful amputations upon Austria-Hungary, a reform of the Prussian electoral system, dethronement of the Hohenzollerns, dissolution of the German Empire into its principalities, the surrender of the German navy, and so on in a series without end."

Lippmann and Croly supposed that the British propagandists and politicians of the new Lloyd George ministry were trying to restore Britain's damaged "prestige." That was understandable. Naturally they wanted to "retrieve the loss, to erase the impression of blunder and muddle."

But Germany, they wrote, was now offering "imperial Britain peace without victory." The German terms would be "moderate." True, such a moderate peace would cement German power over "Middle Europe." That was reasonable, they thought, since Germany saw that such a future "requires a peaceful world."

The British should accept these moderate terms, a compromise peace. If they did not, "if through vanity or stubbornness they are unable to face the facts, then a refusal to negotiate is an abominable waste of life." The statesman who "refuses peace now will have to answer for it next summer, perhaps a year from next summer. Woe to him if he orphans and widows and starves a million homes and is then forced to negotiate the same peace which is offered to him now."

In other words, the editors concluded, "once Germany offers peace on moderate terms, and steals the clothes of the liberals, Mr. Lloyd George will have to perform the staggering task of explaining to the British people the politics of prestige."[9]

———

As this "Peace Without Victory" editorial was being published, the American embassy in Berlin secretly reported its own estimate of German peace terms. Germany had decided not to convey them officially. But the embassy felt it could gauge them reasonably well. "The year 1916 has seen a definite step in the growth of liberal ideas in Germany," chargé Joseph Grew concluded. The prevailing militarism of 1914–1915 had dissipated. New forms of government would probably evolve as the failures of militarism became evident.

"As a basis for discussion," Grew and his team found that "well-informed Germans" talked about certain concessions: "Belgium and northern France to be given up; France to be compensated with a part of Alsace and Lorraine; England to be compensated with certain colonial possessions." On the other hand, Germany hoped to be allowed to pursue economic development in the Middle East, "to have an influential position in the Balkans," and for "the independent Kingdom of Poland [declared in November 1916] to be continued as a buffer state" between Germany and Russia. Noting the change, Grew added, "In 1915 it would not have been possible to find a German voice to speak of the ceding of a square foot of Alsace-Lorraine."

Wilson reflected on Grew's analysis. He found it "most significant."[10]

In that same week before Christmas, Wilson also saw another interesting perspective on peace terms. This one came from London. It was relayed through private channels by maverick American diplomat William Hepburn Buckler to House and then from House on to Wilson. Buckler was passing along an analysis from a respected Liberal member of Parliament, Noel Buxton. Buxton, an occasional adviser of Lloyd George with a great deal of experience in Europe, had publicly supported Wilson's peace note.

Buckler shared a memo about war aims that Buxton had circulated to Lloyd George's new War Cabinet. In it, Buxton argued that total subjugation of Germany was both unnecessary and unwise. "The policy of aggression and the influence of the military leaders are discredited already." In fact, "the internal development of Germany towards liberal institutions would not be hastened, but would be checked by further exhaustion."

Limited terms of peace would be enough. "The renunciation of conquered lands by negotiation would be recognised in Germany as the complete failure of aggression." On the other hand, "further humiliation," Buxton warned, "would produce a degree of resentment and bitter feeling of revenge." That reaction "would obscure the unpopularity of the military school and revive aggressive policy."[11]

THE DAY after Christmas, House asked Ambassador Bernstorff to come up to see him in New York. Together they could talk about a plan for what to do next.

Bernstorff promptly took the train to New York. The next morning, Wednesday, December 27, he made his familiar way to House's apartment home in Manhattan.

House suggested what Lippmann and Croly had just recommended in the *New Republic*. The object was to set up a peace conference.

For the first time, Bernstorff was able to get down to practical work with House. The two men spoke of the need for "prior confidential negotiations" to set up a peace conference. These negotiations would set favorable conditions for Allied acceptance of the conference proposal.

On what those preconditions should be, House tracked exactly what Lippmann and Croly had recommended in the December 23 *New Republic* issue. House told Bernstorff that he did not need to hear from Berlin

*The spider in his web: House in his apartment*

about territorial offers. Those issues House called "unimportant." To Berlin, Bernstorff cabled, "As I have reported often before, Wilson attaches relatively little importance to the territorial side of peace conditions."

Instead, as Lippmann and Croly had just argued, House said the essential precondition was Germany's willingness to give the desired "guarantees for the future." If Germany could give that assurance, Bernstorff reported home, Wilson believed "he could bring the peace conference into being, for our enemies' main argument would thereby be disarmed."

House did not spell out what these "guarantees for the future" would be. Bernstorff thought he knew what was required. As he reported to Chancellor Bethmann Hollweg, "Your Excellency knows the Wilsonian ideas about such guarantees. They consist, first of all, of a limited disarmament on land and water (freedom of the seas), adjustments [of future disputes] by arbitration, and a league for peace." Recalling Bethmann's public Reichstag speech of November 8, Bernstorff was sure Germany could support all these measures.

Bernstorff noted again that the Americans had not asked, "and we shall not be obliged to agree," that the United States would take part in *all* the negotiations. The United States would not be part of the direct negotiations among the warring powers to end the war with a "preliminary peace."

The Americans were asking only that Germany bind itself to "the guarantees" that would be settled at the broader, general conference to establish postwar security and make the peace last. Then, as House had explained, Wilson would have what he needed to call for the peace conference.

These preliminary negotiations to set up the peace conference would be "absolutely confidential," House promised. Only Bernstorff, House, and Wilson would know about them. Bernstorff reported, "House is thinking of going perhaps to England himself [to conduct these talks], since there is no confidence here in the British Ambassador" (Bernstorff did not know that Wilson had been asking House to do this for more than a month).

Bernstorff asked House to confirm that Wilson approved this plan. Reporting to Wilson, House told the president that German agreement on plans for postwar security "would give us a working basis with the Entente, and would put Germany in an unassailable position." House felt "sure, if we are persistent and ingenious enough, a start can be made, and having once started, final negotiations will follow."

Wilson approved. The next day, House telegraphed the green light: "I can now advise you to proceed."[12]

With that, Bernstorff sent his report to Berlin. He asked the chancellor to give him authority to complete negotiation of the conditions for the peace conference.

At last the practical work to call the peace conference was getting under way. Bernstorff thought this was the most important diplomatic exchange with the Americans so far.

Only Wilson, he reminded Berlin, could exert the "strong pressure" to persuade the Allies to negotiate. Aside from the Belgian question, on which he already knew Germany would have to agree to a withdrawal, Bernstorff felt America's view of postwar issues would tend to be "to our advantage" because the Americans "now for the first time have found out the meaning of England's domination of the seas."

Bethmann then gave his green light. He authorized Bernstorff to proceed. But that back-and-forth took about two weeks, partly because of the roundabout processes they had to use in sending coded telegrams to each other.[13] Bernstorff did not talk to House again, armed with Bethmann's authorization to negotiate the peace conference conditions, until January 15.

## Checking In with the British

As Bernstorff was reporting to Berlin about his important meeting with House, the new prime minister of Great Britain was continuing to muse about whether, when, or how to exercise the American peace option. On December 29, about a week and a half after Wilson's peace note and a week after Wiseman had secretly confirmed that the American promise to help get moderate peace terms was still valid, David Lloyd George decided it was time to call in the American ambassador, Walter Hines Page, to set up a channel for a possible peace move.

This was Page's first meeting with Lloyd George as prime minister. Sitting in his unassuming, high-ceilinged office at Ten Downing Street, Lloyd George and the ambassador had a "very long and earnest" conversation.

Wilson's peace note had been "premature," Lloyd George told Page. He "wished that some understanding could have been reached about it before it was sent." He explained: The Allies cannot talk peace when, "as it appears on the map the Germans now have the advantage." If he consented to a peace conference under those conditions, Lloyd George said, "his Government would be swept out of power over night, and the people would become ferocious."

Lloyd George conceded that some German leaders really did want peace. Bethmann, he knew, "did not want this war" and "now withstands as best he can the fierce war spirit of his people." Even the kaiser did not want the war. Lloyd George blamed "the vast and strong military caste." They "must be defeated and permanently driven from power."

Lloyd George then came to his main point. Now that he was prime minister, he returned once again to the very argument in favor of American mediation that he had believed, and made to House, a year earlier. Wilson, the prime minister said, was "the only man in the world to bring this carnage to an end when the time for it to end should come." Only Wilson "could bring sufficient pressure on both Germany and the Allies to force an end of war."

When would that time come? Page asked.

"That's what I am coming to," Lloyd George replied. But the prime minister did not specify a time. What he wanted, for now, was "to establish a relation of confidential privacy" with Page as Wilson's representative, so that they might "talk so to speak, in an extra-ambassadorial way. I wish if the President will permit me to know his mind through you and I will open my mind to him through you." Then, when the time was right, Lloyd George would use this channel to inform Page "when conditions seem to me to call for the President's good offices."

Page reported this conversation in a message he sent directly to President Wilson, bypassing Lansing. In a supplemental message, aside from a breezy prediction that the Germans would "give in within a year—perhaps within half-a-year," Page added, "Lloyd George is one of the most energetic projectiles that I've ever watched or come in contact with. He said more in half an hour yesterday than Asquith ever told me in his life."[14]

BY TRYING to set up this channel to activate Wilson's mediation, while Arthur Balfour was also establishing his new channel in Washington, to House through William Wiseman, Lloyd George was covering his bets.

In public, of course, the new government was all about the "fight to the finish." In private, Lloyd George knew how bad the situation really was.

He had just finished a couple of days of consultations with his French allies. He was keenly aware of the financial problems. He had been there for all the recent alarms. Those had come up in the just concluded conference with the French.

Also, Lloyd George knew that all his hopes for the supposed "knockout blow" depended on persuading the generals to press for it in Italy, the Balkans, or under French command—anything but the planned offensives on the western front. Energetic and ingenious, during the coming six weeks Lloyd George would use all his guile to try to redirect the whole thrust of British military strategy.

He would fail. Part of the devil's bargain that Lloyd George had made to gain power was that he now relied on Conservative politicians and the Northcliffe press. That gave the generals ample political clout to veto Lloyd George's impractical Italian or Balkan alternatives.

Lloyd George did not yet know that his hopes for a new strategy would be dashed. Still, knowing what he did, Lloyd George could see how much could go wrong. The money to buy from America was running out, the existing military plans seemed futile, and the situation in Russia looked worse every day. So, he was preparing his American peace parachute.

———

ON THE other side of the Atlantic, House tried again to encourage the British to ask for peace mediation. In the new year, he had lunch in New York with the British ambassador, Cecil Spring-Rice, and Captain Wiseman.

If the Allies would at least "consent to peace parleys," House promised, yet again, they would have enough American political support to "get practically what they were contending for—at least Great Britain and France would." After all, "[American] sympathies were with them and would continue to be provided they were moderate in their demands."

House then added an important idea, one that had come up before with Wilson back in November. All the professionals who had looked at peace talks issues had puzzled over the problem of indemnities for damaged Belgium and other occupied countries. Each side wanted the other to pay for the damages. Payment of indemnities implied fault and punishment.

House "was in favor of the United States rehabilitating Belgium, Poland and Serbia, if by doing so we could facilitate the making of peace." The United States might help break the coming logjam about who would pay for recovery and reconstruction.

This was not an exotic idea. With the particular leadership of Herbert Hoover, the United States was already playing an unprecedented role as an impartial provider of private humanitarian relief in Belgium and northern France. The United States was trying to extend that precedent to Poland. House's suggestion could not only help address a big potential problem in the peacemaking but also give the United States added indirect leverage in the conference of the belligerents about how to end the war.

House directed most of these renewed assurances to Spring-Rice, who was senior to Wiseman. However, Spring-Rice does not appear to have reported any of this back to London.[15]

## Wilson Has a New Idea

As the new year, 1917, began, Lippmann and Croly had a new set of peacemaking ideas. They detailed them in the lead editorial of their December 30 issue of the *New Republic*.

First, they wrote, as they had in the previous issue, that Germany must "pledge that she will join a league of nations, and that she will solemnly agree to submit all disputes to inquiry before acting." These guarantees for future security, they said, were more important than "territorial details." This language mirrored what House had told Bernstorff on December 27. That is probably no coincidence, since House and Lippmann had conferred together on December 28.

The editors then added three other conditions they thought that Germany must accept "as an earnest of good faith." These were (1) "the principle of no annexation of invaded territory except as part of an exchange," (2) "willingness to restore Belgium," and (3) "readiness to consider a reduction in armaments." These were reasonable arguments. They did not know it, but Germany had already secretly conceded the Belgium point to Wilson. Bernstorff had just asked for permission to agree to the third point, and the first was plausible, consistent with language in Bethmann's November 8 Reichstag speech.

In this editorial though, Lippmann and Croly did not set these up—as they had the last time—as practical preconditions to persuade the Allies to accept a peace conference. This time they offered a very different strategic concept. They argued that Wilson should set these as *his* conditions for *American* consent to get involved in the peace process at all. These principles could be set as "the minimum conditions on which the United States will consent to participation in European politics," they said, striking a lordly pose.

Also, the editors expected Wilson's next move would be some sort of public pronouncement of these conditions for American involvement. Instead of the "absolutely confidential" negotiation of preconditions for a peace conference, the diplomatic work that House and Bernstorff had discussed, the editors were calling for a big presidential speech. In this speech, the editors thought the president should "continue to address the peoples behind the governments" and thus "do an immense propaganda for international good faith."

The editors were thus offering no plan for secret diplomacy at all. Theirs was a plan to influence public opinion, including opinion in America. But the editors, in this issue, offered no apparent follow-on idea of just how this speech was supposed to then lead to peace talks.[16]

———

RIGHT AFTER the new year, Wilson again summoned House to Washington to work with him on the president's next peace move. House and his secretary arrived at the White House on January 3. House joined Wilson's wife and one of his daughters at dinner that evening. Then, after dinner, he and the president got to work.

Wilson read aloud to House the long, confidential message he had received from Page in London, the report about the meeting with Lloyd George, in which the prime minister revived his interest in Wilson's mediation and urged setting up a confidential channel, through Page, to work on this when the time was right. Page began the message by noting he was writing "at midnight." House poked fun at this melodramatic tone. He wondered if Page was going to give them "a Sherlock Holmes recital." He found Page's report "long" and "rambling."

To Wilson, Page's message seemed unimportant. House, for all his scorn for Page, was very attentive to news about Lloyd George's thinking. He must have noticed the significance of the prime minister's turnabout on Wilson's mediation and his effort to reopen a channel for peace discussions. For his diary, he said only that Page's report had "more importance I think than the President accorded it."

Wilson ignored Lloyd George's message. He never responded directly to the prime minister or to Page.

The message did prompt Wilson again to think of asking Page to resign. Mrs. Wilson was sitting in on this conversation. She suggested that House take Page's place. The President seconded her suggestion.

"However," House dictated later, "it did not take me three minutes to persuade him it would not be wise since it would confine my activities to Great Britain and I would not even be able to go to France in the event it were necessary for me to do so, much less, to Germany."

Wilson ended up just leaving Page in place.[17]

Then, Wilson presented to House a whole new peace plan idea. The president wanted to lay out his general principles for a settlement of the war. The "keystone of the settlement arch" would be plans for postwar security. That would be the focus of the plan, "letting territorial adjustments be subordinate to the main purpose." Wilson would present these as the principles that would justify American participation in such a postwar system. He would explain all this in a public statement.[18]

Wilson was outlining to House the same approach Lippmann and Croly had just advocated in the *New Republic*. Tracking Lippmann and Croly, Wilson pushed to one side the territorial issues involved in ending the war itself and framed the ideas as principles for American participation in the postwar settlement.[19] Still mirroring Lippmann and Croly, he ignored, or at least put off, the issue of actually convening a peace conference. His principles were conditions for *American* involvement, not for getting the warring powers to the peace table. Also, in line with Lippmann and Croly's most recent proposal, he would do all this as a public speech, not a plan for secret preliminary negotiations.

House entirely endorsed Wilson's new plan. He was "enthusiastic" about it. What is more, he took credit for it. Probably because Wilson was so strongly emphasizing the postwar guarantees, not the territorial issues to end the war, he thought Wilson had outlined "the exact proposal I outlined to Bernstorff."

With such happy concord about what to do next, the two men then had a long, airy discussion about what general principles Wilson should endorse in the speech, such as self-determination. They wondered if they should throw in support for an independent Poland, since both sides seemed to be conceding that. Obviously, Belgium and Serbia would become independent countries again. "Alsace and Lorraine we were not quite certain of, but we agreed that Turkey should cease to exist." This last comment led to a digression about whether the US ambassador to Constantinople should be given time "to flee the country" before the president made such a statement.

Since Wilson would just be giving a speech, they thought the ideas "would be largely our own concern" and "could not be construed as meddling" in the peace terms of the warring powers. Wilson's speech would only be setting up *American* preconditions, "a statement of the terms upon which we would be willing to join in a league to enforce peace."

House urged Wilson to go all out. He should turn his speech into the most high-profile public event possible, an address to Congress. "You are now playing," House said, "with what the poker players term 'the blue chips.'"

Wilson agreed. His December peace note, now two weeks old, was put behind them. They turned their focus to "this other and more important move."[20]

––––––––––

HOUSE DICTATED to his diary that Wilson's speech plan was "the exact proposal I outlined to Bernstorff." It was not. It was not at all what Bernstorff thought they had discussed.

To the chancellor, Bernstorff had excitedly cabled agreement on a reasonably clear, practical way to proceed. The Germans were to agree to conditions that the United States would use to win Allied agreement to a peace conference.

As to those conditions, Bernstorff had carefully noted, and House's diary agrees, that the Germans were asked to agree to support postwar security plans, "guarantees for the future." The Germans were not asked to agree in advance on any territorial adjustments, except to withdraw from

Belgium. In the December 27 meeting, House was echoing the December 23 issue of the *New Republic* in the context of conditions for a peace conference.

Yet Wilson's new plan, which he presented to House in their January 3 meeting, had nothing directly to do with preparing the way for a peace conference at all, at least not in the immediately foreseeable future. Wilson's new plan had no diplomatic action attached to it. He was not winning German agreement to the conditions that would help him sell peace talks to the Allies. He was setting up conditions for whether America would deign to participate in peacemaking at all. If anything, the new American language had taken a step backward from actively engaging in the resolution of the conflict.

Setting conditions on American participation was equally likely to disturb the Allies. They already wondered whether they could credibly rely on the United States to help with postwar security. Couching the planned speech in this lofty way, telling the belligerents how to earn American involvement, certainly did not make a future US role *more* credible.

House does not appear to have grasped either of these potential concerns, among the Germans or among the British and French. He did not tell Wilson that a very different sort of plan was now in motion with the German government, a plan that Bernstorff thought had been expressly approved by Wilson.

It is possible that House and Bernstorff had simply misunderstood each other, despite some evident common understanding on some of the substantive points. Since childhood, Bernstorff had been quite fluent in English, and he was a deeply experienced diplomat. He probably understood House. Yet it is possible that House did not quite understand the operational side of the diplomacy in the way Bernstorff did, which could explain why House's report about it to Wilson was so fuzzy and vague.

Another, more cynical theory is that House could not have been so incompetent. In this theory, House instead was cleverly and deliberately sabotaging the peace process, conniving to drive America into the war. The question, which comes up in more than one episode in this story, can be boiled down to, Was House a fool or a villain?

A bit of both, perhaps. House did want a compromise peace. Yet he did dissemble. He was an observant man and a gifted player of people.

But his analysis of the world situation was dilettantish and superficial. The quality of his thought did not approach that of Wilson or men of ideas like Lippmann and Croly. Nor was he gifted or experienced in the craft of making or executing policy, such as the construction of a negotiation to end the war. On those sorts of operational tasks, he was usually influenced or instructed by others.

Wilson's reliance on House was a measure of Wilson's aloofness and conceit. Both men recognized the good quality of advice they were getting from some of the diplomats in the immature American service, men like Buckler and young Grew, but they did not empower such men or elevate them into positions of operational responsibility. They did flirt briefly with the idea of putting Buckler in place of Page at the embassy in London but did not act on it.

House was consistent in at least one respect: at all times he sought to avoid a confrontation with British leaders, especially the English Liberals with whom he and Wilson had long identified. Unlike Wilson, though, House would much rather go to war with Germany than have trouble with Britain. Also, if the British leaders were not ready to make peace, House, unlike Wilson, was content to wait until they were. If that led to American involvement in the war, House was philosophical. So, to House, if Wilson wanted to give a high-minded speech, with principles that House liked, so much the better.

After the evening conversation at the White House on January 3, Wilson embarked on preparing for the peace speech. Lloyd George's plea to open a confidential channel was ignored. In Germany, the leaders debated how to respond to Bernstorff's request for authority to negotiate a different sort of peace plan they thought Wilson had endorsed.

## Wilson's Realistic, Conservative, Surreal Proposal

For a week, Wilson worked on the draft speech. By January 11, he was satisfied and showed it to House, who made only a couple of minor suggestions. Through Senate Foreign Relations Committee chair William Stone, the Senate agreed to hear the president's address. Wilson arranged with Lansing to send the text out ahead of time to the major foreign capitals.

This was still an age in which such public papers were meant primarily to be read, not heard.

"We shall have no voice in determining" the terms for ending the war, Wilson said in his address. But the peace terms could influence whether a future league could keep the peace. "There must be," Wilson contended, "not a balance of power, but a community of power, not organized rivalries, but an organized common peace."

That meant, above all, that there had to be a "peace without victory," not a peace of conquest and humiliation. The peace had to accept "the principle that governments derive all their just powers from the consent of the governed, and that no right anywhere exists to hand peoples about from sovereignty to sovereignty as if they were property."

Wilson also proposed "that all nations henceforth avoid entangling alliances which would draw them into competitions of power, catch them in a net of intrigue and selfish rivalry, and disturb their own affairs with influences intruded from without." His core principles were "consent of the governed," "freedom of the seas," and "moderation of armaments." They were the foundation for later, more elaborate versions of such principles, like the set that, a year later, would be issued as his "Fourteen Points."

Wilson leaned on the phrase "peace without victory." He had borrowed it from the title of the essay, so critical of the British, in the December 23 issue of the *New Republic*.[21] But Wilson's diagnosis of the world situation was his own.

As in his earlier peace note, Wilson was realistic in his general analysis of the war and of American interests. He was realistic in assessing how difficult it would be for either side to win an absolute victory. "I am seeking," he wrote, "only to face realities and to face them without soft concealments."

Wilson was realistic, too, in arguing that a compromise peace might be more durable than a peace built on conquest and humiliation. "Only a peace between equals can last."

Wilson's approach to the European settlement, like that of the moderates in Berlin, Vienna, London, and Paris, was also fundamentally conservative. He did not endorse the official Allied call for a "reorganization of Europe." Instead he deferred the question of territorial terms to a negotiation among the warring powers, urging respect for the sovereignty of all organized nations, large and small.

Wilson emphasized the importance of the "consent of the governed" as a basis for enduring peace, but he did not criticize any existing empire or its constitutional arrangements. His only illustration of this principle was to endorse a "united, independent, and autonomous Poland." This was actually the Germans' official position, since they had just re-created a Polish state. It was not the official position of the Allies (among whom Russia still wanted its Polish territories back).

Wilson did implicitly criticize the Ottoman as well as the Russian Empire by also saying that some "security of life, of worship, and of industrial and social development" should be granted to people living "under the power of governments devoted to a faith and purpose hostile to their own." But, in saying that, Wilson made clear that he was not trying to "exalt an abstract political principle."

Instead, he wished "frankly to uncover realities," because "any peace which does not recognize and accept this principle will inevitably be upset." This was not an unreasonable reading of the recent history of the Balkans or the Ottoman domains.

Wilson was not seeking to overthrow and reorder the Austro-Hungarian Empire. He was certainly not hoping to reorganize Germany. Such extravagant Allied war aims were exactly what Lippmann and Croly had ridiculed in their essay "Peace Without Victory."

Wilson did advance an important concept for the future of international relations. In an age when warfare had become so terrifying and encompassing, a "community of power" might, he thought, actually be more viable, in the long run, than reliance on endless rivalries. The notion of a "community of power" might seem idealistic. It was not idealistic to appraise the unprecedented catastrophic wreckage of the world at war and conclude that a different sort of system might be worth a try.

It might seem that Wilson was being more radical in his call for a postwar league of nations. Yet that idea had not originated with him; nor was he its lead developer. One key originator, the British government, through then foreign secretary Edward Grey, had moved from private encouragement to public endorsement of the league idea in October 1916.

Responding, the German government, through Bethmann, had endorsed it as well a couple of weeks later.[22]

But in another sense, Wilson's draft speech was surreal. It was simply detached from the diplomatic realities. Nothing in it was practically connected to an actual negotiation. Nothing in it actually advanced a plan or exerted direct pressure to get the warring powers to the peace table anytime soon.

As Wilson was drafting his speech, he did keep hearing clamor for a more practical peace move. In their January 6 issue, Lippmann and Croly came back to their earlier stress on preconditions for a peace conference, the restoration of Belgium leading the list. Wilson's job now, they wrote, was to prepare the negotiations.[23] But Wilson was already launched in a different direction, the one they had advocated a week earlier.

During House's January 11 visit to look over the draft speech, Wilson read to him another letter he had received from Buckler, his London embassy contact. The "negotiation group" in Britain's Parliament favored secret preliminary negotiations to set up the conditions for a peace conference, Buckler reported.

It "would save time and misunderstanding," the British parliamentarians suggested, "if certain bedrock principles (e.g., evacuation of France and Belgium) could be fixed at the outset, [with] no negotiations to begin until this minimum had been accepted by Germany."[24] This was exactly the sort of plan for a preliminary negotiation that the Germans had been ready for since August, including the anticipation of this very request.

But these more practical suggestions made no visible impression on Wilson. He had drafted his speech. He would deliver it to the Senate on January 22. At that moment he had no other diplomatic plan to end the war.

––––––––

BRITISH INTELLIGENCE officer Captain Wiseman checked in again with House. He came up to House's pleasant Manhattan apartment, calling on a Saturday morning, January 13. He wondered what was going on. Was Wilson still working on making peace? Now that the Allies had responded to Wilson's December peace note, was that chapter closed?

Oh no, House assured him. There was much more to come. "We had just begun."

The war would go on for some time, House expected. He and Wilson believed it was probably entering a last phase until the two sides were finally ready to seek peace. Maybe, he told Wiseman, that would take "another six months, ten months, or a year." House "thought the Allies would have plenty of time to find out whether their spring and summer offensives would be effective"—not that he or America's military advisers expected the coming offensives to make any great change.

House had settled back into his usual diffident, philosophical perspective, waiting for the British to make a move. Two weeks earlier, he and Bernstorff had agreed that the German ambassador was to get authority to agree to the conditions that Wilson could take to the Allies, to help persuade them (along with other American leverage) to sit down to peace talks. Then, House had seemed to share Bernstorff's sense of urgency. He spoke of possibly going to England to carry out this mission. But here he was, two weeks later, resignedly imagining another year of war.

Bernstorff had immediately sought the authority to cut the deal on preconditions for a peace conference. The reply from Berlin could come at any moment (in fact, it had just arrived). But House had done nothing to prepare any new mission to Europe. He had not even raised the possibility of such a mission with Wilson, even as Wilson discarded Lloyd George's request to set up a back channel to discuss Wilson's possible mediation.

Instead, House told Wilson he might take a vacation that month. He wanted to visit friends and family in Texas. Either he did not quite comprehend what Bernstorff was doing or he did not care much, since the British were silent. Wilson asked House to stay around at least until after the big speech. House agreed.[25]

———

To some on the other side of the Atlantic on that wintry day, to those closer to the battlefields, closer to the daily grinding of the deadly mills, this casualness might have been hard to understand. On January 21, the day before Wilson delivered his address to the Senate, his ambassador to Paris, William Graves Sharp, relayed a plea for action. Sharp knew of Wilson's planned address, which he thought was good. But Sharp pressed Wilson to get the German terms and move.

Sharp had been prodded by a senior conservative minister in the French government. That minister hoped all would go well for the Allies.

However, he "still earnestly deplored the fact that unless terms of peace could be quickly agreed upon, the coming months would witness a terrible sacrifice of life on both sides." The French minister did not think his side could win a complete victory or that such a victory would yield a permanent peace. Wasn't there more Wilson could do?

This plea made a deep impression on Sharp. To the French minister, "terrible sacrifice of life on both sides" was no remote abstraction. He had already "lost two most promising sons in this war." And sentiment like this, the ambassador observed, was growing. More and more French leaders were privately hoping Wilson would act very soon. Once the great offensives began again, "another million lives will have been given up before any pause can be made to heed a further call to peace."[26]

"Another million lives" might have sounded a bit extreme. It turned out to be a large understatement.

# CHAPTER 9

# Roads Not Taken

## The Chancellor Authorizes Bernstorff to Make the Deal

Berlin is a cold city in the winter. The days tend to be windy, cloudy, and wet. Night comes early. "The weather is most depressing," the American ambassador wrote home. "Dark and rain every day. All hands seem cross."

Berlin gossip was that the kaiser "was losing his mind and spent all his time praying and learning Hebrew." Food was short. "Potato" ration cards had to be presented in restaurants and hotels. To save fuel, all apartment houses closed by nine and turned out their lights.

For months, Chancellor Bethmann Hollweg had fought to keep the peace road open. But the military leaders were now pressing their plans for 1917. The generals and admirals thought Bethmann and his diplomats had had their chance. Public opinion and political opinion in the Reichstag wanted to let the U-boats loose, to starve the enemy as Germans were being starved.[1]

To these military leaders and their conservative allies, it seemed that the Allies had dismissed the Central Powers' December offer to open peace talks. Wilson seemed reluctant to do anything. His peace note struck them as pious nonsense or part of a British plot. It had gone nowhere.

Very well then, if there would be no peace, then in 1917 the military leaders were determined to take charge of the war. They drew up their plans, an odd mix of confidence and despair. On the ground, the army would go on the strategic defensive. It would trim its lines in the West, readying itself to be the anvil, to break whatever hammer was swung against it—in the West or East.

Yet the military leadership was also worried and impatient. To just tough it out, to let the other side wear itself out, went against their grain. Culturally, they were believers in a decisive blow, tending to regard a defensive posture as a recipe for defeat.

For the German high command, the path to victory in 1917 was at sea. The navy had built many more submarines. Before Christmas, the naval staff had worked up an analysis that predicted a probable victory with the U-boat weapon within six months. Paul von Hindenburg and Erich von Ludendorff were in complete agreement.[2]

This, they thought, was now an issue for the military to decide. They reported to the kaiser, not to the chancellor. It was time to put their boots down. If Bethmann resisted, he would have to go.

————

AROUND CHRISTMASTIME, Bethmann started hearing about these fresh military plans being readied in Pless. There was finally no alternative but to take another long trip to Pless in person and see if he could hold off Hindenburg and Ludendorff. He, Vice-chancellor Karl Helfferich, and his deputy at the Foreign Office, Arthur Zimmermann (who had replaced Gottlieb von Jagow in November), took the overnight train down to Pless on the night of December 28–29.

They were prepared to make a concession to the navy. They would tell the Americans that U-boats should be able to sink *armed* merchant ships without warning. A U-boat that surfaced in range to warn a targeted ship would also be in range of guns on such a ship. More and more merchantmen were being armed in just that way. Such an exception to the *Sussex* pledge would allow most of the attacks the navy might want.

Bethmann, Helfferich, and Zimmermann trudged into the Pless palace, amid all the uniforms, and met with Hindenburg and Ludendorff. The field marshal and the general were haughty, barely civil. The military pocketed the "armed merchantmen" concession and then insisted that anyway, by February, the full unrestricted submarine campaign must commence.

That was not all. The high command now also had a view on peace terms or, as they saw it, war aims. The army and navy now had an expansive list of demands. For instance, just in Belgium, they wanted Germany to retain control of the Flanders coast so as to be able to wage a maritime war against England if need be.

Bethmann had received a preview of the coming renewal of a push for large war aims. Just the previous week, the Prussian leader of the right-wing Conservative Party group in the Reichstag, Count Kuno von Westarp, had tried out the same "Flanders coast" idea.

Bethmann was having none of it. He had rounded fiercely on Westarp. He was "quite astonished" by such a suggestion. "Do you really believe that the peace and the future of Germany can only be maintained by war-like threats and by fear?" After a war like this, "in the next twenty to thirty years, no one could lead [Germany] to war again." It was a mistake to set war aims that would throw away any good chance for peace. And, Bethmann added, these were political matters. On such issues, the authority of the "political branch" of the government was clear.[3]

But now he faced the commanding generals. To Hindenburg, the U-boat war was a matter of military strategy. The war aims were a matter of military necessity. The generals insisted they had the authority to decide. If the kaiser did not agree, Hindenburg threatened to resign. He would absolve himself of responsibility for a war effort he could not lead.

This was a powerful threat. Hindenburg, more than any other person, had become the patriotic symbol of the war effort to most Germans. At this stage of the war, given his stature, a breakup of the imperial government would be a shattering blow.

The dispute was left unsettled. Heading back from Pless to Berlin on the long, winter train ride, Bethmann could see that, this time around, he had few cards left to play, unless the peace option came to life.

———

THIS WAS the grim background when, on January 3, a few days after this confrontation, Bethmann received Ambassador Bernstorff's cable about his breakthrough meeting with House. It was a ray of sunshine in the winter gloom. Bernstorff reported that he and House had agreed on a possible deal that would allow the Americans to go to the Allies and prepare a peace conference. Bethmann leapt at this opportunity.

Though Wilson's December peace note had not started a peace process, Wilson's rhetoric, implying a compromise peace, had struck a resonant chord in the German press. Editors in the political center and on the left encouraged Germany to respond positively to Wilson's call for a compromise peace.

Preparing his reply to Bernstorff, Bethmann promptly drafted a summary outline of notional peace terms, not only for Germany but for all the Central Powers. He still assumed that any statement of peace terms had to include room for give-and-take. He counted on Bernstorff's promise that Wilson would treat this information with "absolute discretion."[4]

Hindenburg had chided Bethmann for his willingness to be flexible. He insisted on knowing Bethmann's bottom line, his "minimum territorial demands."

Bethmann refused to state them. "Policy," he replied, "was always the art of the attainable." Once "the time comes for us to take our places" at the conference table, the main job would be to take advantage of opportunities that arose in the negotiations. "The exercise of moderation in our demands in one direction would naturally make it possible for us to increase our demands in the other."[5]

---

BERNSTORFF HAD said the Americans were interested in assurances about Germany's stand on "guarantees for the future" and that Wilson continued to put "relatively little value on the territorial side of peace negotiations." Zimmermann thus persuaded Bethmann that, given this American disinterest, he did not need to send a full outline of the territorial peace terms to Bernstorff.

Bethmann approved Zimmermann's redrafted instructions, which gave Bernstorff the authority he had requested to make the deal with Wilson. As House and Bernstorff had discussed, Wilson's direct mediation in the actual peace talks of the warring powers was still not desired or expected. Bernstorff did not yet need to get into discussion of all the territorial peace terms.

Bernstorff was given authority to agree on all the "guarantees for the future" that Wilson might want. The Germans expected that these guarantees would be handled in the other set of negotiations at the peace conference, what they called the "second convention," on postwar security. Germany would support arbitral settlement of disputes, a league of peace, work on disarmament, and freedom of the seas.

Germany was even willing to proceed now to sign an arbitration agreement and a "Bryan treaty." This was a form of bilateral treaty that, in 1913 and 1914, the Wilson administration had successfully concluded with a number of states, including Britain and France, promising that conflicts would be examined by an arbitral commission for a year before any dispute would then be resolved with force.

If Wilson or House did ask about the territorial peace terms to end the war, Bernstorff was authorized to say that Germany's terms would be "very moderate," reasonable in contrast to those just announced by the Allies in their reply to Wilson's December note. For instance, Berlin reminded Bernstorff that Germany did not want to annex Belgium.

Assuming that Bernstorff would have no trouble making the deal for Wilson to go to work on the Allies to set up the peace conference, Berlin wanted to know how Wilson planned to proceed. What pressure would he exert on the Allies to get them to accept peace negotiations? How would the United States use its ample leverage?

Only such pressure, Bethmann warned, mindful of his recent confrontation with Hindenburg, could eliminate the German "necessity" to proceed with unrestricted submarine warfare. And if there was any way to go ahead with such a U-boat war without a break with America, Berlin would be glad to hear of it.[6]

## "Peace Much More Quickly Than I Thought Possible"

As soon as he received the message with this green light from Berlin, Bernstorff contacted House. He arranged to come up to New York to see House on Monday morning, January 15.

Bernstorff had already given Secretary of State Robert Lansing the German note stating that, from now on, U-boats would attack armed merchant ships without giving warning. Having delivered that message, Bernstorff asked Berlin to delay, if it could, actually torpedoing any civilian ships without warning at such a delicate time.[7]

Reading the instructions asking what Wilson planned to do to pressure the Allies, the ambassador was struck, again, that Berlin still did not seem to have grasped the significance of the Federal Reserve Board warning against Allied loans on November 28. Bernstorff understood that "in this way the American source of funds was practically cut off."[8] Berlin did not seem to comprehend this. Bernstorff felt the pressure to find some other way to reassure Berlin that the Americans were preparing to act—soon.

Sitting in House's living room on that Monday morning, the two men spoke for an hour. Somehow, Bernstorff jolted House into realizing just what had been set in motion by their conversation back on December 27. House appeared to grasp, perhaps for the first time, that there was really no reason why Wilson could not, right away, just demand that the Allies go to a peace conference.

House was electrified. He wrote to Wilson, "To my mind, this is the most important communication we have had since the war began." It "gives a real basis for negotiations and for peace." To his diary he added that the German readiness was more forthcoming than any statement "made by any of the belligerents."

Using his instructions, Bernstorff assured House that, as to territorial terms to end the war, Germany's were "very moderate," and they did not intend to take "any part of Belgium." Bernstorff also suggested that one way to finesse differences between the two sides was to talk about the principle of "mutual" restoration of territory, reparations, and indemnities, so that it was clear both sides would make concessions.

As for the postwar "guarantees" that Wilson and House had stressed, Bernstorff gave them the full set. Germany, he said, would support a league of nations, support limiting armaments, and support arbitration of disputes. It was willing, right away, to sign a "Bryan treaty."

None of these points—as on Belgium or the league—actually reflected any change in the positions of the German government. As Bethmann and Bernstorff and as the American embassy in Berlin had consistently reported, the United States had or could have obtained assurances like these at any time since September.

Believing he had met all of Wilson's preconditions, Bernstorff pressed for the president to now do his part. He should "submit a *program* for a peace conference." Wilson could specify the date, the place, like The Hague, and any conditions, using the assurances Bernstorff had provided. Germany was ready to accept.

House, who had been so passive a few days earlier when he mused about the war continuing through 1917, was suddenly energized. Later that day, British intelligence agent Captain William Wiseman also came around to House's apartment. House told Wiseman how excited he was. He was effusive about what must be happening in Germany. The liberals in Berlin "must now be in the ascendancy." Germany "is determined to make peace." Wiseman promptly reported this to London.

————

HOUSE FOLLOWED up the next day with another note to Wilson, as still more evidence came in about London's possible readiness for a peace move. Letters arrived from William Hepburn Buckler, his diplomatic contact in London, and others. Buckler spotlighted Britain's financial vulnerability.

Another letter House relayed to Wilson, from an American friend, re-counted a long talk with Reginald McKenna, Britain's former Treasury secretary. McKenna "said the President could force the Allies to their knees any time in a moment." The Lloyd George government would try to "jolly the President along" at least through the next big offensives in the spring, McKenna predicted. But those offensives were likely to fail, McKenna thought, except for some more wearing down of the hungry Germans.

House also seemed to awaken, again perhaps for the first time, to just how much leverage America had over Britain. He was quite taken with McKenna's line about the power to "force the Allies to their knees." All in all, he had to admit, he wrote to Wilson, "it seems to me that…you stand in a position to bring about peace much more quickly than I thought possible."

The Germans were consenting "to almost everything that liberal opinion in democratic countries have demanded." Their government was now "completely in the hands of the liberals," the war had "cut so deeply into the very heart of the nation that their entire attitude seems changed," and the Germans were taking "a stand as advanced as any of the democracies."

"It was a nice question," House wrote Wilson, whether it would be better to wait and try to make peace later in 1917. If they waited, the British might be humbled some more after another spring and summer of fruit-less offensives and "unbridled" German submarine warfare. House recom-mended, though, that Wilson act immediately.

House told a visiting British MP that Wilson's aim "was to reach an end of the war before the next offensive took place." With German escala-tion of submarine warfare added in, England might well lose a continued "war of exhaustion." Britain could not win the war on the battlefield. "He knew it and England knew it."

House told Wilson he was ready to write to Lloyd George and Foreign Secretary Arthur Balfour and to tell them of this German interest in making peace. He was already thinking again of following up with a trip to London. "In my opinion, the best interests of the Allies and ourselves would be met by taking Germany at her word and concluding peace as speedily as possible."[9]

———

BERNSTORFF REPORTED back to Berlin. He said he did not yet know what Wilson would do, aside from a planned speech to summon support from the American people. "Only this much is certain," he wrote, "that, at the moment, the President has no other idea but to promote peace, and toward this end he is striving with utmost energy and all possible means."

Bernstorff believed Wilson did not want a conflict over submarines: "I hope also for a *modus vivendi* on the question of armed merchant ships."

Bernstorff urged his government to be deliberate, to take its time. Events were moving in Germany's direction. Even the mere threat of a loss of American supplies would "suffice to force our enemies to a conference." The leaders in Berlin should be cautious, he warned, "so that no conflict breaks out before the President has taken further steps."[10]

Bernstorff had assessed the situation correctly. He was right that Wilson did not want to pick a fight over a submarine incident. The new German position was that its U-boats would not warn armed merchant ships and that more and more such ships were being armed. Even Lansing found this hard to deny.

Lansing endured an awful confrontation with the British ambassador, Cecil Spring-Rice, on the issue of armed merchant ships. As a neutral country, America was not supposed to host armed ships of either side. Lansing therefore thought it was wrong for Britain to man its cargo ships with trained gunners.

Spring-Rice lost control of himself. " 'You mean to say then,' the British ambassador cried in a hoarse voice, 'that, while scores of lives are being taken by those damned submarines, you propose to prevent our guns from being properly served and so deprive us of our only means of protection...'

His face twitched, his eyes blazed, and his hands clenched until the knuckles showed white."

Lansing said nothing.

Both men stood up. Spring-Rice leaned toward Lansing and "fairly hissed out," "You and the President will be personally responsible" as "helpless people are murdered."

Lansing asked Spring-Rice to think about what he was saying.

Spring-Rice sat down, teared up, and, twitching, profusely apologized for his outburst.[11]

––––––––––

THE BOTTOM line, House confided frankly to Wiseman the following week, was clear. "During peace conversations, and while there is any chance of peace, the submarine issues now pending will not be pressed by the United States."[12]

Wilson was as steadfast as ever in his determination not to let America get pulled into the war. He would not be provoked by some submarine incident.

Earlier in January, at a lunch just of the two men and Mrs. Wilson, House had mentioned that the United States was unprepared, if a war did start. Wilson did not accept the premise.

"There will be no war," Wilson replied. "This country does not intend to become involved in this war. We are the only one of the great White nations that is free from war today, and it would be a crime against civilization for us to go in."[13]

## The Confused President Tries to Reset

While House was getting excited, Wilson was preoccupied with his planned "peace without victory" speech to the Senate. That speech was set for delivery the next week. Reading the flurry of reports and letters coming from House in New York, at first, he found the news "more than I have yet been able to digest."

Adding to the confusion, House garbled the news that Germany was ready to sign a "Bryan treaty," agreeing to set up a process to arbitrate international disputes. House wrote that Germany was "willing to submit to *arbitration* as a means of peace," seeming to imply an arbitration to end the whole world war. This did not seem plausible to Wilson, who asked for clarification.

House was telling him that Wilson should now proceed to set up the peace conference. What was he supposed to do? Wilson did not know. He did not seem to grasp that the ball was in his court—that he should draft the peace conference call and persuade Britain and France, at least, to accept it. "It is most difficult," he wrote to House, "to see now what our next move should be with regard to the German proposals—how we should handle the changed case [though its substance had not really changed] which Bernstorff has put in our hands."

Wilson asked House to help him. What should he do? How should he guide Congress?

But House was confused too. As for Wilson's "originating a programme" for a peace conference, Wilson did not understand that either. "I suppose he meant merely a plan."

Wilson did not quite understand the concept of a preliminary negotiation about conditions for a peace conference. Nor had he given any thought to the possibility of an armistice while a conference took place or to the terms for such a cease-fire.

Instead, Wilson thought he was being asked to devise a plan for his leadership at the peace conference itself. But he did not get that this first meant he had to set up the conference. "I take it for granted [Bernstorff] did not mean that his government would like me to outline [peace] terms which form a basis for discussion." So, the president was puzzled.[14]

---

BERNSTORFF, BACK in Washington, tried to clear up all this confusion. He and House exchanged a rapid series of letters delivered by couriers to and from House, who as usual was in New York. Bernstorff cleared up that a "Bryan treaty" would not affect the current war or inhibit American complaints about submarine issues.

Bernstorff then went over how the peace conference would have to work, with its two sets of negotiations. The first set, a "conference of the belligerents," would lead to a preliminary treaty of peace. Wilson should also "submit a program for the general conference," which would go beyond just the warring powers and include major neutrals, "concerning the guarantees for the future." Germany had been asked to support the "guarantees," and so it had.

Meanwhile, House was also consulting with the British through Wiseman. House was more and more impressed with the young officer, considering him, as he wrote Wilson, "the most sensible Englishman... connected with the Embassy here since the war began."

Wiseman, of course, wanted to know about the territorial terms to end the war. At a minimum, if just to have the intelligence, he wanted to know what terms the Germans would propose.

A few weeks earlier, House had told Bernstorff such territorial terms were "unimportant" to the United States. He and Wilson cared only about German agreement on "guarantees for the future."

Now House changed his position. He decided the Germans had not really given the Americans what they needed to know. "They are only definite as to the future," House wrote to Wilson, "and it is the present you must know about before you can act."

House presented this new demand to Bernstorff. He wanted to know Germany's territorial terms to end the war. The German ambassador did not bother to chide House about this shift. He wrote to him only, "I am afraid it will be very difficult to get any more peace terms from Berlin at this time."

"The situation in Berlin is getting out of our hands," Bernstorff cautioned House. Public opinion in Germany was infuriated by the (just published) formal Allied answer to Wilson's December peace note. This Allied answer called for "the reorganization of Europe" with national liberation. Bernstorff warned that these "exorbitant demands" were hurting "our peace plans."

The Germans "are slippery customers" was the way House summarized this to Wilson. "It is difficult to pin them down to anything definite." In fact, the German communications had been reasonably clear. House was still upbeat, though, believing "that at the moment the liberal element [had] control of the German Government."[15]

The better news, House reported to Wilson, was that he was working with Wiseman on what to do next. House was now beginning to meet or talk with Wiseman almost every day.

To a remarkable, peculiar degree, the British officer was indeed guiding House on how to proceed. House sought his advice on "how to outwit the German diplomacy."

Wiseman, who had no evident instructions on how to guide President Wilson's adviser, made suggestions quite similar to what Bernstorff or British parliamentarians had also proposed, explaining how to conduct the preliminary negotiation to set up peace talks. The United States could propose a peace conference, Wiseman explained, and could set certain conditions for convening such a peace conference, conditions "which would have to be very carefully drawn up."

As to the conditions the United States might set, Wiseman suggested agreements in principle that the conference would take up things like "limitation of armaments and arbitration," as well as territorial settlements "on the basis of nationalities." Perhaps they should commit to "a warm sea port" for Russia. They discussed how to handle "freedom of the seas."

Wiseman was against an armistice. "The war should go on just the same while the conference was sitting."

House argued that Britain should accept such a peace conference "almost immediately." It should not wait until the spring and summer offensives were done. The British people, House argued, were wrong to think the 1917 offensives would produce a decisive victory. If the offensives failed, "a terrible reckoning" would await the British and French governments.

House, like Wilson, also thought that even the attempt to attain a decisive victory was unwise. "The worst thing that could happen would be a decisive victory for either side." Wiseman worried that at a peace conference, in direct negotiations, Germany might split the Allies. Yet the two men nonetheless seemed to be coming together on a tentative plan. Just convening the conference would be the decisive event, House wrote to Wilson. "If a conference is once started it can never break up without peace."[16]

---

THIS WAS where matters stood, for Wilson and for House, when on January 22 the president delivered his solemn address to the US Senate and to the world, calling for a "peace without victory." The speech was nobly crafted. "Wilson aimed to give a great speech, and he succeeded."[17]

Press reaction in the United States was overwhelmingly positive. Progressive senator Robert La Follette called the speech "the greatest message of a century." The editors at the *New Republic*, Walter Lippmann and Herbert Croly, were understandably ecstatic. Croly told House the speech "was the greatest event in his own life."

Opinion around the world split predictably. Pope Benedict, at least, called Wilson's speech "the most courageous document which has appeared since the beginning of the war," one that "revives the principles of Christian civilization."[18]

Outside America, the main issue was whether to accept "peace without victory." Inside America, the main issue was whether America should commit to a postwar league. Opposition to such a league, which might commit America to war, was voiced on the right by Senator Henry Cabot Lodge and on the left by William Jennings Bryan.

Beyond the enormous public commentary, however, the professionals noticed that Wilson's speech did no real diplomatic work. It had ended up saying very little about peace terms. The president had not called for a peace conference. Because he had called for no specific action, it was easy to read about and then ignore his address. Thus, to the British government at least, Wilson's big peace speech "demanded little official attention."[19]

## Wilson Starts to Figure It Out

During the last week of January, after the "peace without victory" speech, Wilson and House finally began figuring out how to devise a diplomatic plan to make peace. They still had no operational advice from anyone in their government. House was processing what he was working out in his exchanges with Bernstorff and Wiseman. He then happened upon another source of advice, Herbert Hoover.

An experienced mining engineer and manager, Hoover had won an enormously positive worldwide reputation for his tremendous work in organizing humanitarian relief, especially in Belgium and northern France. He was someone who knew how to get things done. At about the same time that Wilson was giving his big speech, Hoover visited with House while traveling through New York, seeking more money for the relief work.

Hoover warned House (who warned Wilson) that "both France and England are greatly alarmed over the Russian situation." They were right to be alarmed. At this point, czarist rule in Russia had only another seven weeks left to live.

Hoover then quickly sketched for House how to go about preliminary negotiations for a peace conference. Like Bernstorff and Wiseman, Hoover explained that Wilson could seek a preliminary agreement on certain principles. As examples, Hoover pointed to the ones in Wilson's speech. If the warring powers agreed to these principles, Wilson could call for the conference.

Hoover put his finger on a German commitment to evacuate Belgium and France and agree to some sort of understanding about reparations to rebuild. If they just did that, he said, that alone would open the way to peace. If the Germans made such a commitment, it would be "impossible" to hold "the English and French people to a continuation of the war." Hoover, of course, did not know that, for months, the Germans had already offered such a commitment to the Americans.[20]

House reported Hoover's proposal to Wilson. This latest suggestion helped Wilson see what he should do. "Hoover convinces me," he wrote House, "that if Germany really wants peace she can get it, and get it soon, *if she will but confide in me and let me have a chance.*"

Reacting to House's most recent spin, Wilson said he did not think much of what the Germans had offered so far. But, he wrote, he could "bring things about" if Germany would give him "something reasonable to suggest." "Do they in fact want me to help? I am entitled to know because I genuinely want to help and have now put myself in a position to help without favour to either side."

House arranged to see Bernstorff the next day. House heartily agreed with the president that "the time has arrived when Germany should be pushed to declare her terms," to "give you material to work on in the furtherance of peace."

Bernstorff might have puzzled over all this. This Wilson-House exchange took place on Wednesday and Thursday; House was to see Bernstorff on Friday, January 26. Yet on Monday of that same week, in his "peace without victory" address, Wilson had repeated, as he had always said before, "[The United States] shall have no voice in determining what the terms [of peace] shall be," only in how to make the peace last.

What had happened was that finally, five months after the Germans had requested Wilson's mediation, Wilson had figured out a plan to start a preliminary negotiation with the Allies to hold a peace conference. He did not really need to know all the German peace terms. He was only seeking preliminary agreement on a few principles, a few preconditions, not yet specified, although obviously Belgium would head the list.

Still a little confused, Wilson and House seemed to be blaming the Germans for not having given them enough to work with. This was thoughtless, since in fact the Germans had already indicated agreement, in some cases for several months, on practically all the key points that would likely form such preconditions. And, as House at least should have known, the Germans had been entirely responsive to what they had been asked to commit to (support for the "future guarantees of security") a month earlier.[21]

---

BACK TO New York came Bernstorff, on Friday, January 26. Back to House's familiar Midtown apartment, back to the familiar living room. The German ambassador was under more strain than House knew. Bernstorff could tell House only that the military factions were gaining the upper hand in Germany, "with von Hindenburg and Ludendorff at the head." They, he said, not the kaiser, now had effective control.

House delivered Wilson's latest offer: confidential mediation for peace on the basis of the president's address to the Senate, which, as Bernstorff reported to Berlin, meant "without becoming involved in the territorial conditions of peace." For the second peace conference, the one about postwar plans, both Germany and the United States seemed to have similar concepts. Wilson hoped Germany could accept the principles of Wilson's address.

The main issue now was to set conditions so that both sides would agree to the first conference, the one among the belligerents to end the war. Wilson wanted to call for this conference "quickly enough to prevent unnecessary bloodshed in the spring offensives." House and Bernstorff agreed on the need to act before heavy fighting started again. Otherwise, there would be no peace at least until the autumn, Bernstorff thought. House said it was worse than that. The Allies would want to continue their block-ade through the winter, into 1918.

Wilson wanted more to be able to persuade the Allies to agree to the talks to end the war. He wished to understand, more fully, Germany's terms to end the war. Specifically, House asked for assurance that Germany "would be willing to completely evacuate both Belgium and France" and that it would agree, borrowing a phrase Bernstorff had used before, to "'mutual' restoration, reparation, and indemnity." This, he said, would give Wilson "something definite to work on and immediately."

Bernstorff, of course, had no quarrel with moderate peace terms; he had already offered as much. The final terms, he thought, would "leave the map of Europe pretty much as it was before the war, with the exception of perhaps a new Poland, the [inter]nationalization of the Dardanelles and some minor changes." Over time, he thought, this peace would delegiti-mize the militarists in all the warring powers so that, eventually, "none of the belligerent governments can survive such a peace as must necessarily be made." But it was the only way out.[22]

After Bernstorff left House's apartment, Wiseman stepped in, presum-ably after a decent interval—otherwise the ins and outs would have resem-bled a French farce. With Wiseman, House went through the whole plan he had just given to Bernstorff.

Wiseman reassured House, confidentially, that he was in good touch with London, though not through the ambassador. House had already guessed as much.

House said he now envisioned a preliminary conference on the precon-ditions, "to find whether a conference [was] possible." In the meantime, Wiseman reported to London, House did not think the United States was likely to be drawn into the war. House also still thought the war would end in a draw.

Wiseman recommended Spain as the site for the peace conference. House still preferred The Hague.[23]

Wilson and House authorized the State Department to relay Bern-storff's coded report, requesting the fuller statement of German peace terms, back to Berlin urgently, over the weekend.

The Americans had no concrete plans for what to do after the Germans gave them the necessary "material" to use in pressing the Allies to agree to a peace conference. They had not yet worked out how to approach the Allied side, though House assumed Wiseman was keeping London informed.

On Wednesday, January 31, Bernstorff got his answer from Berlin. The chancellor had quickly prepared and sent to him the very material Wilson had sought: a reasonably full statement of the territorial peace terms the Central Powers would seek in ending the war.

Bernstorff had to try to present that prompt, trusting, and forthcoming news, however, under the worst possible circumstances.

## Germany Sets Off Toward Both War and Peace

When Bernstorff visited House on January 26, he had been under great strain because he knew, as House did not, that his government was planning to tear up the *Sussex* pledge. He knew Germany intended to resume unrestricted submarine warfare on February 1. Berlin had instructed Bernstorff to hold this information until the last possible moment, so the U-boats would have maximum military advantage.

Since the summer of 1916, the German government had seen the peace road as the alternative to the road toward a wider war, a full U-boat war. Once the Central Powers had tendered their own public peace offer and the Allies had decisively rejected it, only the Wilson peace option was left.

By January 1917, practically every senior official in the German government, besides Bernstorff and Bethmann himself, had given up on Wilson. Even those, like Vice-chancellor Helfferich, who were still against the wider U-boat war did not trust Wilson. Helfferich preferred that Germany stay on the defensive and outlast its weary enemies.

Bethmann had gotten a preview of what was coming in his frosty confrontation at Pless with Hindenburg and Ludendorff on December 29. He had hoped to buy sufficient time by moving ahead with agreement to U-boat attacks without warning on armed merchantmen, a measure that the Americans were prepared to accept.

But, beginning on January 5, the navy chief, Henning von Holtzendorff, formally demanded completely unrestricted U-boat warfare to begin on February 1. He deployed a detailed memo, in preparation for weeks, laden with numbers, presuming to show that such a campaign could win the war within months. Holtzendorff insisted on immediately bringing the issue to the kaiser.

On January 8, Hindenburg and Ludendorff told the admiral they completely agreed with him. Hindenburg said, "We reckon on the war with America and have made preparations for it. It cannot be worse.... The war must be brought to an end by the use of all means as soon as possible."[24]

Receiving word of the military decision, Bethmann at once left on another long journey to Pless to try to stop it. "What happens now, I don't know," Bethmann's aide, Kurt Riezler, wrote in his diary. "Great tension as the decision is being made."[25]

First, Bethmann met with the high command. That was fruitless. Next, in the early evening on January 9, Bethmann and Helfferich filed in for their conference at the palace with a "pale and excited" kaiser. Helfferich, who was also the finance minister and perfectly able to do calculations, had reinforced Bethmann, cabling in a sharp critique of the navy's reasoning. Helfferich especially emphasized that there was no need for such hurry, no need to rush.

It did not matter. The kaiser, given his "basic incompetence," would not overrule the united military demand. "England would be prostrate within six months," Holtzendorff promised. The kaiser did not want to see the government break up over this issue.

At this crucial moment, Bethmann had nothing to offer as an alternative. His peace move with the Americans had been pending since August. The kaiser had written personally to Wilson about it in October. At the beginning of December, the kaiser had issued a special order to submarine commanders to avoid any incident that could disrupt the peace process. The outreach to Wilson had not yet produced any tangible outcome.

"I was wholly powerless," Bethmann later testified, "to dissipate the deep distrust of the Supreme High Command of the Army for President Wilson."[26]

The kaiser ruled in favor of Holtzendorff. Unrestricted submarine warfare would begin on February 1. Wilson was to be informed on January 31.

———

ON THE SURFACE, this triumph of the military high command seems a complete validation of all the worries about Germany being dominated by Prussian militarism, warmongering plutocrats, and authoritarian gentry.

Those worries were never baseless or foolish. In the country palace and military headquarters of distant Pless, on January 9, those factions had their way.

Yet, for a year and a half, Chancellor Bethmann Hollweg had beaten back assault after assault from the factions that sought this wider war. He had seen off the most politically powerful admiral in the country, Alfred von Tirpitz. He had obtained the dismissal of the previous commander of the army, Erich von Falkenhayn. For months, he had been seeking a compromise peace with the support of the kaiser, Germany's key allies, and a critical mass of civilian political and opinion leaders. In this phase of the war, the military leaders and their conservative allies were not all-powerful.

But it is hard to beat something with nothing. So far, Bethmann had nothing to show.

Hindenburg, Ludendorff, and Holtzendorff had chosen their moment to make another assault. This time they had carried the day. One of the hard questions for them, posed in different ways by Bethmann, Helfferich, and Bernstorff, was essentially this: Why the rush?

Time was on Germany's side, at least for a while. The occupation of Romania had eased some of the resource constraints. Russia was clearly tottering. The British financial situation was cloudy, though the German high command understood little about that.

Drawn to the U-boat panacea, eager to find some way to end the war, the German military men were unduly pessimistic about their ability to hold out and exhaust their enemies. Events in 1917 would show that, from a strategic defensive position, the anvils actually *were* stronger than the hammers. That year, standing on the strategic defensive, Germany and its allies crippled French offensive power, knocked Russia out of the war, turned Britain's offensives into muddy bloodbaths, and almost knocked Italy out of the war as well.

Why not at least wait a few more months and just escalate the U-boat campaign with the freedom to attack armed merchantmen (or merchant ships alleged to be armed)? That was a step the Americans were willing to tolerate. The Germans could then see how that went. There was some advantage to trying to choke off Allied war supplies before they were assembled for new offensives, but why not escalate in stages?

The only possible conclusion is that at some level, beyond the surface military arguments, the high command was just yearning to have it out with the chancellor, to have this test of political strength and show who was in charge at long last. In fact, right after they won the kaiser's approval for the unrestricted U-boat campaign, the high command immediately followed up by asking for Bethmann's dismissal. This the kaiser would not do.

In addition to the unnecessary rush, the political rush, the high command had also made two enormous misjudgments. One was big: the assumption that the British (with American help) could not eventually find countermeasures (like convoying) to mitigate the U-boat danger.

The other misjudgment was not just big; it was catastrophic. This was the underestimation of the United States.

In the history of warfare, it is not hard to come up with lists of bad decisions. Yet there are few, in all the history of warfare, that turned out to be as epically bad as this one. "Of all the grand miscalculations of the German High Command," Winston Churchill later wrote, "none is more remarkable than their inability to comprehend the meaning of war with the American Union."

With their narrow-minded understanding of power, typical among the German military elite, Hindenburg and Ludendorff had ignored the role, or fragility, of American finance in sustaining the Allied war effort. They also regarded the American military as a "negligible quantity."[27] By November 1918, when the US Army had already put two million soldiers in France with at least a million more on the way, no one would probably have used the word "negligible" to describe the quantity.

———

In Washington, DC, Bernstorff was told what was coming by secret cables, relayed to him in the channel made available by the US State Department and the American embassy in Berlin. The first of these war messages, concerning the planned February 1 commencement of all-out submarine warfare, went out from Berlin on January 16. Following it was another, fateful cable that was meant to be relayed onward to Mexico City.

That other message, designed to tempt Mexico to join in a war against the United States by offering to help regain lands lost in the 1846–1848 US-Mexican war, would become known as the infamous "Zimmermann telegram." The British, routinely intercepting and decoding the American cable traffic from Berlin, had at last also broken the new German diplomatic code. They were therefore able to read both of the messages that Berlin sent to Washington on January 16. It took a few weeks for the British to figure out a way to leak the "Zimmermann telegram" without revealing how they originally intercepted it.[28]

After he received the January 16 message with the submarine warfare plan, Bernstorff had replied immediately. He pleaded for delay. Wilson, he warned, could not tolerate such a personal affront. He asked Berlin to give Wilson more time. He assured his government that the American president was "preparing to go ahead [with a peace move] in the immediate future."

It did not help. Bernstorff was ordered to deliver the U-boat note on January 31, just a few hours before unrestricted U-boat warfare resumed.[29]

On January 26, House had met with Bernstorff to ask for a full set of Germany's territorial peace terms so that Wilson might set just the right conditions to get the Allies to agree to the peace conference. House had emphasized Belgium and "mutual" restorations of territory and payments of indemnities.

Bernstorff used his report of the meeting to make another, desperate plea to keep the peace option alive. He risked sending a quick coded message that could reach Berlin instantly over wireless: "After having had very important conference, request most urgently postponement" until he could send the details.

In his longer, follow-up message, Bernstorff explained what House and Wilson now wanted. He asked Bethmann to give them the German terms right away. The Allies had publicly announced their terms, which included their vague goal of a "reorganization of Europe." Those were obviously unacceptable. Wilson regarded the Allied goals as a "bluff." Wilson's "peace without victory" theme would allow Bethmann to show how much more moderate Germany's aims were.

But if the U-boat war was commenced, Wilson would see this as a "slap in the face." Instead, Germany could empower Wilson to move on peace. "It is only a matter of a short delay in order to improve our diplomatic position," Bernstorff argued. "We shall attain a better peace through the conferences [to end the war and set the postwar arrangements] than if the United States joins our enemies."[30]

———————

IN BERLIN during January, after their defeat in Pless, Bethmann and his aides reflected sadly on the lost possibility of peace. The chancellor's aide, Riezler, noted, "It would be tragic, if we could have had the peace with the West through Wilson, but the prospect for it and the insight will have been offered a week too late."[31]

Then, a couple of weeks later, Bethmann received the wireless "heads-up" message and the follow-on cable in which Bernstorff described his meeting with House on January 26 and pleaded for the chancellor to share Germany's relatively moderate peace terms with Wilson. Bethmann grabbed this news as just the scrap of hope he was looking for. Wilson was at last making an offer to mediate, if only Germany would confide in him.

Bethmann still controlled the "political" branch. He was still the chancellor. It was late on a Sunday night, January 28. At 10:00 p.m. he summoned Vice-chancellor Helfferich and showed him Bernstorff's report. "The Chancellor saw hope light up once again that war with America could be avoided and perhaps even peace achieved." Bethmann "was in a state of excitement like I had never seen."[32]

Bethmann immediately relayed Bernstorff's message to General Headquarters at Pless. Then, following up later that very night, Bethmann arranged for a special train to take him and Zimmermann on the long, overnight, wintry trip to see the kaiser. Along the way, as the train clattered over the rails, Bethmann himself drafted what he hoped would be a forthcoming reply to Wilson. He set it up as a message from the chancellor to the president.

Arriving in Pless, the audience was unfriendly. The kaiser thought he had already set the course. He was annoyed about being pressed "once again" to make a decision. Bethmann asked the kaiser to approve his draft telegram to Wilson.

Bethmann pitched his argument in terms that would appeal to the military men and to the kaiser (who had given up on Wilson). Look, he argued, at least my message might keep America from entering the war immediately.

At this point, the kaiser no longer shared Bethmann's hope that Wilson wanted to make peace. But he went along. The kaiser and the military leaders grudgingly approved Bethmann's message. It went out right away, coded but sent wirelessly (ensuring that anyone could instantly intercept the transmission) in order to save time.[33]

"Germany is ready to accept the mediation [President Wilson] offers in confidence for bringing about a direct conference of the belligerents," Bethmann cabled Bernstorff. It "will recommend the same course to its allies." The American president could now reset the political situation by getting a peace process under way.

––––––––

BETHMANN OUTLINED Germany's preferred peace terms for the American president. He asked that these not be announced publicly, since their moderation—in comparison to what the Allies had announced—would be "a sign of a weakness that does not exist, and this would only prolong the war." No other leader of a warring power had confided in Wilson this way.

It was not easy for Bethmann to draft these terms, literally on the move, practically overnight. As usual, he had to leave room for concessions and trades, yet show Germany's basic readiness for a compromise peace, all in service of practicing the "art of the attainable." What he wrote must be read with these considerations in mind.[34]

Bethmann's peace terms, as passed to House and Wilson, were

- restoration of Belgium, with guarantees for German safety, to be decided by negotiations with Belgium;
- restitution of German-occupied France, reserving possible strategic and economic frontier adjustments and financial compensations;
- restitution of the part of upper Alsace occupied by France;
- a frontier to protect Germany and Poland economically and strategically against Russia;[35]
- restitution of German colonies in proportion to population and economic interests;
- economic and financial mutual compensation based on exchange of territories conquered by both sides and returned when peace was made;
- compensation for damages to German business and private property;
- abandonment of obstacles to normal commerce, replaced by reasonable commercial treaties;
- freedom of the seas;

- peace conditions of Germany's allies on the same lines; and
- German participation in the proposed conference on postwar security on the basis of the principles in Wilson's "peace without victory"
  address.

Germany, Bethmann added, would postpone the submarine blockade, if possible, but the preparations could not be cancelled. At that time
U-boats were already taking up positions in the Atlantic, and it would
be difficult to contact or recall them. The German government hoped its
retaliatory submarine blockade would soon end the war.

But in the meantime, the German government "begs the President to
continue his efforts to bring about peace." It "would end the submarine
blockade as soon as it was evident that his efforts would bring about an ac-
ceptable peace." In a postscript, Bernstorff explained that this meant "that
the [submarine] blockade will be terminated, if a [peace] conference can
be brought about on reasonable terms."[36]

Bernstorff was being asked to deliver two messages at the same time,
representing the schizophrenic "military" and "political" halves of the
German government. The military message, about the resumption of unrestricted submarine warfare, was confrontational. Bethmann's message,
sharing Germany's planned peace terms with President Wilson, was con-
ciliatory and constructive.

In Berlin, Bethmann's aide, Riezler, prayed that Wilson would suppress
his anger at the first message and grasp the opportunity in the second message, the one from Bethmann. On January 31, he wrote in his diary that
"the fate that hangs over everything are thoughts about what Wilson is
going to do." If Wilson could press on the peace terms message, "it would
be a hundred times better than the U-boat war."

The extraordinary situation, Riezler reflected, was that by laying these
two messages in front of Wilson, one beckoning a wider war and one
moving toward peace, "Germany has put its signature on a piece of paper,
about which one doesn't know whether it contains one's own death sen-
tence or the receipt of an inheritance of millions." Germany had left it to
Wilson to choose whether the kaiser would be remembered as "Wilhelm
the very great or Wilhelm the last."[37]

## No Exit from the Warpath?

The U-boat note and Bethmann's proposed peace terms were both delivered to Wilson and House late on January 31. The U-boat note, with its shattering news—that Germany was abandoning its earlier pledge and resuming unrestricted submarine warfare the very next day—was soon public knowledge, a sensation.

Neither House nor Wilson bothered to seriously analyze Bethmann's message or the peace terms that Bethmann had confided to Wilson. Nor did they consider how to pursue this further.

House's first reaction, after the earlier news of the day, was a dismissive wave of the hand. "It is absurd to call it an answer to our request for terms."

The next day, February 1, House and Wilson met together at the White House. After breakfast, Wilson read Bethmann's letter aloud. Wilson too was dismissive, or so House thought.

Wilson was reacting, above all, in just the way Bernstorff had feared he would. He took the German U-boat move as a "slap in the face." The manner was so brusque, so sudden.

It was one thing to have submarine incidents with quarrels over what had happened. Wilson had been willing to grant Germany the slack to go ahead with attacks on armed merchantmen, a loophole that would have allowed Germany to torpedo much of the shipping in the restricted zone near Britain and France without warning. Yet Germany had announced, ostentatiously, that it would tear up the pledge that Wilson had extracted—at the brink of war—in May 1916.

Later that day, February 1, Wilson and House decided that relations with Germany had to be broken. The State Department told Bernstorff he had to go home.

House wrote Bernstorff to say how deeply disappointed Wilson was "at the sudden turn in the situation. It seemed as if peace was near by and could be reached by concessions here and there on both sides."

The German submarine measures had made peace negotiations "impossible," House wrote. "The suddenness with which the new undersea warfare was put into force makes it impossible for the President to propose mediation. I cannot tell you how deeply I regret the turn matters have taken, for there was every reason to believe that within a short time the belligerents would be discussing peace."[38]

With this, Bernstorff made his way back to Germany. Joined by his embassy colleagues and their families, he embarked on a Danish liner, granted safe conduct to return to Germany through neutral Holland. Until the day of his departure, he recalled, "all Americans behaved towards me with perfect propriety and courtesy."

A correspondent from the anti-German *New York Tribune* wrote a kind of obituary on his departure. She remarked that reporters would miss Bernstorff's "amazing charm and the easy candor of his talk...his melancholy eyes, his gently cynical estimates of most dreamers' hopes." However, "over one circumstance he has been always hopeful." Bernstorff had "clung always," the reporter wrote, "to the hope that America neutral would be a leader in the erection of peace machinery." Bernstorff's real regret in leaving, the reporter felt sure, was that he would never again "turn over a communication from the American State Department, to read a faint hope of peace between the lines."[39]

--------

THAT COULD seem to be a simple end to the story. There had been "every reason to believe that within a short time the belligerents would be discussing peace," House had written on February 2. That was now gone. America would now go to war with Germany.

Except for one thing: Wilson really, really did not want to take America into the war. He had quite genuinely wanted to bring peace. He still did. Quite a large portion of the American people and the Congress also did not want war.

The German U-boat message on January 31 hit Wilson very hard. He had not expected it, thinking he still had a good deal of time to make peace. With the president at the White House on February 1, House found him "sad and depressed." Nothing would lift his spirits.

Wilson had believed he could have had peace talks up and running within a month. House thought he had laid down some of the groundwork on the British end already, with Wiseman, and that the Germans "seemed eager for it."

Now, Wilson was deeply disturbed. He did not understand what had happened. He could not figure out what had gone wrong. At one point that day, sitting in the White House, Wilson looked at House. He told him he "felt as if the world had suddenly reversed itself; that after going from east to west, it had begun to go from west to east and that he could not get his balance."

Wilson felt a sense of doom. He believed that US intervention in the war would produce the very victor's peace he had just denounced so eloquently in front of the world, the kind of peace that would only produce more disasters. "He reiterated his belief that it would be a crime for this Government to involve itself in the war to such an extent as to make it impossible to save Europe afterward."[40]

Weeks went by. Wilson did not rush to war. He tried out an option of "armed neutrality." More developments helped further inflame American opinion. Ships were sunk carrying Americans. The next sensation was publication, in March, of the "Zimmermann telegram"—the British intercept of the clumsy German effort to tempt Mexico into joining a war against the United States.

---

THE CORE problem was that, even though Wilson still wanted to find an alternative to the wider war, his own hasty actions had wrecked the peace option. By immediately breaking relations with Germany, sending Bernstorff home, and closing the US embassy in Berlin, Wilson had cut off his channel to negotiate with the German government.

As a start, Wilson could have studied more carefully the message that Bethmann had sent. It contained the material on all the principles that Wilson and all those advising him had been discussing during the last month as the right preconditions for peace talks. If those included restoration of Belgium, endorsement of a postwar league, or other postwar principles, those German offers had been on the table for a long time, but now they were being reaffirmed, directly by the chancellor, in response to Wilson's request. If there were concerns about some of the language that Bethmann had crafted to leave himself some room to maneuver, discussing that with Bernstorff would not have been hard.

If there were doubts about Bethmann's good faith, whether he would actually deliver agreement on the necessary preconditions, that is what negotiations are for. A main purpose of diplomacy is to clarify and test a country's intentions, where there is doubt and uncertainty, by setting concrete terms and specifying actions. As for actions, Bethmann had promised that Germany would stop the U-boat war if a peace conference could be arranged.

Wilson could have responded on both tracks—ostentatiously preparing for war while also planning for peace talks. The world would have perceived the planned preconditions—above all, on Belgium—as a major concession and show of good faith by the German side. Wilson could have claimed, with cause, to have extracted this.

Wilson could have demanded that Bethmann make good on his offer to end the U-boat blockade as soon as peace talks convened. This too could have been portrayed as a victory for American diplomacy and readiness to go to war.

Instead, on the first day, Wilson—influenced by House—had reacted spasmodically. Then, with Bernstorff gone and relations broken, the president found himself trapped. For nearly two months, he agonized over taking the warpath. But he had closed off his most viable exit from it.

Wilson continued to muse about ways to revive peace talks, perhaps through Austria-Hungary. But that had no prospects. He was out in the open, besieged and bombarded by pro-war opinion every day, week after week, with no way out.

Wilson took his final decision for war later in March, with the unanimous approval of the cabinet. By that time, he had concluded that his peace efforts had failed because of the very Prussian militarism that he now felt had to be destroyed. He spoke to the Congress on April 2. A few days later both houses voted overwhelmingly to declare war against Germany. The spring offensives had already begun. The great battles had resumed in Europe and across the world. It would be a long time before the guns fell silent.

# And That Has Made All the Difference

## The Descent

On April 6, 1917, Good Friday, the United States of America declared war on Germany.

In France, with his battery, near the northern town of Arras, the English poet whose peace-versus-war dilemma had inspired the poem "The Road Not Taken" had chosen his road. Edward Thomas had just turned thirty-nine. He got a letter from Robert Frost. Frost's publisher in America had agreed to print a volume of Thomas's poems.

Neither item of news from America made much impression on Thomas. His unit was at the front. Everyone knew something big was coming. In his underground shelter that Easter weekend, sitting on the valise he used to carry his gear, Thomas jotted a letter to his wife. "The artillery is like a stormy tide breaking on the shores of the full moon that rides high and clear among white cirrus clouds....I simply watched the shells changing the landscape."

"The pretty village among trees that I first saw two weeks ago," he wrote, "is just ruins among violated stark tree trunks. But the sun shone and larks and partridge and magpies and hedgesparrows made love and the trench was being made passable for the wounded that will be harvested in a day or two."

On Easter Monday, a shell fell two yards from where Thomas was standing. It was a dud. His men ribbed him about his luck.

The next morning, another shell killed him. On the last page of his war diary, in pencil Thomas had written,

> *Where any turn may lead to Heaven*
> *Or any corner may hide Hell*
> *Roads shining like river up hill after rain.*

His remains are in France.[1]

————

THOMAS WAS one of millions whose lives would be cut short by the war in that year. Some losses came right to Lloyd George's War Cabinet. One of Bonar Law's sons was killed that same month, April, in faraway Palestine. Law's eldest son, a flier, was killed in France in September.[2]

That spring of 1917, the Allied offensives achieved little. The agony of the French offensive finally pushed many thousands of French soldiers to the point of exhaustion and refusal. That would be the last major offensive France would undertake that year. The massive British efforts in the autumn, in Flanders, were a disaster.

By the autumn of 1917, Allied victory was nowhere in sight. Another Italian offensive had pushed Italy's army near collapse; when the Germans and Austrians counterattacked, the collapse came, and the Italians retreated a hundred miles.

As the war continued, the new Provisional Government that took power in Russia in March 1917 tried to whip its disintegrating army into another offensive in the summer. If not for the war, the Provisional Government had a reasonable chance of effecting a democratic transition of power in Russia. To destabilize Russia, in April the German government had arranged for the leader of the Bolsheviks, an extreme revolutionary faction of the broader socialist movement, to return to Russia from his Swiss exile. In July, the leader they had smuggled in, Vladimir Lenin, led a Bolshevik uprising. The Provisional Government defeated this revolt. Lenin had to flee Russia for neighboring Finland.

But, as the war continued, the Provisional Government began to collapse under the strain. Its summer offensive completed the process of military disintegration and collapse. By the autumn, the Germans were overrunning as much of the Russian Empire as they wished.

In October 1917, Lenin returned, and the Bolsheviks staged a coup, not a mass uprising, against the broken Provisional Government. They took power in Petrograd (modern-day Saint Petersburg) and Moscow. From that base, the Bolsheviks proceeded to make peace with Germany, conquer the rest of Russia, and then go to war against the independent Polish state. These new civil and international wars cost millions more lives, left wreckage from Warsaw to Vladivostok, and installed a gigantic Communist state, the Soviet Union, that—without a continuation of the Great War—would never have come into existence.

Even after the United States came into the war, the war situation was so desperate for the Allies by the autumn of 1917 that, when the Germans made another set of peace moves, this time through Spain, Lloyd George was inclined to accept. His War Cabinet was deeply divided. Only the prospect of growing US military aid offered enough hope to keep Britain and France in the war. And, at the same time, the Germans too had lost a key part of their incentive to push hard enough for peace, as Russia was about to quit the war, which emboldened the Germans to think of what they might do once they transferred troops from the eastern front for new exertions in the West.[3]

Though relatively successful on the battlefield during 1917, the Central Powers were also staggering, half starved and exhausted. Austria-Hungary wanted and needed to quit, but its rulers felt ever more tethered to and dependent on their German ally. The Bulgarians and Turks could stay in the fight, but only just.

During 1918, as the war and its brutalization continued, the Austro-Hungarian and Ottoman Empires staggered toward their own disintegration, and the revolutionary chaos would eventually sweep over Germany too. "In more recent years," the historian Robert Gerwarth observes, "a growing body of scholarship on the late Ottoman, Hohenzollern and Habsburg empires has disputed the black legend that the Central Powers were simply rogue states and anachronistic 'people's prisons.' This reassessment has been an emphatic one for both Imperial Germany and the Habsburg Empire, which appear in a much more benign (or at least ambivalent) light to historians today than they did in the first eight decades after 1918."

The result was a violent "reorganization of Europe" (to borrow the phrase from the January 1917 Allied war aims) that spawned bloody civil and international wars in most of central Europe and the Balkans and a war between Greece and Turkey that led to the massacres and expulsion of ancient communities on both sides of the Aegean Sea. "Not since the Thirty Years War of the seventeenth century," Gerwarth adds, "had a series of interconnected wars and civil wars in Europe been as inchoate and deadly as in the years after 1917–18."

In November 1918, Germany, sliding toward defeat, went through a set of revolutions—the first deposed the kaiser; another created a short-lived socialist republic in Bavaria. The final act in this sequence was a revolt in 1923 led by the new Nazi Party, whose leader, an embittered war veteran named Adolf Hitler, had allied himself with Erich von Ludendorff. Hitler ended up in jail, where he plotted his next steps, while admiring the nearby success of the Fascist takeover in Italy in 1922, led by another bitter war veteran, Benito Mussolini.

In other words, the failure to end the Great War in 1916–1917 was much more than a human tragedy for Edward Thomas and the millions like him. It became a turning point in world history. As the Great War itself descended into new depths of savagery—for instance, in the spring of 1917, Germans, withdrawing from parts of France to shorten their lines, began systematically destroying or poisoning everything they left behind—the governments and peoples changed.

Unlike the Great War, "which was fought with the purpose of forcing the enemy to accept certain conditions of peace (however severe)," Gerwarth points out, "the violence after 1917–18 was infinitely more ungovernable. These were *existential* conflicts fought to annihilate the enemy, be they ethnic or class enemies—a genocidal logic that would subsequently become dominant in much of Europe between 1939 and 1945."[4] And that logic would extend well beyond Europe.

## Was It Wise to "Fight to the Finish"?

Two years before an armistice stopped the part of the fighting in Europe that we now call the First World War, the leaders of the core Allied government discussed whether the war should go on. In November 1916, the British war crisis came to a head, and the cabinet squared off for the secret war-or-peace debate. At its meeting on November 22, there were two big issues. Could Britain's military deliver a knockout blow? Could Britain sustain the Allied war effort?

Lloyd George had associated himself loudly and publicly with the cause of a "fight to the finish." But at that cabinet meeting, Lloyd George admitted that if the answer to either of those questions was no, Britain needed to find a way to make peace.

Those two questions were answered in 1917.

No, the Allied military strategy could not deliver a knockout blow. The French, British, Russian (the desperately quixotic "Kerensky offensive" of Russia's new Provisional Government), and Italian hammers all failed to dislodge the German and Austrian positions.

No, Britain could not sustain the Allied war effort. As long predicted by those in the know, Britain ran out of dollars in the spring of 1917.

The money was about to run out in February–March 1917 because of the continuing effect of the November warning of the Federal Reserve Board. After the United States broke relations with Germany, the Federal Reserve Board issued a new statement to change the red light to green, to encourage loans to the Allies.

"We should have found it impossible" to get the Fed's November warning against Allied loans reversed, a Foreign Office mandarin gratefully noted, "if the German Govt had not, as usual, been more stupid than ourselves in our dealings with the U.S."[5] J. P. Morgan & Co. and the US Treasury also advanced hundreds of millions of dollars.

Yet that huge fresh infusion of funds was not enough. When America entered the war in April, Britain had "only three weeks' supply of dollars in hand or anticipated to pay for goods ordered in the U.S." By the late spring, Britain simply had to ask the US government to open the spigots and provide a flood of money to pay the Allied bills.

As the dollars actually ran out, the tone of panic rose and rose. By late June, the Foreign Office, through the Wiseman-House channel, sent a private message directly to Wilson from Lloyd George. "We seem on the verge of a financial disaster," the prime minister wrote, "which would be worse than defeat in the field." Britain, he explained, would have to abandon the gold exchange; "all purchases from U.S.A. would immediately cease, and Allies credit would be shattered. These consequences which would be of incalculable gravity may be upon us Monday next, if nothing effective is done in the meantime. You know I am not an alarmist," Lloyd George wrote, "but this is really serious."

House relayed a message back from Wilson that they would start doing all they could. House was working on nothing else.

That further help did not come fast enough. In mid-July, Bonar Law, at Treasury, wrote, "Our resources available for payments in America are exhausted. Unless the United States government can meet in full our expenses in America, including exchange, the whole financial fabric of the alliance will collapse. This conclusion will be a matter not of months but of days."

By rapidly supplying a flood of unsecured loans directly from the US government, the Americans barely averted the British and Allied financial collapse. The United States spent what it had to spend to sustain an Allied war effort of which it was now such a vital part.[6]

––––––––

IF THE United States had not come into the war, the Lloyd George coalition, put in office in December 1916 to "fight to the finish," would have led the Allied cause to defeat. At the time they made their arguments in November 1916, Lord Lansdowne, Edward Grey, Reginald McKenna, Walter Runciman, Lord Crawford, and the others open to peace had judged the situation correctly.

A defender of Lloyd George and his coalition partners, looking back over a century, can admire their spirited, even desperate resolve to crush Prussian militarism, whatever the cost. They were right to care about the plight of France and Belgium. Back then, the inspirational analogy for the "fight to the finish" group was Britain's stoic resolve to defeat Napoleon. Today, the analogy most likely to grab audiences would be Winston Churchill's desperate, admirable determination in 1940 to fight on against Hitler.[7]

Yet it is not right to analogize Lloyd George's 1916–1917 choice to "fight to the finish" with Churchill's 1940 determination to fight on. The Germany of 1916 was not remotely as pathological and dangerous to the world as the Germany of 1940. In 1940–1941, Churchill could look to a supportive "arsenal of democracy" in America; in 1916–1917, Lloyd George could not rely on America, with its stance of studied neutrality, requiring payments in full. Churchill might also hope for diversion in a German-Soviet conflict. In 1917, Germany was about to slowly wind up a two-front war as its Russian enemy collapsed.

The defender of Lloyd George might then turn to another argument, suggesting that the British prime minister had gambled and won on a brilliant wager. Aided by the British intelligence intercepts, perhaps Lloyd George bet that the Germans would escalate their submarine warfare after all. Perhaps he gambled, correctly, that this would bring America into the war. In this view his colossal, secret bet paid off—with final victory.

There are two problems with such a "brilliant gamble" defense. One is that it is rarely wise to bet that the enemy will make a gigantic mistake. For instance, what if the German high command had realized the seriousness of the Allied financial trouble? Or what if they had waited to let the "armed merchantmen" campaign play out for a few months? Or what if they had held off escalation because the Americans began making more energetic peace moves? Or what if they had delayed for some other reason and then recalculated all their options once the revolution in Russia swept out the czar (in March 1917)?

———

THE OTHER problem with the argument that Lloyd George's brilliant gamble paid off is a question that cuts very deep indeed. Was it really wise for Britain (or France or Russia) to even *want* to continue the war "to the finish"?

In November 1916, General William Robertson predicted that his strategy probably would not work until the end of 1918, at the earliest. Even if that was feasible (as it then was not), were the gains really worth the costs of two more years of horrific warfare, however those costs were measured?

That was the very question that Lansdowne posed so lucidly in November 1916.

After the war, the former foreign secretary, Edward Grey, thought about that question. Understandably, his first instinct was to blame the Germans. Looking back in his memoir, Grey thought "Germany missed a great opportunity for peace." If Germany "had accepted the Wilson policy, and was ready to agree to a [peace] Conference," he wrote (not knowing what had actually happened), "the Allies could not have refused."

But Grey did not just blame the Germans. He considered the deeper question. "Did the Allies also miss an opportunity?" he wondered. "The condition of Europe is sufficiently disappointing," Grey observed, writing in 1925, "to make it interesting to imagine what the course of events might conceivably have been if the Allies and Germany in 1916 had told President Wilson that they were ready for the Conference he was prepared to summon."

A compromise peace would "have demonstrated the stultification and failure of Prussian militarism." That would have been enough. "If a Wilson peace in 1916 had brought real disillusionment about militarism, it would have been far better than what actually happened."

If the war had ended then, not only would the losses of life, treasure, and national strength have been saved (including the life of one of Grey's favorite nephews, he did not add), but, Grey also thought, Europe would have been more likely to recover. Its prospects for future peace would have been better, including better relations with a United States that by then had become fraught with disillusionment on both sides.[8]

Retired, his life ebbing away, Grey kept thinking about how peace might have been made. "So disappointing have events been since 1919, so dark are the troubles still, that we are tempted to find some relief in building castles in the air; and, if the future is too clouded for this, we build them in the past."[9]

## How Germany Saved Its Enemies

History offers few ironies greater than this: The arrogant high command of the German army and navy, besotted with their victory mirage, actually rescued their bitterest enemies from defeat. And they insured their own.

Germany and her allies were short of food. But Britain and her allies were even more short of the money to *buy* food—and munitions. Historian John Milton Cooper Jr. astutely noticed, long ago, that "Germany resorted to submarine warfare to cut the Allied lifeline of overseas supplies—just when finances were about to accomplish the same result." This left Cooper a bit bewildered. "Why the Germans chose to make the only move that could save their enemies is an intriguing question."

It was partly an intelligence failure. John Maynard Keynes talked to many of the Germans after the war. He concluded that "the Germans were totally unaware of our financial difficulties."

The alarming details were kept very close between the Morgan bankers and the British officials who worked with them. But the general seriousness of the situation was no great secret.[10] There was a narrowness of mind among the generals. Ludendorff in Germany, like Robertson in Britain, did not really want to understand financial issues.

It is also important to notice that, as the high command sought a confrontation over the issue of unrestricted submarine warfare, the Americans were easing restrictions on the U-boats. Bethmann had constructed the compromise of allowing attacks on armed merchant ships and informed the Americans, and the Wilson administration was going to tolerate it. Since it was increasingly common for the Allies to arm merchantmen, this offered more scope for U-boats to act on suspicion that they were so equipped. House admitted to British intelligence agent William Wiseman that, while peace efforts were under way, Wilson would not let a submarine incident derail them.

In other words, Bethmann's "armed merchantmen" compromise was working, at least for a time. The navy could have tried it. It did not really wish to because, it seems, the military demand was also partly political, even cultural—an effort to reclaim and demonstrate power over the chancellor, at last.[11]

FROM ANY perspective, the U-boat option won because the other choice, the peace option, lost. But that failure was *not* Germany's failure.

The Germans had done what Grey wanted them to do. To borrow Grey's words, they had "told President Wilson that they were ready for the [peace] Conference he was prepared to summon." Between August 18, 1916, and January 31, 1917, the German government said that many times.

The German chancellor, Bethmann, rarely attracts historical praise. He carries his share of blame for the outbreak of war in 1914. His contemporaries were frequently irritated and impatient with him—with his "vacillating." He can seem like a dutiful, temporizing bureaucrat, a pedantic communicator, not a slashing orator. He was no Bismarck, many complained.

And yet, throughout 1916 and January 1917, he did not vacillate. Like a seawall buffeted by wave after wave, for more than a year he firmly resisted effort after effort to widen the U-boat war and draw America into the

conflict. He was the object of unremitting political attack by the conservatives. He not only resisted; he fought back, obtaining the dismissal of key
military leaders in the government.

He developed the peace option. He won the kaiser's approval for it. He
launched it. He prepared his key political allies for it. And he held the option open for months, despite the ambiguous and dispiriting reports, some
of them false, about Wilson's delay and supposed doubts. Even at the very
end of January 1917, he made the last desperate effort to throw out a lifeline that Wilson, amid his anger about the U-boat note, might still grasp.

Bethmann was indeed not a charismatic spellbinder. He was no Lloyd
George, no Wilson, if those are the standards for emulation. But neither
was he a man without qualities.

Should Bethmann, and Berlin, have done more to tempt others to talk
peace? They could have publicized German willingness to withdraw from
Belgium. On December 17, after the peace talks offer by the Central Powers and just before Wilson's peace note, Pope Benedict XV, through his
representative, told the German and Austro-Hungarian governments that
Wilson was about to make a peace move. The pope "had good ground
to believe the Entente was inclined to peace negotiations" if the Central
Powers "would disclose 'something' concerning [their] peace conditions,"
particularly "a guarantee for the restoration and complete independence
of Belgium."[12]

From at least the end of July 1916 until the end of January 1917, Bethmann was willing to offer that concession. Wilson had been told this by
Bethmann, by Ambassador Bernstorff, by the American embassy in Berlin,
and by British reports about Austrian peace feelers.

Why not just make that offer publicly, then, and in an unconditional
way?[13] Why not go further, perhaps, and even publicly offer to withdraw
from all of occupied France, not just the portion of northern France ad-
joining Belgium?

Bethmann had to weigh three factors against such an unconditional
public concession. First, he wanted to use such an offer to get something
in return—at least an Allied commitment to sit down at the peace table.
This was the deal he was arming Wilson to negotiate. Second, he counted
on persuading Belgium's restored government to guarantee Belgium's future military and economic neutrality. Third, he was trying not to provoke

his political opponents, who had earlier, and would later (beginning again in February 1917), prefer to secure Germany by annexing large chunks of Belgium.

Germany and its allies might well have been better off if Bethmann had made public offers so bold that they could not be refused, so bold that Wilson and House would have needed only to smile with satisfaction and send out the conference invitations forthwith. Instead, however, the German behavior was more normal—more watchful of domestic politics, more anxious to trade concessions for visible outcomes, and more uncertain about Wilson's intentions. Bethmann hoped he had given Wilson enough to work with to close a preliminary deal with the Entente and call the peace conference.

Indeed, Bethmann *had* given Wilson enough to work with. In the failure to make peace at the most opportune moment, no one failed, and failed the world, more than President Wilson. His was the most consequential diplomatic failure in the history of the United States.

## The American Failure

Wilson also commands sympathy and no small degree of respect. Bernstorff rightly judged that, at least from May 1916 until January 31, 1917, Wilson was genuinely neutral and passionate about making peace.

Wilson also was realistic. Informed by American military attachés and others watching the war, he was realistic about the prospects for either side to gain a decisive victory. He was realistic in not setting himself up as a moralistic judge of who was at fault for the war. He did not let passion about submarine incidents or Belgian deportations sway him from the central task of trying to end the conflict. One reason he was so eager to make peace as soon as possible was that he judged, also realistically, that failure meant America might be forced into a war he and most of the country fervently did not want to join.

Wilson was realistic in his modesty about trying to reorganize Europe. At that time, in 1916 and early 1917, one of the reasons he deferred engagement in the territorial peace terms, one of the reasons he sought a "peace without victory," was to encourage a reasonably conservative settlement, to avoid a series of annexations and humiliations that would only plant the seeds for future conflicts. In this respect, his fundamental outlook on Europe's evolution was similar to that of statesmen like Bethmann and Grey.[14]

Wilson was realistic when he accepted Grey's argument that the United States had to take part in a postwar league of nations to reassure the Allies that a compromise peace could last. Wilson was not only realistic, he was also deeply perceptive, when he explained—in his peace note and his January 1917 speech—that a peace without victory was the best, and perhaps the only, way to secure a peace that might endure.

Having predicted, correctly, that a peace accompanying bloody victories and humiliating defeats would probably not last, Wilson was condemned, like some figure in a Greek tragedy or myth, to suffer the prolonged and painful validation of his own dark prophecy. The process began during the armistice negotiations in late 1918. Wilson and House were outmaneuvered by the French and British, and that preliminary peace gave the Allies the overwhelming advantage that carried over into the spirit of the famous peace conference in 1919.[15] Thus, in 1919, Wilson found himself orating fruitlessly against the doom he had himself once prophesied. Then, after his physical breakdown in September 1919, Wilson had to watch the ruin continue until death took him early in 1924.

———

IN 1916–1917, Wilson failed to make peace not because he was too encumbered by ideals. He failed because he simply did not know how to do it. He was the rookie who sits down at the poker game and, dealt a hand with three kings, throws back two of them in the hope of getting better cards.

By September 1916, all the stars were in alignment for Wilson's peace move. Leaders on both sides were pessimistic about their prospects in the war and worried about their ability to continue. The Germans had formally asked Wilson to act and had secretly volunteered the restoration of Belgium to show their readiness to reach a compromise peace.

The British and French were reluctant to make a peace based only on the mid-war status quo. It was a measure of their desperation that a significant faction was willing to contemplate even that. Others open to peace, like Arthur Balfour, needed more.

They could have had more. Wilson could have brokered a peace conference conditioned on a plain German commitment to restore Belgium and withdraw from at least most of occupied France. He could have gone further and attempted to arrange armistice lines, while talks were under way, that accomplished most of those withdrawals in a civilized manner, perhaps accompanied by relaxation of the sea blockades on both sides. Just the Belgium condition alone would have utterly transformed the politics surrounding peace in Britain, at least.

Instead, for two months, from September to November 1916, Wilson did nothing because of the happenstance that 1916 was a presidential election year and he could not move until he was reelected. Then, for another month, a vital month from mid-November to mid-December, Wilson did nothing—even though he felt the urgency to act—because he was effectively delayed and deflected by House and Secretary of State Robert Lansing, and because his government had made no plans and offered no advice for what Wilson should do after he was reelected.

After setting the stage with powerful added pressure on Britain at the end of November (the Federal Reserve Board warning and the strong Wilson-directed letter from House to Grey), Wilson then issued an ineffectual peace note late in December that was a misfire. The note, apparently inspired by newspaper editorials, took no practical action, since House persuaded him to remove his call for a conference.

Then followed about six weeks of hectic, confused efforts to get a better peace move going. Bernstorff (and Wiseman, probably without instructions) attempted to guide House. Wilson meanwhile came up with another plan inspired by essays in the *New Republic*. Bernstorff followed through on the peace plan he thought he had agreed upon with House and Wilson. Wilson and House—startled, encouraged, and further instructed, including by British parliamentarians and Herbert Hoover—finally reset that plan so that, by the last week of January, Wilson was at last starting to construct the plan to set up peace talks that had actually been available to him for at least the last five months.

When, on January 31, 1917, he discovered that his efforts had failed to ward off the expanded U-boat war, Wilson was stunned. Shocked and reeling, he then angrily brushed past Bethmann's effort to keep the peace option alive.

Wilson still did not want to bring America into the war. Yet, having sent Bernstorff home, Wilson found that war was the only option he had left, his only remaining card.

WILSON THOUGHT he knew how to play the game. He did not know what he did not know. He thought he could figure it all out on his own, borrowing ideas from newspapers and magazines, without any real study of diplomacy, not even seeking to learn from recent experience, such as how Theodore Roosevelt had successfully played the game in ending the Russo-Japanese War in 1905.

It is possible to be realistic about problems and incompetent to solve them. And Wilson's incompetence was specific to this problem; it was not general.

The American president displayed real skill in orchestrating the Federal Reserve Board warning of November 1916. In handling the diplomacy of notes on submarine warfare, Wilson used Lansing's clerkish, lawyerly skills to advantage, while firmly calibrating substance and tone. On the second-most important foreign policy issue of 1916, the civil war raging in Mexico, Wilson also displayed both skill and judgment, mainly in warding off foolish proposals. He handled congressional issues with skill and judgment too.

In all those matters, Wilson was judging and reacting, not designing and implementing. In the Federal Reserve Board case he had competent partners on the board. He had competent partners in Congress.

On the other hand, in the peacemaking to end the Great War, he had Edward House.

The Wilson-House relationship always attracted attention. The most famous psychoanalyst in the world, Sigmund Freud, even ended up coauthoring a book to puzzle over it.

House was a sympathetic receptacle for Wilson's general hopes. But House was not all that influential on the substance of most policy issues. He had not even comprehended what Wilson had done with the Federal Reserve Board.

House mainly worked on two vital subjects. One was picking people to work in the Wilson administration, mastering the politics of patronage, in an age when the two went hand in hand. The other was European politics and the war. Starting with his annual trips from 1913 onward, building on his old travel habits, House had carefully cultivated the impression and occasional reality of being Wilson's bridge to Europe—above all, to London.

Yet the greatest failing in Wilson's foreign assessments was not his judgment of the situation in Germany—on which he received good, understandable reports. The great failing was in his understanding of the situation *in London*.

Relied on as the supposed conduit to and expert about London, House (though not Wilson) was thrown off by Lloyd George's adamant public stance. House delayed and deflected Wilson's peacemaking during the vital autumn of 1916 and dissembled about this to the German government.

House and therefore Wilson were ignorant and heedless of the desperate war/peace arguments that divided, and eventually broke, the Asquith coalition. They could have thrown lifelines to the powerful group of would-be peacemakers in London. Instead those ministers thrashed and sank.

Even as, in December 1916, House warmed again to the peacemaking project, his illusions about Lloyd George starting to fade, he had no constructive ideas for what to do. Only in the last weeks of January 1917 did he and Wilson, reacting to prodding and suggestions from others, including Bernstorff, Wiseman, and Hoover, finally, slowly begin to figure out how they might proceed. Then they ran out of time, in part because they discarded Bethmann's last lifeline.

One of the few benefits of American entry into the world war is that House's role became relatively less important. Others became indispensable in the much wider effort. Once Wilson and House actually started working together in the field, during the Paris peace negotiations of 1919, Wilson could finally really take House's measure. The two men then grew apart, until Wilson refused to see or speak to his onetime friend ever again.[16]

## The Logic of War

If no peace road had beckoned, the entry of the United States of America into the Great War might not have been wrong, given the German submarine campaign, the "Zimmermann telegram," and much understandable sympathy with the Allied cause. Even in far retrospect, that is a close question on which reasonable people can disagree.

But the entry of the United States into the Great War was unnecessary. It was unnecessary because the United States, and President Wilson specifically, had the will, the means, and the power to instead bring the war to an end. The United States could have made peace and did not do it. It thus left itself only the much harder choice of whether to acquiesce in the ensuing German actions.

Once the United States of America had embarked on the logic of war, another sequence of events put it on its own strange new path, with undreamt-of consequences, not just for the United States but for the nature of postwar Europe and the world.

First, the German behavior in gambling on the U-boat war, plus episodes like the Zimmermann telegram, understandably pushed Wilson not only to war but also to war aims that had to include the destruction of German "militarism."

Second, when America went to war, the government had not necessarily envisaged sending anyone to Europe to fight. A more limited engagement might have meant no more than helping on the seas and bankrolling supplies.

At the time Congress declared war, in the first week of April 1917, the American government had no obvious intention to send even one unit of troops to Europe. Even after war was declared, a knowing and powerful senator, chair of the Appropriations Committee, simply stated, "Congress will not permit American soldiers to be sent to Europe."[17]

At the turn of 1917, the Wilson administration had no war plans for fighting in Europe. None. The administration had mistakenly believed the Allies were in reasonably good shape. Once again, House's failure to understand the situation in London had deceived Wilson and the government in Washington into believing that they could perhaps participate in the war with no more engagement than money, ships, and supplies. Wilson took the precaution, however, of readying a plan for wartime conscription, the first since the Civil War.

Third, in the late spring and summer of 1917, after having entered the war, the administration finally learned the truth about the desperate Allied financial and military situation. It realized that the Allies were actually in quite serious trouble.

The Allied leaders crossed the ocean to visit Washington, the British mission led by Balfour, the French mission dominated by Marshal Joseph Joffre. They, especially and most effectively the French, pleaded for all the help they could get, as soon as they could get it. If the Allies did not get the help, they might actually lose the war.

America and Wilson had not joined the Allies in order to be on the losing side. A losers' peace in 1917–1918 would be much worse than what the Allies had been considering in 1916–1917.

Fourth, the US government *then* decided it had to mobilize everything it could, as fast as it could. An initial thought of an expeditionary force to France of about a division, perhaps a few tens of thousands, hastily evolved later in 1917 to plans to send millions. Two million were in France by the end of 1918, and many more were in train to follow if, as was expected, the war went on through 1919.

More than fifty thousand Americans died in battle, as many as the dead of the later Vietnam War, but taken from an America half as populous. Even more died in the service from disease. Another two hundred thousand were wounded physically. The war also helped propagate the awful global influenza pandemic, which—though called the "Spanish" flu—first surfaced at an American army camp in March 1918.

Most of the American combat losses came in three months of intense fighting near the end of the war. Only then did the United States suffer the kind of monstrous monthly casualty rates the other major warring countries had been suffering, month in and month out, for over four years.

Fifth, such a titanic mobilization of America, a vast commitment of men and blood, escalated hopes for the peace to bring a comparably titanic reward. The idea for a league of nations would redeem all. The stakes for the peacemaking became much higher, as a kind of salvation.

Wilson had not originated the overwhelming emphasis on a postwar league of nations with which he would later, and forever, be associated. The ideas came mainly from British Liberals (such as Grey) and internationally minded American Republicans. Wilson had originally joined the cause in 1916 as a necessary measure in his main effort—the peace effort to end the war. Then the league idea grew until it became the signature contribution that America could bring to the postwar settlement.

At the peace conferences that began in 1919, American influence on the peace terms was limited, but it was about all that could reasonably have been expected. After all, Britain, France, and Italy also were victorious.

They actually lived full-time in Europe. The doughboys were headed home, and the US government's wallet was going back in its pocket.

Even if the folks back home had been more interested and supportive, which they were not, America's peacemakers in 1919 could never have told everyone what to do. There were so many details in the various treaties with Germany, with Austria-Hungary, and later with the remnants of the Ottoman Empire or with Turkey. The American influence ended up being important, yet still modest.

The various postwar settlements concluded between 1919 and 1923—with Germany, Austria-Hungary, Bulgaria, and the Turkish state that emerged from the wreckage—can of course be criticized on various points. But the situation at the end of 1918 was so ruinous that no postwar arrangements could have produced a happy ending. It is hard to come up with a set of plausible outcomes that would have been much better, in light of the circumstances the peacemakers faced in 1919 and afterward.[18]

Sixth, when Icarus fell to earth, when the peace results were not so satisfying, it was a very hard fall. Americans reacted with disgust to the spectacles of war and revolution in Europe, as well as to the jolt of a postwar economic recession.

The US Senate refused to ratify the Treaty of Versailles. Wilson would not accept qualifications that might have allowed it to be ratified. The United States did not join the League of Nations.

But it would not have mattered that much, even if the United States had ratified the treaty and participated in the League of Nations. Currents of public and congressional opinion, wide and strong, were already defining the limits of future American participation in European politics and world trade.

League member or not, postwar American statesmen like Secretary of State Charles Evans Hughes fully tested the limits of the American international engagement possible in this forbidding domestic environment. They did so on issues from disarmament to economic reconstruction to the future of East Asia.

The collective security provisions of the League of Nations were moribund until the 1930s, when they failed entirely. But distant US membership undercut by popular domestic indifference would not have saved them.[19]

Practically everything about the Great War seemed to turn out paradoxically. America entered the war to save democracy in Europe from militarism. By the early 1930s, democracy had almost disappeared from Europe, and militarism was rampant even, as in Italy and Romania, in nations that had been on the Allied side.

Americans were disillusioned, and in their disillusionment, they swung during the 1930s to isolationism. That American isolationism ended up endangering the whole world as never before. It would bring on a second world war, the worst war in human history.

## The Exile

In his last face-to-face meeting with House, on Friday morning, January 26, 1917, Count Bernstorff had offered his prediction for how a negotiated peace, a true peace of understanding, would turn out. Bernstorff's prediction, as House relayed it to Wilson, was that such a peace would "leave the map of Europe pretty much as it was before the war."[20]

This would have been, Bernstorff noted after the war, "a sort of Hubertusburg Peace," using the 1763 analogy Bethmann and other Germans had drawn on so often during 1916, the peace that saved Prussia as a major power. For Bernstorff, that was good enough.

Given the situation on the ground in 1916, Bernstorff believed "a peace unfavourable to ourselves was unthinkable." In any case, he thought, a peace without victory would have been better than "the world of the Peace of Versailles, blooming with starvation, Bolshevism and nationalistic hatred."

"Naturally, we should have had to restore Belgium and accept the disarmament programme, etc.," Bernstorff acknowledged. "But we had already declared ourselves ready to take these measures, and, as regards disarmament, etc. this reform was inevitable, in view of the economic position of the countries concerned."[21]

---

PROTECTED BY his safe conduct, Bernstorff arrived back in Berlin in February 1917. He observed the widespread "ignorance and undervaluation of America." He concluded that the chief problem for the peace option had been that so many of his colleagues in Berlin had distrusted Wilson.

In April, after America entered the war, Bernstorff made an appointment to talk directly with General Ludendorff. Both men came to the point.

"In America, you wanted to make peace," Ludendorff said. "You evidently thought we were at the end of our tether."

"No, I did not think that," Bernstorff replied. "But I wanted to make peace *before* we came to the end of our tether."

"We, however, did not want to," answered Ludendorff.

Bernstorff warned Ludendorff that, in a year, the Americans would be ready to send very large forces to fight in France.

Ludendorff waved this off. "The U-Boats will force peace in three months." He repeated this claim, adding that he had "absolutely certain information on this point."[22]

Three months later, as such illusions faded, the political compromise that had held together majority support for the war in the German Reichstag broke down. The parties of the Left and the Center, having abandoned their illusions about the U-boat war, openly supported a "peace of reconciliation," what the centrist leader, Matthias Erzberger, called a "peace which brings no forcible oppression of peoples or border areas." This would be a peace of "no annexations, no reparations." The Reichstag approved such a peace resolution by a vote of 212 to 126, with 17 abstentions.

In the short term, the only result of this resolution was the final downfall of the already crippled chancellor, Bethmann. The military leaders insisted that the chancellor clearly could no longer control the Reichstag, and the kaiser gave in.

The Reichstag was interested in Bernstorff as a possible successor to Bethmann as the new chancellor. Both Bethmann and the kaiser's civil adviser, Rudolf von Valentini, suggested him.

The kaiser, however, would only go along with a Chancellor Bernstorff if the generals agreed, "which of course," Bernstorff commented, "they did not." Bernstorff was instead sent out of Germany, to become the ambassador in Constantinople.[23]

After the war was over, the kaiser exiled to spend the rest of his life in Holland, Bernstorff returned to political life. He became an elected member of the Reichstag in the new German republic. He returned to diplomacy during the 1920s, working with old adversaries, like Robert Cecil, at the new League of Nations.

———

WHEN HITLER came to power in 1933, however, Bernstorff had not only no place in government but no place in Germany. Hitler blamed Bernstorff, among others, for Germany's humiliation in the Great War. Bernstorff was driven into exile.

Living out the rest of his life in Switzerland, in Geneva, he had time to reflect on the past. He had already published a memoir of his ambassadorship in America, and he read what other former officials published, including the book that House worked on with Yale historian Charles Seymour.

Knowing less about the inner debates within the British government, Bernstorff reflected mainly about Germany and America. Amid the restful mountains and lakes of his home in exile, in 1935 Bernstorff wrote another book to reflect some more on what he had learned. As he wrote, all of Europe was worried about the possible coming of another terrible war. Looking back, Bernstorff had no doubt that Germany had made a fateful mistake early in 1917.

Germany, he believed, should have wholeheartedly accepted Wilson's potential mediation. That would have been "the salvation of Germany's position in the world, and the avoidance of the misery in which Europe is now plunged." Bernstorff still believed Wilson would have been a fair arbiter of any peace process.

Wilson's later "spiteful censure and treatment of us, both during the war and at Versailles, may be explained psychologically," Bernstorff explained, "by the fact that we rejected his efforts as a mediator, and declared the U-Boat war." Wilson had "never forgiven the German Government for having caused the failure of his peace-policy of 1916–17, which was supported by public opinion in America." Wilson's "personal sensitiveness and egocentric nature played an essential part in all the negotiations." Wilson was neutral right up to the U-boat note of January 31, 1917. After that, though, Wilson "saw red whenever he thought of the Imperial Government, and his repugnance against it knew no bounds."[24]

———

As HE neared the end of his life, having read the books published after the war, Bernstorff felt he could analyze the American peacemaking too. He had thought and thought about the months of fruitless effort that started in August 1916.

Wilson, he wrote, "desired the best, but could not achieve his end, because he was lacking in the necessary force of statesmanship." Bernstorff found much that he admired in Wilson. "Nature had equipped him with brilliant gifts." Sadly, in Bernstorff's view, "they were not the gifts called for by his position at that time, and were rendered even more ineffective by the President's incapacity for personal negotiation."

This incapacity, Bernstorff thought, explained part of Wilson's otherwise baffling reliance on House, "whom Wilson got to negotiate for him as often as was practicable." Meanwhile, the president "was too thoughtful, and too slow in decision. Added to the rest was his overweening self-confidence and his dislike of allowing subordinates to work on his behalf."

Nonetheless, Bernstorff was sure Wilson still had peace within his grasp, before it slipped away. "No doubt the course of world history would have been quite different," Bernstorff concluded, "if Wilson, in the year 1916, had made us his offer of mediation one month sooner."

But Wilson did not. None of the principal powers were able to make peace. "The War lasted two years more, and did not end until Europe was plunged into ruin."

What would have happened if the opportunity for peace had been grasped? "That," wrote the old exile, "is the great, unfathomable mystery of world history."[25]

ACKNOWLEDGMENTS

As mentioned in the introduction, this project grew out of discussions with the late Harvard historian Ernest May. In deciding, nearly ten years later, whether to develop a lengthy initial paper into something more, I'm especially grateful for the encouragement of a fellow historian, Frank Gavin, and early reactions of other colleagues to the way the work was taking shape. I'm also grateful for some good strategic advice from my agent, Andrew Wylie.

This is not only one of the most important historical episodes I have ever studied closely; it is also one of the strangest. After a presentation at Harvard, Calder Walton put me in touch with his Cambridge friend, Dan Larsen, who, along with Holger Afflerbach, helped reassure me that what I was finding might really be true.

At PublicAffairs, I owe a tremendous debt to Clive Priddle. He "got" the story and shared my interest in it. It was Clive who called my attention to the linked story of Edward Thomas and Robert Frost. His editorial advice was exceptionally engaged and thoughtful, and if this book works, he deserves much of the credit. He was aided by his assistant, Anupama Roy-Chaudhury, and the very professional production team at HBG. Jen Kelland has been the kind of conscientious copyeditor any author would be lucky to have. Patti Isaacs did a lucid, meticulous job with the map and the diagrams.

This is a work that builds upon a foundation of archival and documentary collections carefully compiled by people in several countries and institutions, some of them long gone, like Hugo Sinzheimer's team working for the Reichstag in 1919–1920 and the Carnegie Endowment team that helped translate and preserve their work, the French team that assembled more of the German records after World War II, and the simply remarkable group that worked on the 1916–1917 portion of the Papers of Woodrow Wilson. I believe that group believed they were discovering quite a bit of new information in the course of their work, venting about it only in the occasional suggestive footnote. Having worked at times as a hewer of wood and drawer of water in such projects, I do not take such work for granted. The institutions of knowledge of particular importance for this project included the excellent National Archives of the United Kingdom, the Bodleian Library at Oxford, the Churchill Archives Centre at Cambridge, the Morgan Library in New York, the US State Department's Historian's Office, the Library of Congress, the Hoover Institution at Stanford University, the US National Archives, Yale University, and naturally my home base, the University of Virginia, its Department of History—where Rachel Goretsky helped me with some of the early research—and the Miller Center of Public Affairs.

# NOTES

Sources are cited fully on first usage in the notes and in short form thereafter. To help distinguish government documents from published materials, I cite such documents with abbreviated dates (e.g., 28 Nov 16). Unpublished documents from collections of personal papers give, on initial usage, the name of the collection, the library where it is located, and the relevant box number. Unpublished documents from The National Archives of the United Kingdom are cited with record references: CAB for Cabinet Office files; FO for Foreign Office files; HW for War Office files (in that era); ADM for Admiralty files.

## Introduction: Two Roads Diverged

1. Frost and Thomas quoted in Matthew Hollis, *Now All Roads Lead to France: A Life of Edward Thomas* (New York: W. W. Norton, 2012), 206, 229–231 (pagination from the Kindle edition, which differs slightly from pagination in the print edition).

2. Frost-Thomas correspondence, June and July 1915, quoted in ibid., 233–235. "The Road Not Taken" was published early in 1916 as the lead poem in Frost, *Mountain Interval* (New York: Henry Holt).

3. Edward Thomas, "Roads," 22 Jan 16, available online from the *Poetry Foundation*.

4. Bethmann to Bernstorff, Berlin 260, 18 Aug 16, in André Scherer and Jacques Grunewald, eds., *L'Allemagne et les Problèmes de la Paix Pendant la Première Guerre Mondiale: Documents Extraits des Archives de l'Office Allemand des Affaires Étrangères* (Paris: Presses Universitaires de France, 1962), 1:438 (hereinafter *APP*, with volume and page number).

5. See, generally, Konrad Jarausch, *The Enigmatic Chancellor: Bethmann Hollweg and the Hubris of Imperial Germany* (New Haven: Yale University Press, 1973).

6. Theodor Wolff, *Tagebücher 1914–1919*, ed. Bernd Sösemann (Boppard am Rhein: Harald Boldt Verlag, 1984), 1:156–157 (entry for 9 Feb 1915).

7. Hans Peter Hanssen quoted in David Welch, *Germany, Propaganda and Total War, 1914–1918* (London: Athlone, 2000), 179.

8. Poincaré "preoccupied": J. F. V. Keiger, *Raymond Poincaré* (Cambridge: Cambridge University Press, 1997), 225. A newsreel records Poincaré coming to see the king at Haig's headquarters. Imperial War Museum, "The King Visits His Armies in the Great Advance," available online.

9. In Chapter 4, I elaborate on this episode, which was later reported to the British cabinet's War Committee. Biographers of Poincaré, including Keiger, appear to be unaware of this discussion. See also, for example, François Roth, *Raymond Poincaré* (Paris: Fayard, 2001), chap. 3. The king's account of his August 12 meeting with Poincaré is in a handwritten diary entry Bertie composed the day he saw the king, 17 Aug 16, in the Bertie Papers, FO 800/190, UK National Archives. But Bertie omitted this material from his published diary. *The Diary of Lord Bertie of Thame, 1914–1918*, ed. Lady Algernon Gordon Lennox (London: Hodder & Stoughton, 1924), 2:14 (entry for the August 17 audience with the king).

10. Private memorandum by Bertie, 11 Aug 16, Bertie Papers, FO 800/171.

11. Edward Mandell House diary, 4 Jan 17, House Papers, Yale University (presented as a direct quote) (hereinafter House diary).

12. Georges-Henri Soutou, "Briand et l'Allemagne au Tournant de la Guerre (Septembre 1916—Janvier 1917)," in Karl Ferdinand

Werner, ed., *Media en Francia…: recueil de mélanges offerts á Karl Ferdinand Werner* (Maulévrier: Hérault, 1989), 485; "a decisive turning point": Jörn Leonhard, *Pandora's Box: A History of the First World War*, trans. Patrick Camiller (Cambridge: Harvard University Press, 2018), 547. Leonhard adds a masterly summary of these trends. Ibid., 542–547. "For the historian": Bentley Brinkerhoff Gilbert, *David Lloyd George: A Political Life*, vol. 3, *Organizer of Victory, 1912–1916* (Columbus: Ohio State University Press, 1992), 367.

13. "Pivotal year": Roger Chickering, *Imperial Germany and the Great War, 1914–1918* (Cambridge: Cambridge University Press, 2nd ed., 2004), 65. For a view of the disturbing precedents the war created and modeled even in the United States, see David Kennedy, *Over Here: The First World War and American Society* (New York: Oxford University Press, 25th anniv. ed., 2004).

14. Robert Gerwarth, *The Vanquished: Why the First World War Failed to End* (New York: Farrar, Straus & Giroux, 2016), 12–13.

15. German officials doctored the Reichstag's documentary and testimonial record about the July crisis in 1914 and earlier matters. But this other Reichstag report, on the 1916–1917 peace moves, was conscientiously conducted. The Reichstag's investigative team, led by one of Germany's leading left-wing international lawyers and Reichstag delegates, Hugo Sinzheimer, obtained documents and took testimony from all the key principals under oath (with the principals knowing that the investigators had the records). It obtained analysis from several experts and published a report. The witnesses were carefully cross-examined and challenged repeatedly. Sinzheimer's work was honest, and he enlisted some good experts to help. Sinzheimer later died from maltreatment in a Nazi concentration camp. The investigative records and associated documents were published, in English translation, by the Carnegie Endowment for International Peace, in *Official German Documents Relating to the World War* (New York: Oxford University Press, 1923) (cited in the notes as *OGD*).

After the Second World War, French historians prepared a documentary archive of all captured German records related to peace moves during the First World War. This is another invaluable documentary collection, overlapping with but not identical to the records from the Reichstag work, edited by André Scherer and Jacques Grunewald, the *APP* collection cited above.

16. This debate over German war aims blurs into another debate, in which proponents of the "Fischer school" denounce historians like Gerhard Ritter and argue that German peace moves in 1916 were undertaken in bad faith and therefore had no chance. In fact, the evidence shows significant fluctuations in German war aims, depending on the time, the military circumstances, the political context, and which leaders were driving the action. For a nice summary, see Holger Afflerbach, " '…eine Internationale der Kriegsverschärfung und der Kriegsverlängerung…': War Aims and the Chances for a Compromise Peace During the First World War," in Afflerbach, ed., *The Purpose of the First World War: War Aims and Military Strategies* (Berlin: DeGruyter/Oldenbourg, 2015), esp. 243–244. Afflerbach divides the main phases into (1) establishment of war aims after the war began, (2) growing realism, and (3) growing despair. I would slightly modify Afflerbach's description to stress that German war aims escalated again in 1917–1918, with the ascension of the Hindenburg-Ludendorff de facto dictatorship and the German military successes during 1917–1918. Then they contracted again, with growing despair.

17. *9/11 Commission Report* (New York: Norton, 2004), 339.

18. Daniel Larsen has a useful critique of the problematical older historiography in his article "War Pessimism and an American Peace in Early 1916," *International History Review*, vol. 34 no. 4 (2012): 795, 796–798, 800–801. At that point Larsen was focused on the Anglo-American angle early in 1916. Larsen's full, important study is scheduled for publication as *Plotting for Peace: American*

*Peacemakers, British Codebreakers, and Britain at War, 1914–1917* (Cambridge: Cambridge University Press, 2021).

## Chapter 1: Wilson Makes a New Peace Move

1. House to Wilson, 29 May 14, in Arthur Link, David Hirst, John Little, Frederick Aandahl, et al., eds., *Papers of Woodrow Wilson* (Princeton: Princeton University Press, 1966–1994), 30: 109, also published in a digital edition by the Rotunda imprint of the University of Virginia Press. The volumes most relevant to this narrative were published from 1980 to 1983 (referred to hereinafter as *PWW*, with volume and page number from the print edition). For the literature on American entry into World War I, see Justus Doenecke's fine bibliography in his *Nothing Less Than War: A New History of America's Entry into World War I* (Lexington: University Press of Kentucky, 2011).

2. House thought the problem was just to get the kaiser together with British leaders and they would reconcile their differences. The kaiser expressed impulsive interest, since he could not understand why Britain would want to side with "Slavs" (Russians) or "Latins" (French). House did not understand that, in the first half of 1914, relations between Britain and Germany were already improving, as the earlier naval rivalry was receding into the background. On the 1914 House trip, see Charles Neu, *Colonel House: A Biography of Woodrow Wilson's Silent Partner* (New York: Oxford University Press, 2015), 125–131. Neu's work is the best biography of House.

3. House to Wilson, 1 Aug 14, *PWW*, 30:327.

4. For those who wish to dive into that story, a well-judged guide—in a large literature—is T. G. Otte, *July Crisis: The World's Descent into War, Summer 1914* (Cambridge: Cambridge University Press, 2014).

5. Hew Strachan, "The Ideas of 1914," in *The First World War*, vol. 1, *To Arms* (Oxford: Oxford University Press, 2001), esp. 1125–1129.

6. A fine recent portrait of the evolution of pro-Allied public opinion in America is Michael Neiberg, *The Path to War: How the First World War Created Modern America* (New York: Oxford University Press, 2016). Despite the book's title, it is not about the diplomatic side of that story.

7. For the views, organizations, and supporters of each of these three broad factions, see Ross Kennedy, *The Will to Believe: Woodrow Wilson, World War I, and America's Strategy for Peace and Security* (Kent: Kent State University Press, 2009), 1–64. Kennedy labels the three camps as "pacifists," "liberal internationalists," and "Atlanticists." A valuable chronology of editorial opinion throughout the war, in relation to Wilson's views, is James Startt, *Woodrow Wilson, the Great War, and the Fourth Estate* (College Station: Texas A&M University Press, 2017).

8. "Unique mission": Arthur Link, *Wilson: Confusions and Crises, 1915–1916* (Princeton: Princeton University Press, 1964), 24; "fruit of our thoughtless youth": Wilson (4 Nov 15), quoted in ibid., 20.

9. "Americans for Big America": Wilson (2 Sep 16), quoted in Arthur Link, *Wilson: Campaigns for Progressivism and Peace* (Princeton: Princeton University Press, 1965), 95.

10. Rightly stressing Wilson's flexibility is John Thompson, "More Tactics Than Strategy: Woodrow Wilson and World War I, 1914–1919," in William Tilchin and Charles Neu, eds., *Artists of Power: Theodore Roosevelt, Woodrow Wilson, and Their Enduring Impact on U.S. Foreign Policy* (Westport: Praeger, 2006), 95–105 (on the period before America joined the war). A thorough review of the attitudes on the submarine question remains Patrick Devlin, *Too Proud to Fight: Woodrow Wilson's Neutrality* (London: Oxford University Press, 1974), 156–216, 283–430, 472–500.

11. See Stephen Wertheim, "The League That Wasn't: American Designs for a Legalist-Sanctionist League of Nations and the Intellectual Origins of International Organization, 1914–1920," *Diplomatic History*, vol. 35 no. 5 (2011): 797, 802–818.

19. Holger Afflerbach, *Auf Messers Schneide: Wie das Deutsche Reich den Ersten Weltkrieg verlor* (München: C. H. Beck, 2018), 291.

12. A very good review of the literature on American preparedness debates before the war is Ross Kennedy, "Preparedness," in Kennedy, ed., *A Companion to Woodrow Wilson* (New York: John Wiley, 2013), 270–285.

13. John Milton Cooper Jr., *Woodrow Wilson: A Biography* (New York: Knopf, 2009), 7; see also John Milton Cooper Jr., *The Warrior and the Priest: Woodrow Wilson and Theodore Roosevelt* (Cambridge: Harvard University Press, 1983).

14. For analysis of Roosevelt's choreography in the Russo-Japanese mediation, see Robert Zoellick, *America in the World: A History of U.S. Diplomacy and Foreign Policy* (New York: Twelve, 2020), 112–124.

15. Tarbell published the article based on her interview in *Collier's* magazine. *PWW*, 38: 327–328. An excellent analysis of Wilson as a pragmatist, embedding this in the American philosophical tradition most influentially developed by William James, is Trygve Throntveit, *Power Without Victory: Woodrow Wilson and the American Internationalist Experiment* (Chicago: University of Chicago Press, 2017), esp. 125–126, although Throntveit appears unaware that Wilson openly acknowledged, to Tarbell, that he classed himself as a "pragmatist."

16. Cooper, *Woodrow Wilson*, 201.

17. See Charles Neu, "Woodrow Wilson and His Foreign Policy Advisers," in Tilchin and Neu, *Artists of Power*, 77–84. The relationship between Franklin Roosevelt and Harry Hopkins, for instance, was quite different from that between Wilson and House. Aside from the very different personalities involved, Hopkins was usually on the public payroll in some office or another, often in quite powerful official positions. And, unless on a mission, he always stayed close to his boss, in his last years usually living right in the White House.

18. Jonathan Daniels, *The End of Innocence* (Philadelphia: J. B. Lippincott, 1954), 50.

19. Neu, *Colonel House*, 53, 56.

20. The story of the novel, and the material from Lippmann, is in ibid., 70–74.

21. Lippmann, 1938, quoted in Ronald Steel, *Walter Lippmann and the American Century* (New York: Routledge, 2017, orig. 1980), 109.

Steel, who had access to Lippmann and his papers, also does not seem to be aware of the connection between the "Philip Dru" book, Lippmann, and House, presumably because Lippmann gave no sign of having made the connection. If Lippmann had made the connection, he might have called this out during the period when he was quite critical of Wilson, before 1916. Nor is there any sign that, when House and Lippmann became friends, in 1916, House recalled the review or made the connection between it and Lippmann.

22. Waldo Heinrichs Jr., *American Ambassador: Joseph C. Grew and the Development of the United States Diplomatic Tradition* (New York: Oxford University Press, 1966), 24.

23. On the origins of the House mission to Europe at the end of 1915, the exchanges with Grey, Wilson's instructions, and quotes through December 1915, unless otherwise cited, see Link, *Confusions and Crises*, 100–114, and Neu, *Colonel House*, 216–221. See also the background on the Grey-House relationship in Nicholas Ferns, "Loyal Advisor? Colonel Edward House's Confidential Trips to Europe, 1913–1917," *Diplomacy & Statecraft*, vol. 24 (2013): 365–382.

24. Grey to Spring-Rice, 22 Dec 14, reprinted in George Macaulay Trevelyan, *Grey of Fallodon* (Boston: Houghton Mifflin, 1937), 356.

25. In June 1915, Grey's influential private secretary, Eric Drummond, had drafted papers for Grey arguing for creation of a postwar "League of Peace." William Mulligan, *The Great War for Peace* (New Haven: Yale University Press, 2014), 125–126.

26. The leader of this movement in England was Lord James Bryce. On the founding of the League to Enforce Peace (LEP), whose first president was William Howard Taft, see Warren Kuehl, *Seeking World Order: The United States and International Organization to 1920* (Nashville: Vanderbilt University Press, 1969), 181–216; Wertheim, "The League That Wasn't," 802–818; and Thomas Knock, *To End All Wars: Woodrow Wilson and the Quest for a New World Order* (Princeton: Princeton University Press, 1992), 56–57. By 1915, Wilson also had ambitious ideas for a

postwar system that would end wars of conquest, guaranteed by an "association of nations" bound to preserve the peace. His ideas, though, remained private and undeveloped. Cooper, *Woodrow Wilson*, 176; Kuehl, *Seeking World Order*, 224–227.

Wilson's eventual views were not identical to those of the LEP. That group leaned toward allying with Britain and seeking German defeat as their necessary precondition. Wilson thought that such a one-sided outcome would make a lasting peace harder to attain. He preferred a mediated settlement.

Later, other important differences would emerge between the "great power concert" and "collective security" versions of these league ideas. See Kuehl, *Seeking World Order*; Kennedy, *The Will to Believe*, 44–47; and Wertheim, "The League That Wasn't." In 1915 and 1916 these differences were not yet clear.

27. The instruction letter: Wilson to House, 24 Dec 15, *PWW*, 35:387.
28. Tumulty memo, 4 Jan 16, *PWW*, 35:424.
29. Simon Heffer, *Staring at God: Britain in the Great War* (London: Random House, 2019), 479–480.
30. For an overview, see George Cassar, *Asquith as War Leader* (London: Hambledon Press, 1994), and the standard biography, Roy Jenkins, *Asquith* (London: Collins, rev. ed., 1978). On Asquith "spent" and "carried on the current," see Page to Wilson, 2 Jul 15, *PWW*, 33:550–553.
31. Michael Fry, *Lloyd George and Foreign Policy*, vol. 1, *The Education of a Statesman, 1890–1916*

## Chapter 2: The British Are Tempted

1. House to Wilson, 30 Jan, 1 and 3 Feb 16, *PWW*, 36:52, 85, 122–123, 125. The two men had a private code. Wilson would decode the telegrams himself and type them out. Their private code posed no hindrance to British intelligence, which was intercepting and reading these telegrams. But House and Wilson were security conscious enough to be relatively careful in what they put into these cables.
2. When House predicted American entry into the war, later in the year, on the Allied side, the French foreign minister, Jules Cambon,

(Montreal: McGill-Queen's University Press, 1977), 12–13.
32. Page to Wilson, 2 Jul 15, *PWW*, 33:550–553.
33. Jenkins, *Asquith*, 338. The corruption crisis was the "Marconi" scandal, involving allegations of insider trading in Marconi shares by Lloyd George, among others.
34. Trevor Wilson, ed., *The Political Diaries of C. P. Scott, 1911–1928* (Ithaca: Cornell University Press, 1970), 163 (entry for 14 Dec 15).
35. House diary, 14 Jan 16, in Edward Mandell House Papers, Yale University (hereinafter House diary); and House to Wilson, 15 Jan 16, *PWW*, 35:484–485.
36. *Political Diaries of C. P. Scott*, 164–165 (entry for 15 Dec 15), 177 (entry for 28 Jan 16).
37. House diary, 15 and 19 Jan 16.
38. House diary, 28 Jan 16. The assault on Verdun began on February 21.
39. House diary, 27 and 28 Jan 16. For the German record of what they heard in two of their meetings with House, see Solf to Jagow, 28 Jan 16, and Bethmann's memo, 28 Jan 16, both in Carnegie Endowment for International Peace, *Official German Documents Relating to the World War* (New York: Oxford University Press, 1923) (hereinafter *OGD*), 2:1280–1283; see also Gerhard Ritter, *The Sword and the Scepter: The Problem of Militarism in Germany*, vol. 3, *The Tragedy of Statesmanship—Bethmann Hollweg as War Chancellor (1914–1917)*, trans. Heinz Norden (Coral Gables: University of Miami Press, 1972, orig. 1964), 152–153.

asked how that would happen. According to the French record, House replied, "It would be necessary for an incident to occur that would cause all the American people to rally behind the President." What sort of incident? House then turned to submarine issues. Jules Cambon report, 2 Feb 16, *PWW*, 36:125n1. In a second meeting with French leaders, House explained his expectation that America would intervene later in the year whether the Allies did well or poorly. Presumably he thought both situations would produce a call for American mediation, which he thought the Germans would reject.

House was not fully revealing his scenario for American intervention to the French. His references to intervention did not just mean military intervention. But he did not fully explain his peace mediation plan. Also, because House was casually assuming that the Germans would play into this scenario by rejecting mediation, his references to intervention were even blurrier. The French heard this as a promise of military intervention if things went badly, redoubling the confusion. Cambon memo, 7 Feb 16, *PWW*, 148n1. This understanding they passed to Lord Bertie, the British ambassador in Paris.

Bertie, an ardent Conservative who loathed Wilson, also was contemptuous of House. Bertie passed the French report on to Edward Grey. Grey showed Bertie's report to House, who by that time was back in London. House spotted the flaws and pointed them out to Grey. Grey sent the corrections back to Bertie. House discusses this in his diary. Larsen also reviews this episode in *Plotting for Peace*, chap. 3. Good historians criticizing House have seized on this episode to fuel their scorn for him (e.g., Cooper, *Woodrow Wilson*, 316–317) or at least their unease with his conduct (Neu, *Colonel House*, 231–232).

3. Jenkins, *Asquith*, 95, 335–336. Asquith wrote up this little play in March 1915.

4. To simplify, the diagram omits the admiral leading the navy and includes Grey, who was not a formal member of the War Committee but attended whenever diplomatic issues were on the agenda, which was usually the case.

5. David Woodward, *Field Marshal Sir William Robertson: Chief of the Imperial General Staff in the Great War* (Westport: Praeger, 1998), 30.

6. The biography is Stephen Roskill, *Hankey: Man of Secrets* (London: Collins, 1970); volume 1 covers 1877 to 1918. Hankey was a lieutenant colonel on the retired list. Regulations allowed him to continue to wear his uniform in this government service. "Most useful man": Jenkins, *Asquith*, 412.

7. Robertson had made the basic proposal for the offensive in December 1915. Balfour's essential response came on December 27. The War Committee debated the issue on January

13. See minutes of War Committee meeting, 13 Jan 16, CAB 42/7/5, or 22/3/2, attaching earlier memoranda. Grey's memo, 14 Jan 16, is in the Edward Grey Papers, FO 800/96. Balfour's reply, "The Present Military Position, and Opinions in the War Committee," 21 Jan 16, is at CAB 37/141/17. Robertson's comment, "The Question of Offensive Operations on the Western Front," at CAB 42/7/1, circulated on 5 Jan 16.

8. "Political chaplain": Gilbert, *Organizer of Victory*, 21.

9. The Asquith comment, on July 1915, is from Martin Farr, *Reginald McKenna: Financier Among Statesmen, 1863–1916* (London: Routledge, 2008), 326.

10. McKenna's comment in the War Committee meeting, 23 Aug 15, is quoted in ibid., 306. The import and French spending estimates are both from Larsen, *Plotting for Peace*, intro. and app. 1.

11. Farr, *McKenna*, 320.

12. Grey to War Committee, 17 Feb 16, "The Position of Great Britain with Regard to Her Allies," in Grey Papers, FO 800/96.

13. *America and Munitions: The Work of J. P. Morgan in the World War* (internal history, privately published by J. P. Morgan & Co., 1923), 269, available at the Morgan Library, New York City. The study's author is not given but was F. Carrington Weems, an associate of the firm and a US Army officer in the war. The outstanding source on Morgan's work and Anglo-American finance was written by Vincent Carosso. Carosso, a meticulous outside scholar, was given full access to the firm's archives. His 920-page initial volume, *The Morgans: Private International Bankers, 1854–1913* (Cambridge: Harvard University Press, 1987), was to be followed by a comparably voluminous second volume. Carosso passed away as that volume, which details the wartime period, was in final typescript. His excellent manuscript is available in the Vincent Carosso Papers, Morgan Library, New York City; it is cited hereinafter as Carosso MS, with chapter and manuscript page. A much briefer but also well-judged account of the financial story is in Kathleen Burk, *Britain, America and the*

*Sinews of War, 1914–1918* (Boston: George Allen & Unwin, 1985). Unfortunately, the relatively sanguine picture of British finances in a recent survey of the economics of World War I does not adequately reflect what is in the archives of the British government or its American banker. Stephen Broadberry and Peter Howlett, "The United Kingdom During World War I: Business as Usual?" in Broadberry and Mark Harrison, eds., *The Economics of World War I* (Cambridge: Cambridge University Press, 2005).

14. "Marked a turning-point": Carosso MS, 4:86–87; see also ibid., 4:87–102; Burk, *Britain, America and the Sinews of War*, 67–75. At first, in September 1915 McKenna and his talented aide, Keynes, were too pessimistic, seeing the dollars running out in six months. Lloyd George, who had been more confident, remembered that undue pessimism. As Treasury devised new expedients, McKenna revised his estimates of when the dollars would run out, projecting dollar bankruptcy sometime in the first half of 1917. Those early 1916 estimates turned out to be close to the mark.

15. Farr, *McKenna*, 312–316, 321. McKenna was invariably joined by Runciman in his arguments to find some way to limit or end the war.

16. Kitchener outlined this theory in detail to a member of the cabinet, Lewis Harcourt, when the two men dined alone on January 3. Harcourt cabinet diary, 3 Jan 16, in Lewis Harcourt Papers, Bodleian/Weston Library, MS. Eng. C. 8271, Oxford University (hereinafter cited as Harcourt cabinet diary).

17. War Committee minutes, 13 Jan 16, CAB 42/7/5.

18. Larsen, *Plotting for Peace*, chap. 3, drawing on the proceedings of this Military-Finance Committee, January 1916, at CAB 27/4.

19. Balfour's analysis was in a memo for the cabinet, "Irresponsible Reflections on the Part Which the Pacific [Peaceful] Nations Might Play in Discussing Future Wars," 19 Jan 16 (not referring specifically to House or Grey but written just after he discussed these ideas with them), CAB 37/141/11.

20. House diary, 10 Feb 16; House cable and letter to Wilson, 10 Feb; Wilson cable to House,

12 Feb, *PWW*, 36:166–168, 173. British intelligence was intercepting some of House's cables (which were not as revealing as the letters being sent by diplomatic pouch and not intercepted). The naval officer running those operations, Captain Reginald Hall, tried to use those intercepts to sabotage House's efforts. Larsen, *Plotting for Peace*, chap. 3; Daniel Larsen, "British Intelligence and the 1916 Mediation Mission of Colonel Edward M. House," *Intelligence and National Security*, vol. 25 no. 5 (October 2010): 682–704. But, in this phase, Hall's intrigues do not seem to have influenced the War Committee debates.

21. House diary, 10 and 12 Feb 16.

22. Farr, *McKenna*, 328 (as of the January 13 argument about the offensive plan); Hankey diary, 12 Feb 16, in Maurice Hankey Papers, Churchill Archive Centre, Cambridge University, Box 1/1 (hereinafter cited as Hankey diary).

23. House diary, 14 Feb 16.

24. On the limited to nonexistent British interest in breaking up Austria-Hungary at this point, near the midpoint of the war, see William Anthony Hay, "A Problem Postponed: Britain and the Future of Austria-Hungary, 1914–18," *Diplomacy & Statecraft*, vol. 13 no. 3 (2002): 57–62.

25. House diary, 15 and 17 Feb 16; the text of the House-Grey memorandum is at *PWW*, 36:180n2.

26. The historical understanding of British policy on the peace option has long been confused. The memoirs were unreliable and incomplete, although at least Grey's was not actively untruthful. The historiography and evidence up until 1973 are well summarized in John Milton Cooper Jr., "The British Response to the House-Grey Memorandum: New Evidence and New Questions," *Journal of American History*, vol. 59 no. 4 (1973): 958–966 and the documentary attachments at 966–971.

27. War Committee minutes, 22 Feb 16, beginning on 25–26, CAB 42/9/3 or CAB 22/8.

28. *Lloyd George: A Diary by Frances Stevenson*, ed. A. J. P. Taylor (London: Hutchinson, 1971), 101–102, 93 (entries for 21, 23, and 1 Feb).

29. Grey discussion with Hankey in Hankey diary, 16 Mar 16; Hankey's earlier view in

Hankey diary, 11 Mar, and also, in a slightly different version, in Lord Hankey, *The Supreme Command: 1914–1918* (London: George Allen & Unwin, 1961), 2:479.

30. "Humbug": Asquith to Hankey, Hankey diary, 16 Mar 16; Grey to Asquith, circulated to War Committee, 15 Mar 16, in Herbert Henry Asquith Papers, Bodleian Library, Oxford University, Box 29.

31. Hankey warned Robertson: Hankey diary, 14 Mar 16; War Committee minutes, 21 Mar 16, CAB 42/11 and 22/13, reprinted with helpful explanation in Cooper, "The British Response," 959n2, 967–970.

32. Harcourt cabinet diary, 19 Apr 16 (his notes for preceding days document the buildup and the "passages" between McKenna and Lloyd George).

33. Hankey diary, 24 Apr 16.

34. Larsen, *Plotting for Peace*, chap. 4.

35. Hankey diary, 27 Apr (re Seely) and 2 May 16.

36. Quoted in Larsen, *Plotting for Peace*, chap. 4.

37. McKenna to cabinet, 19 May 16, CAB 37/148/6, and his May 17 attachment.

38. See House diary, 8, 12, 19, and 29 Mar 16.

39. See Devlin, *Too Proud to Fight*, 473–483; Link, *Confusions and Crises*, 256–279.

40. House to Wilson, 9 May 16, with enclosed cable from House to Grey, 10 May; House letter to Grey, 11 May; House to Wilson, 14 May, enclosing 12 May cable from Grey and proposed reply; Wilson to House, 16 May, *PWW*, 37:6–7, 21, 42–44, 57–58. Wilson defined wars of aggression as wars "begun either a) contrary to treaty covenants or b) without warning and full inquiry,—a virtual guarantee of territorial integrity and political independence."

41. Tumulty to Wilson, 16 May 16, *PWW*, 37:58–59 (emphasis in original). Tumulty then developed the argument about timing in some detail. The next day, Wilson welcomed his note and said his views were similar. Ibid., 62.

42. House diary, 17 May 16.

43. House to Wilson, 17 May 16, with enclosed draft cable to Grey; Wilson to House, 18 May, approving the draft, which was sent on May 19, *PWW*, 37:62–64, 68.

44. Spring-Rice to London, 18 May 16, *PWW*, 37:73.

45. "Black financial outlook" and the vote count in Hankey diary, 24 May 16. See also Larsen, *Plotting for Peace*, chap. 4; Larsen, "War Pessimism and an American Peace in Early 1916," 795, 810–811; David French, *British Strategy and War Aims, 1914–1916* (London: Allen & Unwin, 1986), 195; John Turner, *British Politics and the Great War: Coalition and Conflict, 1915–1918* (New Haven: Yale University Press, 1992), 98–100.

46. A good summary of the Allied dilemmas on Poland at this point in the war is in Mulligan, *The Great War for Peace*, 114–116.

47. Balfour's redrafted reply to House, 24 May 16, CAB 37/148/28.

48. Curzon's note: Larsen, *Plotting for Peace*, chap. 4. Curzon was not yet a regular member of the War Committee but appears to have been invited to attend that day's meeting because of his work on air and shipping issues.

49. "Most important": House to Wilson, 18 May 16; Wilson's note to himself on the four points, 24 May 16; and the speech are at *PWW*, 37:68, 102, 113–117.

50. Wilson to House, 18 May 16, *PWW*, 37:68–69.

51. House to Wilson, 27 May 16, in ibid., 37:117.

52. The House to Grey letter, 27 May 16 (probably received during the first week of June), is mentioned in a footnote in Link, *Campaigns for Progressivism and Peace*, 32–33n113.

53. Wilson to House, 29 May 16, in ibid., 37:118.

54. On the British reaction, see Hankey diary, 29 May 16; Larsen, *Plotting for Peace*, chap. 4; and Grey's May 29 reply to House (rec'd May 31), *PWW*, 37:131–132. For the French argument, including both House's account and the French record of the discussion with House on June 1, see *PWW*, 37:134–137 and note 2.

House blamed Wilson for the inflammatory language on indifference to the causes of the war. But the problems with the speech went much deeper than that, and House was principally responsible for them, since he was the one Wilson had looked to for advice on how to win over the British peacemakers.

55. Carosso MS, 4:127–128, 137–147.

56. Devlin, *Too Proud to Fight*, 463.
57. Wilson to House, 22 Jun 16, *PWW*, 37: 280–281; House diary, 23 Jun 16. House added, "It is stupid to refuse our proffered intervention on the terms I proposed in Paris and London."

## Chapter 3: The Germans Secretly Seek a Compromise Peace

1. Prince Rupprecht of Bavaria, quoted in Alexander Watson, *Ring of Steel: Germany and Austria-Hungary in World War I* (New York: Basic, 2014), 325.
2. A concise summary of the three major European campaigns of that year (Verdun, Brusilov offensive, Somme) is Robin Prior, "1916: Impasse," in Jay Winter, ed., *The Cambridge History of the First World War*, vol. 1, *Global War* (Cambridge: Cambridge University Press, 2014), 89–109.
3. The German observer was Moritz Julius Bonn, a professor of political economy who worked for the German government during and after the war. He served on the German delegation at Versailles and other postwar conferences. He knew Bethmann and other leading officials. He was one of the experts appointed to advise the 1919–1920 German parliamentary investigation into why the German peace move failed. The quote is from his final expert opinion on the peace issues, 23 Jun 20, *OGD*, 1:188–189.
4. Pless is now Pszczyna. The castle has been restored and has a museum. On Daisy's impressions, see "History of the Castle," Castle Museum in Pszczyna, http://www.zamek -pszczyna.pl/english/history.
5. Holger Afflerbach, "Wilhelm II as Supreme Warlord in the First World War," in Annika Mombauer and Wilhelm Deist, eds., *The Kaiser: New Research on Wilhelm II's Role in Imperial Germany* (Cambridge: Cambridge University Press, 2003), 195, 206.
6. "Conception of peace": Mulligan, *The Great War for Peace*, 162. On Bethmann's readiness for a negotiated peace by 1915, see Jarausch, *The Enigmatic Chancellor*; Karl Helfferich, *Der Weltkrieg*, vol. 2, *Vom Kriegsausbruch bis zum uneingeschränkten U-Bootkrieg* (Berlin: Ullstein, 1920), 291–296.

But House then slid back to his old 1915 insistence that the war had to end "militarism and navalism." He wondered if that was "where the shoe pinches" for the British.
58. Wilson to House, 22 Jun 16, cited above.

7. Kurt Riezler diary, 29 Apr 16, in Riezler, *Tagebücher, Aufsätze, Dokumente*, ed. Karl Dietrich Erdmann (München: Vandenhoeck & Ruprecht, new ed., 2008), 350; see also his entries for 30 Apr and 7 May, 351–355, just before the *Sussex* pledge settlement.
8. Riezler diary, 14 Jun 16, in ibid., 359.
9. Bavarian ambassador's report, 29 May 16, in Jarausch, *The Enigmatic Chancellor*, 198. In May, after settling the submarine issue, Bethmann felt ready to ask Wilson for help. Then, at the beginning of June, the military situation improved momentarily, and Bethmann yielded briefly to his foreign secretary Gottlieb von Jagow's advice that Wilson was too pro-British and naive. At that time, Jagow preferred to keep the Americans out of the peace talks and to hold out for one of the Entente allies to cut a separate deal. Karl Birnbaum, *Peace Moves and U-boat Warfare* (Uppsala: Almquist & Wiksells, 1958), 73–108.
10. The main salvo to belittle Bethmann's reputation as a liberal came from Fritz Fischer, *Germany's Aims in the First World War* (New York: W. W. Norton, 1967). Fischer argued, with good evidence, that Bethmann had been more of an opportunist, going along with the more ambitious war aims early in the war (and again, more weakly, in the spring of 1917). The usual lead counts in this indictment are Bethmann's behavior in the July crisis of 1914 and his part in the September 1914 development of an annexation program developed at the height of Germany's opening victories. On these two issues, balanced perspectives are offered in T. G. Otte, "The Limits of the Possible: Some Reflections on Chancellor Bethmann Hollweg and the July Crisis of 1914," *H-German*, December 17, 2014, https://networks.h-net.org/node/35008 /discussions/55746/ann-h-german-forum -first-world-war-otte-december-2014; and Wayne Thompson, "The September Program:

Reflections on the Evidence," *Central European History*, vol. 11 no. 4 (1978): 348–354.

Fischer is so concerned to show that Bethmann was always in tune with the annexationists that he tends to omit the evidence showing that he was not, especially as the war progressed. He also separates his U-boat chapter from his 1916–1917 war aims chapter; yet, since the U-boat and peace options were the two main choices, these two topics were actually closely intertwined. By 1916, the split between Bethmann and the German conservatives had become open and notorious, a constant subject of public comment and debate. The split was obvious on both the U-boat issue and the issue of war aims/annexations (linked to hopes of a compromise peace). Since Bethmann's peace efforts can only be understood in the context of understanding this linked debate, which so many Germans at the time could see, Fischer's selective use of evidence to blur this fundamental debate undermines his work on the 1916–1917 period. For this particular period, I find that historians like Ritter and Afflerbach are better guides, in addition to the primary sources.

11. Bethmann testimony, 4 Nov 19, *OGD*, 1:392.
12. Riezler diary, 29 Jun 16, in *Tagebücher*, 360–361.
13. Von Müller diary, 2 Jul 16, in Walter Görlitz, ed., *The Kaiser and His Court: The Diaries, Note Books and Letters of Admiral Georg Alexander von Müller Chief of the Naval Cabinet, 1914–1918*, trans. Mervyn Savill (London: Macdonald, 1961), 180.
14. Holger Afflerbach, *Falkenhayn: Politisches Denken und Handeln im Kaiserreich* (Munich: Oldenbourg, 1994), 198.
15. Bethmann to Lyncker, 23 Jun 16, quoted in Ritter, *Tragedy of Statesmanship*, 188; Bethmann with the kaiser and his staff, Müller diary entries, 26–27 Jul 16, in Görlitz, *The Kaiser and His Court*, 187–188; Afflerbach, *Falkenhayn*, 435.
16. "A great war weariness": Harry Kessler quoted in Leonhard, *Pandora's Box*, 113; see Afflerbach, *Auf Messers Schneide*, 231–233; "only a miracle": from Lyncker to his wife, October 1916, at 232.

17. Count Bernstorff, *Memoirs of Count Bernstorff*, trans. Eric Sutton (New York: Random House, 1936), 24.
18. Bernstorff was on the shortlist to become chancellor after he had to return to Germany under a cloud in 1917, after the United States went to war against Germany. Plessen diary, 13 Jul 17, in Holger Afflerbach, ed., *Kaiser Wilhelm II. als Oberster Kriegsherr im Ersten Weltkrieg: Quellen aus der militärischen Umgebung des Kaisers 1914–1918* (München: Oldenbourg, 2005), 907.
19. David Nickles, *Under the Wire: How the Telegraph Changed Diplomacy* (Cambridge: Harvard University Press, 2003), 140–142.
20. "The most brilliant," "he does not devote," and comments on Gerard: Count Bernstorff, *My Three Years in America* (London: Skeffington & Son, 1920), 7, 247–248; "audiences" and "obstinate dogmatism": Bernstorff, *Memoirs*, 133–134; "absolutely honorable": Bernstorff testimony, 21–22 Oct 19, *OGD*, 1:234, 283.
21. Bernstorff, *My Three Years in America*, 220.
22. See Bernstorff to Foreign Office, no. 44, 2 Jun 16 (rec'd 7 Jun) and Jagow to Bernstorff, 7 Jun 16 (sent on 12 Jun), probably delivered via cargo submarine in mid-July, *APP*, 1:354–355, 359–360; *OGD*, 2:1294, 976–977 (mislabeled in this source as a telegram); Jagow to Bernstorff, 12 Jun 16, *OGD*, 2:978; Bernstorff, *My Three Years in America*, 219.

In mid-June, Bernstorff was so worried about possible German resumption of unrestricted submarine warfare that he apparently tried a fictional effort, using a story of having met a well-placed person from England, to induce House to encourage the German government to appoint someone (likely to be Bernstorff) to meet with someone the English might then send. With this odd and desperate device, Bernstorff may have been trying to show Berlin that there might be some action on the peace alternative. In fact, he knew that House had put this on ice for the summer. See Birnbaum, *Peace Moves and U-boat Warfare*, 111–114. In June, Bernstorff similarly tried to stop a tearing up of the *Sussex* pledge, and likely war with America, by reporting, incorrectly, that Wilson's mediation offer was "to be definitely expected in the course of the summer, from election prospects if for no other reason." Bernstorff to Foreign Office, 19 Jun 16 (rec'd 22 Jun), *OGD*, 2:979.

23. Bernstorff to Bethmann, 13 Jul 16 (rec'd 16 Aug), *APP*, 1:405–407; *OGD*, 2:979–981. Another message to similar effect, written on 28 May, was possibly sent back via cargo submarine and did not arrive in Berlin until 30 Aug. Ibid., 982–983.

24. Bethmann to Bernstorff, *APP*, 1:438; *OGD*, 2:981–982 (my translation differs slightly from the translation in *OGD*). Bethmann rewrote a more conservative Foreign Office draft that would have kept the neutrals out of the peace conference. Birnbaum, *Peace Moves and U-boat Warfare*, 126–127.

25. On Bethmann's thinking, see Afflerbach, *Auf Messers Schneide*, 278; on the discussions with the kaiser, see Müller diary, entries for 25 and 27 Aug 16, in Görlitz, *The Kaiser and His Court*, 197–198.

26. For the difficult end-of-August discussions with the military about U-boat warfare, see the detailed notes of the 31 Aug 16 meeting in Pless, *OGD*, 2:1154–1163. Bethmann's chief aides in this work were Jagow and Karl Helfferich. Helfferich held the interior and finance portfolios and was also vice-chancellor. Helfferich had initially preferred to hold out and try harder for a separate peace with Russia, offering up Poland. But Bethmann and Jagow convinced him that the Russia-only option had no chance. Afflerbach, *Auf Messers Schneide*, 233–237, 278; Birnbaum, *Peace Moves and U-boat Warfare*, 128–129.

For the instruction, see Bethmann to Bernstorff, 2 Sep 16, *APP*, 1:465–466; *OGD*, 2:983 (*bedingte Wiederherstellung* is mistakenly translated as "unconditional" in *OGD*). As to what Bethmann meant by "conditional" restoration of Belgium, the Germans had already reviewed several of their ideas with King Albert. See the details on the German-Belgian discussions in 1916 about future security assurances in Ritter, *Tragedy of Statesmanship*, 240–245, 546n24, and in Birnbaum, *Peace Moves and U-boat Warfare*, 107n8. I discuss this Belgian issue further in Chapter 5.

27. Bernstorff, *Memoirs*, 107–108.

28. House diary, 3 Sep 16; Bernstorff, *My Three Years in America*, 242–243; Bernstorff telegrams to Foreign Office, undated (probably early on 8 Sep) and 8 Sep 16, *APP*, 1:466–467; *OGD*, 2:983–984. Both of these were cabled using the Buenos Aires–Stockholm roundabout. The *OGD* translation refers to whether Wilson will "enter into" territorial questions; I translate *einmischen werden* as shown in the text. On the significance of Belgium to American opinion, see also Bernstorff testimony, in *OGD*, 1:253–254.

29. Birnbaum, *Peace Moves and U-boat Warfare*, 130.

30. Von Marschall, a deputy to Lyncker, 28 Aug 16, quoted in Ritter, *Tragedy of Statesmanship*, 205.

31. On the growing strength and attitudes of Hindenburg and navy commander Holtzendorff, see Birnbaum, *Peace Moves and U-boat Warfare*, 131–144.

32. Ernest May, *The World War and American Isolation, 1914–1917* (Cambridge: Harvard University Press, 1959), 290–291, quoting Joseph Grew and Theodor Wolff.

33. See ibid., 294–301; Ritter, *Tragedy of Statesmanship*, 271–274.

34. On the kaiser's continued determination to avoid the full U-boat war, see Grünau to Foreign Office (from the kaiser's train), 5 Oct 16, *OGD*, 2:1171.

35. Bethmann to Bernstorff, 25 Sep 16 (telegrams 90–92), *OGD*, 2:984–986; for background on the back-and-forth in the drafting process at Imperial Headquarters in Pless, see Birnbaum, *Peace Moves and U-boat Warfare*, 155–158.

36. Berlin 4375, 25 Sep 16 (rec'd in Washington the next day), in Department of State, *Papers Relating to the Foreign Relations of the United States, 1916: Supplement, the World War* (Washington, DC: Government Printing Office, 1929), doc. 69 (cited hereinafter as *FRUS 1916, World War*, with document number only, since this reference series is available in electronic and print forms). For the German background of the renewed late-September pleas through both Bernstorff and

Gerard, see Bethmann to Wilhelm II, 23 Sep 16 (negotiated with navy chief Holtzendorff), and subsequent exchanges, *APP*, 1:469–474; Birnbaum, *Peace Moves and U-boat Warfare*, 153–154.

37. Link believes House regarded Bernstorff's further push and his instructions from Bethmann as "routine." This is how Link explains why House did not tell Wilson about it. It is more likely that House thought he had put the matter off until after the election. Link does not mention the message from Gerard in Berlin. Link, *Campaigns for Progressivism and Peace*, 170–172. On September 30, Lansing relayed Gerard's message to Wilson at his home in New Jersey, where the president often stayed during the closing phase of his reelection campaign. *PWW*, 38:313–314.

38. Bernstorff to Foreign Office, 10 Oct 16 (about a meeting on 9 Oct), *PWW*, 38:390–392 (with a better translation than the one in *OGD*); House diary, 11 Oct 16. Bethmann put it thus: "A spontaneous appeal for peace, toward the making of which I request that he be further encouraged, would be gladly accepted by us." Bethmann to Bernstorff, 14 Oct 16, *OGD*, 2:989.

39. Bernstorff to Foreign Office, 20 Oct 16 (rec'd 24 Oct), *APP*, 1:521; *OGD*, 2:990 (with slightly different translation).

40. House diary excerpt, 19 Oct 16; House to Wilson, 20 Oct, with attached message from Bernstorff and the kaiser's note, in *PWW*, 38:493–496. Berlin had left it to Bernstorff to decide whether it was best to give the kaiser's memo to Wilson. Bernstorff decided to give it to House—along with a cover letter stating, as instructed, that the message was "not intended as a threat with more drastic U-Boat warfare on our part"—and let him decide.

41. Wilson to William Edlin, 4 Nov 16; Wilson to Edith Reid, 10 Nov 16, both quoted in Ray Stannard Baker, *Woodrow Wilson: Life and Letters*, vol. 6, *Facing War, 1915–1917* (New York: Charles Scribner's Sons, 1937), 365, 296–298.

42. See Afflerbach, *Auf Messers Schneide*, 237–238, 284–285; Ritter, *Tragedy of Statesmanship*, 277–279; Jarausch, *The Enigmatic Chancellor*, 251; for Bernstorff's similar articulation of the "Hubertusburg" analogy, see Bernstorff, *Memoirs*, 139–140.

43. Manfried Rauchensteiner, *The First World War and the End of the Habsburg Monarchy, 1914–1918*, trans. Alex Kay and Anna Güttel-Bellert (Wien: Böhlau Verlag, 2014), 655. The Austrian side did not trust Wilson's attitude toward the Dual Monarchy. The Germans and Austrians kept discussing whether to rely on the American channel or make a direct, public peace offer.

44. Bussche to Foreign Office, 12 Jul 16, attaching Czernin's memo, *APP*, 1:401–403.

45. "League of Nations": Jarausch, *The Enigmatic Chancellor*, 250; and, noting the disclaimer of interest in Belgian annexation, Wolff, *Tagebücher 1914–1919*, 1:455 (entry for 9 Nov 16).

46. Ritter, *Tragedy of Statesmanship*, 277–279; Fritz Fischer, *Griff nach der Weltmacht: Die Kriegszielpolitik des kaiserlichen Deutschland 1914/18* (Dusselldorf: Droste, 1961), 257–258.

47. "We are not leading": Bethmann to Stumm, 28 Oct 16, *APP*, 1:534–535.

48. "The Chancellor has promised me": quoted in Z. A. B. Zeman, *The Gentlemen Negotiators: A Diplomatic History of the First World War* (New York: Macmillan, 1971), 123; see also Fischer, *Griff nach der Weltmacht*, 260. For more on the German-Austrian negotiations, see Rauchensteiner, *First World War and the End of the Habsburg Monarchy*, 671; also, the main documents for these intra-alliance and internal negotiations are in *OGD*, 2:1053–1072; Wolfgang Steglich, *Bündnissicherung oder Verständigungsfrieden: Untersuchungen zu dem Friedensangebot der Mittelmächte vom 12. Dezember 1916* (Berlin: Musterschmidt, 1958); Ritter, *Tragedy of Statesmanship*, 282–292; Birnbaum, *Peace Moves and U-boat Warfare*, 190–200.

The Germans believed they could counter British rhetoric calling for national self-determination. They could cite British and French imperial acquisitions, the

Anglo-French bullying of Greece to make way for their wartime expedition into Salonika, and Britain's recent suppression of the uprising in Ireland. Germany and Austria proceeded (in November) to announce the restoration of an independent Poland in the territory they occupied, although this was really their way of separating it from Russia and into a country they could dominate. The Germans hoped to install a German monarch, perhaps from the royal house of Bavaria, on the Polish throne. To them, the big argument against granting independence to Poland was that it would complicate a separate peace with Russia. By the end of the summer of 1916, the Germans had given up, at least for the time being, on concluding a separate peace with Russia. On Bethmann's conceptions and the German/Austrian debates, see Mulligan, *The Great War for Peace*, 170–173; Martin Kitchen, *The Silent Dictatorship: The Politics of the German High Command Under Hindenburg and Ludendorff, 1916–1918* (London: Croon Helm, 1976), 89–94.

49. "Thick book" and Bethmann's reasoning: Afflerbach, *Auf Messers Schneide*, 280–282; for examples of Bethmann explaining the problems of "maximum" and "minimum" positions, see Bethmann to Wedel, 1 Nov 16, *OGD*, 2:1057–1058; Bethmann's explanations to the Bundesrat: quoted in Ritter, *Tragedy of Statesmanship*, 281; "get Asquith and Grey": former chancellor Bülow describing Bethmann's views to Theodor Wolff, in *Tagebücher 1914–1919*, 1:439–440 (entry for 9 Oct 16).

50. Bethmann's 1916 comments to Hindenburg and to his aide, Kurt Riezler, quoted in Ritter, *Tragedy of Statesmanship*, 292; Bethmann testimony, *OGD*, 1:339. See also Jarausch, *The Enigmatic Chancellor*, 250, 487n56; Birnbaum, *Peace Moves and U-boat Warfare*, 194–196. Fischer makes his case about the extreme nature of Bethmann's aims in this period by omitting much of the material I have mentioned, while leaning heavily on the papers written by such "nameless staff officers." To understand Bethmann's political strategy is also to understand why he made various tactical concessions in his internal war aims negotiations with Hindenburg and others. Those documents would be irrelevant once the conference began. Bethmann, not the generals, would be in charge at the negotiating table.

## Chapter 4: The British Debate Reaches Breaking Point

1. Woodward, *Robertson*, 52–55.

2. Ibid., 56–57; Cassar, *Asquith as War Leader*, 191–192; and see Jim Beach, *Haig's Intelligence: GHQ and the German Army, 1916–1918* (Cambridge: Cambridge University Press, 2013), 202–217.

3. Raymond to Diana Manners, 11 Dec 15; to his wife, Katharine, 15 Apr 16; "more tired of the war": to Katharine, 28 May 16; "don't look ahead": to Katharine, 11 Jun 16, in John Jolliffe, ed., *Raymond Asquith: Life and Letters* (London: Collins, 1980), 226, 257, 264, 268.

4. To Manners, 10 Jul 16, ibid., 272–273.

5. "Dent" and "disaster" (commenting on the Australian-British attack near Fauquissart, usually referred to as the Battle of Fromelles): to Katharine, 4 Aug 16; "senselessness": 10 Jul 16; "being a success or not": 9 Aug 16, in ibid., 281, 282, 274, 284. Back in May, Raymond and Churchill had taken a long walk together, and Churchill had confided his fear that "it would be madness to have an offensive this year." Raymond to Katharine, 3 May 16, ibid., 262.

6. Foreign Office (Ralph Paget and William Tyrrell), "Suggested Basis for a Territorial Settlement in Europe," 7 Aug 16, CAB 42/17/4.

7. War Committee minutes, 10 Aug 16, CAB 42/17/5.

8. Robertson "very anxious" and Balfour: Hankey diary, 23 and 25 Aug 16. On August 23, Hankey raised "the peace question" at dinner. Montagu was "strongly supportive"; Asquith and Grey more noncommittal. Ibid.

9. In addition to his conversation with Grey, recounted in the introduction, on August

15 Bertie lunched with Balfour, Cecil, and Hankey, all of whom engaged their unsympathetic visitor in musings about peace terms. *Diary of Lord Bertie*, 12–13.

10. Bertie to Hardinge, 24 Aug 16, FO 800/59/284–89. Lord Hardinge had recently returned from his viceroyalty in India to become Grey's permanent undersecretary. Bertie finally sent his report about Poincaré and Briand to Hardinge. Bertie knew that Asquith would himself be seeing Briand that day and might hear from Briand about the prime minister's confrontation with Bertie. So Bertie might have judged that he could not bury the king's report any longer. Hardinge shared Bertie's distaste for the American peace idea. But he circulated Bertie's report with the War Committee.

11. Larsen, *Plotting for Peace*, chap. 5.

12. Hankey diary, 24 Aug 16.

13. Page to Wilson, 17 Mar 18, quoted in Larsen, *Plotting for Peace*, intro.

14. Larsen provides some examples of this. Bertie, Hardinge, and Hall schemed to deflect the American peace move, also involving the American embassy in this. *Plotting for Peace*, chap. 6.

The British navy's codebreaking unit was Room 40. The army's equivalent, in the War Office, was MI1b. The two units did not necessarily coordinate their work. The main human intelligence effort, the forerunner of the secret intelligence service MI6, was in the War Office, MI1c. The head of "C" was also known as "C," Mansfield Smith-Cumming. A good summary is Christopher Andrew, *The Secret World: A History of Intelligence* (New Haven: Yale University Press, 2018), 509–512, 532–533.

15. Larsen, *Plotting for Peace*, chap. 5; Hankey diary, 25 Aug 16.

16. Grey to House, 28 Aug 16 (emphasis added), *PWW*, 38:89–92.

17. War Committee minutes, 30 Aug 16, CAB 42/18/8.

18. Montagu, "The Problems of Peace," 29 Aug 16 (but with a postscript indicating it was circulated after the August 30 War Committee meeting), CAB 29/1.

19. Hankey, *The Supreme Command*, 2:512–513; Raymond, letter to Katharine, 7 Sep 16, in Jolliffe, *Raymond Asquith*, 293–294; Jenkins, *Asquith*, 413; on the briefings from Haig, see Cassar, *Asquith as War Leader*, 194–196.

20. The period after the failure of the Somme became a turning point in "the emergence of the pessimistic, even defeatist critique which was to have such an impact on British war policy in the war's last years." Brock Millman, *Pessimism and British War Policy, 1916–1918* (London: Frank Cass, 2001), 26.

21. Jolliffe, *Raymond Asquith*, 296–297.

22. For Margot's account, see *Margot Asquith's Great War Diary, 1914–1916*, ed. Michael and Eleanor Brock (Oxford: Oxford University Press, 2014), 288–289 (entry for 17 Sep 16). See, generally, Jenkins, *Asquith*, 413, 415; Cassar, *Asquith as War Leader*, 193, 196–197; Gilbert, *Organizer of Victory*, 490n114; "bankrupt in pride and life": Asquith to Pamela McKenna, 20 Sep 16, in Farr, *McKenna*, 334. One of the points that infuriated Reginald McKenna about Lloyd George was that, as McKenna and his wife were consoling Asquith about his loss, they believed Lloyd George had seen to it that his own sons were sent to staff positions where they were "well-sheltered" from the war. Larsen, *Plotting for Peace*, chap. 6.

23. War Committee minutes, 28 Sep 16, CAB 42/20/9.

24. Roy Howard, "Lloyd George Calls All Peace Talk Unfriendly," United Press International, September 29, 1916; carried in newspapers around the world.

25. Howard, writing in December 1916, quoted in Larsen, *Plotting for Peace*, chap. 6.

26. See ibid. and Gilbert, *Organizer of Victory*, 369.

27. A. J. P. Taylor, *English History, 1914–1945* (London: Oxford University Press, 1978), 62.

28. Gilbert, *Organizer of Victory*, 368; John Grigg, *Lloyd George: From Peace to War, 1912–1916* (London: Methuen, 1985), 432–433; "cost is concealed": George Riddell (later Baron Riddell), *The Riddell Diaries, 1908–1923*, ed. J. M. McEwen (London: Athlone, 1986), 168 (entry for 19 Sep 16). Riddell, a wealthy

and well-connected editor of the *News of the World* Sunday paper, was especially close to Lloyd George.

29. *Margot Asquith's Great War Diary, 1914–1916*, 270 (entry for 26 Jun 16).

30. See Link, *Campaigns for Progressivism and Peace*, 175–176.

31. At least some of the War Office decrypts of American reports are in HW 7/17. The Room 40 decrypts of German cables are in ADM 223/745 (again, it is hard to tell if the collection is complete). The American decrypt is dated 25 Sep 16, 7 p.m.; quotes in the text are from this. The file of German decrypts does not include Bethmann's September message offering the restoration of Belgium. There is no documentary evidence that, at this time, British leaders were aware of this offer. It is possible that Bethmann's message was decrypted and Hall did not distribute the decrypt, but I cannot prove that. There is a decrypt in the file of Bernstorff's reply, stating that America would insist on the restoration of Belgium.

32. To put this more positively, as Grigg does, is to say that Lloyd George was trying to knock out what Grigg calls the "defeatists" in the British government, like Lord Lansdowne. Grigg, *From Peace to War*, 430–432. If in late September, acting at the behest of someone like Lord Northcliffe, Lloyd George was aiming at other British politicians, his targets were fellow Liberals, including War Committee colleagues like McKenna, Grey, a Conservative like Balfour, or even Asquith. But, at the time, only someone like Northcliffe would label such men, or Lansdowne, as "defeatists."

33. Grey exchange with Lloyd George: Larsen, *Plotting for Peace*, chap. 6; Gilbert, *Organizer of Victory*, 370.

34. *Diary by Frances Stevenson*, 114 (entry for 30 Sep 16); "ghastly failure" and on Robertson: ibid., 120 (entry for 31 Oct). On Northcliffe's role, see Fry, *Lloyd George and Foreign Policy*, 232–233.

35. Lansing had alerted Wilson to Lloyd George's interview on September 30, while Wilson was at his home and campaign headquarters in Shadow Lawn, New Jersey, at the same time that he forwarded Gerard's September 25 message about German readiness for an American peace move, the message that, though the Americans did not know it, had helped prompt Lloyd George's assault. *PWW*, 38:313.

36. On Lloyd George's false statements to Parliament during the debate that followed Asquith's speech of October 11, see Larsen, *Plotting for Peace*, chap. 6.

37. "Indefinite war" and "sheer lunacy": McKenna to Liberal *Guardian* editor C. P. Scott, in Wilson, ed., *Political Diaries of C. P. Scott*, 227–228 (entry for 2–3 Oct 16).

38. [Weems], *America and Munitions*, 309; see also Carosso MS, 4:162.

39. Carosso MS, 4:165. Morgan was using a figure of $2.1 billion in American exports so far in 1916, writing to Davison in September.

40. The best picture of the securities/loan expedients in 1916 and the emergencies emerges from the detail in the Carosso MS, 4:159–178. The "rifles crisis" is sifted in ibid., 4:179–182; also see the War Committee minutes, 18 Oct 16, CAB 42/22.

41. On Davison's breakfast with Asquith, see [Weems], *America and Munitions*, 311. Weems, the anonymous author of this internal history, was an associate of the firm, a US Army officer in the war who then returned to banking. Carosso does not have this account in his history, probably because it was undocumented. Weems, who was a careful chronicler, likely got this directly from Davison.

42. On the origin of the short-term loan plan, "if only to avoid the continuous scratching for dollars of the past few months," see Carosso MS, 4:188–192.

43. At the then prevailing exchange rate, £2 million a day was about $286 million a month. McKenna, "Our Financial Position in America," 24 Oct 16 (attaching an 18 Oct report of an Anglo-French financial committee prepared by that committee's secretary, John Maynard Keynes), CAB 24/2. This was supplemented by further supporting papers,

including an October 10 note by Keynes quoted in the text, circulated to the War Committee on 6 Nov 16, CAB 42/23. A few American firms, like Bethlehem Steel, did join in buying British bonds to help sustain their business. But, as the Treasury papers said, such loans were not nearly sufficient.

44. Robertson, "General Staff Memorandum Submitted in Accordance with the Prime Minister's Instructions," 31 Aug 16, CAB 29/1.

45. Crawford (Earl of Crawford and Earl of Balcarres), "Conditions of an Armistice," 17 Sep 16, CAB 29/1. Crawford was the minister for food and agriculture. The two Liberal ministers looking after the rest of the civilian economy were McKenna at Treasury and Walter Runciman, president of the Board of Trade (trade and industry).

46. Balfour, "The Peace Settlement in Europe," 4 Oct 16, CAB 29/1. The uniformed naval leaders had an expansive wish list. The admirals mainly wished to stress that, if the peace was "inconclusive," Britain would need to invest huge sums in peacetime preparedness—in other words, in building up the navy. Admiral Henry Jackson, "Note on the Possible Terms of Peace," 12 Oct 16, CAB 29/1.

47. Cassar, *Asquith as War Leader*, 202.

48. See Hankey, "The General Review of the War," 31 Oct 16, CAB 24/2; see also Roskill, *Hankey: Man of Secrets*, 308, 311–312; Hankey, *The Supreme Command*, 2:556 (diary entries for 28 Oct, 1 and 11 Nov 16); Woodward, *Robertson*, 63–72. The precise numbers for estimated casualties in Hankey's cabinet paper were "108,000 men a month for fifty-four divisions in the field, and 133,000 men a month for a force of sixty-two divisions in the field during the summer months."

49. Hankey, "General Review of the War."

50. David French, *British Strategy and War Aims, 1914–1916* (Boston: Allen & Unwin, 1986), 230. For a similar conclusion on Britain's profound "strategic crisis" after the failure of the 1916 offensives, see Turner, *British Politics and the Great War*, 126–127.

51. War Committee minutes, 3 Nov 16, CAB 42/23/4 (which includes Robertson's paper, emphasis added on the "at least"). Hankey

reconstructed what was said at the meeting with help from Asquith and Lloyd George, who reviewed and edited his draft for accuracy. On Robertson's plan to raise the military age, see Cassar, *Asquith as War Leader*, 206.

52. On Asquith's praise, see Riddell, *The Riddell Diaries*, 173 (entry for 5 Nov 16); "damning": *Diary by Frances Stevenson*, 121 (entry for 4 Nov 16). Lloyd George's "brief against the generals was as long on criticism of the 'Westerners' as it was short on specific recommendations." David Woodward, *Lloyd George and the Generals* (London: Routledge, 2nd ed., 2004), 120.

53. Roskill, *Hankey: Man of Secrets*, 1:313–314. Hankey omitted any mention of this letter in his memoirs.

54. "Memorandum by Lord Lansdowne Respecting Peace Settlement," 13 Nov 16, CAB 29/1. Lansdowne specifically praised Lord Crawford's September argument that an American armistice proposal could not just be rejected. The biography is now Simon Kerry, *Lansdowne: The Last Great Whig* (London: Unicorn, 2017); "decisive at critical moments": Zara Steiner, *The Foreign Office and Foreign Policy, 1898–1914* (Cambridge: Cambridge University Press, 1969), 47.

In the historiography, Lansdowne is best known for a letter urging peace that he published in the press a year later, in November 1917, when he was out of government. At that time there was little chance that his arguments would prevail. His secret effort in November 1916 was much more significant. On the background of Lansdowne's "stunning" 1916 memorandum, see Kerry, *Lansdowne*, 262–263; Douglas Newton, "The Lansdowne 'Peace Letter' of 1917 and the Prospect of Peace by Negotiation with Germany," *Australian Journal of Politics and History*, vol. 48 no. 1 (2002): 16, 26–29; "usual quiet ruthlessness": Jenkins, *Asquith*, 418.

55. Quoted in Larsen, *Plotting for Peace*, chap. 7.

56. "Too late" and "nothing but disaster": *Diary by Frances Stevenson*, 122 (entries for 13 and 14 Nov 16).

57. Robert Doughty, *Pyrrhic Victory: French Strategy and Operations in the Great War*

(Cambridge: Harvard University Press, 2005), 300, 317.

58. For a nice summary of the political maneuvers surrounding the Allied conference at Chantilly, part of which included Lloyd George's effort to get Robertson shipped off on a mission to confer with the Russians (on which Kitchener had set off in June 1916 and gone down with his ship), see Cassar, *Asquith as War Leader*, 202–205; "surly scowl": ibid.,

205. On Lloyd George's disappointment at being "crushed" at the strategy conference (Haig's term), see Woodward, *Lloyd George and the Generals*, 122; "Very depressed": Riddell, *The Riddell Diaries*, 173 (entry for 19 Nov 16). The day before, Lloyd George also told Stevenson that he was "very, very depressed at the outlook" (*Diary by Frances Stevenson*, 123 [entry for 18 Nov 16]).

## Chapter 5: How to End a Great War

1. Polk to Page, 19 Jan 17, in Frank Polk Papers, Yale University, Box 11.

2. Richard Pipes, *The Russian Revolution* (New York: Random House, 1990), 250, 255.

3. "Longstanding tradition": Georges-Henri Soutou, "Diplomacy," in Jay Winter, ed., *The Cambridge History of the First World War*, vol. 2, *The State* (Cambridge: Cambridge University Press, 2014), 495.

4. "High death toll actually reinforced": Leonhard, *Pandora's Box*, 405; Soutou makes a similar point in the above-cited essay.

5. Baker, *Facing War*, 362; "devoted above all things": Joseph Gerard, *My Four Years in Germany* (New York: Hodder & Stoughton, 1917), 253; "if he could not force an early peace": Joseph Gerard, *My First Eighty-Three Years in America* (Garden City: Doubleday, 1951), 242. Wilson had also heard that Russia's czar was interested in a peace move, the point having been conveyed to Gerard by William Bayard Hale, a journalist friendly to Wilson who had helped the president on Mexican issues but was also notorious for his pro-German sympathies. Berlin 4458, 11 Oct 16, in *FRUS 1916, World War*, Doc. 73.

6. I have only noted information that would have been readily available at the time. For modern analysis of this peacemaking, see, as cited earlier, the analysis of Roosevelt's method in Zoellick, *America in the World*, 112–124; and I. V. Lukianov, "The Portsmouth Peace," and Eugene Trani and Donald Davis, "Roosevelt and the U.S. Role: Perception Makes Policy," both in Steven Ericson and Allen Hockley, eds., *The Treaty of Portsmouth and Its Legacies* (Hanover: University

Press of New England, 2008), 41–76; Raymond Esthus, *Double Eagle and Rising Sun: The Russians and Japanese at Portsmouth in 1905* (Durham: Duke University Press, 1988); Eugene Trani, *The Treaty of Portsmouth: An Adventure in American Diplomacy* (Lexington: University Press of Kentucky, 1969).

7. On the American struggle to help alleviate the agonizing conditions in occupied Russian Poland, which was obstructed by both sides in various ways, but especially by British reluctance to ease their blockade, see M. B. Biskupski, "The Diplomacy of Wartime Relief: The United States and Poland, 1914–1918," *Diplomatic History*, vol. 19 no. 3 (1995): 431–451.

8. House tossed out such a reconstruction idea to Wilson later in December. Wilson reacted with interest, but nothing then was done with it. House diary, 14 Dec 16 (about a discussion on December 13). House elaborated the idea further, with the British ambassador on January 2, also to no effect. House diary, 2 Jan 17.

9. On such matters, see, e.g., Janice Gross Stein, ed., *Getting to the Table: The Processes of International Prenegotiation* (Baltimore: Johns Hopkins University Press, 1989); Janice Gross Stein, "Getting to the Table: The Triggers, Stages, Functions, and Consequences of Prenegotiation," *International Journal*, vol. 44 no. 2 (1989): 475–504.

10. Bethmann to Erich Marcks, 16 Mar 16, in Jarausch, *The Enigmatic Chancellor*, 215, 484n40.

11. Bernstorff, *My Three Years in America*, 220.

12. Bernstorff testimony, 22 Oct 19, *OGD*, 1:254; see also Bernstorff, *My Three Years in America*, 244. Bethmann had previewed the Belgium

assurance, as a way to gain American mediation, with the kaiser's staff as early as July 27, as mentioned in Chapter 3. Bethmann made a similar point to Ambassador Gerard before Gerard's return to America in October. Although Bethmann's formal instruction to Bernstorff had referred to "conditional" restoration of Belgium, a point discussed later in this chapter, Bernstorff never used this caveat with House, and House never pressed for details on this. House (and Wilson) assumed all along that the Germans were prepared to give up Belgium and more. They would later get other evidence of this from their embassy in Berlin.

13. Drummond to Cecil, 13 Dec 16, quoted in Newton, "The Lansdowne 'Peace Letter,'" 22.

14. "Strong probability" and "strong peace sentiment": House to Polk, 28 Jul 16, Polk Papers, Box 8. House reaffirmed this message in another letter to Polk on August 8, sent before Bernstorff conveyed the German request for mediation.

15. Polk to Coudert, 6 Oct 16, Polk Papers, Box 4.

16. House warned Polk of these plans to go to Congress, 25 Jul 16, Polk Papers, Box 8.

17. Polk to House, 6 Jun 16, reporting the French ambassador's worries about "peace being forced on France when it was not ready for it." Ibid.

18. Quoting Zimmermann to German embassies in Madrid, Stockholm, and others, 14 Dec 16, *OGD*, 2:1074; Bethmann cautioned the Austrians along these lines about a public Belgian or Serbian offer, noting the similar need for their enemies to agree both to the peace conference and to a specific place and time. Bethmann to Wedel, 15 Dec 16, *OGD*, 2:1075; *APP*, 1:617–618.

19. Frederic Coudert to Polk, 19 Sep 16 (from Paris), Polk Papers, Box 4.

20. The Peace of Amiens was concluded in the autumn of 1801 but was not formally ratified until 1802. The parallel peace treaty with Austria was signed at Lunéville in 1801 to end the wars of the Second Coalition against France. The wars resumed in 1803. A fine modern study is John Grainger, *The Amiens Truce: Britain and Bonaparte, 1801–1803* (Woodbridge: Boydell & Brewer, 2003).

21. A foundational survey is Jonathan Helmreich, *Belgium and Europe: A Study in Small Power Diplomacy* (The Hague: Mouton, 1976); see also Michael Palo, "Belgium's Response to the Peace Initiatives of December 1916: An Exercise in Diplomatic Self-Determination," *The Historian*, vol. 42 no. 4 (1980): 583.

22. "Guarantees," e.g., Bethmann to Hindenburg: 4 Nov 16, *APP*, 1:542–543. This is an example of Bethmann's desire, as mentioned in the last chapter, to keep the military at bay with positions as vague as possible, until he could get to the peace table and go to work. In this case, Hindenburg told Bethmann's man in Pless that he wanted much more from Belgium and gave him a list on this and various other topics. Bethmann soothingly instructed his agent to tell Hindenburg he agreed with all his suggestions on this and other topics, except one actually demanding indemnities from the Belgians. Grünau to Foreign Office, 5 Nov 16; Bethmann to Grünau, 6 Nov 16, *APP*, 1:548–551. In practice, Bethmann then ignored Hindenburg's positions on Belgium and everything else. Bethmann's actual indifference to Hindenburg's wishes became apparent when these territorial issues came up again, in January 1917.

23. Some explorations, which indicate the great pressure Prime Minister Briand felt to consider peace possibilities, began, quite secretly, in Switzerland in December 1916 between two "cultural" officials, French professor Émile Haguenin and German count Harry Kessler. Both Haguenin and Kessler had excellent contacts at the top of their governments. The main focus was some creative solution for Alsace and Lorraine, perhaps in a novel governance structure, and much more. See Soutou, "Briand et l'Allemagne," 485, 491–498; Landy Charrier, "À la recherche d'une paix de compromise: Kessler, Haguenin et al diplomatie officieuse de l'hiver 1916–1917," *Histoire@Politique*, no. 11 (2010); Soutou, "Diplomacy," in Winter, ed., *Cambridge History*, 2:514–515.

24. "The Germans were basically ready to go back to the status quo of 1914 in the West, limiting their gains to the East, at the expense of a weakening Russia. Actually, the majority of

the ruling classes and of the general population were keener to achieve gains in the East than in the West. It would roll back the much feared Russian Empire, and provide more opportunities for colonization than heavily populated Western Europe. And the new resources and power bases gained in the East would be enough to establish a definitive secure position for Germany." Soutou, "Diplomacy," in Winter, ed., *Cambridge History*, 505. Revealingly, in late 1917, when Lloyd George mused about possible peace moves, he would think of restoring the status quo ante in the West, perhaps adding territorial concessions for France, while compensating an otherwise intact Germany and Austria-Hungary in the East, at Russian expense. The army's general staff was mainly concerned about preserving a sufficiently strong position in the Middle East. Woodward, *Lloyd George and the Generals*, 240–241; Woodward, *Robertson*, 120–121.

25. Tumulty transcript of Wilson with American Neutral Conference Committee, 30 Aug 16, *PWW*, 38:108–117, quoting 115–117.

26. Bonn testimony, *OGD*, 1:193–194; see also 188.

### Chapter 6: "Peace Is on the Floor Waiting to Be Picked Up!"

1. "Wilson Welcomed Back to Washington," *New York Times*, November 13, 1916, 1.

2. This set of assaults is usually known as the Battle of the Ancre. "Snow and sleet": Alan Wakefield, "How Did the Battle of the Somme End?," Imperial War Museum, June 14, 2018, online essay; "bloody cigarette": George James Spears, *The Satire of Saki* (New York: Exposition Press, 1963), 94.

3. "Say to all": Baker, *Facing War*, 368 (emphasis in original); "we were now approaching": Joseph Tumulty, *Woodrow Wilson as I Know Him* (Garden City: Doubleday, 1921), 248.

4. Howard dispatch relayed, House to Wilson, 20 Oct 16; House to Wilson, 6 Nov 16, *PWW*, 38:496–497, 619.

5. House diary, 14 Nov 16. This entry is also reprinted in *PWW*, 38:645–647.

6. "Lansing Cables Remonstrance on Exile of Belgians," *New York Times*, November 15, 1916, 1.

7. On the German labor deportations in Belgium, see Jens Thiel, "*Menschenbassin Belgien": Anwerbung, Deportation und Zwangsarbeit im Ersten Weltkrieg* (Essen: Klartext, 2007), and the summary in Isabel Hull, *Absolute Destruction: Military Culture and the Practices of War in Imperial Germany* (Ithaca: Cornell University Press, 2005), 236–241.

8. For Lansing's defense of his behavior, see Lansing to Wilson, 15 Nov 16, *PWW*, 38:650–653.

9. House diary, 15 Nov 16. Also in *PWW*, 38:656–659. Lansing's desk diary confirms his meeting with House and Polk this day about Wilson's "peace demand." Lansing diary, Robert Lansing Papers, Library of Congress.

10. Clifford Carver to House, 3 Oct 16, quoted in Larsen, *Plotting for Peace*, chap. 7.

11. House diary, 16 and 18 Nov 16.

12. Ibid.

13. Jagow to Bernstorff, 16 Nov 16, *APP*, 1:564–565; *OGD*, 2:991–992.

14. Jagow to Bernstorff, 8 Nov 16; Bernstorff to Foreign Office, nos. 152 and 153, 17 and possibly 18 Nov 16, *OGD*, 2:990, 992–993.

15. House to Wilson, 20 Nov 16, *PWW*, 40:4–6.

16. Bernstorff to Foreign Office, 21 Nov 16 (rec'd 24 Nov) (my translation), *APP*, 1:575–576; *OGD*, 2:993–994. The message was sent through the State Department–Embassy Berlin channel. Wilson's first major biographer also noticed, with astonishment, that House's statement to Bernstorff was "exactly the reverse of the real fact!" Baker, *Facing War*, 6:369.

17. Thomas Boghardt, *The Zimmermann Telegram: Intelligence, Diplomacy, and America's Entry into World War I* (Annapolis: Naval Institute Press, 2012), 95–96; Nickles, *Under the Wire*, 146.

18. House to Wilson, 20 Nov 16; with this portion repeated in House's memo of the meeting passed to Polk at State, see Department of State, *Foreign Relations of the United States: The Lansing Papers* (Washington, DC: Government Printing Office, 1939), 1:573.

After the war, House would later "forget" this and all other indications of German readiness to make territorial concessions. His later claim, influencing a generation of historians, was that the German side had only been interested in dictating a victors' peace from their current position of advantage. House made this argument in his frequently unreliable de facto memoir, for which he used the Yale historian Charles Seymour as his conduit. For House's claim on German attitudes, see the editorial comments at, for example, Seymour, ed., *The Intimate Papers of Colonel House*, vol. 2, *From Neutrality to War* (Boston: Houghton Mifflin, 1926), 386, 389, 405. Seymour based his own impressions on what House had told him as they worked together on these volumes. The claims about German attitudes were sustained in the Seymour book by taking care that any mention of Bernstorff's proffered concessions was edited out of the documentary excerpts.

House did not know it, but Bernstorff was leaning forward in including France so generally in such a broad evacuation commitment. The ambassador actually had no formal instructions authorizing this reference, though a Belgian evacuation would necessarily force the Germans to leave most of the territory they occupied in France. Bernstorff obviously judged that Bethmann would back him up if the United States pressed the issue. The Germans would bargain hard, though, about the details of cease-fire lines or the future Franco-German borders in eastern France.

19. Wilson to House, 21 Nov 16, with three enclosures, *PWW*, 40:20–24.

20. This is the Tarbell interview quoted in Chapter 1, published in *Collier's* on 3 Oct 16, *PWW*, 38:327–328.

21. The Austrian move was reported to the United States in a memo dictated by the counselor of the British embassy at the State Department, 19 Nov 16, in *FRUS 1916, World War*, Doc. 82. The information, gleaned in late October, reflected the extensive work on peace preparation going on between Berlin and Vienna that month, alluded to in Chapter 3. The Austro-Hungarian emperor, Franz Josef, died in November, which redoubled Vienna's interest in peace.

22. On the meeting with Bethmann, Berlin 4636, 22 Nov 16 (rec'd on 24 Nov), ibid., Doc. 89. References to the message show up in later cables and discussions. When he returned to Washington on November 26, House seems to have been shown this message by Polk. On Bethmann and no "retention of Belgium": Berlin 4652, 25 Nov 16, in *FRUS 1916, World War*, Doc. 90. See also Heinrichs, *American Ambassador*, 28. Twenty-five years later, Joseph Grew would be the US ambassador, serving in Tokyo, at another difficult time.

23. House to Grey, 24 Nov 16, House Papers, Box 53, Yale University. Historians should notice that this letter by House, the Wilson letter that directed it, and any mention of discontent with the British were omitted from Seymour, *Intimate Papers of Colonel House*, 2:392–393 (which covers this period).

24. The House letter was carried to London by Australian-born Captain Guy Gaunt, RN, whose ship home sailed the next day. House had been working all year with Gaunt, acquiescing in British intelligence and counterintelligence work in the United States. German agents were actively engaged in their own intelligence operations, including sabotage efforts against munitions shipments. The Americans, like the British, kept careful tabs on German diplomats and officials (including Bernstorff) and German activities. Polk, at State, helped look after this work.

25. A detailed proposal from Norman Angell was passed to Wilson by Norman Hapgood, a prominent writer and journalist Wilson admired. *PWW*, 40:10–19. On the *Times* material being passed to Wilson by Tumulty and House, see ibid., 24, 30. Wilson's dislike for Nicholas Murray Butler was palpable; that same week he crossed Butler off the invitation list for a gala dinner, hosted by New York City's mayor, to celebrate Wilson's re-election. Wilson to Tumulty, 22 Nov 16, *PWW*, 40:35. The first two "Cosmos" pieces (there were more in the series, published in 1917 as a book) ran under the continuing title "All Want Peace: Why Not Have It Now?," *New York Times*, November 20, 1916, 12, and November 21, 1916, 10. The *Times* editorial

ran on the same page, on November 21. The American embassy in Berlin had reported on Bethmann's speech. Berlin 4889, 10 Nov 16 (rec'd 12 Nov), *FRUS 1916, World War*, Supplement, Doc. 80.

26. Baker, *Facing War*, 383, shows a photostat of Wilson's marked-up typescript of part of his initial draft of a peace note, showing his drafting style.

27. Wilson "Prologemon," draft peace note, and note to House, c. 25 Nov 16, *PWW*, 40:67–74. The editors of the *PWW* were uncertain about the exact date. The draft paper published in the *PWW* includes a paragraph in which Wilson says that he is not making a peace proposal or proposing mediation. Since House says in his diary that he suggested this change on November 26, this paragraph probably was not in Wilson's original November 25 draft. This draft still calls for a peace conference, language Wilson would later remove.

28. "Creditors": Wilson's final campaign address, 4 Nov 16, *PWW*, 38:613–614.

29. [Weems], *America and Munitions*, 317.

30. For general background on the extreme, by this point, British dependence on the United States during this period, see the discussions earlier in this book in Chapters 2 and 4, as well as Carosso MS, 4:188–194; Burk, *Britain, America and the Sinews of War*, 77–95; and the excellent essay by John Milton Cooper Jr., "The Command of Gold Reversed: American Loans to Britain, 1915–1917," *Pacific Historical Review*, vol. 45 no. 2 (1976): 209–230.

31. Harding to Benjamin Strong, 16 Nov 16, quoted in Cooper, "The Command of Gold Reversed," 222. On the board's existing qualms, including the "calamity" of Davison's November 18 meeting with the board, where, as Jacob Brown of Brown Brothers put it, Davison "invited disaster and got what he deserved," see Carosso MS, 4:194–196.

32. Hamlin diary, 25 Nov 16 (Hamlin was a member of the Federal Reserve Board); Wilson to Harding, 26 Nov; Hamlin diary, 27 Nov; Harding to Wilson, 27 Nov; Wilson to Harding, 27 Nov, *PWW*, 40:76–78, 87–88. For fine background on the Federal Reserve Board in

this formative period of its history and how and why the British credit situation came to Wilson's attention, see Priscilla Roberts, "'Quis Custodiet Ipsos Custodes?' The Federal Reserve System's Founding Fathers and Allied Finances in the First World War," *Business History Review*, vol. 72 no. 4 (1998): 585, 611–616.

33. "Dark": Carosso MS, 4:203; on the lasting impact, see ibid., 4:202–207; "irreparable": quoting Richard Crawford in Washington, ibid., 4:210; "folly": quoting Lord Percy, 4 Oct 16, in Cooper, "The Command of Gold Reversed," 219.

34. "Something in the air": Carosso MS, 4:198; Bernstorff to Foreign Office, 1 Dec 16 (rec'd 4 Dec), *OGD*, 2:997; Spring-Rice to Foreign Office, 3 Dec 16, *PWW*, 40:77–80, 87–88, 136–137. For more on the finger-pointing afterward and the exchange on "German Jews," see Carosso MS, 4:196–197, 200–202.

35. House diary, 25 Nov 16.

36. Seymour (with House), *Intimate Papers of Colonel House*, 2:394.

37. Lansing diary (memos to himself), "What Will the President Do?," 3 Dec 16, and "The President's Attitude Toward Great Britain and Its Dangers," Sep 16, Robert Lansing Papers, Library of Congress.

38. Wilson draft to Lansing, 28 Nov 16; Lansing to Grew, State 3621, 29 Nov 16; see also Lansing to House, 1 Dec 16, *PWW*, 40:94–95, 106–107, 118. On the leakage of the note and finger-pointing from Lansing at Gerard, see Lansing to Wilson, 2 Dec 16; Wilson to Lansing, 3 Dec, *PWW*, 40: 122–123, 130.

39. House to Wilson, 30 Nov 16, and note 1, *PWW*, 40:110–111. Wilson was getting contrasting evidence about British interest in peace (e.g., Gavit to Wilson, 2 Dec 16, *PWW*, 40:124–127).

40. Wilson to House, 3 Dec 16, *PWW*, 40:131–132.

41. Quoted in Neu, *Colonel House*, 201; see also 210.

42. House repeated some version of his conversation with Daniels to President Wilson. His point was to again urge Wilson not to do anything that would upset the Allies. He did not record Wilson's reaction. House diary, 14 Dec 16, reprinted in *PWW*, 40:238.

43. House to Wilson, 3 Dec 16, *PWW*, 40:133; House diary, 7 Dec.

44. Berlin 4671, Grew to Lansing, 1 Dec 16 (rec'd 2 Dec), *FRUS 1916, World War*, Doc. 98; relayed in Wilson to House, 5 Dec, *PWW*, 40:160–161.

45. Müller diary, entry for 2 and 3 Dec 16, in Walter Görlitz, ed., *Regierte der Kaiser? Kriegstagebücher, Aufzeichnungen und Briefe des* Chefs des Marine-Kabinetts Admiral George Alexander von Müller, 1914–1918 (Göttingen: Musterschmidt, 1959), 238–239.

46. House diary, 2 Dec 16; Bernstorff to Foreign Office, 4 Dec 16 (rec'd 7 Dec), *OGD*, 2:997–998; there is an analogous translation of the same message in Bernstorff, *My Three Years in America*, 264.

## Chapter 7: What Is Wilson Trying to Do?

1. See Larsen, *Plotting for Peace*, chap. 7, including for evidence that Grey was developing his ideas working with Runciman (who was also McKenna's ally) and with Lansdowne. On November 14, Lansdowne talked to his Conservative colleague, Crawford, about their common interest in peacemaking and possible armistice terms. Crawford diary, 14 Nov 16, in John Vincent, ed., *The Crawford Papers: The Journals of David Lindsay, 27th Earl of Crawford and 10th Earl of Balcarres, 1871–1940* (Manchester: Manchester University Press, 1984), 365.

2. On the November 22 meeting, see Crawford diary, separate memo on cabinet meeting of 22 Nov 16, in Vincent, *Crawford Papers*, 366–367; Harcourt cabinet diary, 22 Nov 16. On the manpower issues at that moment, see, e.g., War Committee conclusions circulated to cabinet on the Man-Power Distribution Board's conclusions, 21 Nov 16, CAB 37/160/7; on some of the shipping and food issues and discussion of food rationing, see, e.g., pp. 3–5 of the War Committee conclusions, 23 Nov 16, CAB 37/160/13.

3. Hankey diary, 22 Nov and 4 Dec 16. Lloyd George still had no use for Robertson's and Haig's emphasis on the western front. "We have been talking of 'great victories' [on the western front] for the last few months, but in the end it only means that we have advanced five or six miles." *Diary by Frances Stevenson*, 127 (entry for 23 Nov 16).

4. On the background, including "succumb," see Woodward, *Robertson*, 71–72, 77–78. The journalist was Charles Repington of the London *Times*. Woodward assumes—like many British historians—that German war aims were so extreme that there was no other choice but to "fight to the finish."

5. Robertson paper for the cabinet, 24 Nov 16, CAB 37/160/15.

6. Cecil paper, 27 Nov 16, CAB 37/160/21. Bertie to Grey, 2 Dec 16 (rec'd 5 Dec), circulated in CAB 37/161/7.

7. War Committee approval of extension of compulsory national service, 30 Nov 16, CAB 37/160/33; on use of foreign labor, see, e.g., Ministry of Munitions, "Importation of Labour from Abroad," 7 Dec 16, CAB 42/26/7.

8. Lansdowne cabinet paper, 27 Nov 16, CAB 37/160/22; Asquith to Lansdowne, quoted in Larsen, *Plotting for Peace*, chap. 7.

9. Grey cabinet paper, 27 Nov 16, CAB 37/160/20.

10. War Committee minutes, 28 Nov 16 (6 p.m. meeting), CAB 42/26/2. A week later, Spring-Rice and the French ambassador in Washington, Jusserand, were still uncertain about Wilson's role in the board warning. Spring-Rice was more suspicious but (mistakenly) thought Lansing had something to do with it. Jusserand (mistakenly) did not think Wilson had anything to do with it or even understood it. Spring-Rice to Grey, 5 Dec 16, circulated to the cabinet, CAB 37/161/8. Later, Spring-Rice (mistakenly) put most of the blame on pro-German Jewish financiers, who were also regarded as Wilson's principal supporters in the Wall Street community, the Christian bankers having supposedly voted for Hughes in the election. Spring-Rice to Grey, 5 Dec 16, circulated to cabinet on 30 Dec, CAB 37/161/37.

11. Harcourt cabinet diary, 29 Nov 16.

12. Spring-Rice to Grey, 24 Nov 16, circulated to cabinet on 7 Dec, CAB 37/160/18.

Spring-Rice continued to warn Grey, and the cabinet, about the intensity of American hostility toward Britain. Spring-Rice to Grey, 5 Dec 16, cited above. Britain, he wrote, should be thankful for what it could get. The Americans "could do us much more harm than they are doing, and, in fact, their power of mischief is incalculable. And we had better not count too much on their goodwill."

13. Grey to Spring-Rice, 26 Nov 16, FO 115/2090; also in Trevelyan, *Grey of Fallodon*, 368. Lord Crawford, having worked armistice terms for a cabinet paper back in September, was also attentive to armistice terms in December. His notion was relatively modest: "prompt evacuation of portions of occupied territory… as a guarantee of German good faith, and to ensure that they treat our counterproposals with a wholesome respect." Vincent, *Crawford Papers*, 368.

14. Grey memorandum from late November or early December, quoted in Larsen, *Plotting for Peace*, chap. 8.

15. Watson, *Ring of Steel*, 443–444.

16. Johannes Hürter, "Die Staatsekretäre des Auswärtigen Amtes im Ersten Weltkrieg," in Wolfgang Michalka, ed., *Der Erste Weltkrieg: Wirkung, Wahrnehmung, Analyse* (Munich: Piper, 1994), 225; Birnbaum, *Peace Moves and U-boat Warfare*, 216–217.

17. Riezler, *Tagebücher*, 384 (entry for 22 Nov 16).

18. Bethmann to Hindenburg, 27 Nov 16 (my translation), from Birnbaum, *Peace Moves and U-boat Warfare*, 226n7.

19. Müller diary, 2 and 3 Dec 16, in Görlitz, *Regierte der Kaiser*, 238–239.

20. Birnbaum, *Peace Moves and U-boat Warfare*, 233.

21. Ibid., 234–246.

22. Notes taken during Bethmann briefing, 11 Dec 16, quoted in Steglich, *Bündnissicherung oder Verständigungsfrieden*, 145–146.

23. Cecil, "Note on the German Offer of Peace," Appendix IV to minutes of War Cabinet meeting, 18 Dec 16, CAB 23/1/10.

24. Quoted in Sterling Kernek, "Distractions of Peace During War: The Lloyd George Government's Reactions to Woodrow Wilson, December 1916–November 1918," *Transactions of the American Philosophical Society*, vol. 65 no. 2 (1975): 1, 15.

25. On momentary disappointment, see House diary, 14 Dec 16 (on events of 12–13 Dec); Link, *Campaigns for Progressivism and Peace*, 214–215; Grew to Lansing, Berlin 4725, 12 Dec 16 (rec'd late on 13 Dec and probably passed to Wilson on 14 Dec), *FRUS 1916, World War*, Doc. 121.

26. House to Wilson, 5 and 6 Dec 16, discussing views of Whitehouse and also Charles Philips Trevelyan, *PWW*, 40:172, 178–180.

27. For an obituary summary of Buckler's career, see "Necrology," *American Journal of Archaeology*, vol. 56 no. 3 (1952): 179; see also the William Hepburn Buckler Papers, Yale University. Buckler was a half brother of another renowned American diplomat, Henry White.

28. House to Wilson, 7 Dec 16, enclosing draft message to Lloyd George and message from Buckler to House, 7 Dec, *PWW*, 40:185–187.

29. Wilson to House, 8 Dec 16, *PWW*, 40:189. House described Lloyd George's earlier proposal as having been that, in the autumn of 1916, Wilson would "demand that the war cease. He said the Allied governments would demur but that later they would yield." Lloyd George, according to House, "also had the theory that you could dictate the terms of peace and he outlined what he thought you could do." House to Wilson, 9 Dec 16, ibid., 201. Wilson's "we cannot go back to those old plans" may have referred to such speculations, since by then he appears to have understood that he could not just "dictate the terms of peace."

30. The final version of the note is at ibid., 273–276. Though he suggested various edits, Lansing had no real substantive comments on the draft note. He told Wilson he was "not at all sure what effect this communication would have," but the United States might as well do this, since the next step was probably to come into the war. Lansing to Wilson, 10 Dec, ibid., 209–210. Wilson did not bother to tell Lansing how wrong he was about this "verge of war" assumption, an omission that probably contributed to Lansing's mistaken reliance on this theory when he explained the

note after it was issued the following week. "Has nearly destroyed": House diary, 20 Dec 16.

31. Stone quoted in Link, *Campaigns for Progressivism and Peace*, 221.

32. Link, *Campaigns for Progressivism and Peace*, 220–239, provides a good summary of Wilson's anger about Lansing and the peace note. Arthur Link, *Woodrow Wilson: Revolution, War, and Peace* (Wheeling: Harlan Davidson, 1979), 57, argues that Lansing committed "one of the most egregious acts of treachery in American history in an effort to torpedo Wilson's peace move." That argument was later supplemented by the material in the long footnote in *PWW*, 40:307–311 (published in 1982).

It is also possible to read Lansing's statement more as an honest, ignorant blunder rather than a deliberate effort to "torpedo Wilson's peace move" (see note 30 above). Lansing's later pleas to House show how little he understood what Wilson was doing. See also the weighing of the evidence in Kernek, "Distractions of Peace," 16–17.

The *PWW* note in 1982 added evidence implying that House told Roy Howard that the "verge of war" rationale was right. This would thus implicate House as an accomplice in Lansing's supposed betrayal. The Howard evidence is hard to explain. Perhaps Howard overinterpreted some Delphic comment by House. I do not believe House thought Wilson was, or should be, on the "verge of war."

33. Kaiser's marginal note on cabled report, 22 Dec 16, and Zimmermann comment in message to Vienna about the Wilson note, 23 Dec, quoted in Steglich, *Bündnissicherung oder Verständigungsfrieden*, 165.

34. "Profound disappointment": Birnbaum, *Peace Moves and U-boat Warfare*, 255. On December 19, Zimmermann told chargé Grew that Bethmann "would adopt no basis [for peace] which it would be impossible for the Entente to accept, [but] had particularly avoided giving any intimation as to what their basis would be, as this, among other

reasons, might have demoralized the troops in the field who would have believed that there was no further purpose in fighting." On December 21, Zimmermann explained the point again, as quoted in the text. Berlin 4753 and 4764, 19 and 21 Dec 16, *FRUS 1916, World War*, Docs. 152, 156; see also Afflerbach, *Auf Messers Schneide*, 288–289.

35. Wilson to Lansing, 23 Dec 16, *PWW*, 40:324–325; Bernstorff to Foreign Office, 21 Dec 16 (rec'd 25 Dec), *OGD*, 2:1004–1005; on German leak fears, see Birnbaum, *Peace Moves and U-boat Warfare*, 260.

36. For the breakfast meeting and the German Foreign Office suspicion that Wilson was actually trying to stop direct peace negotiations, see Birnbaum, *Peace Moves and U-boat Warfare*, 256–258, 263–265; and Wedel (German ambassador in Vienna) to Foreign Office, 26 Dec 16, *OGD*, 2:1089 (recounting the Zimmermann analysis that he relayed to the Austrians).

37. The German reply to Wilson's peace note was conveyed both through Bernstorff and in Berlin. Zimmermann to Bernstorff and Zimmermann to Gerard, 26 Dec 16, *OGD*, 2:1005–1006. The US ambassador to Germany, Gerard, was back in Berlin. He complimented Zimmermann on the German reply to Wilson's note: "a damned good note, a fine note, short and sweet." Zimmermann to the Kaiser, 26 Dec 16, *OGD*, 2:1089.

38. Hardinge to Spring-Rice, 21 Dec 16, quoted in Kernek, "Distractions of Peace," 21. Cecil to Spring-Rice, 20 Dec 16, CAB 37/161/44.

39. "To put a stop": Cecil, "Proposed Action in Regard to American Note," 22 Dec 16, attached to Minutes of War Cabinet meeting, 23 Dec 16, CAB 23/1, 4.

40. For the final version of the Allied response to Wilson's peace note, see Sharp to Lansing, 10 Jan 17, *PWW*, 40:439–441; on Allied plans for Poland and the French-Russian understanding in December 1916, see Jeffrey Mankoff, "The Future of Poland, 1914–1917: France and Great Britain in the Triple Entente," *International History Review*, vol. 30 no. 4 (2008): 741–767.

41. Kernek, "Distractions of Peace," 31.

42. "Baffling" and "pro-German Jews": Victor Rothwell, *British War Aims and Peace Diplomacy, 1914–1918* (Oxford: Clarendon Press, 1971), 61–62; for "prig": Michael Graham Fry, *And Fortune Fled: David Lloyd George, the First Democratic Statesman, 1916–1922* (New York: Peter Lang, 2011), 91, 93.

43. Agreement to reexamine British dependence on America, conclusion of War Cabinet, 21 Dec 16, CAB 37/162/3; for the review of the House-Grey memorandum and further round of papers on American dependence, which came to depressing conclusions similar to those reached in the October review, see the summary in Kernek, "Distractions of Peace," 21–23.

44. Balfour, "Suggestion for a British Reply to the Peace Note from the President of the United States," undated [Dec 1916], CAB 37/162/31. Balfour granted that the warring powers would arrange terms among themselves. He wanted Wilson to find some way of assuring that a few key principles were respected. For example, respect for small states implied at least some German commitment to the restoration of Belgium, Serbia, and Montenegro, since "the Central Powers can hardly desire to inaugurate the new era, in which small states are to be secure against aggression, by wiping three small States out of existence."

45. On Wiseman's background, see William B. Fowler, *British-American Relations 1917–1918: The Role of Sir William Wiseman* (Princeton: Princeton University Press, 1969), 14–19; Keith Jeffery, *The Secret History of MI6, 1909–1949* (New York: Penguin, 2010), 110–113; Richard Spence, "Englishmen in New York: The SIS American Station, 1915–21," *Intelligence and National Security*, vol. 19 no. 3 (2004): 511–537. Wiseman deposited his papers, which include his copies of some of his secret messages to and from headquarters, at Yale University.

Later, during the war, Wiseman worked quite directly with the Foreign Office, usually through Drummond. Some accounts, and even Fowler to some extent, treat Wiseman

or Cumming as freelancing in their early policy interactions with House. It is evident from the documents that both Wiseman and Cumming were working closely with Drummond and Balfour from the start. In January 1917, Wiseman confided to House that he had his own direct line to the Foreign Office. This was truthful, even if he did not explain that his line ran through Cumming.

Earlier in the war, House had occasionally met with a Royal Navy captain, Guy Gaunt, to work on counterintelligence issues. Wiseman established his relationship with House while Gaunt was home on leave. House never opened himself to Gaunt on policy matters the way he did, from the start, with Wiseman. When Gaunt returned to the United States, in January 1917, he attempted to dislodge Wiseman, without success. Fowler, *British-American Relations*, 21–22. Since Wiseman worked for MI1c (in the War Office), while Gaunt worked for naval intelligence, Gaunt had no direct authority over Wiseman even though he nominally outranked him in service terms. Ambassador Spring-Rice was aware of some of Wiseman's activities and protected him.

46. Wiseman to Cumming, no. 457, 15 Dec 16, in William Wiseman Papers, MS 666, Yale University, Box 4.

47. House diary, 17 Dec 16; House to Wilson, 17 Dec 16, *PWW*, 40:262. Cumming had asked Wiseman to get the German peace terms from the Americans. "We have already received outline of these." He should use House or anyone else to get the details, doing his utmost, and cable if he needed money. After Wiseman had his meeting with House, London told Wiseman that Lloyd George was going ahead with his speech and that Balfour thought "it better that no action should be taken." C no. 349, 16 Dec 16; Wiseman to C, no. 460, 17 Dec; C no. 350, 18 Dec, in Wiseman Papers, Box 4.

48. Wiseman to C, no. 468, 22 Dec 16, in Wiseman Papers, Box 4. Attempting to reconstruct the background of Wilson's peace note, a British agent in Washington picked up a story

about a US cabinet meeting in which most members, but not Wilson, were on the verge of war with Germany. Years later, Wiseman penciled a note on the reverse side of this document, commenting that in this case he and Spring-Rice "gave bad information" about American policy. Wiseman to C, no. 469, 23 Dec 16, and notes on reverse side, in ibid.

49. Soutou, "Diplomacy," in Winter, ed., *Cambridge History*, 2:514; for more details, see Soutou, "Briand et l'Allemagne au Tournant de la Guerre," 491–499.

50. Even in those western front plans, Lloyd George broke with Robertson and Haig. The prime minister tended to favor the plans and leadership of the new French military commander, Robert Nivelle. He schemed with the French to place Nivelle in command over Haig. These further schemes by the prime minister foundered in February and March 1917. See Woodward, *Lloyd George and the Generals*, 128–156.

51. Minutes of the War Committee meeting, 28 Nov 16; "half in love": impressions of Sir Henry Wilson in Basil Collier, *Brasshat: A Biography of Sir Henry Wilson* (London: Secker & Warburg, 1961), 253 (emphasis in original).

52. Quotes from Carosso MS, 4:223, 226; see also ibid., 4:215–247, and the brief summary, including more about Keynes's recollections and the "last bean," in Burk, *Britain, America and the Sinews of War*, 86–87.

## Chapter 8: Peace Without Victory?

1. House diary, 20 Dec 16; see the discussion of the House meetings with Horace Plunkett on December 20 and 22 and House to Wilson, 20 Dec, in Link, *Campaigns for Progressivism and Peace*, 225–227; Wilson to Baker, 26 Dec 16, *PWW*, 40:330–331.

2. Wilson to Lansing, 23 Dec; Lansing to Wilson, 24 Dec, *PWW*, 40:324–325, 326–327; Christmastime for the Wilsons in Baker, *Facing War*, 408–409; the informal British responses in Page to Lansing, London 5363, 22 Dec 16 (rec'd 23 Dec); Page to Lansing, London 5374, 26 Dec 16 (rec'd 27 Dec), *FRUS 1916, World War*, Docs. 153, 164.

3. Lippmann to Mabel Dodge, 14 Dec 16, quoted in Steel, *Walter Lippmann*, 109; see also the "before it is too late" tone in Wilson to Lansing, 17 Dec 16, *PWW*, 40:256.

4. House diary, 23 Dec 16.

5. House diary, 2 and 4 Jan 17.

6. House diary, 3, 11, and 12 Jan 17 (I have slightly changed the punctuation of the last quotation).

7. "A forum" and "inside of my mind": Steel, *Walter Lippmann*, 76, 102. The best work tracing the interactions and influence of Lippmann and Croly with Wilson and his circle, reinforcing their common evolution of a "pragmatist internationalism," is Throntveit, *Power Without Victory*, esp. 124–129, 152–153, 163–179, 187 (agreeing with Wilson on Mexico), 195–209. My book dials up the microscope on their very consequential interactions of ideas and action during December 1916 and January 1917.

8. House to Wilson, 29 Dec 16 (conveying Croly letter); Charles Merz report to Lippmann on "The President's Conference," 8 Jan 17, *PWW*, 40:359–360, 423 ("entire agreement" was in all caps in the original).

9. *New Republic*, vol. 9 no. 112 (December 23, 1916), quotes from 198–199, 201–202. Lippmann and Croly were not outliers. They reflected a "progressive consensus" in favor of a compromise peace with moderate terms. John Thompson, *Reformers and War: American Progressive Publicists and the First World War* (Cambridge: Cambridge University Press, 1987), 142–149. Lippmann was himself the American-born son of German Jewish immigrants, a family that tended to identify with German liberals and dislike Prussia. Lippmann's biographer, Ronald Steel, *Walter Lippmann*, 109–110, presents him as consistently pro-Ally, joining with House and leading America to war, and the "Peace Without Victory" essay as an attack on Prussian militarism. Steel must not have read the essay.

10. Grew to Lansing, Berlin 4916, 21 Dec 16, *FRUS 1916, World War*, Doc. 156. This message was sent by pouch, not cabled, so Wilson did not see it until January 10. Lansing called "special attention" to the last section,

which is quoted in the text. Wilson promptly read it and wrote to Lansing about its significance. Lansing to Wilson, 10 Jan 17; Wilson to Lansing, 11 Jan 17, *PWW*, 40:428, 442.

11. Buxton's speech was on December 21. He had already circulated the memo, "Notes on American Opinion Regarding the War," on December 16. House's contact at the American embassy in London, Buckler, sent Buxton's memo to House by mail on December 22, and House relayed it to Wilson on January 5. *PWW*, 40:413–416.

12. Bernstorff's and House's accounts of their December 27 meeting dovetail, though Bernstorff's report is more detailed. Compare Bernstorff to Bethmann, Washington 192, 29 Dec 16 (rec'd 3 Jan 17), *OGD*, 2:1010–1011; *PWW*, 40:362–365 (quotes in the text are from this English translation), and Bernstorff, *My Three Years in America*, 276–278 (including his slightly different translation of his report), with House diary, 27 Dec 16; House to Wilson, 27 Dec 16, *PWW*, 40:337.

Wilson wrote back to House that he had already encouraged governments to communicate their terms confidentially to him and that House's report was consistent with that. This was the confirming message that led House to cable Bernstorff that the plan had been approved. Thus, I believe Wilson did not really understand exactly what Bernstorff and House had asked him to approve. Wilson to House, 28 Dec 16, *PWW*, 40:343. "I can now advise": House to Bernstorff, 28 Dec 16, House Papers, Yale University, Box 12.

13. The process was further delayed, by at least a couple of days, because Bernstorff had received Wilson's permission to send his coded messages to Berlin directly, relayed for him by the State Department to/from the US embassy in Berlin. In this case, Lansing saw no need to hurry in transmitting Bernstorff's message, and Bernstorff finally had to complain to House in order to get his message relayed. The Americans had given permission to use this channel for messages related to peace negotiations. See Bernstorff to House, 30 Dec 16, House Papers, Box 12. In January, Lansing continued to try to slow or obstruct the German messages through this

channel. Link's statement that Bernstorff's December 29 cable was sent through the Buenos Aires/Stockholm roundabout is incorrect. Link, *Campaigns for Progressivism and Peace*, 249.

Although it was intercepting the American State Department's cable traffic between Washington and Berlin, the British government was not aware of this exchange. As mentioned earlier, the German embassy in Washington had updated its main diplomatic code during November. British intelligence had not yet broken the new one. The old code was designated as 13040; the new code was 7500.

14. Page to Wilson, London 5390, 29 Dec 16; letter from Page to Wilson, 30 Dec 16 (rec'd in Jan 17), *PWW*, 40:355–358, 366–368.

15. House diary, 2 Jan 17. I have not been able to locate a meaningful report on this meeting by Spring-Rice. Compare the material in the text with the fragmented and barely coherent report in Spring-Rice to Foreign Office, 4 Jan 17, in *PWW*, 40:406–407.

16. *New Republic*, vol. 9 no. 113 (December 30, 1916): 225–226. All House noted in his diary about his meeting with Lippmann was that he had urged Lippmann to be more sympathetic to the British (presumably asking the editors to tone down the sharp criticisms of the "Britain of Northcliffe" voiced in the previous issue). House diary, 28 Dec 16. In the December 30 issue, the editors also criticized the *New York Times* for being too pro-Ally by treating the president's demand for war aims as really only addressed to the Germans. The Allies, they wrote, had plenty to explain too. "It is just vacant amiability to pretend that the world knows whether for example the retrocession of Alsace-Lorraine and the Russian occupation of Constantinople are minimum terms. Certainly the *Times* does not know what the Allies have decided upon as to the future of Poland, or as to the future of the captured German colonies, or as to the indemnities they will ask." Ibid., 226–227. They also criticized other pro-Ally commentary and the baneful influence of the Northcliffe press, both in the lead editorial and in a separate essay, "Beneath the Outcry." Ibid.,

231–232. Lippmann and Croly added a further, forceful endorsement of Wilson's peace note with a separate essay titled "Americanism." This cast Wilson's note as a refreshingly and distinctively American policy, not just a policy of choosing to back one of the two sides in the war. Ibid., 228–231.

17. House diary, 3 Jan 17. The "At midnight" heading for London 5391 does not appear in the published version of the message and might not have been part of the decoded typescript. More than a week later, on January 11, at Wilson's direction, Lansing wrote to Page that his message had been received and deciphered, promising that Wilson would "endeavor to send a comment on it very soon." *PWW*, 40:442–443, 444. No further response is evident in the record.

18. House diary, 3 Jan 17.

19. Wilson had received a suggestion for concentrating on territorial terms. A couple of the best-informed foreign policy experts in the British parliament who were not in the government, Josiah Wedgwood and Noel Buxton, had written directly to House, praising Wilson's peace note. Then a radical Liberal MP, Wedgwood was also serving as an army officer in various posts. Wedgwood and Buxton, like some Germans, thought Wilson was getting ready to try to dictate peace terms. They actually liked that idea. They encouraged Wilson to lay down the proposed terms "in the most exact possible detail" to suit Wilson's ideals, ideals these men shared. House had relayed the Wedgwood/Buxton letter, but he derided it as "fantastic." Why, Wilson asked, did House think these ideas were "fantastic"? Did he disagree with the assumption that Wilson

was the only person who could set the terms? No, House said he agreed with that. He just added lamely that he had disagreed with some of the details about how to dispose of some colonies. House to Wilson, 29 Dec 16, *PWW*, 40:361–362.

20. House diary, 3 Jan 17.

21. Another sign of Wilson's borrowing from Lippmann and Croly appeared in the working draft of the speech, begun on January 5, which he called "Americanism for the World." This directly tracked the idea in their essay "Americanism," published in the December 30 issue.

22. Quotes from the final version of the address, as delivered on 22 Jan 17, in *PWW*, 40:533–539. For emphasis on the realism of Wilson's address, also see Adam Tooze, *The Deluge: The Great War, America and the Remaking of the Global Order, 1916–1931* (New York: Penguin, 2014), 53–54.

23. *New Republic*, vol. 9 no. 114 (January 6, 1917): 252–253. Lippmann and Croly met with House again on January 15. By this time, the United States had received the formal Entente reply to Wilson's December peace note. See Sharp to Lansing, 10 Jan 17, *PWW*, 40:439–441.

24. House diary, 11 Jan 17; the Buckler letter was to House, 27 Dec 16, in House Papers and quoted in *PWW*, 40:446–447n4.

25. On the House-Wiseman meeting, see House diary, 13 Jan 17, and Wiseman to C, no. 500, 16 Jan 17, in Wiseman Papers, Box 4. On House's vacation plan, see House diary, 11 Jan 17.

26. Sharp to Wilson, 21 Jan 17, conveying the views of Denys Cochin, a longtime political figure among the Catholic conservatives and a top deputy in France's Foreign Office, *PWW*, 40:532–533.

## Chapter 9: Roads Not Taken

1. "The weather": Gerard to Lansing, 3 Jan 17, *PWW*, 40:554. The kaiser's "losing his mind" supposedly originated with retired admiral Alfred von Tirpitz and was recounted to Gerard by someone who had talked to Tirpitz.

Earlier in December, Hindenburg had demanded that the public peace offer of the Central Powers be linked to agreement that

unrestricted submarine warfare would resume at the end of January. Bethmann had rejected this demand and carried the day. Bethmann did promise that, if the Allies rejected the public peace offer of the Central Powers, the "political branch" would press the United States to accept unrestricted attacks on armed merchant ships. Hindenburg note from meeting with the kaiser, 8 Dec 16 (indicating a request to the kaiser, not that the kaiser had accepted this demand), relayed to Berlin on 10 Dec; Bethmann reply (undated, probably 10 Dec), *OGD*, 2:1071–1073; *APP*, 1:609, 610–611; on the conclusion in Bethmann's favor, see Birnbaum, *Peace Moves and U-boat Warfare*, 242.

2. The navy's analysis, Holtzendorff to Hindenburg, 22 Dec 16, is at *OGD*, 2:1214–1277.

3. On the December 29 meeting in Pless and some background on the military staff work on war aims and U-boat pressure during December 1916, see Steglich, *Bündnissicherung oder Verständigungsfrieden*, 155–158 (mainly on war aims); Birnbaum, *Peace Moves and U-boat Warfare*, 276–280 (on the U-boat issue). On Bethmann and Westarp: Kuno von Westarp, *Konservative Politik im letzten Jahrzehnt des Kaiserreiches* (Berlin: Deutsche Verlagsgesellschaft, 1935), vol. 2, 79. Riezler saw the basic issue as "peace or U-Boats and another ½ to 1 year of war, which the enemy may struggle with while we will certainly be completely exhausted." Germany would then have to beg for peace from an America engaged with England. *Tagebücher*, 390 (entry for 29 Dec 16).

4. Bethmann's draft, probably 4 Jan 17, *APP*, 1:659–660. Bethmann's original draft stressed preserving the "territorial integrity" of Germany and her allies. The notional peace terms he planned to share with Wilson, to signal moderation but allow room for bargaining, were as follows:

From Belgium, Germany would ask for cession of the border fortress of Liège. It would try to reach political, economic, and military understandings with the Belgian king to restore Belgian neutrality and keep Belgium from joining an anti-German military or economic bloc.

In eastern France, Germany would try to trade border adjustments near Metz and control of the Briey ore fields and offer, in return, cession of territory back to France in upper Alsace. In his meeting with Hindenburg on December 29, Bethmann had conceded that Germany might not be able to keep the Briey ore basin that it had occupied during the war, but it would at least try to use

it in bargaining. Since December, Bethmann had been carrying on extremely secret, unofficial negotiations with an emissary of the French prime minister, Briand, about some sort of arrangement on Alsace and Lorraine that might also involve mineral concessions. This was done through the Kessler-Haguenin channel in Geneva, mentioned in Chapter 5, note 23.

In the East, the Central Powers, in connection with the new Kingdom of Poland, would try to restore to Poland the borders of old "Congress Poland" by separating parts of Lithuania and Courland from Russia. In return, Russia would be conceded clear passage through the Dardanelles strait. Austria-Hungary would seek border adjustments with Serbia, Montenegro, and Romania. Bulgaria would seek border adjustments with Serbia and the Dobruja.

Germany would also try to get back some colonies in Africa to secure maritime bases.

5. Hindenburg-Bethmann exchange and policy as the art of the attainable (*Da die Politik immer die Kunst des Erreichbaren bleiben wird*): Hindenburg-Bethmann, 31 Dec 16, and Bethmann-Hindenburg, 4 Jan 17, *APP*, 1:653–654, 658; *OGD*, 2:1095–1096. The context of their argument was Bethmann's expectation that, though it would try, Germany would not be able to keep the Briey ore basin it occupied in eastern France.

In Bethmann's alliance talks with the Austrians, the main issue was what to do about Poland. The Austrians feared that a restored Poland would threaten Austrian rule over the Galician Poles. But after the experience of being invaded by Russia in 1914, the Germans insisted on creation of a Polish "buffer state" on the long German-Russian border, oriented "neither to the East nor the West." Notes of German-Austrian discussions on January 6, 7 Jan 17, *APP*, 1:663–667.

6. Zimmermann to Bernstorff, no. 149, 7 Jan 17 (relayed to Washington, in code, on January 8 by the US embassy in Berlin), probably relayed by the State Department to Bernstorff on 11 Jan, *APP*, 1:668–669; *OGD*, 2:1012–1013. Just inferring from the documents, Birnbaum

mistakenly argued that this message was substantially rejecting the American offer to push for a peace conference. He assumes this because Bethmann did not send the earlier, more fulsome draft, discussed above in note 4. Link then followed Birnbaum's negative inference. Birnbaum, *Peace Moves and U-boat Warfare*, 297–299; Link, *Campaigns for Progressivism and Peace*, 256.

What Birnbaum (and therefore Link) misunderstood was that, while Bethmann had been thinking back to Wilson's original peace note asking for a general statement of terms, Zimmermann's redraft, which Bethmann approved, was actually more responsive to Bernstorff's latest message. Bernstorff had correctly reported Wilson's and House's open disinterest in such territorial terms, as House had explained on December 27. Reviewing the matter in his memoir, Bernstorff, who was no particular friend of Zimmermann, rightly added, "The refusal contained in this telegram was only concerned with a demand [to participate in or dictate the outcome of the talks among the warring powers] which had never been made by the United States." Bernstorff, *My Three Years in America*, 282.

Wilson's renewed disinterest in territorial issues would also have allayed Zimmermann's earlier suspicion, his fear that Wilson was trying to dictate peace terms, *in place of a peace conference*. Also, Birnbaum does not consider, as the German officials would have, the difficulty and delay involved in getting Bethmann's draft outline of territorial terms cleared by all the relevant parties, possibly including Germany's allies. Bethmann's authorization to Bernstorff was cleared by Hindenburg and the head of the navy, Admiral Holtzendorff. Hindenburg commented grudgingly, "We should only say that we don't want to annex Belgium." *APP*, 1:669n3. As events would show, Bernstorff had no problem using the authority he was given to discuss peacemaking conditions. His problem was the U-boat issue.

7. Zimmermann to Bernstorff, no. 145, 4 Jan 17; Stumm to Bernstorff, 5 Jan (both rec'd 9 Jan); Bernstorff to Foreign Office, nos. 22 and 205,

9 and 14 Jan, *OGD*, 2:1011–1014, 1017. For the "armed merchantmen" note delivered on January 10, see *PWW*, 40:447–453.

8. Bernstorff, *My Three Years in America*, 283.

9. House to Wilson, 15, 16, and 18 Jan 17 (with enclosed letters from Buckler, Buxton, and Hapgood), *PWW*, 40:477, 493–497 (emphasis in original); House diary, 15 Jan 17. House confirmed with Bernstorff the invitation to Wilson to offer a program for the peace conference. House to Bernstorff, 17 Jan 17, House Papers, Box 12. "Liberals now in ascendancy": Wiseman to C, no. 500, 16 Jan 17, Wiseman Papers, Box 4 (this part of Wiseman's report is omitted from the excerpt, which is listed a bit misleadingly as being sent to the Foreign Office, in *PWW*, 40:503–504). The visiting Englishman was J. Howard Whitehouse, a Liberal MP and former aide to Lloyd George. Wilson's aim "to reach an end of the war": Whitehouse diary, 18 Jan 17, quoted in Link, *Campaigns for Progressivism and Peace*, 258–259.

10. Bernstorff to Foreign Office, no. 212, 16 Jan 17 (relayed to Berlin through the State Department on 17 or 18 Jan, rec'd 21 Jan), *OGD*, 2:1020–1021; *APP*, 1:675–676; *PWW*, 40:504–506 (I have quoted the translation in *PWW*, with one small exception). From the number of code groups referred to elsewhere, the original of this message appears to have had about 1,000 words; the second portion of the original message has been lost.

11. "Reasonable arguments": Lansing to Wilson, 17 Jan 17, *PWW*, 40:509; the confrontation with Spring-Rice is from Lansing's diary, recounting a meeting on January 18. At that point the specific issues were two: (1) The British were further tightening the screws in the blockade by cutting off neutral use of British coal if neutrals did any business with their enemies. (2) The United States had trouble, as a neutral power, with rising British and French arming of merchant vessels. Such vessels could be regarded as warships and, under existing understandings of neutral rights, a neutral power could not supply the warships of belligerent powers. Lansing had insisted on obtaining written assurances that the ships

would not use their arms offensively against submarines; now he was adding questions about whether trained military personnel were manning the guns. Link, *Campaigns for Progressivism and Peace*, 261–264.

12. Wiseman, "Further Notes on Conversation with A. (House)," 26 Jan 17, in Wiseman Papers, Box 4. See also Link, *Campaigns for Progressivism and Peace*, 283–284 (that Wilson was not going to go to war over the issue of attacks on possibly armed merchantmen).

13. House diary, 4 Jan 17, presented as a direct quote.

14. Wilson to House, 16 and 17 Jan 17; House to Wilson, 17 Jan 17, Wilson to House, 19 Jan 17, *PWW*, 40:491, 507–509, 524. On the "Bryan" treaty confusion, Wilson first asked House whether this meant Germany wished to submit the peace terms for the *current* war to arbitration. Then, the next day, he wrote another letter asking House whether perhaps the Germans had meant that, if Germany signed a "Bryan" treaty, any dispute with America about a submarine incident would have to go through the arbitration procedure, which would mean a yearlong "cooling off" period pending the arbitral commission's investigation.

15. "Most sensible Englishman": House to Wilson, 16 Jan 17; "present you must know": House to Wilson, 19 Jan 17, relaying Bernstorff to House, 18 Jan; House to Wilson, 20 Jan, relaying Bernstorff to House, 20 Jan, *PWW*, 40:525–528. As mentioned in Chapter 7, the published Allied reply to Wilson's December peace note had declined to detail Allied war aims. It called for the restoration of all occupied territories "with just reparation." It also called for "the reorganization of Europe" based on national liberation, including the liberation of Italians, Slavs, Romanians, and Czechoslovaks from "foreign domination," as well as the end of "bloody" Turkish tyranny and the expulsion of the Ottoman Empire from Europe.

16. House to Wilson, 20 Jan 17, *PWW*, 40:527–528; Wiseman, "Notes of an Interview with A. (House)," 21 Jan 17 (recounting a meeting on January 19), Wiseman Papers; House diary, 19 Jan 17. I have put in names where, in the original, there are code letters, which Wiseman

usually annotated on the copies of the papers he preserved in his files. As part of their conference plan, they agreed that if one of the belligerents, like Germany, broke international law during the conference, all the neutrals—including the United States—would go to war against the violator. That way, House explained to Wilson, the peace conference might "tie up Germany...so that she cannot resume her unbridled submarine warfare."

17. Cooper, *Woodrow Wilson*, 371. The text is in *PWW*, 40:533–539.

18. For a summary of the reaction, see Link, *Campaigns for Progressivism and Peace*, 268–277; "greatest event": House to Wilson, 22 Jan 17; see also Croly to Wilson (urging him to make the public case for the league idea); Wilson to Croly, 25 Jan 17 (noting how much he was in debt to the editors), *PWW*, 40:539, 559, 41:13.

19. Kernek, "Distractions of Peace," 33.

20. House to Wilson, 22 and 23 Jan 17, *PWW*, 40:540, 558.

21. Wilson to House, 24 Jan 17; House to Wilson, 25 Jan 17, *PWW*, 41:3–4 (emphasis in original), 17–18. For some indication of the tangle over Bernstorff's efforts to get the State Department to relay his coded messages to Berlin during this hectic period, see Lansing to Wilson, 25 Jan 17, with House to Lansing, 24 Jan, ibid., 18–19.

22. House to Wilson, 26 Jan 17 (two letters), *PWW*, 41:49–51; Bernstorff to Foreign Office, no. 239, 27 Jan 17 (rec'd 28 Jan); *APP*, 1:684–685; House diary, 26 Jan 17.

23. House to Wilson, 26 Jan 17 (two letters); *PWW*, 41:49–51; House diary, 26 Jan 17; Wiseman, "Notes of a Conversation with A. (House)" and "Further Notes on Conversation with A. (House)," 26 Jan 17, along with a very brief summary report to C, no. 518, 27 Jan 17, Wiseman Papers, Box 4. There are some small discrepancies between Wiseman's and House's summaries. For example, Wiseman got the impression that House did not think peace could be made before the offensives began. He thought, according to Wiseman, that the Germans would "await the result of the Allies' Spring offensive before

trying again. They think the Allies will fail, and that they will then be able to obtain good terms." This may be a misunderstanding of what House feared would happen, not what he expected. The text treats the House report to Wilson as the best source.

24. For Hindenburg's agreement with the navy, see the conference record, 8 Jan 17, *OGD*, 2:1317–1319 (with a slightly different translation of Hindenburg's comments).

25. Riezler, *Tagebücher*, 393 (entry for 9 Jan 17).

26. Afflerbach, *Auf Messers Schneide*, 291–293; Birnbaum, *Peace Moves and U-boat Warfare*, 304–327; Bethmann's 1919 testimony, *OGD*, 1:344, 370; "Basic incompetence": Wilhelm Deist, "Strategy and Unlimited Warfare in Germany," in Chickering and Förster, *Great War, Total War*, 279.

27. Winston Churchill, *The World Crisis*, vol. 3, *1916–1918* (New York: Scribner's, 1927), pt. 1, 229–230. There is a nice summary of the U-boat decision and its aftermath in Watson, *Ring of Steel*, 416–449 (leading with a section titled "The Worst Decision of the War"). Other good overviews of the U-boat decision remain May, *World War and American Isolation*, esp. 277–301, 387–415, and Ritter, *Tragedy of Statesmanship*.

As panaceas go, the German navy's argument was a relatively tempting one. On the surface, the numbers and staff work might seem convincing. But it was still a panacea, not a real solution. On close examination, many of the estimates did not hold up. And once the British later decided to endorse the convoy system, the most optimistic assumptions—which assumed no reactive British behavior—disappeared. For a fine analysis of the German navy's promises and what went right and wrong, see Holger Herwig, "Total Rhetoric, Limited War: Germany's U-boat Campaign, 1917–1918," in Chickering and Förster, *Great War, Total War*, 193.

28. The best account is now Boghardt, *The Zimmermann Telegram*, 94–128.

29. Bernstorff to Foreign Office, nos. 222, 225, 228, 19, 21, and 23 Jan 17, *OGD*, 2:1021, 1027, 1045–1046.

30. Bernstorff to Foreign Office, nos. 60 (sent via wireless, not cabled) and 239, 26 and 27 Jan 17, *OGD*, 2:1046–1048; no. 239 is also in *PWW*, 41:51–52 (this translation is the one quoted).

31. Riezler, *Tagebücher*, 397 (entry for 12 Jan 17).

32. Helfferich, *Der Weltkrieg*, 2:417–418.

33. Observer comments from Admiral Müller in Görlitz, *Regierte der Kaiser*, 253–254 (entries for 28 and 29 Jan 17). This "urgent" message was sent directly by radio telegram from the powerful Eilvese wireless station to the one in Tuckerton, New Jersey, using the 7500 code. Stumm to Bernstorff, no. 64, 29 Jan 17, *OGD*, 2:1048. The Germans tended not to use this wireless method of transmission because, among other issues, it guaranteed immediate interception, which then put that much more reliance just on the code. Also, the more messages intercepted, the easier it is to break a code. That they used the wireless for such an important message is a sign of their desperate sense of urgency.

34. The chancellor had, however, tried his hand at summarizing possible peace terms for the Central Powers in the telegram he had drafted for Bernstorff on January 4. As mentioned in note 6, he had not needed to use that draft. His January 29 draft was more forthcoming on some points.

35. The Central Powers had restored a Kingdom of Poland in November on the Russian-Polish lands they had occupied.

36. Bernstorff to House, 31 Jan 17, *FRUS 1917, World War*, Supplement 1, Doc. 30. I use this language since it is the version Wilson and House actually saw. Bernstorff crafted it based on Bethmann to Bernstorff, no. 65, 29 Jan 17, *PWW*, 41:59–64; *APP*, 1:685–686; *OGD*, 2:1048–1050.

37. Riezler, *Tagebücher*, 403–404 (entry for 31 Jan 17).

38. House diary, 31 Jan and 1 Feb 17; House to Wilson, 2 Feb 17 (enclosing House to Bernstorff, 2 Feb), *PWW*, 41:95–96. Ambassador Gerard saw Bethmann, then Zimmermann, on February 3, after the United States had announced it had broken diplomatic relations.

Bethmann said "that nothing but peace on admirably modest terms would do." Bethmann said that Wilson had Germany's peace terms. Yet Gerard, quite angry, claimed in his report that he knew the real terms. In Gerard's version, and Bethmann did not trust Gerard, these were "Germany to give up Belgium but retaining so-called guaranties such as railroads, forts, a garrison, ports, commercial control etc.; a slice of France through rectification of frontier; will only give back a small part of Serbia, and Bulgaria can do as she likes with Roumania and everybody must pay indemnities to Germany, etc. If Bernstorff has given President any other terms, he is fooling him, but do not quote me to Bernstorff." Gerard added, "These people have only one God—Force." Gerard to Lansing, 4 Feb 17 (rec'd 5 Feb), *FRUS 1917, World War*, Supplement 1, Doc. 105.

House showed this cable to Wiseman a few days later. Wiseman passed the contents on to London. Wiseman to C, no. 539, 8 Feb 17, Wiseman Papers, Box 4. The British should, however, have already had in their possession the decrypt of Bethmann's actual January 29 message to Bernstorff, since they should have been able to intercept it and they had then broken the relevant code. I have not come across that decrypt in the archives, however.

39. "Perfect courtesy": Bernstorff, *My Three Years in America*, 336; "amazing charm": Ernestine Evans, "Diplomacy and Friendship: Twin Arts of Bernstorff," *New York Tribune*, February 14, 1917, 3.

40. House diary, 1 Feb 17. Part of Wilson's hesitation about war had a racial element. When Wilson presented the issue of a break with Germany to his cabinet on February 2, one of the cabinet secretaries, David Houston, recalled the president saying that "if he felt that, in order to keep the white race or part of it strong to meet the yellow race—Japan, for instance, in alliance with Russia, dominating China—it was wise to do nothing, he would do nothing, and would submit to anything and any imputation of cowardice." Houston was in favor of war. But another southern cabinet secretary, Josephus Daniels of North Carolina, told Wilson how much he sympathized, "for my feeling that we are the trustees of the civilization of our race is so strong that the possibility of becoming involved in the world's struggle makes me unable to sleep." Both quoted in Link, *Campaigns for Progressivism and Peace*, 296–297.

## Epilogue: And That Has Made All the Difference

1. Hollis, *Now All Roads Lead to France*, 324–325, 331–334. On the circumstances of his death, see "The Poet and the Forensic Scientist: The Mysterious Death of Edward Thomas," Cardiff University podcast, October 19, 2017.
2. Heffer, *Staring at God*, 563.
3. See Fry, *And Fortune Fled*, 96–100.
4. Gerwarth, *The Vanquished*, 6, 7, 13.
5. Sperling, Feb 17, quoted in Cooper, "The Command of Gold Reversed," 227.
6. "Three weeks": Kathleen Burk, "Money and Power: The Shift from Great Britain to the United States," in Youssef Cassis, ed., *Finance and Financiers in European History, 1880–1960* (Cambridge: Cambridge University Press, 1992), 361; "financial disaster": Lloyd George to Wilson, via Drummond to Wiseman for House, 25 Jun 17; Wilson to Lloyd George via same channel, 29 Jun 17, Wiseman Papers, Box 1; "whole financial fabric of the alliance will collapse": Law memo in Page to Lansing, London 6780, 20 Jul 17 (rec'd 21 Jul), *FRUS 1917, World War*, Supplement 2, vol. 1, Doc. 457.

7. See David Reynolds, "Churchill and the British 'Decision' to Fight on in 1940: Right Policy, Wrong Reasons," in Reynolds, *From World War to Cold War: Churchill, Roosevelt, and the International History of the 1940s* (New York: Oxford University Press, 2006), 75–98.

8. A stimulating counterfactual exploration of American nonintervention in the war is Manfred Berg, "'He Kept Us Out of War!' A Counterfactual Look at American History Without the First World War," *Journal of the Gilded Age and Progressive Era* (2017):

16:2–23. Berg implicitly recognizes the significance of the 1916–1917 turn, including for Allied fortunes. But Berg did not analyze the failed diplomacy of that pivotal phase. He suggests a possibility that American intervention might have been inevitable because of America's financial dependence on the Allies, relying on Hew Strachan's work. Berg may have misunderstood Strachan's argument. The dependence did not really run equally both ways. As British experts realized when they analyzed this issue, in 1916 and later, the American economy was not actually so dependent on Allied war orders. The Allied orders were competing against and crowding out adequate and rapidly growing domestic demand.

9. Viscount Grey of Fallodon, *Twenty-Five Years, 1892–1916* (New York: Frederick Stokes, 1925), 2:134–137.

10. For Cooper, including the Keynes quote, see "The Command of Gold Reversed," 228. Bernstorff grasped the financial issue and reflected strongly on it in his memoirs. But, at the time, he did not spotlight it in his reports as much as he could have. It is worth noting that, had the German Jewish bankers like Paul Warburg really been as pro-German as some of the British officials (and Jack Morgan) thought, they could have helped the German government understand the Allied weaknesses much better than it did.

11. In emphasizing the U-boat battle as a political and cultural struggle as much as, or more than, a purely military one, this argument is sympathetic not only to the general theme in Ritter's multivolume history *The Sword and the Scepter* (*Staatskunst und Kriegshandwerk* in the original) but also to the argument about German "military culture" and its particular impatience with restraint in Isabel Hull's *Absolute Destruction*. This observation reinforces some appreciation for what Bethmann was able to accomplish, against the determined efforts of these forces, for more than a year. And, as the British case shows, Germany was not alone in facing a powerful military faction in wartime.

12. Wedel (German ambassador to Vienna) to Foreign Office, 17 Dec 16 (rec'd 18 Dec), *OGD*, 2:1079.

13. The Reichstag subcommittee that investigated German handling of Wilson's peace moves criticized Bethmann on this point, suggesting that "if Germany had seized this moment [the Entente's extreme demands in answering Wilson's peace note] for coming forward with moderate war aims and with a peace aim which the world could justify for Germany, together with an absolutely unambiguous declaration concerning the unconditional return and restoration of Belgium," in the sense of Bethmann's original admission to the Reichstag that Germany's invasion of the country, though he thought it justified, had indeed violated Belgian neutrality, then this would have brought Germany's peace efforts "to the highest pitch of efficiency." Report of the Reichstag's Second Subcommittee of the Committee of Inquiry, "Wilson's Peace Move of 1916–1917," 23 Jun 20, *OGD*, 1:144–145.

14. This interpretation complements the more improvisational interpretation of Wilson in Thompson, "More Tactics Than Strategy," 95–115, as well as in Cooper's biography of Wilson and in Throntveit, *Power Without Victory*. Wilson's views on the future of the Habsburg domains were still ill formed at this phase. See, generally, Nicole Phelps, *U.S.-Habsburg Relations from 1815 to the Paris Peace Conference: Sovereignty Transformed* (Cambridge: Cambridge University Press, 2013).

15. A superb account of the armistice negotiations is Bullitt Lowry, *Armistice 1918* (Kent: Kent State University Press, 1997).

16. The best appraisal of the Wilson-House relationship in the Versailles peace talks of 1919 is Inga Floto, *Colonel House in Paris: A Study of American Policy at the Paris Peace Conference 1919* (Princeton: Princeton University Press, 1980). Floto describes the "necessity of untangling the threads" of the peace conference crisis of April 1919. In Paris, House displayed "obvious weaknesses as a negotiator." By this time, House was thoroughly disillusioned

with Lloyd George. He fell under the sway of French premier Georges Clemenceau. "House appreciated [what Wilson was trying to achieve] far better than any of Wilson's other advisers, yet every time it really mattered, he gave in." Ibid., 239, 242.

17. Senator Thomas Martin (D-VA), quoted in Edward Coffman, *The War to End All Wars: The American Military Experience in World War I* (Lexington: University Press of Kentucky, rev. ed., 1998), 8.

18. Among the best appraisals to reach this conclusion are Margaret Macmillan, *Paris 1919* (New York: Random House, 2002), 493–494, and Zara Steiner, *The Lights That Failed: European International History, 1919–1933* (London: Oxford University Press, 2005), esp. 67–70, 123–125.

19. Adam Tooze sees a decade of failed American hegemony, beginning in the last months of 1916 and early 1917. Tooze also sees more continuity in American international engagement after the war. Despite the US failure to join the League of Nations, "the actual structure that emerged by the early 1920s was an ironic fulfillment of Wilson's ambition... making America into a de facto 'super-State', exercising a veto over the combined decisions of the rest of the world." *The Deluge*, 516.

20. House to Wilson, 26 Jan 17, *PWW*, 41:25. Austrian historian Lothar Höbelt comes to a similar conclusion. "Mourir pour Liège? World War I War Aims in a Long-Term Perspective," in Afflerbach, ed., *The Purpose of the First World War*, 143–159. In the long run, Bernstorff mused to House, "None of the belligerent governments can survive such a peace as must necessarily be made."

21. Bernstorff, *My Three Years in America*, 334, 326, 330, 334.

22. Ibid., 269, 334, 344, 352 (the quotations from the exchange with Ludendorff are from notes Bernstorff made later that day).

23. On the Reichstag peace resolution and Erzberger, see Watson, *Ring of Steel*, 457–460. The Reichstag resolution still masked a variety of issues about compromise war aims, especially in the East, that would have had to be addressed in negotiations. On Bernstorff's candidacy to replace Bethmann, see Bernstorff, *Memoirs*, 154.

24. "Salvation": Bernstorff, *Memoirs*, 134; "spiteful...repugnance": Bernstorff, *My Three Years in America*, 315–316, 53.

25. Bernstorff, *Memoirs*, 137–138, 134.

# INDEX

PHILIP ZELIKOW is the White Burkett Miller Professor of History and J. Wilson Newman Professor of Governance at the Miller Center of Public Affairs, both at the University of Virginia. A former career diplomat, he was the executive director of the 9/11 Commission. He worked on international policy in each of the five administrations from Ronald Reagan through Barack Obama.

PublicAffairs is a publishing house founded in 1997. It is a tribute to the standards, values, and flair of three persons who have served as mentors to countless reporters, writers, editors, and book people of all kinds, including me.

I. F. STONE, proprietor of *I. F. Stone's Weekly*, combined a commitment to the First Amendment with entrepreneurial zeal and reporting skill and became one of the great independent journalists in American history. At the age of eighty, Izzy published *The Trial of Socrates*, which was a national bestseller. He wrote the book after he taught himself ancient Greek.

BENJAMIN C. BRADLEE was for nearly thirty years the charismatic editorial leader of *The Washington Post*. It was Ben who gave the *Post* the range and courage to pursue such historic issues as Watergate. He supported his reporters with a tenacity that made them fearless and it is no accident that so many became authors of influential, best-selling books.

ROBERT L. BERNSTEIN, the chief executive of Random House for more than a quarter century, guided one of the nation's premier publishing houses. Bob was personally responsible for many books of political dissent and argument that challenged tyranny around the globe. He is also the founder and longtime chair of Human Rights Watch, one of the most respected human rights organizations in the world.

·　　·　　·

For fifty years, the banner of Public Affairs Press was carried by its owner Morris B. Schnapper, who published Gandhi, Nasser, Toynbee, Truman, and about 1,500 other authors. In 1983, Schnapper was described by *The Washington Post* as "a redoubtable gadfly." His legacy will endure in the books to come.

Peter Osnos, *Founder*